FIRST EDITIONS:
A GUIDE TO IDENTIFICATION

FIRST EDITIONS:
A GUIDE TO IDENTIFICATION

Statements of selected North American,
British Commonwealth, and Irish publishers on their
methods of designating first editions

SECOND EDITION

Edited by
Edward N. Zempel
and Linda A. Verkler

The Spoon River Press

Our special thanks to Julie Hartman.

Published by
The Spoon River Press
P. O. Box 3676, Peoria, Illinois 61614

ISBN 0-930358-08-2

Manufactured in the United States of America

INTRODUCTION

This new expanded edition of *First Editions: A Guide to Identification* has a complex history. Essentially, it is a compilation of publishers' statements regarding their methods of designating a 'first edition.' For some, the term 'first edition' has an unclear meaning. To most librarians, bibliographers, and book collectors, however, it means 'the first printing or first impression of a first edition.' Here, a printing or impression is considered to be all the copies of a book printed in one continuous operation from a single makeready.

In this reference are assembled and coordinated the publishers' statements previously published in five books, all now out of print. Each of these books was a standard reference for bibliographers, librarians, book dealers, and book collectors. This book, then, holds the statements from the first, second, and third editions of H.S. Boutell's *First Editions of To-day and How to Tell Them*. It contains also the publishers' statements from *A First Edition?*, published in 1977, and from the first edition of *First Editions: A Guide to Identification*, published in 1984. The last two books were compiled and edited by the editors of the book at hand. A brief publishing history of each of these books may help the reader appreciate the way in which the information is here presented.

The first edition of Boutell's valuable reference was published in 1928. It held statements from American and British publishers regarding their methods of designating their first impressions. As Boutell stated in his introductory note:

> Generally speaking, the collector of first editions is really a collector of first impressions, a first impression being a book from the first lot struck off the presses, and a first edition comprising all books which remain the same in content and in format as the first impression. A second impression is a second printing. A second edition postulates some alteration of text or format. But these terms are, unfortunately, not strictly adhered to.

Revised and enlarged, Boutell's book was published in a second edition in 1937. The third edition, again a revision and enlargement of the previous edition, was published in 1949. A fourth edition was published in 1965. All of these editions are now out of print.

As well as including the publishers' statements from the first three editions of Boutell's *First Editions of To-day and How to Tell Them*, this book contains also publishers' statements from two other books: *A First Edition? Statements of selected North American, British Commonwealth, and Irish publishers on their methods of designating first editions* and the first edition of *First Editions: A Guide to Identification*. Each of these books was compiled and edited by Edward N. Zempel and Linda A. Verkler, the editors of the work at hand.

A First Edition? was published in 1977. This book was a work separate from the various editions of Boutell's work. Now out of print, *A First Edition?* held statements from over 550 publishers.

The first edition of *First Editions: A Guide to Identification* held statements from over 1,000 publishers. As well as containing the information in the first three editions of the Boutell references and *A First Edition?*, it contained statements from many publishers outlining the 1960 practice of designation. It also held publishers' statements from 1981 or 1982. The statements regarding 1960 practices were gathered to fill a gap that might otherwise have resulted in an inventory of publishers' designation practices. The 1981 and 1982 statements were sought in an attempt to update and possibly expand previous statements.

This new edition of *First Editions: A Guide to Identification* has been expanded to include statements from nearly 1,700 publishers and publishers' imprints. It includes publishers' statements for 1988 or 1989. The reference has been expanded to include statements from over 550 publishers and publisher's imprints not listed in the first edition of *First Editions: A Guide to Identification*.

Publisher's statements have, with one exception, been gathered from English-language publishers. Publishers' statements are dated by year. Often the reader is referred to another statement (for example, 1928 Statement: *See* 1937 Statement). Frequently, the statement referred to incorporates insubstantial revisions made at the publisher's request. More generally, the statement referred to is a verbatim rendering of an earlier statement, adding only the valuable information on when the designation practice was begun.

Most of the statements in this book are enclosed in quotation marks. Such statements were printed as received or as they appeared when published in the first three editions of Boutell's reference, *A First Edition?*, or the first edition of *First Editions: A Guide to Identification*.

A few statements in this book bear no quotation marks. These statements were abstracted from information provided by the publisher. Information was presented in this fashion only when the publisher did not provide a formal statement or when the publisher did not wish the statement to be printed verbatim.

With one exception, publishers listed in this book were drawn from those in the United States, the British Commonwealth, and the Republic of Ireland. All publishers other than those from the United States are identified by country. Publishers are listed alphabetically. Generally, changes in the style of a company's name are reflected in this book.

One of the strengths of the first edition of *First Editions: A Guide to Identification* was thought to be its inclusion of the first printing designations of so many small publishers. That interest was retained in compiling the statements for the present reference.

This new edition includes a brief primer on identifying book club editions. This section, "Identifying Book Club Editions," begins on page 305, immediately after the publishers' statements.

We would like to express our appreciation to those publishers who responded to our queries. Again, their patience was equal to our persistence. Statements from nearly 1,700 publishers and publishers' imprints are included in this reference. As will be seen from the statements published herein, this book is a wide inventory of publishers' methods for designating their first printings.

A

ABACUS (ENGLAND)
1988 Statement: *See* 1988 Statement of Sphere Books Limited (England)

ABARIS BOOKS, INC.
1988 Statement: "We have very short press runs (1,000-3,000). Most of our titles are art reference books. The 2nd edition is marked 'Second Edition' and so on for all later editions."

ABBEVILLE PRESS, INC.
1981 Statement: "For the most part, we simply print 'first edition' on the copyright page of books we expect will go into subsequent printings or revisions. We have no policy on this."

1988 Statement: "Our first printings bear the words 'First edition' on the copyright page. Subsequent printings are identified by number: e.g., 'Second printing.' Revisions are identified as 'Second edition,' and reprints are indicated as above."

ABELARD-SCHUMAN LIMITED (ENGLAND)
1976 Statement: "We do not identify first editions in any special way but indicate a reprint on the copyright page."

1988 Statement: *See* 1988 Statement of Blackie and Son Limited (United Kingdom)

ABINGDON PRESS
1937 Statement: "First editions of Abingdon Press publications can be identified by examining the copyright page. There does not appear on the bottom of the copyright page of first editions a statement as to the number of the edition and when printed. This statement does not appear until the second edition and thereafter."

See also Abingdon-Cokesbury Press

1981 Statement: "We distinguish between first editions and revised editions by designating 'Revised' or 'Revised and Enlarged,' but we have no system for designating the various printings of a book."

1988 Statement: "We distinguish between first editions and revised editions by designating 'Revised' or 'Revised and Enlarged.' Reprints are identified on copyright page beginning with the second printing. This new method of designating reprints was begun around 1983."

ABINGDON-COKESBURY PRESS
(Abingdon Press, The Stockton Press, and Cokesbury Press were merged in 1940 to form Abingdon-Cokesbury Press.)

1947 Statement: "Quite some time ago we discontinued using identifying marks for the first printings of our books. We found that they served no useful purpose and were the source of considerable trouble and some unnecessary cost.

"A few first printings may have been identified by showing 'First Edition' on the copyright page in late 1940 or early 1941. We have given very little attention to this matter and long since have decided that identifying first printings is of no value except in very special publications."

WILLIAM ABRAHAMS

1988 Statement: *See* 1988 Statement of E. P. Dutton & Co., Inc.

HARRY N. ABRAMS, INC.

1976 Statement: "I'm afraid we have had no special policies about citing editions. When we've done it, it's been mostly on textbooks. We are now tending more toward putting First Edition on the copyright page. Again, mostly on textbooks (*History of Art* by Janson, for one) we give printings and their dates."

1988 Statement: "I'm afraid we have had no special policies about citing editions. When we've done it, it's been mostly on textbooks."

BEN ABRAMSON, PUBLISHER

1947 Statement: *See* Argus Books, Inc.

ACADEMIC PRESS, INC.

1981 Statement: "Identification of a first edition is actually achieved by the absence of a qualifying notation. This compares with subsequent editions, which always carry (e.g.) 'Second Edition' on the half-title and title page as well as anywhere on the case or jacket where the title appears.

"The copyright page carries a line that appears as follows:

80 81 82 83 84 85 9 8 7 6 5 4 3 2 1

The far left gives the year and the far right the number of the printing. A book that had no specific Edition designation and that carried the above line as is would clearly be a copy from the first printing of the first edition. Subsequent printings would have the far right digit deleted and as many of the far left numbers as appropriate. For instance, a book whose title had no edition designation and a line that appeared

81 82 83 84 9 8 7 6 5

would be the first printing, done in 1981.

"The edition designation policy has been in effect since the founding of the company. The printing designation has changed several times. In earlier years it was the practice to say (e.g.) 'Fifth Printing, 1965' on the title page. During the years from about 1972 through 1976, we designated printings by a vertical column of numbers in the gutter margin on the last page of the book to carry any printing (usually being the last page of the index). That column appeared as follows:

A	5
B	6
C	7
D	8
E	9
F	0
G	1
H	2
I	3
J	4

"The column displayed would indicate that the first printing (A) was done in 1975. Subsequent printings would drop the top letter and/or numeral as appropriate. This system depends on looking at the copyright page to determine the applicable decade. All Academic Press books that appeared during those years carry that form of designation, but subsequent printings of those titles have been converted to the horizontal designation on the title page as described previously.

"Other imprints of Academic Press follow the same policies."

1988 Statement: *See* 1981 Statement

ACADEMIC PRESS INC (LONDON) LIMITED (ENGLAND)

1976 Statement: "We do not have any special method of identifying first editions of our titles."

1981 Statement: *See* 1976 Statement

ACADEMY CHICAGO PUBLISHERS

1988 Statement: "Academy Chicago Publishers do not identify the first editions of their original properties in any special way—no 'First Edition' notations are used. However, when we do a second printing we usually state that and include the date for this new edition. If a copyright page does not say 'Second printing' on it then you may assume it is the first printing of the first edition and the only one extant.

"This policy has been used throughout the twelve years that the company has been in business."

ACADEMY EDITIONS (ENGLAND)

1976 Statement: "Our first editions carry the following statement on the title verso:

First published in Great Britain in 19.. by Academy Editions
Following reprints have in addition: Reprinted in 19..
New editions are similarly indicated with: Second edition 19.."

1981, 1988 Statements: *See* 1976 Statement

ACE / PUTNAM

1989 Statement: *See* 1989 Statement of G. P. Putnam's Sons

BERNARD ACKERMAN, INC.

(In July, 1946, became Beechhurst Press, Inc.)

See Beechhurst Press, Inc.

ACROPOLIS BOOKS LTD.

1976 Statement: "We only indicate those printings or editions after the first."

1981, 1988 Statements: *See* 1976 Statement

ACS BOOKS (AMERICAN CHEMICAL SOCIETY)

1988 Statement: "We do not designate first printings or first editions. For subsequent printings we indicate the number of the printing and the year. This is placed on the bottom of the copyright page, which is the reverse side of the title page."

ACS PUBLICATIONS INC.

1988 Statement: "We print the date of publication on the copyright page. We do not explicitly identify a first edition although sometimes we do include 'First Printing, month, year' on that page.

"Whenever we reprint a book, whether new material is added or not, we add 'First printing, month, year' and 'Second printing, month, year', ('Third printing, month, year') etc. Some books have 'Revised' on the title page to indicate a substantial revision that would warrant a new ISBN."

THE ACTINIC PRESS (ENGLAND)
1976, 1981 Statements: *See* 1976, 1981 Statements of J. Garnet Miller Ltd. (England)

ADDISON HOUSE, PUBLISHERS
1976 Statement: "I am afraid that our first edition is probably the same thing as a first printing as most of our books will not warrant change over the years."

ADDISON-WESLEY PUBLISHING COMPANY
1976 Statement: "Our present method of identification on printings is merely an alphabetical and numerical code. This applies to both our children's books and to our adult trade books. For instance, on the copyright page of a new book the code would be listed:
ABCDEFGHIJK   7987
(this indicates a first printing in the year 1977)
"As each reprint is done, one letter of the alphabet is dropped and the last number if in a different year. For instance, a second printing would have
BCDEFGHIJK   798
(a second printing in 1978)
"We do not indicate 'first edition,' 'second edition.' Some of our earlier children's books have 'first printing,' 'second printing,' etc. Some have no designation whatsoever."
1981, 1989 Statements: *See* 1976 Statement

ADIRONDACK MOUNTAIN CLUB
1988 Statement: "We do not always indicate First Edition on the copyright page, but *lack* of identification marks them as such.
"All future printings and/or editions are noted on the copyright page."

ADLARD-COLES LTD. (ENGLAND)
1976, 1981, 1988 Statements: *See* 1976, 1981, 1988 Statements of Granada Publishing Limited (England)

ADVENTURE TRAILS PUBLICATIONS
1947 Statement: "We seem to have no standard rule for first editions, except that they are limited in number, and three of them have been hand numbered.
"The first edition of *The Vengeance of the Vixen*, for instance, was limited to 1500 copies, numbered by hand. Of *How the Eggplant Came To Be* there were only 1000 copies of the first edition, numbered. There were two thousand copies of *Peanuts* printed in the first edition, hand numbered. There were 1500 copies of *Chiquito* printed and the number is mentioned in the first edition. The second edition of *The Vengeance of the Vixen* is marked 'second edition.' "

AFRICANA PUBLISHING COMPANY
See Holmes and Meier Publishers, Inc.

AGATHON PRESS, INC.
1988 Statement: "No special designation for first printing."

AHSAHTA PRESS

1988 Statement: "Our practice of designating different printings and editions has remained constant since our founding in 1974. First editions contain simply the copyright notice. Subsequent printings contain the following notice, '(X)Printing, (Month) (Year),' beneath the original copyright notice. If substantial revisions (corrections, deletions, additions) are made, we note '(X)Printing, (Month) (Year),' beneath the original copyright."

ALASKA NORTHWEST PUBLISHING COMPANY

1976 Statement: "I'm not sure how regular we've been until the last couple of years, but our current method of designating 1st editions is *not* to designate them. A second printing will be marked:

First printing, date
Second printing, date

And so on until we do a revised edition. Then it's

Revised edition, date
Second printing, revised edition,
date."

1981, 1988 Statements: *See* 1976 Statement

ALBA HOUSE

1988 Statement: "We print a strip of code numbers on the copyright page to designate the printing. For a first printing it reads:

1 2 3 4 5 6 7 8 9 10"

THE ALBYN PRESS (ENGLAND)

1947 Statement: "Regarding our method of indicating first and subsequent printings of our books, we have to say that this information is contained on the reverse of the title page and reads—

First published 19..
By The Albyn Press
42 Frederick Street
Edinburgh, 2

"Subsequent printings are noted beneath this as—

Reprinted...............
New Edition..........."

ALFRED PUBLISHING CO. INC.

1988 Statement: "First editions are not marked in any particular way. Usually, when second and further editions are issued of the same title, they are so marked."

ALICE JAMES BOOKS

1981 Statement: "We do not identify first editions as such. We designate second printings by the words 'Second Printing' and the date. We have not changed our method of identification."

1988 Statement: *See* 1981 Statement

PHILIP ALLAN & CO., LTD. (ENGLAND)
(Out of business.)

1937 Statement: "It is our practice to put the date of publication of any book either on the title page or on the back of the title page. If the book is reprinted, the date of the reprint appears on the back of the title page beneath the date of the first printing. Subsequent editions and reprints are similarly printed on the back of the title page."

J. A. ALLEN & CO. LTD. (ENGLAND)

1976 Statement: "Please be advised it is our custom to indicate the date of original publication on the verso of the title page. Where there is a new edition or reprint, it will be indicated below the original copyright notice."
1981, 1988 Statements: *See* 1976 Statement

W. H. ALLEN & CO., LTD. (ENGLAND)

1976 Statement: "This Company does not have any special method of identifying first editions. So far as I can ascertain, the Company, which dates back to the eighteenth century, has never used any identifying designation."
1981 Statement: *See* 1976 Statement
See also 1989 Statement of W. H. Allen & Co., PLC (England)

W. H. ALLEN & CO., PLC (ENGLAND)

1989 Statement: "I can only confirm the [1976 and 1981] statements [of W. H. Allen & Co., Ltd.]. However, a first edition could probably be recognised by the absence of a notice saying 'Reprinted 19XX.' "

ALLEN & UNWIN AUSTRALIA PTY. LTD. (AUSTRALIA)

1988 Statement: "All first editions of our books are printed with copyright notice and date (© author 1988) and the words 'first published in 1988.' Reprints and second editions also have the words 'reprinted' or 'second edition' with the date.

"This method of designation has been standard practice for many years, and is applied to all imprints and subsidiaries."

GEORGE ALLEN & UNWIN, LTD. (ENGLAND)

1928 Statement: "It is our practice in the first edition to print the words 'First Published in...' (the year of issue) and in subsequent impressions or editions to add the additional dates."
1937 Statement: "It is our practice in the first edition to print the words 'First Published in ....' (the year of issue) and in subsequent impressions or editions to add the additional dates. With translations we give the original title, date and place of publication.

"We began using our present method of identifying first printings about 1914."
1947 Statement: *See* 1937 Statement
Statement for 1960: "We can confirm that between 1949 and 1976 the bibliographic designation of first printings was the same [as that given in the 1976 statement]."

GEORGE ALLEN & UNWIN (PUBLISHERS) LTD (ENGLAND)

1976 Statement: "We identify all our books on the back of the title page by a bibliographical note which declares the date of first publication. Subsequent impressions or editions are noted as and when they occur. A first edition, by which is normally meant a first impression of a first edition will have only a single line entry of first publication with the appropriate date."
1981 Statement: "We have not changed the method by which we denote the first edition of a work and it is still as printed in the original edition of your book."
1988 Statement: *See* 1988 Statement of Unwin Hyman, Limited (England)

ALLIANCE BOOK CORPORATION
(Established 1938. Out of business prior to 1949.
Ziff-Davis Publishing Co. acquired their publications.)
1949 Statement: *See* Ziff-Davis Publishing Company

ALOES BOOKS (ENGLAND)
1976 Statement: "We don't have a hard or fast rule on editions. We hardly ever mention state of printing, merely if it's our second print & so on."
1981 Statement: "We try to be concise on this point and not clutter up the colophon with facts that would tend to make the book an object and not a thing to read. We do clarify if the piece has appeared elsewhere in magazine or book format. If we are lucky enough to go into a second printing then the cover usually carries this information now. In the past some reprints have just had colour changes or board changes for the cover."

ALYSON PUBLICATIONS
1988 Statement: "We designate the first printing of a first edition on the copyright page. We have used this method since our founding in 1977."

AMERICAN ASSOCIATION FOR STATE
AND LOCAL HISTORY PRESS
1988 Statement: "First editions of our books are not specifically identified as first editions *on original publication*. We simply use a regulation copyright notice, showing the date of each book's first appearance:
    Copyright © 1975
    The American Association for State and Local History
    All rights reserved . . . Printed in the United States of America
"However, if we publish a *second* edition, we *do*, in the copyright notice for the *second* edition, list and identify the first edition and its date, followed by the dates when the first edition was reprinted, and by the date and identification of the *second* edition:
    Copyright © 1975, 1983, by the American Association for
    State and Local History. All rights reserved . . . Printed in
    the United States of America . . . .
    First Edition published 1975
    Second Printing 1976
    Third Printing 1978
    Fourth Printing 1979
    Second Edition, revised and expanded, 1983
"I must confess, at this point, that we're not always scrupulously consistent about including in our 'second edition' notices the printing history for the first edition. Now and again, we leave that out and simply say:
    First Edition published 1975
    Second Edition, revised and expanded, 1983
"Since the responsibility for seeing that that copy is included on the copyright pages of our second editions has, at various times, been freely passed around among editors, production managers, staff designers, and press directors, it's sometimes difficult to say who okayed these occasional variations, unless we talk with the staff historian. We frown on the inconsistencies, but we do have some."

AMERICAN BAR FOUNDATION
1988 Statement: "During the years when the American Bar Foundation had a publishing program (1960-86), first editions were not so identified.

Only later editions carried any identification as to edition. Second printings, which have been rare, have usually been identified.

"We have no imprints or subsidiaries."

AMERICAN COUNCIL ON PUBLIC AFFAIRS

1949 Statement: *See* Public Affairs Press

AMERICAN HISTORY PRESS

1988 Statement: *See* 1988 Statement of Northwoods Press

AMERICAN INSTITUTE OF CHEMICAL ENGINEERS

1988 Statement: "The American Institute of Chemical Engineers does not identify first printings, but when a book is reprinted it carries a line on the reverse of the title page that reads, for example, 'Second Printing 1988.' "

AMERICAN INSTITUTE OF PHYSICS

1988 Statement: "No designation of first printing or first edition is used. If there are later printings or editions, the information is listed on the copyright page with the year of the printing or edition."

AMERICAN LIBRARY ASSOCIATION

1988 Statement: "We have no written policy concerning the identification of first editions. In answer to your question:

1. We do not state 'first edition' or
'first printing' on the copyright page
2. Printings (up to March of 1988) have been
indicated on the copyright page; in the future
they will be indicated *only* when corrections
are made in the book itself
3. Revised or second, third, etc., editions are
always indicated on the copyright page."

AMERICAN PHILOSOPHICAL SOCIETY

1988 Statement: "The American Philosophical Society does not identify first editions. We do, however, specify second editions or reprintings. We have no subsidiaries."

AMERICAN POETRY AND LITERATURE PRESS

1988 Statement: "Our company designates the first printing of a first edition by: 'First Printing'. . . and the date. Subsequent printings are listed: 'Second Printing' . . . and the date, etc.

"A Revised version is designated, 'Second Edition' and the date. There is a clear differentiation between the two terms. A new 'printing' is a reprint. A new 'edition' has to be revised and have changes in it.

"This method of designation was first adopted in 1979. It does not differ from any previously used.

"In designating first printings, imprints and subsidiaries would follow our practices."

AMERICAN SOCIETY OF CIVIL ENGINEERS

1988 Statement: "No special marking of first printing."

AMPERSAND PRESS

1976 Statement: "The only designation is the date of publication. Subsequent editions or printings would be indicated as such."

AMPHOTO

1976 Statement: "No special way of indicating *first* editions, but *second* & subsequent editions are so noted. Therefore, absence of *any* indication (or of multiple copyright dates) usually indicates a first edition. It may also indicate a reprint *(unrevised)* of the 1st, but this, too, is usually noted."
1981 Statement. *See* 1976 Statement

ANANSI (CANADA)

See House of Anansi Press Limited (Canada)

ANDREWS AND McMEEL, INC.

1981 Statement: "I have slightly revised our company's entry in your book *A First Edition?* Please note that the company's name is now Andrews and McMeel, Inc. The entry should read as follows:

"In the normal course of things, we do not consider minor changes sufficient to refer to a new printing as a new edition. Thus, I will refer to first printings and second printings rather than first editions and second editions.

"We have no special identifying mark for a first printing. The only way one could tell a first printing would be the absence of information on subsequent printings. Our present policy is as follows: When a book goes into a second printing we then introduce on to the copyright page the word 'First printing' and the date and 'Second printing' and the date. A new line is added for each subsequent printing. Thus, as I said, a first printing is actually identified by the lack of such a line."
1988 Statement: *See* 1981 Statement

ANGUS & ROBERTSON PUBLISHERS (AUSTRALIA)

1988 Statement: "Angus & Robertson Publishers designates first editions on the imprint page with the words:

First published in Australia by Angus & Robertson
Publishers in ... (year of publication)

"If these words are *not* followed by a list of reprint dates, then the reader can assume that the copy he or she holds is the first edition. However, the wording above, which is used to denote the first-ever edition, anywhere in the world, of a particular title, is also used to denote the first *Australian* edition. Because of this ambiguity, the reader can only be absolutely certain that he or she is looking at the first Australian edition, though in the majority of cases it would also be the first edition world-wide."

ANTAEUS

See The Ecco Press

THE ANTHOENSEN PRESS

1947 Statement: "With very few exceptions there is only one printing of our books. All information about first or subsequent editions can be found in the colophon. There are noted: number of copies; some production details—binding, paper, etc. Also facts like limited editions, numbered editions, date and designer are in the colophon. There are three imprints under which our books might appear: The Southworth Press, up to the year 1934; The Southworth-Anthoensen Press up to the year 1947. Since January of 1947 the Press has become The Anthoensen Press.

"In the rare cases of second editions, type from the first edition (we use letterpress) is always used, though it might be abridged, or differently bound."

ANTHROPOSOPHIC PRESS, INC.

1976 Statement: "Because of the particular nature of our publications, we do not identify editions. Even reprintings, when they have continued for decades, are not noted."

1981 Statement: "For the time being I will retain the policy indicated in the [1976 statement]."

1988 Statement: *See* 1981 Statement

ANTIQUE COLLECTORS' CLUB LTD (ENGLAND)

1988 Statement: "Our first printings carry the usual copyright line with date of first publication on the reverse of the title page. When a book is reprinted information is added along the lines of—

    First published 1982
    Reprinted 1984, 1986, 1988

The final date always designates the latest printing.

"Updated editions are also clearly marked such as—

    First edition 1982
    Reprinted 1984, 1985
    Second edition 1986
    Reprinted 1987, 1988

Once again the final date is the latest printing.

"Where a book originated elsewhere and we are reprinting it, usually as a revised edition, this is also clearly indicated. This represents our current practice, and on checking back there are a few minor variations, but none are significant or likely to lead to confusion. We do not currently use other imprints or have subsidiaries."

ANTONSON PUBLISHING LTD. (CANADA)

1976 Statement: "Our only means of designating a first edition is the listing of 'First Printing' and the date of this first printing. We date each additional printing. Usually, this relates to the year shown for the current copyright. Our dating as indicated above is consistent."

ANVIL PRESS POETRY LTD (ENGLAND)

1988 Statement: "In our first editions, first printings the year of publication only is stated; in subsequent editions and printings particulars of all editions and printings to date are given."

APERTURE

1988 Statement: *See* 1976 Statement of Aperture, Inc.

APERTURE, INC.

1976 Statement: "First printings are usually identified with either 'First Edition' or 'first printing.' Sometimes, as in the case of *Ghana*, the c/r is used for more than one edition. (There is an English edition as well.) We'll omit the printing; but even here, no absolute rule.

"The phrase 'first published in....' usually means that this is *not* the point of first publication—as, 'first published in Great Britain by Smithy' implies that Smithy is not the first publisher of the book, but the book may be simultaneously published in the U.S. and the book was a U.S. creation.

"When reprint numbers are used, the idea is to simply delete the lowest number from the plate (we don't have to make a new plate) for a reprint. When this method is used, the lowest printing number that can be read is the right one."

1981 Statement: *See* 1976 Statement

1988 Statement: *See* Aperture

APPALACHIAN CONSORTIUM

1988 Statement: "First printings have a standard copyright notice and subsequent printings are indicated as:

Second Printing, 19__

Third Printing, 19__

and so forth."

APPALACHIAN MOUNTAIN CLUB

1988 Statement: "We always designate the edition of the book on the copyright page, whether it is first, second, etc. Printings are indicated by stone-offs—for example, for the second printing, in 1988, we would stone-off the number 1 (we begin by listing numbers 1-10) and the year 87 (we begin by listing six years). We began using this method of designation years ago, although it's only recently that we've used it consistently."

D. APPLETON & CO

(Merged with Century Co. to form D. Appleton-Century Co., Inc., on May 31, 1933.)

1928 Statement: "Our first editions are designated by a small numeral one in parentheses (1) at the foot of the last page. Later as we reprint the book this numeral is changed according to the number of the reprinting, that is, (2), (3), etc."

See also D. Appleton-Century Company, Inc.

D. APPLETON-CENTURY COMPANY, INC.

(Merged on January 2, 1948, with F. S. Crofts and Co., to form D. Appleton-Century-Crofts, Inc.)

1937 Statement: "Our first editions are designated by a small numeral one in parentheses (1) at the foot of the last page. Later, as we reprint the book, this numeral is changed according to the number of the printing, that is, (2), (3), etc. This numbering was inaugurated by D. Appleton and Company in 1902."

1947 Statement: "The practice of our New York house is to print the figure 1 within brackets at the end of the last printed page on any book issued by them. When a second printing takes place this figure is, of course, changed to the figure 2, etc., etc.

"In addition our New York house invariably dates the title page and the American copyright law requires the year of first publication to be on the back of the title page, in order to preserve the copyright. This numbering was inaugurated by D. Appleton & Company in 1902."

See also D. Appleton-Century-Crofts, Inc.

D. APPLETON-CENTURY-CROFTS, INC.

1948 Statement: "The merger became effective on January 2, 1948. We do not intend to use the Croft's imprint on any of our books. We have revised our colophon to include another 'C' for Crofts. No change will be made in the method of identifying first printings. We shall continue to place the number of the printing on the last page of the book, and all Croft's books will follow our method."

1982 Statement: "We carry a string of numbers: at left, a series of numbers (last two digits of year), slash, then numbers ten to one in that order to right. Farthest left digits represent year of publication or reprint date; farthest right digit is reprint number. Example below.

82 83 84 85 86 87/10 9 8 7 6 5 4 3 2 1"

1988 Statement: *See* 1988 Statement of Appleton & Lange

APPLETON & LANGE

1988 Statement: "We carry a string of numbers: at left, a series of numbers (last two digits of year), slash, then numbers ten to one in that order to right. Farthest left digits represent year of publication or reprint date; farthest right digit is reprint number. Example below.

82 83 84 85 86 87/10 9 8 7 6 5 4 3 2 1"

THE APPLETREE PRESS LTD PUBLISHERS (IRELAND)

1981 Statement: "To get right to the heart of the matter the only thing which distinguishes Appletree Press first editions is the absence of any mention of reprints. The one exception is our *Nationality and the Pursuit of National Independence*. The first edition has a black and blue cover, subsequent editions have a straightforward black and white cover."

1988 Statement: "Appletree Press first editions may normally be distinguished by the wording 'First published in (year) by The Appletree Press Ltd.' Subsequent editions may also include this wording but will, in addition, include additional information about more recent editions."

THE AQUARIAN PRESS LIMITED (ENGLAND)

1988 Statement: *See* 1988 Statement of Thorsons Publishing Group Ltd. (England)

THE AQUILA PUBLISHING COMPANY LIMITED
(UNITED KINGDOM)

1976 Statement: "Our normal practice is to publish books in at least two editions at the same time, occasionally three. These are pamphlet and signed pamphlets (limited edn.) and paperback, hardback (And in most cases signed ltd. hardback). Where a signed edition is published this is taken by the British National Bibliography and the British Library (formerly the publications division of the British Museum) as the first edition, but legally all three (or two) editions are 'first edition'. When we reprint this is always stated in the book, either on the back cover or on the verso title page. Where a second edition is concerned this is also shown. The legal definition of an edition as opposed to a reprint/impression is that an edition must be re-set either in its whole, or in important parts. The corrections of errors, or small author's revisions are normally not enough to make this a new edition, so long as these are of a very minor nature. First editions (not anthologies) are always marked as such on the verso title, and Anthologies have this information usually in the form of a codicil to the copyright notice."

1988 Statement: *See* 1976 Statement

ARCADIA HOUSE

1937 Statement: *See* 1937 Statement of Hillman-Curl, Inc.
1947 Statement: *See* 1947 Statement of Samuel Curl, Inc.

DENIS ARCHER (ENGLAND)

1947 Statement: *See* 1947 Statement of Selwyn & Blount, Ltd. (England)

ARCHITECTURAL BOOK PUBLISHING COMPANY INC.

1988 Statement: "Our first editions do not usually have an indication that they are a first edition.

"However, whenever we have a reprint, we list the date of the new printing on the copyright page and also, if it is a new edition, we also indicate that on the copyright page."

THE ARCHITECTURAL PRESS LTD (ENGLAND)

1976 Statement: "The form of words is: First published (year) by the Architectural Press, Ltd."

1981 Statement: *See* 1976 Statement

1988 Statement: *See* 1988 Statement of Butterworth Architecture (England)

ARCHWAY PRESS

1947 Statement: "First editions bear no identification, as such. Subsequent editions bear full identification (i.e., second edition, third edition) and the date of the edition."

THE ARGUS BOOK SHOP, INC.

1937 Statement: "Later printings are indicated on the verso of the title page in all our publications. We have used this method since 1926."

ARGUS BOOKS, INC.
(Formerly The Argus Book Shop, Inc.)

1937 Statement: "Later printings are indicated on the verso of the title page in all our publications. We have used this method since 1926."

1947 Statement: "When I first began to publish I used the imprint Argus Books. In 1945 when I first moved to New York I used the imprint Ben Abramson, Publisher. Since June of 1946 the imprint has been Argus Books, Inc. In every case of a reprint it is indicated by being marked 'second printing' or 'third printing,' etc."

ARGUS COMMUNICATIONS

1976 Statement: "Our first printing is coded on the copyright page in the following way: 0 1 2 3 4 5 6 7 8 9. Each time we go back to press one numeral is deleted starting on the left-hand side."

1981 Statement: "Our code has been reversed, as indicated below. I have not been able to determine when the change was initiated.

"Our first printing is coded on the copyright page in the following way: 0 9 8 7 6 5 4 3 2 1. Each time we go back to press one numeral is deleted starting on the right-hand side."

1988 Statement: *See* 1981 Statement

THE ARION PRESS

1988 Statement: "Almost all of our publications are reprints of classical literature. They are limited in number and never go beyond our first edition. The occasional original work that we publish is marked in no way except by a copyright date."

ARIS & PHILLIPS LTD (ENGLAND)

1988 Statement: "Each book has the copyright notice—including date—on the title verso, with all the bibliographic details. If the book is reprinted without alteration or corrections this is not indicated. Corrected or revised editions are so designated beneath the copyright statement—Second (corrected) edition & date."

ARK (ENGLAND)

1988 Statement: *See* 1988 Statement of Associated Book Publishers (UK) Ltd. (England)

ARKANA (ENGLAND)

1988 Statement: *See* 1988 Statement of Associated Book Publishers (UK) Ltd. (England)

ARKHAM HOUSE

(Also uses the imprints Mycroft and Moran, and Stanton and Lee.)

1947 Statement: "Arkham House, Mycroft & Moran, Stanton & Lee publish *only* first editions; any book bearing any one of these imprints *is* automatically a first edition. Most books carry a colophon setting forth the number of books printed."

Statement for 1960: "All Arkham House books are limited (first) editions with the exception of the collected works of H.P. Lovecraft, the subsequent reprintings of which are acknowledged in the end colophon to each volume. This is and always has been the Arkham policy."

ARKHAM HOUSE PUBLISHERS, INC.

1976 Statement: "All Arkham House books are limited (first editions) with the exception of the collected works of H.P. Lovecraft, the subsequent reprintings of which are acknowledged in the end colophon to each volume."

1981 Statement: "Initial pressruns of Arkham House books (from 1980 to the present) are identified by the term 'First Edition' on the copyright page. If a title subsequently is reprinted, the 'First Edition' designation either is removed from the copyright page or is replaced by an appropriate acknowledgement such as 'Second Printing,' 'Third Printing,' et cetera."

1988 Statement: "All Arkham House first editions are designated by the term 'First Edition,' which invariably occupies the final line on our copyright pages (p. iv). Should a book enter subsequent printings, this line will be replaced by 'Second Printing,' 'Third Printing,' or whatever notification is appropriate. With the exception of our collected critical Lovecraft edition, Arkham House seldom reprints its titles."

ARLEN HOUSE: THE WOMEN'S PRESS (REPUBLIC OF IRELAND)

1981 Statement: "For a first edition we have in the past said simply:
   'Published by...'
"In subsequent editions we give details of previous editions thus:
   'First published under (title, if previous title different) date.
   'This revised (if applicable) edition (date).' "
This practice is followed by the imprints of Arlen House.

ARLINGTON HOUSE PUBLISHERS

1976 Statement: "Arlington House does not designate first editions. However, reprints are indicated in the usual manner: Second printing, May 1973, for example."

1981 Statement: Arlington House Publishers now uses a sequence of numbers from 1 through 9. With each new printing, the lowest number is deleted.

ARMS AND ARMOUR PRESS (ENGLAND)
1988 Statement: *See* 1988 Statement of Cassell PLC (England)

EDWARD ARNOLD (ENGLAND)
1988 Statement: *See* 1937 Statement of Edward Arnold & Co. (England)

EDWARD ARNOLD & CO. (ENGLAND)
1928 Statement: "We do not designate our first editions of books in any special way. If the book reaches a second edition or second impression we designate it as such on the title page as a rule."

1937 Statement: "We do not designate our first editions of books in any special way. If the book reaches a second edition or second impression we designate it as such on the title page or on the reverse of the title."

1947 Statement: *See* 1937 Statement

1988 Statement: *See* 1988 Statement of Edward Arnold (England)

ARROWHEAD BOOKS
1947 Statement: "The first edition of *Bubu of Montparnasse* by Charles-Louis Phillipe is the only one which has the date at the end of T. S. Eliot's preface. The firm which made the plates used for later editions simply dropped the line and we have not reinserted it.

"The first edition of *Bumarap* can be told by the fact that the copyright date was left out on the page behind the title page. It is to be found in each of subsequent editions.

"The first edition of *Waggish Tales* edited by Norman Lockridge has Alexander Woollcott's name at the end of the introduction. It is omitted in the plates. If there are any further editions the name will not be there."

J. W. ARROWSMITH (LONDON), LTD. (ENGLAND)
1928 Statement: "Our custom is to put on the back of the title page 'First published in 1928,' or whatever the year may be. Reprints are marked 'First published in 1928—Second impression 1928—' and so on.

"May we take this opportunity of pointing out that the words 'First Edition' are invariably misused. What is meant is 'First Impression' as a First Edition may include 20 or 30 impressions and presumably it is only the first which is of value."

1937 Statement: *See* 1928 Statement

1947 Statement: *See* 1928 Statement

ART AND EDUCATIONAL PUBLISHERS, LTD. (ENGLAND)
1947 Statement: "The first editions of all our publications bear the following imprint, verso title page 'First Published' followed, in some cases, by the month but always by the year, and our full name and address. Subsequent editions or reprints are marked with the reprint date or new edition date. It should be perfectly clear therefrom that an edition that does not bear either the reissue date or a new edition date, is the *first edition*."

ART DIRECTION BOOK CO.
1988 Statement: "We indicate first editions as:
'1st printing July 1978'
and by listing subsequent printings as:
'2nd printing July 1985,' etc."

THE ART TRADE PRESS, LTD. (ENGLAND)
1947 Statement: *See* Rockliff Publishing Corporation, Limited (England)

ARTISTS & ALCHEMISTS PUBLICATIONS

1976 Statement: "The books printed today, that do not say 'first printing'—are a first printing—in the future we will indicate such."

1981 Statement: *See* 1976 Statement

ASHER-GALLANT PRESS

1988 Statement: "We do not indicate first editions—only second editions—and we do not indicate first or subsequent printings on any titles. This has been our policy since we started publishing in 1977, under the name Caddylak Publishing."

ASHMOLEAN MUSEUM (ENGLAND)

1988 Statement:

"1. The Ashmolean uses no special identification for *first* editions. The date of publication appears:

    (i) at the bottom of the title page

    (ii) at the bottom of the title page reverse (copyright page)

"2. All subsequent editions are however clearly indicated on the reverse of the title page with the statement

    'First published...'

    'Second edition published...'

"3. If an edition is reprinted the statement will read

    'First published...'

    'Second edition published...'

    'Reprinted...'

"4. In every instance the date of publication will appear at the bottom of the title page and at the bottom of the title page reverse with the name and address of the printer."

ASIA PRESS

See The John Day Co., Inc.

ASPEN PUBLISHERS, INC.

1988 Statement: "In the absence of any designation regarding edition, one can assume a title is a first edition. Second and subsequent editions are so identified on the cover, spine, and title page of an Aspen book. This has always been our practice."

ASSOCIATED BOOK PUBLISHERS (UK) LTD. (ENGLAND)

1988 Statement: "All our books are first editions unless it indicates otherwise on the title verso.

"For your information, we enclose a copy of statement appearing in our imprints, which are as follows: Routledge, Ark, and Arkana.

    First published in 19— by

    Routledge

    a division of Routledge, Chapman and Hall

    11 New Fetter Lane, London EC4P 4EE"

ASSOCIATED BOOK PUBLISHERS (UK) LTD.
(SCIENTIFIC AND TECHNICAL DIVISION) (ENGLAND)

1988 Statement: "We do not use any particular method to identify first editions of our books. There is a simple statement on the biblio page of when the book was first published. If there is no additional information on either reprints or new editions then the book is a first edition."

ASSOCIATED UNIVERSITY PRESSES
(Bucknell University Press, University of Delaware Press, Fairleigh Dickinson University Press, Littman Foundation, Ontario Film Institute, and Philadelphia Art Alliance Press)

1976 Statement: "In addition to this press (Fairleigh Dickinson University Press) we also administer the affairs of Bucknell University Press, The University of Delaware Press, and the Art Alliance Press. The Presses have no particular means of designating first editions or first printings. However, subsequent editions and printings do carry printing histories."
1981, 1988 Statements: *See* 1976 Statement

ATHENEUM PUBLISHERS
1976 Statement: "Atheneum's method of designating a first edition is by clearly indicating such on the copyright page.
"It will invariably be found on the last line on the copyright page, and will say 'First Edition' or 'First American Edition' (the latter in the case of a book which has been issued earlier in a foreign country)."
1981 Statement: *See* 1976 Statement
1989 Statement: *See* 1989 Statement of Macmillan Publishing Co., Inc.

ATHLETIC PRESS
1988 Statement: *See* 1988 Statement of Golden West Books

THE ATHLONE PRESS (ENGLAND)
1981 Statement: "Since 1st February 1979, the Athlone Press has ceased to be the university press of the University of London and we are now everywhere styled as The Athlone Press. Otherwise, there is no change whatsoever to our wording or practice."
See also The Athlone Press of the University of London (England)
1988 Statement: *See* 1981 Statement

THE ATHLONE PRESS
OF THE UNIVERSITY OF LONDON (ENGLAND)
1976 Statement: "We add no words to identify first editions of our books. Indeed the absence of description is the identification since all printings subsequent to the first are identified on the verso of the title page. A first edition would therefore bear on the verso of the title page the copyright line © A.N. Other 1976. The second edition would have the words Second Edition on the title page and this information would also be included in the bibliographical details immediately following the copyright line."
See also The Athlone Press (England)

THE ATLANTIC MONTHLY PRESS, INC.
1937 Statement: "On first editions of Atlantic Monthly Press titles beginning with the fall of 1925 (when they appeared under the Little, Brown and Company imprint) the date at the bottom of the title page coincides with the date of publication printed on the copyright page immediately beneath the copyright notice. Later printings are likewise listed on the copyright page, so that reprints are easily distinguishable.
"Prior to the fall of 1925, however, it is not an easy matter to distinguish first editions of our books. In many instances it has been necessary for us to check back on text corrections to be quite sure, as at that time our title pages carried no dates and our copyright pages did not consistently list reprints of our titles. There is therefore no definite ruling one can give, al-

though in general it is safe to say that such copies containing simply the copyright line on the copyright page are first editions."

1947 Statement: *See* 1937 Statement

1976 Statement: The edition (e.g., First Edition or First American Edition) is indicated on the copyright page. Subsequent printings of the edition are listed.

1981 Statement: *See* 1976 Statement

See also Little, Brown and Company

AUCKLAND UNIVERSITY PRESS (NEW ZEALAND)

1976 Statement: "First editions are marked e.g. 'First published 1976'; subsequent printings are identified 'Reprinted 1976' or '2nd edition 1976' depending on whether there is new matter or not. We have always used this method."

1981, 1989 Statements: *See* 1976 Statement

AUGUST HOUSE INC, PUBLISHERS

1988 Statement: "First Edition, (year)

        10 9 8 7 6 5 4 3 2 1

"With each printing, one number is lifted so that the last number is the number of the printing."

This method of identification was adopted in 1984.

J. J. AUGUSTIN INCORPORATED, PUBLISHER

1976 Statement: "All our books are first editions. We never reprint."

1981 Statement: *See* 1976 Statement

J. J. AUGUSTIN PUBLISHERS CORPORATION

1947 Statement: "We are somewhat hesitant to give a definite statement of the method used to identify first printings of our books, however as far as we can see from our recent publications and older ones at hand, the first editions show the word Copyright and the year in the front of the book, while books with two or more editions list the different editions or reprints, respectively."

AURUM PRESS (ENGLAND)

1988 Statement: "In general we print the date of the first printing on the title-page verso, with dates of subsequent reprintings or new editions where relevant, as in the following example:

    First published 1987 by Aurum Press Ltd

    Reprinted 1988

    New edition 1989"

AVALON PRESS LTD. (ENGLAND)

1947 Statement: "We adopt the same method to identify the first printings of our books as that employed by other leading publishers. The first edition would have the words 'First published 194-' and subsequent editions would have the words 'Second edition 194-' and so on. If the text of a book has been revised the word 'revised' is also inserted."

AVON BOOKS

1981 Statement: "Avon designates the first printing of our books by a copyline which appears on the copyright page, 'First Avon Printing, May, 1981' for example. The copyline reflects the imprint of the title. We have five imprints; Avon (mass market books and trade books), BARD (distinguished fiction, mass market size books), DISCUS (distinguished non-fiction, mass market size also), FLARE (young adult titles, mass market) and CAMELOT (children's books, trade size). The printing line would read, 'First Flare Printing, May, 1981' or whatever is appropriate. This method of designating the first printing has been the one Avon has always used.

"Starting in July, 1981 we will institute a new method for designating second printings and subsequent editions. A line of numbers will be added to the bottom of the copyright page: 10 9 8 7 6 5 4 3 2 1. The last number on the right indicates the current edition. The above example would designate a first edition. A line reading 10 9 8 7 would indicate the book is in its seventh printing. This line of numbers is in addition to the print line, 'First Avon Printing' etc. Previous to July, 1981 we used to designate second editions by an additional line, 'Second Printing, July, 1981.'"

B

BACKCOUNTRY PUBLICATIONS
1988 Statement: *See* 1988 Statement of The Countryman Press, Inc.

BACKGROUND BOOKS, LTD. (ENGLAND)
1947 Statement: "First editions of our publications are printed in the following manner, opposite the title page:
'1st printing 19..'
"Subsequent printings are identified firstly under the heading of 2nd, 3rd, etc. impression' and a second printing is marked in the same manner as the first printing, and so forth."

BAEN PUBLISHING ENTERPRISES
1988 Statement: "Since inception in 1984 Baen Books has indicated first editions on the copyright page with the phrase 'A Baen Books Original.' First, and all subsequent printings, are also indicated on the copyright page with month and year of the printing."

BAILEY BROS. & SWINFEN LTD. (ENGLAND)
1988 Statement: "For your information our first imprints give the date of publication on the copyright page i.e. the verso. Should the book be reprinted, the date of the reprint would be shown on this page also. We would not put second edition unless the book had been altered or amended in any way, thus we would continue with third, fourth, fifth printing, etc. The new edition would name the date as would the reprints."

JOHN BAKER (ENGLAND)
1976, 1981 Statements: *See* 1976, 1981 Statements of Adam and Charles Black Publishers Limited (England)
1988 Statement: *See* 1988 Statement of A & C Black (Publishers) Limited (England)

BAKER BOOK HOUSE
1989 Statement: "Almost without exception, first editions have no printing notice—just the copyright. All later editions are identified as 'second edition' or as a subsequent printing, e.g., 'second printing.'"

BALCH INSTITUTE FOR ETHNIC STUDIES
1988 Statement: *See* 1988 Statement of Associated University Presses

BALD EAGLE PRESS
1988 Statement: *See* 1988 Statement of The Pennsylvania State University Press

ROBERT O. BALLOU, PUBLISHER
1937 and 1949 Statements: *See* Jonathan Cape and Robert Ballou, Inc.

BANTAM BOOKS
1988 Statement: "Our general policy has been to designate hardcover and paperback printings by the number code 9 8 7 6 5 4 3 2 1—the number on the right indicating which printing.

"No one seems to know when this practice was adopted. It does not differ from any previous designation. This designation is for Bantam Books only."

BANYAN BOOKS, INC.
1976 Statement: "Our first editions carry the copyright notice alone; subsequent editions are noted (2nd printing, 19..), (rev. ed. 19..) as the situations warrant."
1981, 1988 Statements: *See* 1976 Statement

BARD
See Avon Books

ARTHUR BARKER LTD. (ENGLAND)
1937 Statement: "It is our general practice to print the number of impressions and editions of our books on the reverse side of the title page.

"The first edition of a book merely has 'first published 1936' or whatever the year happens to be. If the book is reprinted we run a line:
    '2nd impression June 1936
    '3rd impression July 1936,' etc.

"If the author makes any changes between the first printing or second printing, we usually replace '2nd impression' by the words 'revised edition' followed by the date.

"We started this method in 1933."
1949 Statement: *See* 1937 Statement

BARLENMIR HOUSE, PUBLISHERS
1976 Statement: "Barlenmir House's method of identifying first editions in its publications is by identifying 'FIRST EDITION' on the copyright page of the book."

BARN OWL BOOKS (ENGLAND)
1989 Statement: A first printing is indicated in the copyright page by the phrase "First published (date)."

BARNARD & WESTWOOD, LTD. (ENGLAND)
1947 Statement: "We use the following method: First printing—we merely show 'Printed by Barnard & Westwood Ltd.' etc. Subsequent printings are shown 'Second Printing,' 'Third Printing,' and so on."

A. S. BARNES AND COMPANY, INC.
(Including Countryman Press.)

1947 Statement: "First printings of our books can be identified as against subsequent printings. In some cases we do print on the copyright page 'Second printing,' 'Third printing,' et cetera; in other cases we don't. It is really impossible for anyone to actually identify whether or not one of our books is a first edition without intimate knowledge."

1976 Statement: "We make no specific identification of first editions or first printings. Subsequent editions and printings do carry a printing history on the copyright page."

1988 Statement: *See* 1976 Statement

BARNES & NOBLE BOOKS

1976 Statement: "To designate a first edition the words First Edition are used on the copyright page, although often a first edition is not designated. The first printing of an edition is indicated as follows on the copyright page:

76 77 78 10 9 8 7 6 5 4 3 2 1

"The second printing is indicated like this:

76 77 78 10 9 8 7 6 5 4 3 2

"The numbers before 10 indicate years.

"Previously printings were listed as follows:

First printing, July, 1964."

BARNES & NOBLE BOOKS (IMPORTS & REPRINTS)

1988 Statement: "Barnes & Noble Books is strictly an importing operation which specializes in academic title in the humanities. Since we get most of our titles from the British Isles we indicate on the verso of the title page 'First published in the U.S. 19—' followed by our company name and address—even though our imprint appears on the book's title page, spine, and jacket.

"We have been importing academic books since 1949 and the above policy has remained the same. It has not changed over the years. When we have found it necessary to reprint a particular volume we always state 'Reprinted 19—' somewhere on the verso which indicates that that particular copy is not a first edition (printing)."

BARRE PUBLISHING CO., INC.

1976 Statement: "Every printing after the first is listed with the edition on the copyright page. (i.e. on the first edition, first printing, the c/r page says only 1st edition; on 2nd printing, '2nd printing' is added to 1st edition). This method does not differ from any previously used."

BARRIE & JENKINS (ENGLAND)

1988 Statement: *See* 1988 Statement of Century Hutchinson Publishing Group Limited (England)

M. BARROWS AND COMPANY, INC.

1947 Statement: "First printings are identified in our books by these very words appearing on our copyright page. Later printings are also identified in the same manner. Our method for Village Green Press books is the same."

BARTHOLOMEW BOOKS

1988 Statement: "First editions have no identification. Subsequent editions are noted: second, third, etc. No other method is used."

BASIC BOOKS, INC.

1981 Statement: "Generally, when we issue a new edition it is because there is new material in the book. The book will then read, for instance, 'second and revised edition,' 'third and revised edition' etc.

"When there is no change in content, the book will be reprinted. Our normal method of indicating which printing we are making is to remove the digits at the bottom of the reverse of the title page one by one starting with the lowest number.

"This has been our general policy."

THE BASILISK PRESS LTD (ENGLAND)

1988 Statement: "Basilisk books are *not* reprinted. We print an edition of usually 500 copies, and when it is out of print, it is *really* out of print."

B. T. BATSFORD, LTD. (ENGLAND)

1937 Statement: "In all our publications the date appears either on the verso or recto of title-page, or where this is not included on this leaf it is to be found as preface date. Reprints or revised editions are always clearly shown on the recto of title."

1947 Statement: *See* 1937 Statement

Statement for 1960: "The words 'First published 19..' were still used during the 1960s and we continue this style [in 1981]."

1976 Statement: "First printing of the first edition is designated by the words: First published 19...

"The form which this follows is similar to that which has been Batsford's practice for a good many years now."

1981 Statement: " 'First published 19..' is still our method of designating a first edition. Under this we would insert as appropriate 'New edition 19..', or 'Reprinted 19..' if only minor amendments are made."

1988 Statement: *See* 1981 Statement

BATTERY PRESS, INC.

1988 Statement: "We use standard copyright information to designate 1st editions. Subsequent printings or reprints are marked."

WILLIAM L. BAUHAN, PUBLISHER

1988 Statement: "As a rule our books do not contain any specific designation on the copyright page that the book is a first edition. Subsequent printings or revised editions are almost invariably so marked. So it would be safe to assume that a book is a first edition unless otherwise marked.

"This house began as Richard R. Smith publishers on Murray Hill, New York in 1929, and in 1952 Mr. Smith moved the firm to Rindge, New Hampshire. After his death, William L. Bauhan bought the firm in 1959 and moved it that year to Peterborough, N.H. and in 1972 to Dublin, N.H. In 1968 the Smith name was dropped and the present name assumed. Between 1968 and 1972 some books were issued under the imprint 'noone House.'

"Since taking over the firm, William Bauhan has generally specialized in regional New England titles."

BAYLOR UNIVERSITY PRESS

1988 Statement: "Our books carry the usual data on the copyright page indicating the date of publication. If we were to reprint a title this would be added to the information already appearing."

BBC BOOKS (ENGLAND)
1988 Statement: *See* BBC Enterprises Limited (England)

BBC ENTERPRISES LIMITED (ENGLAND)
1988 Statement: "BBC Books is a division of BBC Enterprises, a wholly owned subsidiary of the British Broadcasting Corporation.

"The BBC started publishing books in approximately 1966/67 and used as its title page imprint 'British Broadcasting Corporation.' The verso to the title page read—

Published by the British Broadcasting Corporation,

35 Marylebone High Street, London Wl

First published...

"From March 1987 the title page imprint became 'BBC Books' and the verso to the title page read—

Published by BBC Books, A Division of BBC Enterprises

Limited,

80 Wood Lane, London Wl2 OTT.

First published..."

BEACON NIGHT LIGHTS
1988 Statement: *See* Beacon Press

BEACON PRESS
1947 Statement: "Nothing to indicate first printing. Subsequent printings carry a note on the copyright page as follows:

First printing, June 1947

—printing, October 1947"

Statement for 1960: "The method of designating first printings in 1960 was the statement on the copyright page 'First published by Beacon Press in 1960.' "

1976 Statement: "The method of designating first printings in 1976 was the statement on the copyright page, 'First published by Beacon Press in 1976.' "

1982 Statement: First printings of both hardcover and paperback editions are designated by the following number code:

9 8 7 6 5 4 3 2 1

The number on the right indicates the printing.

1988 Statement: "First printings of both hardcover and paperback editions are designated by a series of impression numbers. The smallest number indicates the most recent printing.

"We first began to use this modified method in 1987, and it is used as well in our Beacon Night Lights imprint."

BEAR FLAG BOOKS
1988 Statement: *See* 1988 Statement of Padre Productions

BEAUFORT BOOKS INC.
1981 Statement: "Our edition code is based on the assumption that a printing run is equivalent to an edition. We use a sequence of numbers on the copyright page running from 1-10. When one edition is completed, a number is deleted. Thus, if a '1' remains, the book is a first edition. If the sequence '2-10' remains but there is no ' 1,' the book is a second edition. And so on.

"In the case of a true revision, 'revised edition' appears on the copyright page."
1988 Statement: *See* 1981 Statement

BEDFORD BOOKS, LTD. (ENGLAND)

1947 Statement: "We are so short of paper that we have only published two books since the war, and they have only gone to press once."

BEECHHURST PRESS, INC.

1947 Statement: "First editions of Beechhurst Press books have no identification marks on the copyright page. Subsequent printings are identified by the words 'Second printing' and the date or 'Third printing' and the date and so forth. Thus the lack of identification on the copyright page would serve to identify the first printing of any of our titles.

"The firm of Bernard Ackerman, Inc., became Beechhurst Press in July, 1946. There was no change in ownership and the policies were continued in effect. Thus the first editions of Ackerman books can be identified in the same way."

THE BEEHIVE PRESS

1976 Statement: "All books are our first editions, unless the copyright page specifically states something like, 'Copyright 1972 by The Beehive Press. Reprinted 1976.' "
1981, 1988 Statements: *See* 1976 Statement

BEEKMAN PUBLISHERS, INC.

1988 Statement: "Our first editions—so far—have been *only* editions. We would designate those editions after the first printing with proper numbering and information. All of our issues are first 'editions.' "

BEHRMAN HOUSE, INC.

1947 Statement: "When we reprint a book we indicate that it is the second or whatever printing. On the first edition we say nothing. In other words, if a book does not refer to any particular printing, you may rightly assume that it is the first printing of the first edition."

BEING PUBLICATIONS

1976 Statement: "The act of publication is our method of identifying a first edition; consecutive editions or printings are so marked.
"We have not used any different methods."
1981 Statement: *See* 1976 Statement
1988 Statement: "We're inactive at present."

CHARLES H. BELDING

1988 Statement: *See* 1988 Statement of Graphic Arts Center Publishing Company

THE BELKNAP PRESS

1988 Statement: *See* 1988 Statement of Harvard University Press

G. BELL & SONS, LTD. (ENGLAND)

1928 Statement: "The title page of the first edition carries the year of publication at the foot, and when it is reprinted the month and year are indicated on the reverse of the title page, e.g.:
First Published (say) February 1928.
Reprinted (say) July 1928."

1936 Statement: "We only indicate the months when a book is reprinted twice in a year. We have used this method of identifying first printings since the Great War."

1947 Statement: *See* 1936 Statement

1976 Statement: "We do not have any common form of words on the title page verso of our books relating to the first edition. We would assume that the copyright line giving the year would provide the necessary information. Sometimes we add 'First published in (year)', with or without our name following."

BELLEROPHON BOOKS

1988 Statement: "First editions are usually the ones with errors; we do not otherwise distinguish them."

BELLEVUE PRESS

1976 Statement: "The colophon page of each of our books clearly states the information any collector would wish to know about any one of our books. Here we note printer, designer or artist when the particular book requires such notes, and the size of our published editions, noting how many are reserved for 'signed' copies, how many are published in the trade edition, and if the book is other than a first edition."

1981 Statement: "Your previous entry is quite sufficient for our press, except that it may be added:

"Since 1979 most Bellevue Press books do clearly state *First Edition* on the copyright page. However the colophon page is still the best source for 'edition' information."

ERNEST BENN, LTD. (ENGLAND)

1928 Statement: "We have two forms of designating first editions, (1) a bibliography printed on the back of the title page stating first published in — and then the year. We use this form mostly. (2) is to have no bibliography on the first edition but to put the year of publication on the front of the title page with our imprint.

"We have used this formula since we first started book publishing in 1923."

1937 and 1947 Statements: *See* 1928 Statement

Statement for 1960: *See* 1976 Statement

1976 Statement: "We follow standard practice, e.g. that adopted by University Presses in always stating date of first publication. We always differentiate between a straight reprint, usually referred to as a 'Second impression' etc. and where any revision has taken place 'Second (corrected) impression', and major revision as a 'Second edition.' "

1981 Statement: "We always state date of first publication. The first line on the title-verso (copyright page) reads, 'First published 1981 by Ernest Benn Limited.' Thereafter a straight reprint is called 'Second impression,' etc. If a reprint has been lightly revised, we call it 'Second (revised) impression,' etc. A major revision is called 'Second edition,' etc."

BERGH PUBLISHING, INC.

1988 Statement: "Our first editions are not marked in any way. Should a second one be printed this of course is mentioned on the cover as well as on the impression page."

BERGIN & GARVEY PUBLISHERS, INC.

1988 Statement: "Bergin & Garvey Publishers, Inc. uses two indicators of first edition status in its books, both of which are found on p. iv of the front matter, the copyright page:

"1. A printed statement, 'First published by Bergin & Garvey . . . .' In the case of a book first published by another publisher, say, in the UK, the reader must infer that another publication took place, as we would use 'First published in the United States by Bergin & Garvey . . . ', by looking at the copyright date also.

"2. We use a number code; the left-hand number indicates the year of publication (890 would mean 1988; 90 would mean 1989; etc.) and the right-hand number, the number of the impression (87654321 would mean first printing; 876543 would mean third printing)."

BERNARDS (PUBLISHERS), LTD. (ENGLAND)

1947 Statement: "Our bibliographical notices follow the usual English practice, namely:
"First printing will be identified:—
　　First published—
"Subsequent printings will be identified with the different number of impressions as follows:—
　　First published —
　　New Impression —."

BESS PRESS

1988 Statement: "We have no special identification method. The copyright date indicates the first printing. Subsequent editions are also recorded on the copyright page."

CORNELIA & MICHAEL BESSIE BOOKS

1988 Statement: Cornelia & Michael Bessie Books follow the practices of Harper & Row Publishers Inc., with an additional imprint logo on the title page.
See 1988 Statement of Harper & Row, Publishers, Inc.

BETTER HOMES AND GARDENS BOOKS

1981 Statement: "Better Homes and Gardens Books clearly designates first printings of its first editions with the words 'First Edition. First Printing.' on the book's copyright page (usually the title page or the page following it). Subsequent editions and/or printings are similarly designated, i.e. 'First Edition. Fourth Printing.' or 'Sixth Edition. First Printing.' "
1988 Statement: *See* 1981 Statement

THE BHAKTIVEDANTA BOOK TRUST

1976 Statement: "The printing history of our books is printed on the copyright page of each book. If a book says First Printing, then it is a First Edition. There is no indication as to when a book becomes a Second Edition."
1981 Statement: "The printing history of our books is printed on the copyright page of each book. If a book says First Printing, then it is a First Edition. Subsequent printings are always indicated on the copyright page and it is assumed that each new printing involves correcting of any mistakes."
1989 Statement: *See* 1981 Statement

BIG SKY
1976 Statement: "I simply say 'First Edition.' "

BINFORD & MORT
1976 Statement: "When first publishing under the imprint of Metropolitan Press, our company used the star method to indicate the number of the printing—though when changes in text were made, the book was then stated to be a second edition, etc. One star indicated the first reprinting; two stars, the second, and so on.

"Under Binfords & Mort, we have some books listed under the name of the Metropolitan Press books. Now, under Binford & Mort, the printing or edition is so indicated on the copyright page."

1981, 1988 Statements: *See* 1976 Statement

BINFORDS & MORT, PUBLISHERS
1947 Statement: "I am afraid that you won't find any mark noting many of our second printings. This was especially true during the war when we couldn't run even one printing all with the same colored cloth for the cover. *Paul Bunyan the Work Giant* was marked with an 'X' as each different printing was made. The first run of that was numbered.

"Our earlier books were published under the firm name of Metropolitan Press."

See also Binford & Mort

JOSEPH J. BINNS, PUBLISHER
1988 Statement: "All 1st editions are so marked. Other editions, i.e., 2nd, 3rd, etc., are so indicated."

BISON BOOKS
1988 Statement: *See* 1988 Statement of University of Nebraska Press

BITS PRESS
1988 Statement: "Our books—from 1974 to date—are all first editions (and first printings). Should we ever have cause to reprint, the copyright page will show 2d Printing or (if there are changes in the text) 2d Edition, and so on.

"In the cases of a few limited editions (e.g., John Updike, *Five Poems*, 1978) books have been published in two states (e.g., on handmade and on machine-made paper, or in somewhat different bindings) as noted in the colophons. These are all, nonetheless, properly first editions also."

H. BITTNER AND COMPANY
1947 Statement: "So far, we have not published any second editions."

BLACK DRAGON
1988 Statement: *See* 1988 Statement of Panjandrum Books

BLACK FARM PRESS
(In 1941 combined with The Press of James A. Decker.)
1947 Statement: *See* The Press of James A. Decker

A. & C. BLACK, LTD. (ENGLAND)
1928 Statement: "Subsequent editions and impressions are so noted."
1947 Statement: "*First Editions* of our publications have the date on the title-page only; Second and Reprints have the date of reprint on the title-page and particulars of all printings in a bibliography on the verso.

"The same particulars would apply to the principal books which we publish over the imprint of S. W. Partridge & Co. Prior to our taking over the business, however, Messrs. Partridge had seldom printed a date on the title-pages of their Juveniles, and as some of these have now been selling for a number of years we are not always giving a bibliography on the reverse of title-pages."

Statement for 1960: Following is an example of the copyright page of a book published by A. and C. Black Ltd.

FIRST PUBLISHED IN ONE VOLUME 1955
BY A. AND C. BLACK LTD
4, 5 & 6 SOHO SQUARE LONDON WIV 6AD
THE BOOK IS ALSO AVAILABLE IN FOUR PARTS
FIRST EDITION 1955
SECOND EDITION 1963
THIRD EDITION 1966
REPRINTED 1968 AND 1970
REPRINTED 1972
ISBN 0 7136 0772 6
© 1966 A. & C. BLACK LTD"

A & C BLACK (PUBLISHERS) LIMITED (ENGLAND)

1988 Statement: "Our current practice is to designate a first edition by the words 'First published (date)' on the biblio page."

ADAM AND CHARLES BLACK PUBLISHERS LIMITED (ENGLAND)

1976 Statement: "We designate a first edition by the words 'First edition (date)' on the biblio page. Subsequently we add the words 'Reprinted (date)' or 'Second edition (date)' etc. These methods of identification do not differ from any previously used, and the same practice is followed by books published by John Baker and Dacre Press."

1981 Statement: *See* 1976 Statement

1988 Statement: *See* 1988 Statement of A & C Black (Publishers) Limited (England)

BLACK SPARROW PRESS

1976 Statement: "The copyright page of first printings carries no identifying notation, but first printings always have a full colophon page, and their title pages are in color.

"Reprints have the title page in black and white only, carry no colophon, and are identified as 'Second printing', 'Third printing', etc., on the copyright page.

"For further details see Seamus Cooney's *A Checklist of the First One Hundred Publications of the Black Sparrow Press* (Black Sparrow Press, Los Angeles, 1971), and its projected successor covering the first 250 titles."

1981 Statement: "The copyright page of first printings carries no identifying notation, but first printings always have a full colophon page, and their title pages are in color.

"Reprints have the title page in black and white only, carry no colophon, and are identified as 'Second printing,' 'Third printing,' etc., on the copyright page.

"For further details see Seamus Cooney's *A Checklist of the First One Hundred Publications of the Black Sparrow Press* (Black Sparrow Press, Los Angeles, 1971), and its successor covering the first 300 titles, *A Bibliography of the Black Sparrow Press: 1966-1978* (1981)."

1988 Statement: *See* 1981 Statement

BLACK SWAN BOOKS LTD.

1988 Statement: "Black Swan Books designates a first printing with the following statement which appears on the verso of the titlepage: 'First edition.' Subsequent printings do not have any designation given, nor does, of course, the above statement appear. First printings of a revised edition are designated 'Revised edition.'

"This method of designation has been used by us from the start of our press and the publication of its first book in 1980."

BLACKBERRY

1976 Statement: "All Blackberry books are limited first editions. Any future reprint will, of course, be noted in the book next to the copyright notice."

BLACKIE & SON, LTD. (UNITED KINGDOM)

1928 Statement: *See* 1937 Statement of Blackie & Son, Limited (United Kingdom)

BLACKIE & SON, LIMITED (UNITED KINGDOM)

1937 Statement: "It is not possible to give a general rule for the detecting of our first editions.

"In the first editions of our more recent educational works and general publications (exclusive of Reward or Story Books) the date appears on the title-page, and if it is a new edition, it is so stated. The dates of subsequent reprints are noted on the back of the title-page.

"We are afraid it is impossible to say just what date we started using this present method."

1947 Statement: *See* 1937 Statement

Statement for 1960: *See* 1976 Statement of Blackie and Son Limited (United Kingdom)

BLACKIE AND SON LIMITED (UNITED KINGDOM)

1976 Statement: "Since the 1957 Copyright Act our imprint or biblio pages have contained the words, e.g.

© John Hume 1974

First published 1974

and this style may be taken to identify a first edition. Subsequent editions would have this information plus the date of the subsequent edition (be it a reprint, revision or new edition)."

1981 Statement: "The [1976] statement is still accurate and the same practice is followed by all our imprints."

1988 Statement: *See* 1981 Statement

BLACKSTAFF PRESS LTD. (NORTHERN IRELAND)

1981 Statement: "Our current practice in designating editions is to give the copyright symbol, the name of the copyright holder and the date of first printing on the imprint page. In subsequent reprintings, if the material is unaltered, this information remains the same i.e. we do not indicate second or third printings. We do however indicate a new (i.e. altered, enlarged or cut) edition by saying after the copyright line something like 'second edition' or 'new enlarged edition' etc.

"This company has only one imprint, i.e. Blackstaff Press."

1988 Statement: "Our current practice in designating editions is to give the copyright symbol, the name of the copyright holder and the first date of printing. In subsequent reprintings, if the material is unaltered, the information on the copyright line remains the same but we do insert a new line which indicates reprint dates (e.g. Reprinted 1985, 1986, 1987 etc.). We also indicate a new (i.e. altered, enlarged or cut) edition by adding the new date to the copyright lines *as well as* inserting a new line which indicates the new edition (e.g. 'second edition' or 'new enlarged edition' etc.) together with the relevant date.

"This company has only one imprint, i.e. Blackstaff Press."

BASIL BLACKWELL (ENGLAND)

1928 Statement: "Our first editions are published without any reference on the title page whatever; all subsequent editions bear the fact on the back of the title page."

1937, 1947 Statements: *See* 1928 Statement

See also Basil Blackwell and Mott, Ltd. (England)

BASIL BLACKWELL LIMITED (ENGLAND)

1988 Statement: "Ten years ago this company was called 'Basil Blackwell and Mott Limited.' About eight years ago it changed its name to 'Basil Blackwell Publisher Limited.' Finally, four years ago it changed its name to 'Basil Blackwell Limited.' No further changes are planned at present!

"It is certainly our practice to print full copyright and printing history details on the verso of the title page.

"Shakespeare Head Press is an imprint of this company."

See also Basil Blackwell and Mott Limited (England)

BASIL BLACKWELL AND MOTT, LTD. (ENGLAND)

1976 Statement: "Before the Universal Copyright Convention of 1957 it was our practice to put the date of publication on either the recto or verso of the title page, but occasionally for reasons of space it was sometimes transferred to the back of the book, but only rarely. Since 1957 of course the international copyright mark and the date of publication appear on the verso of the title page."

1981 Statement: *See* 1976 Statement

1988 Statement: *See* 1988 Statement of Basil Blackwell Limited (England)

BASIL BLACKWELL PUBLISHER LIMITED (ENGLAND)

1988 Statement: *See* 1988 Statement of Basil Blackwell Limited (England)

BLACKWELL SCIENTIFIC PUBLICATIONS LTD (ENGLAND)

1976 Statement: "The first editions of our books are identifiable as such only by the absence of any reference to later editions on the title page, recto or verso."

1981, 1988 Statements: *See* 1976 Statement

WILLIAM BLACKWOOD & SONS, LTD. (SCOTLAND)

1928 Statement: "Although we have no hard and fast rule, our general practice is to omit the notification of the first edition on the first issue of a book, the date of publication appearing below the imprint. Subsequent editions are notified accordingly."

1937 and 1947 Statements: *See* 1928 Statement

1976 Statement: "In the case of a title published by William Blackwood & Sons Ltd., the first edition bears the year of publication below the imprint on the title page. For a reprint the year is removed, and below the copyright note on the verso of the title page, the following note is added: 'Reprinted 19...' Subsequent reprints are recorded in the same way.

"I should stress that this is our current practice. In the past, especially with the large number of books published by the firm up to about 60 years ago, the system was not consistent. However, I think it is true to say that in the case of a reprint, the above notation, or something similar, was always used. Thus any book which does not bear a reprint note may be assumed to be a first edition. But there were possibly exceptions, and I believe in the early 19th century it was the fashion to attempt to 'establish' a new writer by claiming that his book was already in its second edition, whereas in fact it was only the first printing. The first book of John Gibson Lockhart, *Peter's Letters to His Kinsfolk*, was I think treated in such a way."

1981 Statement: "In the case of a title published by William Blackwood & Sons Ltd., the first edition bears the year of publication on the verso of the title page. For a reprint, the following note is added: 'Reprinted 19...' Subsequent reprints are recorded in the same way.

"We changed our method in January of [1981]."

BLANDFORD PRESS, LTD. (ENGLAND)

1947 Statement: "It is rather difficult to give you any hard and fast ruling on how to identify the first printings of our books and to differentiate between them and subsequent printings. Whether we give any indications depends very largely on the type of book. With a technical or semi-technical volume we usually indicate the year of publication and the number of the edition. However, with certain general books it has not been possible to do that during recent years on account of paper restrictions, and shortage of materials, and frequently several printings are made, and we usually have no reason to differentiate between the first, second or third printing, and in certain instances would prefer not to.

"This company was established immediately after the first World War in 1919."

Statement for 1960: Following is an example of the relevant portion of the copyright page of a book in its first printing published by Blandford Press, Ltd., in 1960.

First published in 1960
© Copyright 1960 by Blandford Press Ltd.
16 West Central Street, London, W. C. 1

1976 Statement: First editions are designated by the words: First published 19..

1981 Statement: "I give the wording as it appears in our publications: 'First published in the U.K. 19.. by Blandford Press Link House, West Street, Poole, Dorset, BH15 1LL Copyright © 19.. Blandford Books Ltd.' "

1988 Statement: *See* 1988 Statement of Cassell PLC (England)

GEOFFREY BLES, LTD. (ENGLAND)

1937 Statement. "Our practice is to give the date of the first edition of the book on the title page verso. Subsequent reprints and editions are noted under that, e.g.

FIRST PUBLISHED	FEBRUARY 1933
REPRINTED	MARCH 1933
REPRINTED	APRIL 1933"

1947 Statement: *See* 1937 Statement

BLOCH PUBLISHING CO., INC.

1947 Statement: "There is no special way to identify the first printings of our books, but we differentiate from the first printing by marking the second and subsequent printings to that effect on the copyright page. When a book is reprinted and revised or enlarged, mention of this is made."

BLOODAXE BOOKS (ENGLAND)

1988 Statement: "Bloodaxe Books designates a first edition as being 'first published in X year.'

"Editions after the first are indicated by adding 'second edition' and the year. We designate a title to be in its second edition if there have been changes to the text; otherwise we designate it a second impression.

"We do not designate the first printing. This is designated only for second and subsequent printings (which we designate as impressions).

"All markings are on the back of the title page."

BLUE WIND PRESS

1976 Statement: "Undesignated book = first edition, first printing. The words 'Second Printing' mean 'of the first edition.' We sometimes use the following code:

77 78 79 80 5 4 3 2 1

As is it means first printing, 1977. If we do 2nd printing in 1977 we erase the '1.' If we do 2nd printing in 1978 we erase the '1' and the '77.' And so on. As a rule of thumb I consider a 'new' (2nd, 3rd &c) edition one in which the text has been altered. A new cover is simply a new printing to me. But a book retypeset for a new format (size) but with the text unaltered is also a new edition."

1981 Statement: *See* 1976 Statement

1988 Statement: "Undesignated book = first edition, first printing. The words 'Second Printing' mean 'of the first edition.' We sometimes use the following code:

77 78 79 80 5 4 3 2 1

As is it means first printing, 1977. If we do 2nd printing in 1977 we erase the '1.' If we do 2nd printing in 1978 we erase the '1' and the '77.' And so on. However, we didn't always bother. There are some subsequent printings which aren't noted in any way (except the colors on the cover are often slightly different). As a rule of thumb I consider a 'new' (2nd, 3rd &c) edition one in which the text has been altered. But a book retypeset for a new format (size) but with the text unaltered (or with the title page and cover changed) is also a new edition."

BOA EDITIONS

1981 Statement: "First Editions published by BOA Editions are indicated in the following manner:

"The phrase 'First Edition' appears on the copyright page of the book and the colophon at the end of the book describes the limitations of the various sub-editions of each book, i.e., paper, cloth and specially bound, limited editions signed by the poet.

"Subsequent printings are then indicated on the copyright page: 'Second Printing,' 'Third Printing' etc., generally with a date included."

THE BOBBS-MERRILL COMPANY

1928 Statement: "We are not entirely consistent in our first edition attitude. Whenever we do mark a first edition the distinguishing mark is a bow and arrow at the bottom of the page on which appears the copyright line.

"However, not all of our first editions are marked."

1936 Statement: "We are consistent in our first edition attitude. We print the words 'First Edition' on the copyright page. All of our first editions are so marked."

1947 Statement: See 1936 Statement

BOBBS-MERRILL COMPANY, INC.

1981 Statement. "First editions are designated on copyright pages as first printing, second printing, etc."

THE BODLEY HEAD LIMITED (ENGLAND)

1976 Statement: A first edition is designated by the words: "First published 19.."

1981 Statement: "The only information I can add is that if the text has been published first in another country (say, in USA), we would then describe our first edition as 'first published in Great Britain 19XX.'

"In this case the date of first edition would be included in the copyright line above, on that page."

See also John Lane The Bodley Head, Ltd. (England)

1988 Statement: See 1981 Statement

BOLCHAZY-CARDUCCI PUBLISHERS

1988 Statement: "We do not indicate 'First Edition.' We use 'Reprint' or 'Second / Third Revised Edition.' "

ALBERT & CHARLES BONI INC.

1928 Statement: "We run a note on the copyright page of all our books indicating all subsequent printings after the first."

1937 Statement: See 1928 Statement

BONI & GAER, INC.

1947 Statement: "We do not put distinguishing marks in our first printings. However, all subsequent printings are marked and therefore it is safe for you to assume that one of our publications with no marks is a first printing."

BONI & LIVERIGHT

1928 Statement: "As a general rule we have no marking on the copyright page of our publications to show our first edition although on subsequent editions we print Second, Third, Fourth, Fifth, Sixth edition, etc. We have had one or two books with first edition marked on the copyright page but this is not our general practice."

1937 Statement: (Became Horace Liveright, Inc; later, Liveright Publishing Corporation.) See 1937 Statement of Liveright Publishing Corporation

1947 Statement: See 1947 Statement of Liveright Publishing Corporation.

THE BOOK GUILD LIMITED (ENGLAND)

1988 Statement: "The words 'first published in [date]' indicate that if nothing else is stated then the book is a first edition. This term is used on every one of our books.

"This is standard practice on all of our books and has been from the in-
cept of this Company. We have two other imprints which are *Temple House
Books* which is used for all our paper back editions, and *Seagull Books* which
is used for specialized local works by prominent people."

BOOK PRESENTATIONS
1947 Statement: *See* 1947 Statement of Greystone Press

THE BOOKSTORE PRESS
1976 Statement: "We have no special methods."
1981, 1988 Statements: *See* 1976 Statement

BOREAS PUBLISHING CO., LTD. (ENGLAND)
1947 Statement: "The only identification we are using for our publications
is the little difference in design of our trade mark, which is on all of our
publications.

"Underneath please find our trade mark: The Viking Ship of the first and
every additional edition. The first edition has a stem-post at the end of the
sail, but the other issues are without it."

1st Edition   Following Editions

THE BORGO PRESS
1981 Statement: "We state 'First Edition—Month, Year' on verso of title
page. Subsequent printings are so indicated."
This method does not differ from any previously used. All imprints follow
this same method of identification.
1988 Statement: "We state 'First Edition—Month, Year' on verso of title
page. Subsequent printings are so indicated.

"Subsequent printings state: 'Second Printing—Month, Year'—or delete
first edition statement altogether (no printing or edition statement).

"Reprints of books published originally by other companies state: 'First
Borgo Edition—Month, Year.' "

THOMAS BOUREGY & CO., INC.
1988 Statement: "At this time, the books in our AVALON line have only one
edition. If, in the future, we were to publish subsequent editions, we would
indicate it on the copyright page."

R. R. BOWKER CO.
1947 Statement: "We have no definite system of specifically indicating first
editions of our publications. First editions usually carry only the copyright
notice; subsequent editions or printings usually carry information to this
effect."
1989 Statement: "We have no definite system of specifically indicating first
editions of our publications. First editions usually carry only the copyright
notice; subsequent editions or printings may carry information to this effect."

THE BOXWOOD PRESS

1976 Statement: "All of our publications are original (not reprints) and are first editions. Second editions and reprints are so marked."

1981 Statement: "All of our publications are original (not [from other publishers]) and are first editions. Second editions and reprints are so marked."

1988 Statement: *See* 1981 Statement

MARION BOYARS PUBLISHERS, INC.

1981 Statement: The first printing of a first edition is identified by the lack of any notation other than the copyright date. Printings after the first are identified as such.

BOYDELL & BREWER, LTD. (ENGLAND)

1988 Statement: "Our method is to indicate edition and printing on the copyright page with, e.g.:

First published 1988 by The Boydell Press
an imprint of Boydell & Brewer Ltd
[followed by address]

"Our other imprint is D. S. Brewer and we also publish volumes for other organizations such as The Royal Historical Society, The Suffolk Records Society and The Lincoln Record Society; the same method of designation is used for all of these. Absence of a printing statement should indicate first printing, as the reprint history and further edition details are updated at subsequent printings, e.g.:

Reprinted 1985, 1987
Second edition 1988

"We are currently tightening up our procedures for including reprint history on the copyright page. To date, absence of reprint details cannot be taken as a wholly reliable indication of first printing."

BOYDELL PRESS (ENGLAND)

1988 Statement: *See* 1988 Statement of Boydell & Brewer, Ltd. (England)

BRADT PUBLICATIONS (ENGLAND)

1988 Statement: "First edition copyright [author's name] [date]. Subsequent editions: Second edition [date].

"I've been erratic in applying the above rules: one fourth edition went in as copyright Hilary Bradt 1987 with no mention of earlier editions (1974, 1976, 1980). This provoked a reviewer into writing 'Any book which goes into four editions in one year must be worth buying.' I'm endeavoring to be more accurate now."

BRANDEIS UNIVERSITY PRESS

1988 Statement: *See* 1988 Statement of University Press of New England

THE BRANDEN PRESS, INCORPORATED

1976 Statement: "We do not normally designate a first edition of a book unless it is a limited edition. In this case, the details of the limited edition are explained in some detail.

"On the other hand, we frequently indicate on the copyright page the second edition and so forth after the first printing."

1981 Statement: *See* 1976 Statement

1988 Statement: "For the most part, we specify new editions and/or printing on the copyright page."

BRANDYWYNE BOOKS
1988 Statement: *See* 1988 Statement of Underwood-Miller

CHARLES T. BRANFORD CO.
1949 Statement: "Our system is simple. The first printing has no particular markings, but subsequent printings are marked, e.g., 'second printing' and the date."

BRENTANO'S
(Discontinued publishing in 1933.)
1928 Statement: "Up to the end of 1927 all books published by this company had no edition printed on them unless they reached a second edition. This information would be on the back of the title. From January 1st 1928 the words 'First Printed 1928' were substituted and if the book reached a second edition the words 'second impression April 1928 (or...).' "
1933 Statement: *See* 1928 Statement

BRENTANO'S, LTD. (ENGLAND)
(This English house discontinued by Brentano's in 1933.)
1928 and 1933 Statements: *See* 1928 Statement of Brentano's

D. S. BREWER (ENGLAND)
1988 Statement: *See* 1988 Statement of Boydell & Brewer, Ltd. (England)

BREWER & WARREN
(Succeeded Payson Clarke, Ltd, on Jan. 1, 1930. Became Brewer, Warren and Putnam, Inc., in autumn of 1931. Out of business prior to 1937.)
1937 Statement: "We do not put the actual words 'first edition' on the reverse of the title page for the first edition but when we go into the second printing we say 'first printing such and such a date,' 'second printing such and such a date,' therefore, all copies of a book which do not carry such designation may be taken as being 'firsts.' "

BREWER, WARREN AND PUTNAM, INC.
(Succeeded Brewer and Warren in autumn of 1931. Firm was dissolved on December 8, 1932, and publications were taken over by Harcourt, Brace and Co., Inc.)
1937 Statement (by the former president of the company): "We did not put the actual words 'first edition' on the reverse of the title page for the first edition but when we went into the second printing we said 'first printing such and such a date,' 'second printing such and such a date,' therefore all copies of a book which do not carry such designation may be taken as being 'firsts.' "

BRIMAX (ENGLAND)
1989 Statement: *See* 1989 Statement of The Octopus Publishing Group PLC (England)

THE BRITISH ACADEMY (ENGLAND)
1988 Statement: "An impression is likely to be the first printing of the first edition if there is no mention of succeeding printings/editions on the copyright page (though I know of one or two unfortunate exceptions)."

BRITISH BROADCASTING CORPORATION (ENGLAND)
1988 Statement: *See* 1988 Statement of BBC Enterprises Limited (England)

BRITISH DENTAL JOURNAL (ENGLAND)
1988 Statement: *See* 1988 Statement of British Medical Journal (England)

THE BRITISH LIBRARY (ENGLAND)
1988 Statement: "We give all bibliographical information about our books on the title verso page. Normally we would say 'first published 1988,' or similar, and usually a copyright statement will include the copyright date, i. e., © 1988 The British Library Board. For subsequent editions we state 'reprinted 1988,' or similar."

BRITISH MEDICAL ASSOCIATION (ENGLAND)
1988 Statement: *See* 1988 Statement of British Medical Journal (England)

BRITISH MEDICAL JOURNAL (ENGLAND)
1988 Statement: "British Medical Journal books carry the statement:
British Medical Journal 1988
"Subsequent printings or editions carry the statement:
British Medical Journal, 1983, 1988

. . . .
. . . .
First edition 1983
Second impression (with corrections) 1985
Second edition November 1988
"British Medical Association books carry the statement:
British Medical Association 1988
First Printed July 1988
"British Dental Journal books carry the statement:
Published by the British Dental Association
64 Wimpole Street, London W1M 8AL
Papers from the
British Dental Journal
March 19 to June 25, 1988
Copyright British Dental Journal, 1988"

BRITISH MUSEUM (NATURAL HISTORY) (ENGLAND)
1988 Statement: "It is our practice to include the following on the title verso:
First published ... (date)
British Museum (Natural History),
Cromwell Road, London SW7 5BD
"This holds good for all our titles."

BRITISH MUSEUM PUBLICATIONS, LTD. (ENGLAND)
1988 Statement: "Our first editions bear only the copyright date. Subsequent reprintings bear 2nd (or 3rd) impressions with the date or reprinted with the date. This practice, or something very similar, has been in force since the Company was formed in 1973. When reprinting we would normally take the opportunity of making any necessary alterations."

BRITISH YEARBOOKS (ENGLAND)
1947 Statement: "All Yearbooks published are annual and are marked as such, only in the case of second and third impressions in the same year are these facts recorded in the Prelims."

BROADMAN PRESS

1988 Statement: "We do not identify printings."

BROADSIDE PRESS

1989 Statement: "Example of 1st Printing:
First Edition
First Printing
Copyright © 1988 by *author's name*
"Example of 2nd Printing:
Copyright © 1973 by *author's name*
First Printing, November 1973
Second Printing, February 1976
"This method was adopted in 1965."

BROCKHAMPTON PRESS (ENGLAND)
(Name changed to Hodder & Stoughton Children's Books sometime prior to 1976.)

1976 Statement: *See* 1976 Statement of Hodder & Stoughton Limited (England)

THE BRONX COUNTY HISTORICAL SOCIETY

1988 Statement: "A first edition is noted in the Foreword or Preface. Any subsequent editions are noted on the title page."

BROOKE HOUSE PUBLISHERS, INC.

1976 Statement: "Brooke House books are intended to carry (as an indication of the number of the printing rather than as any indication of edition) a number on the copyright page consisting of an ascending series of ten figures and a descending series of ten figures. The number on the left is the last digit of the year of the printing; the number on the right is the number of the printing. If a printing is made in the same year as the one just before, only the number on the right is deleted in the new printing. E.g., 7890109876 would indicate a 6th printing in 1977. If a 7th printing were to be made, the 6 would be deleted.—A second *edition* would carry some indication, e.g., Revised Edition, Second Edition, etc.; again on the copyright page."

THE BROOKINGS INSTITUTION

1976 Statement: "We do not explicitly identify first editions, because with few exceptions we publish only first editions. We designate printings by a string of numbers on the copyright page, one of which is deleted whenever the book is reprinted, so that the lowest surviving number indicates the printing in hand. Whenever we do publish revised, second, or third, etc., editions, we so label them on the title page, jacket, cover, stamping die, and foreword; successive printings are indicated as I describe above. Instead of the row of numbers we used until [about 1968] the device exemplified by phrases such as 'Second Printing March 1965.' Original printings were not so designated."

1981, 1988 Statements: *See* 1976 Statement

BROWN, SON & FERGUSON, LTD. (SCOTLAND)

1976 Statement: "In the majority of our publications, on the bibliographical page is always printed either 'First Edition' or 'First Printed,' but in some of our older books which are non technical, and which have been running for 30 to 40 years, the original printing date has not been included."

1981, 1988 Statements: *See* 1976 Statement

BROWN UNIVERSITY PRESS

1988 Statement: *See* 1988 Statement of University Press of New England

BRUCE PUBLISHING COMPANY
(Milwaukee, Wisconsin)

1937 Statement: "We follow no regular rule to indicate first editions of books. In the case of trade books, we usually indicate the second and subsequent printings by an appropriate line on the copyright page giving this information."

1947 Statement: *See* 1937 Statement

BRUCE PUBLISHING COMPANY
(St. Paul, Minnesota)

1937 Statement: "The words First printing, Second printing, et cetera, together with notation of the date of printing—7-21-36—are imprinted in 6 point type on the last page of the book in the lower left hand corner. This method has been in use in our printing plant since 1928."

BRUNSWICK PUBLISHING

1988 Statement: "If there is any change in the text, the designation will be *Second Edition*; second or subsequent printing of that edition will carry the designation, e.g.: *Second Edition, Second Printing (and the months and the year)*."

BUCKNELL UNIVERSITY PRESS

1976, 1981, 1988 Statements: *See* 1976, 1981, 1988 Statements of Associated University Presses

BUGG BOOKS

1989 Statement: *See* 1989 Statement of Price/Stern/Sloan Publishers Inc.

BURKE PUBLISHING COMPANY, LTD. (ENGLAND)

1976 Statement: "We confirm that our first editions are identified merely by the bye line 'first published....' which appears above the copyright notice in each book we publish.

"The first printing is clearly identified by the fact that no further bibliographical information appears below, whereas on reprints or new editions similar information is printed under this first line, i.e. reprinted plus the date or revised and reprinted plus the date or second edition plus the date, etc."

1981, 1988 Statements: *See* 1976 Statement

BURNING DECK PRESS

1981 Statement: "We would indicate a *second printing* by having 'second printing' on the © page."

1988 Statement: *See* 1981 Statement

BURNS & MAC EACHERN LTD. (CANADA)

1976 Statement: "We don't designate first editions. We do designate as such all subsequent printings and editions."

BURNS, OATES & WASHBOURNE, LTD. (ENGLAND)

1928 Statement: "We print on the back of the title page of each of our new books:—

First published 19..

40

"All new editions or new impressions of a work bear this same note with the added information about subsequent editions."
1937 Statement: "We print on the back of the title page of each of our new books:
Made and Printed in Gt. Britain 19..
"All new editions or new impressions of a work state First Edition (or impression) 19.. with the added information about subsequent editions."
1947 Statement: *See* 1937 Statement

THORNTON BUTTERWORTH, LTD. (ENGLAND)
1928 Statement: "It is our habit to place on the back of the title page of all our books the date of first publication, thus: 'First Published... 1928.' If the book should be reprinted we add below indented 'Second Impression' and give the date, further reprints are added immediately under. Should another *edition* of the work be issued we add 'Second Edition' with the date not indented ranging with the first line.

    First Published....1928
       Second Impression   July 1928
       Third Impression   Sept. 1928
    Second Edition ....Jan. 1929
       Fifth Impression Aug. 1929"
1937 Statement: *See* 1928 Statement

BUTTERWORTH & CO (PUBLISHERS) LTD. (ENGLAND)
1988 Statement: "We have no particular method of identifying first editions. Unless it states otherwise (eg. Second Edition) then our book is a first edition—but not necessarily a first publishing of a first edition.
"There is no change from our previous practice. Our imprints and subsidiaries use the same system."

BUTTERWORTH ARCHITECTURE (ENGLAND)
1988 Statement: *See* 1988 Statement of Butterworth Scientific Ltd. (England)

BUTTERWORTH SCIENTIFIC LTD. (ENGLAND)
1988 Statement: "The books programme of Architectural Press was taken over by Butterworth Scientific in February 1988 and the new imprint named Butterworth Architecture. The statement used for all Butterworth Scientific first editions, including the Butterworth Architecture and Wright (previously John Wright of Bristol) imprint [is]:
    First published, 19..
    © Butterworth & Co. (Publishers) Ltd, 19.. "

BUTTERWORTHS (CANADA)
1988 Statement: "At this time Butterworths does not identify a first edition or subsequent printings. However, I enclose a photocopy of information included on our copyright pages in the past."
"As a matter of fact this topic was discussed recently in regard to reprints and we may decide to insert this information in the future."
Photocopy of copyright page shows:
    First Published   1954
    Second Edition   1958
    Third Edition   1963
    Fourth Edition 1967

Fifth Edition	1970
First Reprint	1971
Second Reprint	1972
Sixth Edition	1975
Seventh Edition	1980

BUTTERWORTHS PTY LIMITED (AUSTRALIA)

1988 Statement: "Our first editions do not carry any identification as such. Insofar as I can ascertain, this has always been the case. The imprint page carries a copyright line, for example:

© 1988 Butterworths Pty Limited.

"Subsequent editions carry the words 'Second Edition' or whatever on the cover and title page, while the imprint page sometimes, but not always, includes a history. For example a third edition might state: 'First edition 1970, Second edition 1981' on the imprint."

C

CADDYLAK PUBLISHING

1988 Statement: *See* 1988 Statement of Asher-Gallant Press

CADMUS EDITIONS

1988 Statement: " 'First Edition' on the copyright page indicates the first printing of a first edition; subsequent printings of the edition are so marked on the copyright page. If the book was first published abroad, 'First American Edition' will appear on the copyright page.

"The above method was adopted at the outset of publication by Cadmus Editions and has been consistent throughout."

JOHN CALDER (PUBLISHERS) LTD (ENGLAND)

1988 Statement: "All our title pages make it quite clear if it is a first edition, or in the case of translations, a first English edition and the publishing history is added with subsequent reprints.

"Occasionally we do a special de-luxe first edition in advance of the commercial first printing, but this is only for acknowledged authors of classic status and are usually signed by the author."

CALIFORNIA INSTITUTE OF PUBLIC AFFAIRS

1989 Statement: "I looked through some of the 100 or so editions that we've published since 1969 and found that while we are always careful to designate following editions (and printings of editions)—on the reverse title page—we have been spotty about marking first editions—no standard practice."

CALIFORNIA STATE UNIVERSITY PRESS

1988 Statement: "There is no designation of our first edition titles. Only subsequent editions carry the designation 'Second Printing,' 'Third Printing,' and so forth.

"For example, the Copyright page of the 1986 reprint of our 1984 publication of *Frank Lloyd Wright: Letters to Architects* carries the designation: 'Second Printing.' "

CAMBRIDGE UNIVERSITY PRESS (ENGLAND)

1928 Statement: "It is our practice to put the date of the publication of any book on the title-page itself. If the book is reprinted, the date of the reprint appears on the title-page and a bibliographical description on the back of the title, e.g.

> First Edition 1922
> Reprinted 1923
> Second Edition 1924."

1937, 1947 Statements: *See* 1928 Statement

1976 Statement: First printings are designated by the statement "First published 19.." on the verso of the title page. Subsequent printings and editions are indicated.

1981, 1988 Statements: *See* 1976 Statement

CAMDEN HOUSE BOOKS, INC.

1988 Statement: "For Camden House, Inc., 1st editions are indicated by the words: 'First edition' on the copyright page."

CAMELOT

1981 Statement: *See* 1981 Statement of Avon Books

CAMERON & CO.

1976 Statement: "Our method of designating a first edition is simply to print the words 'First Edition' in the book. Subsequent printings are designated as 'Second Edition,' 'Third Edition,'etc."

1981 Statement: *See* 1976 Statement

1988 Statement: "In the past we used First Printing to designate First Edition. Beginning this year with *Above New York* we will use First Edition 1988 in lieu of First Printing. Subsequent printings will be designated as Second Printing 19--, etc. Revisions will be designated but there will not be Second and Third Editions."

JONATHAN CAPE, LTD. (ENGLAND)

1928 Statement: "Our practice is to print on the back of the title page 'First published 1928' or whatever the year may be. When the book is reprinted without revision or alteration, we add to this 'second impression,' again giving the year. Each printing is thus recorded in like manner in the same place. It follows then that a book published by us which has on the back of the title page 'First published 1928' and no other information with regard to further printings, is, ipso facto, a first edition."

1937, 1947 Statements: *See* 1928 Statement

Statement for 1960: "Cape's practice before the UK acceded to the UCC (27 September 1957) was [stated in the 1982 statement], except that no copyright line was printed. The copyright line (*See* [1982 Statement]) was introduced on 27 September 1957."

1976 Statement: "Jonathan Cape's books show their bibliographic history on the verso of the title page (i.e. page iv or 4). The statement begins: 'First published 19..' and it is followed by the copyright line: 'Copyright © 19.. by—.' The date in both lines is identical. If the book was first published elsewhere, we then say: 'First published in Great Britain 19..' and the date in the copyright line will be earlier. For example: 'First published in Great Britain 1976' 'Copyright ©1973 by—.' Dates of subsequent reprints, new editions etc., are listed on the same page."

1982 Statement. "Jonathan Cape's books show their bibliographic history on the verso of the title page (i.e. page iv or 4). The statement begins: 'First published 19..' and it is followed by the copyright line: 'Copyright © 19.. by—.' The date in both lines is identical. If the book was first published elsewhere, we then say: 'First published in Great Britain 19..' and the date in the copyright line may be earlier. It will follow exactly the copyright line used in the edition first published elsewhere. For example: 'First published in Great Britain 1976' 'Copyright © 1973 by—.' Dates of subsequent reprints, new editions etc., are listed on the same page."

1988 Statement: "You will be aware that we are now part of Random House U.K. (as are Chatto and Bodley Head) but we keep our own imprint.

"Our method of designating a first edition is essentially the same as you have in your last edition of the Guide."

JONATHAN CAPE AND ROBERT BALLOU, INC.

(Organized in May, 1932. Out of business at some time prior to 1937. Succeeded by Robert O. Ballou, Publisher.)

1937 Statement (by Mr. Robert Ballou): "Both Jonathan Cape and Robert Ballou, Inc., and Robert O. Ballou, Publisher, made no particular attempt to distinguish first editions. The first edition usually bore a statement on the reverse of the title page just under the copyright line which read 'First published 19...' But I find on checking back through some of my own publications, that this was omitted as often as used. When it was used the year only was mentioned. On subsequent editions there was usually (or always if my memory is right) a statement of the month and year in which each edition was printed. This was also directly under the copyright notice. Thus the second printing of the trade edition of *Roll Jordan Roll* has this statement under the copyright notice:

First Printing December, 1933
Second Printing January, 1934

I have no copy of the first edition of this book so I cannot tell you how it is marked, but it is probably not marked at all, having simply the copyright notice. As a matter of fact the only two books under my own name (Robert O. Ballou, Publisher) which I ever reprinted were Julia Peterkin's *Roll Jordan Roll*, and Henry Roth's *Call It Sleep*. Each of these had two editions and any copies that are not marked as second printings are firsts. Of course a number of my publications were made up of sheets imported from England and I have no way of knowing, in most cases whether these were sheets from the first edition there or not."

JONATHAN CAPE AND HARRISON SMITH, INC.

(Out of business prior to 1932. This firm divided and was succeeded by: Harrison Smith, Inc., organized in November, 1931, and Jonathan Cape and Robert Ballou, Inc., organized in May, 1932.)

1937 Statement: "Although no strict rule was followed, in general it will be found that unless books are marked 'Second printing,' they are first editions."

CAPITOL PUBLISHING COMPANY

1947 Statement: "Our books carry no marks which would distinguish the first edition from the following. The reason for that is that they are picture books for the very young and we did not deem such distinction necessary.

"There is however one exception: *All About Us*, the first title in a new series of books planned by us. In this case the first edition bears no particular imprint whereas the following two editions are defined as such on the copyright page. We intend to continue this practice on the following titles of this series."

CAPRA PRESS

1976 Statement: "We do not designate first editions or first printings, but we do designate successive editions or printings."
1981, 1988 Statements: *See* 1976 Statement

CARATZAS BROTHERS, PUBLISHERS

1976 Statement: "We generally do not have any indication for the first printing of the first edition; subsequent printings of the first edition, or subsequent editions are so indicated on the copyright page and/or the title page (in the case of a second or otherwise revised edition). As we have been in business only for two years there are no past inconsistencies, or few other sins to contend with."
1981 Statement: *See* 1976 Statement

CARCANET NEW PRESS LIMITED (ENGLAND)

1981 Statement: "We distinguish between two kinds of first edition. The first is the 'absolute' first edition where we are the first publisher of the book in the world. After this, we have the 'first British edition' which means just that—usually a book we have bought in from America. In our books we designate the first printing by the prefix 'first published in 19..' or, for the second category, 'first published in Great Britain in 19..' and then proceed to print the address.

"We have always identified our publications in this fashion. All of the imprints of our company follow this pattern."
1988 Statement: *See* 1988 Statement of Carcanet Press Limited (England)

CARCANET PRESS LIMITED (ENGLAND)

1988 Statement: "[The 1981 statement] remains correct in all particulars apart from the word 'New' which must be removed.

"The dropping of 'New' was not a simple terminate act. At times we had certain titles coming out under the proper 'Carcanet Press' imprint and certain titles from the 'New Press' category. This was entirely a financial distinction."

CARDINAL (ENGLAND)

1988 Statement: *See* 1988 Statement of Sphere Books Limited (England)

WILLIAM CAREY LIBRARY

1976 Statement: "We have no particular way of designating first editions of our books. The copyright page will simply have the copyright notice and date, and the ISBN and Library of Congress Catalog number. However, subsequent printings and editions are designated as 'Second printing, [date],' etc."
1981 Statement: *See* 1976 Statement

CAROLINA ACADEMIC PRESS

1988 Statement: "Second (and subsequent) printings as well as revised editions are indicated on the copyright page."

CAROLINE HOUSE PUBLISHERS

1981 Statement: The copyright page carries the numbers 1 through 10. The lowest number designates the printing. Formerly, no attempt was made to designate a first printing.

CAROLINGIAN PRESS

1976 Statement: "All editions are (to date) first and limited to one."

CAROLRHODA BOOKS, INC.

1976 Statement: "In the past, first printings have been designated by the copyright date alone.

"In subsequent printings, the following was added to the copyright entry.
   Second Printing 1977
   Third Printing 1979
   (and so forth)

"We recently have begun adding a number code to the first printing of each book following the copyright entry.
   76 77 78 79 80 10 9 8 7 6 5 4 3 2 1

"When a book is reprinted for the second time, for instance, we remove the '1' and the year of the first printing."

1981 Statement: "In the past, first printings have been designated by the copyright date alone.

"In subsequent printings, the following was added to the copyright entry:
   Second Printing 1977
   Third Printing 1979
   (and so forth)

"We recently have begun adding a number code to the first printing of each book following the copyright entry:

"We now use
   1 2 3 4 5 6 7 8 9 10 90 89 88 87 86 85 84 83 82 81

"When a book is reprinted for the second time, for instance, we remove the '1' and the year of the first printing."

All imprints of Carolrhoda Books, Inc. follow the same practice.

1988 Statement: *See* 1981 Statement, but note that the number code to the first printing now follows the CIP (cataloging in publication) data.

THE CARRIAGE HOUSE PRESS

1988 Statement: "All Carriage House Press books have a colophon at the back of the book which includes the words 'first edition,' and which gives the number of copies printed in both clothbound and paperback editions."

CARRICK AND EVANS, INC.

(Established 1937. Merged with Lippincott January 8, 1941.)

1948 Statement: "First printings of Carrick and Evans titles were identified by placing the letter 'A' directly beneath the copyright line. On subsequent printings the 'A' was removed."

ROBT. CARRUTHERS & SONS (SCOTLAND)

1976 Statement: "We have no special way of identifying any 'first editions' of the few works we publish. In fact, except for 'The Scottish War of Independence' by Evan M. Barron, they are all 'first editions,' and in its case the second edition is identifiable by its long special introduction, which really makes it more valuable historically and authoritatively than the first!

It is also out of print. So in all other cases whatever date may appear with the imprint, or elsewhere, is the date of first publication."
1981 Statement: *See* 1976 Statement

FRANK CASS PUBLISHERS (ENGLAND)

1988 Statement: "This format has been our standard practice for many years:

First published 1987 in Great Britain by
FRANK CASS AND COMPANY LIMITED
Gainsborough House, 11 Gainsborough Road,
London, E11 1RS, England
and in the United States of America by
FRANK CASS AND COMPANY LIMITED
c/o Biblio Distribution Centre
81 Adams Drive, P.O. Box 327, Totowa, N.J. 07511
© 1987 John D. Clarke"

CASSELL & COMPANY, LTD. (ENGLAND)

1928 Statement: "The date of publication of each book issued by this firm appears on the back of the title page; the publication dates of subsequent editions are added as they occur."
1937, 1947 Statements: *See* 1928 Statement
Statement for 1960: *See* 1976 Statement
1976 Statement: "The only means of identification of first editions of our publications is the statement on page iv (the history page): First published 1976.
"The only departure from this is when the book is not first published in this country in which case our history page reads:
First published in Great Britain 1976
"This has always been our practice."
1981 Statement: *See* 1981 Statement of Cassell Ltd. (England)

CASSELL LTD. (ENGLAND)

1981 Statement: "We have not changed our method of designating the first printing of a first edition. However, please note our new company title. All Trade imprints follow the same policy."
See also Cassell & Company, Ltd. (England)
1988 Statement: *See* 1988 Statement of Cassell PLC (England)

CASSELL PLC (ENGLAND)

1988 Statement: "All our imprints indicate the print history as
First published 19__
Reprinted 19__, 19__, 19__ ...
Second Edition 19__
although in the past there will have been some exceptions to this wording."

CATHAY (ENGLAND)

1989 Statement: *See* 1989 Statement of The Octopus Publishing Group PLC (England)

THE CATHOLIC UNIVERSITY OF AMERICA PRESS

1976 Statement: "Most of the books published by our firm are printed on a one-time basis. However, a few have been reprinted or revised. In the case of reprinting, we merely state on the copyright page: 'reprinted (date).' With a revised edition, we place on the title page either the words 'newly revised edition' or 'revised and enlarged edition,' whichever the case may be."

1981, 1988 Statements: *See* 1976 Statement

CAUSEWAY PRESS LIMITED (ENGLAND)

1988 Statement: "We indicate a first edition by the words 'First impression' followed by the year of publication. Reprints are indicated by 'Reprinted' followed by the year of the reprint. A second edition is indicated by 'Second edition' followed by the year of that edition. This has been standard policy since the company was formed in 1983."

CAVALIER PRESS (AUSTRALIA)

1981 Statement: *See* 1981 Statement of Widescope International Publishers Pty., Ltd. (Australia)

THE CAXTON PRINTERS, LTD

1937 Statement: "We do not as a rule designate our first editions by printing the words 'First Printing' or 'First Edition' on the back of the title page, but when we make a reprint, we give the date of the first printing and the date of each subsequent printing, on the back of the title page.

"The purchaser of a Caxton book will know, then, that he is getting a first printing, unless there is information indicating that we have made more than one printing, on the back of the title page.

"In the case of books such as Fischer's works, published jointly with Doubleday, Doran, the first edition may be ascertained by examining the bottom of the title page. If our name appears before the name of the cooperating publisher, at the bottom of the title page, the edition is a Caxton first.

"This procedure has been followed since the first book was published by The Caxton Printers."

1947 Statement: *See* 1937 Statement

Statement for 1960: "You are advised that our method of indicating first printings has been uniform since we started publishing books. The method used in 1960 or 50, or 40, or 30, is in accordance with the [1976 statement]. The absence of any information regarding printings on the copyright page indicates a first printing. In the case of additional printings the printings are listed by the number of the printing and the month and year date."

1976 Statement: "All of our first editions are identified by the absence of any information regarding printings on the copyright page.

"In the case of a second printing or second edition etc., you will find on the copyright page a listing of printings or editions such as this:

First Printing July, 1945

Second Printing August, 1947 etc."

1981, 1988 Statements: *See* 1976 Statement

CELESTIAL ARTS

1976 Statement: Previously, all printings were listed. As of January 1966, the printing, month, and year are given. A numerical system of one through seven and a series of corresponding dates are given as well:

First Printing, May 1976

1 2 3 4 5 6 7 - 80 79 78 77 76

The first number and the last date designate the printing and date of the current publication.

1981, 1988 Statements: *See* 1976 Statement

CENTAUR PRESS, LTD., (ENGLAND)

1976 Statement: "Only by omission, as it were. That is to say, a first edition would carry the line (e.g.) © Centaur Press Ltd. 1976.

"A second or subsequent edition would have a line to say so: E.g.,'Second edition 1978.' "

1981, 1988 Statements: *See* 1976 Statement

CENTER FOR CONTEMPORARY POETRY

1976 Statement: "We only do one edition of 500 copies of each *Voyages.*"

1988 Statement: *See* 1976 Statement. Publisher ceased publication with 1979 edition.

CENTER FOR SOUTHERN FOLKLORE

1976 Statement: "No designation of first printings and/or editions is used. Will be indicated only on printings and/or editions after the first. This hasn't been implemented yet as we are new in publishing."

1981 Statement: *See* 1976 Statement

CENTURY (ENGLAND)

1988 Statement: *See* 1988 Statement of Century Hutchinson Publishing Group Limited (England)

CENTURY BENHAM (ENGLAND)

1988 Statement: *See* 1988 Statement of Century Hutchinson Publishing Group Limited (England)

CENTURY COMPANY

(Merged with D. Appleton and Co., to form D. Appleton-Century Co., Inc., on May 31, 1933.)

1928 Statement: "We have no special mark showing first editions of our publications, except in the case of a few special books. We are planning, however, in the future to put each printing as made on the back of the title pages of all of our publications."

CENTURY HUTCHINSON PUBLISHING GROUP LIMITED (ENGLAND)

1988 Statement: "We still follow the procedure as indicated in 1981 by Hutchinson:

"On checking through books published before 1976 it seems that Hutchinson has never included the month in the relevant statement.

"The normal form is: 'First published year (i.e. 1976)'

"However, we sometimes include 'in Great Britain' in the statement, thus: 'First published in Great Britain year (i.e. 1976).'

"This implies that the book has been published somewhere other than in Great Britain in a different year. However, if the overseas edition and our edition are published in the same year, then we use the first version. The edition in question could either be an entirely reset version, or offset from (usually) the US or sometimes the Australian edition with new prelims prepared here, or it could be bought in from the overseas publisher with our prelims substituted in the country of origin. Unfortunately, it is not obvious from the prelims how the book has been produced, although one could probably distinguish an offset or bought-in edition by looking at the text (points of house style, etc.).

"So far as I know all our imprints use this form, certainly those of the General Books division.

"Century & Hutchinson merged in 1984 to become Century Hutchinson. However, there is no Century Hutchinson imprint. We currently use the following imprints for hardcover and trade paperback first editions:
Century
Rider
Century Benham
Hutchinson
Hutchinson Children's Books
Radius
Barrie & Jenkins
Muller."

CEOLFRITH PRESS (ENGLAND)

1976 Statement: "So far, Ceolfrith Press has only published first editions and this is indicated by simply printing inside the title leaf 'First Edition,' followed by the date.

"However, we also published limited editions of most of our publications (excluding exhibition catalogues) which are numbered and signed by the authors, poets or artists. The reverse of the title leaf of these editions is also designated as follows:
'This is No... of the signed edition' and the numbering is done by hand.

"We also state in our publications how many copies were printed in both ordinary and signed editions."

W. & R. CHAMBERS, LTD. (SCOTLAND)

1928 Statement: "It is our intention to adopt the plan in future of marking the first impression of our general books 'original edition.' We do not intend to do this in the case of school books."

1936 Statement: "We mark the first impression of all books published by us, including school books, 'Original Edition.' "

1947 Statement: *See* 1936 Statement

1976 Statement: "In all our current publications the first date of publication is usually printed on the reverse of the title page along with the copyright notice. Prior to the institution of the copyright notice we normally put in the date of the latest edition or reprint. However in our early publications very often no date was given and therefore first dates of publication are very difficult to identify."

1981, 1988 Statements: *See* 1976 Statement

CHANCELLOR (ENGLAND)

1989 Statement: *See* 1989 Statement of The Octopus Publishing Group PLC (England)

CHANDLER & SHARP PUBLISHERS, INC.

1988 Statement: "We do not designate first printings in any particular way. They are, of course, the first printing run during the year of copyright. Subsequent printings are indicated by number (2nd, 3rd, 4th, etc.) and by year of printing. We have used this method since 1973, when we published our first book. We have no subsidiaries or other imprints."

CHANTICLEER PRESS

1947 Statement: "First editions of our publications are marked as such on the copyright page, and subsequent editions and reprints are also marked on that page."

GEOFFREY CHAPMAN (ENGLAND)

1988 Statement: *See* 1988 Statement of Cassell PLC (England)

CHAPMAN AND HALL

1988 Statement: *See* 1988 Statement of Routledge, Chapman, and Hall, Inc.

CHAPMAN AND HALL (ENGLAND)

1988 Statement: *See* 1988 Statement of Associated Book Publishers (UK) Ltd. (Scientific and Technical Division) (England)

CHAPMAN & HALL, LTD. (ENGLAND)

1928 Statement: "We do not specify either on the title page or on the back of the title that a first edition is a first edition. When the book is reprinted we generally put a bibliographical note on the back of the title page as follows:—

First Impression March 1928
Second Impression April 1928

and so forth."

1937 Statement: "We do not specify either on the title page or on the back of the title that a first edition is a first edition but all our publications are now dated, technical books bearing the date on the title page and general books carrying the date on the verso. It may therefore be taken that a book carrying dates on the title page is a first edition, as well as books carrying the words 'First published 1936.' Any subsequent reprints or editions are shown in the bibliographical note."

1947 Statement: "There has been little change in our practice of dating books since we supplied you with certain information on this point in 1937. As far as all books on general literature and fiction are concerned, we now show the year of publication on the title page, and in the event of any further editions some mention of this would be made on the verso."

CHARLES RIVER BOOKS

1988 Statement: "We usually indicate a second edition on the reverse side of the half title page."

CHATERSON, LIMITED (ENGLAND)

1947 Statement: "All our books have the date of the first edition on the title page or on the back of the title page. All subsequent editions are listed in addition."

CHATHAM PRESS

1982 Statement: "We use the terminology 'First Edition,' followed by 'First or Second or . . . Printing.' "

1988 Statement: "We use the terminology FIRST EDITION for the first printing only. Follow-up printings have the designation 'First or Second . . . or Printing' or 'Revised Edition . . . Printing.' "

"All subsidiaries and imprints follow this practice."

CHATTO & WINDUS (ENGLAND)

1928 Statement: "We use no particular distinguishing sign to mark our first editions with."

1937 Statement: *See* 1928 Statement

1947 Statement: "We have no distinguishing mark, but certainly all contemporary work is easily identified by the fact that all books bear the date of publication either on the title-page or the verso of the title, and in the event of a book being reprinted the information as to whether it is a second impression or a new edition is noted in the biblio."

Statement for 1960: "We see that every book carries the date of first publication, and reprints, whether new impressions or new editions, are clearly listed on the verso of the title page."

1976 Statement: *See* 1976 Statement of Chatto & Windus Ltd (England)

CHATTO & WINDUS LTD (ENGLAND)

1976 Statement: "We have no particular method beyond ensuring that every book carries the date of first publication, and reprints, whether new impressions or new editions, are clearly listed on the verso of the title page."

1981, 1988 Statements: *See* 1976 Statement

CHELSEA GREEN PUBLISHING COMPANY

1988 Statement: "We started in 1984. We have always stated what printing it is. 'First printing, Sept 1987,' for example. Then 'Second printing,' etc. For a paperback reprint, we say 'First paperback printing,' etc. We have no imprints or subsidiaries."

CHELSEA HOUSE
(Out of business prior to 1949.)

1928 Statement: "So far as the cloth-bound book publication goes so few of the books that we have published have run into more than one edition, that we have not been faced with the necessity of marking first editions in any way."

1937 Statement: *See* 1928 Statement

CHELSEA HOUSE PUBLISHERS

1988 Statement: "We use standard publishers' numbers."

CHEROKEE PUBLISHING COMPANY

1988 Statement: *See* 1988 Statement of Larlin Corporation

CHILDRENS PRESS

1976 Statement: "Childrens Press uses the dateline designation. For example:

1 2 3 4 5 6 7 8 9 10 11 12 R 78 77 76 75

"The digits to the left of the letter R (reprint) indicate the printing. The digits to the right of the letter R indicate the year. The above was first printed in 1975. In the following example, in 1975 the title was printed for the 7th time.

7 8 9 10 11 12 13 14 15 16 17 18 19 20 21 22 23 24 25 R 75

"Elk Grove and Golden Gate Junior Books published since we acquired those companies also carry this dateline designation. Titles published prior to our acquisition do not carry any printing designation."

1981 Statement: "Our first printing designation has not changed."

1988 Statement: *See* 1981 Statement

CHILDRENS PRESS, INC.

1947 Statement: "The reason we did not give a statement of our method of identifying first printings is that we have not identified them in this point. We publish only children's books."

CHILTON BOOK COMPANY

1976 Statement: "Chilton Book Company indicates year of publication and number of printing by a numerical code. First number indicates publication year, last indicates printing. e.g.

    7 8 9 0 1 2 3 4 5 6   0 9 8 7 6 5 4 3 2 1
    published in 1977   first printing

"Second and additional revised editions are usually noted on both title page and copyright page."

1981, 1988 Statements: *See* 1976 Statement

CHINA BOOKS & PERIODICALS INC.

1988 Statement: "Historically, China Books has not designated first editions in a consistent manner, though a number of its books do state 'First edition,' or 'First edition' followed by date of publication. However, *later* editions have usually been clearly designated, so it is often safe to conclude that the edition is indeed a first unless otherwise stated. All first editions published after January 1, 1988, will be clearly designated as such."

THE CHRISTOPHER PUBLISHING HOUSE

1947 Statement: "We always state on the title page or copyright page if a book is a second or subsequent edition. All others are first editions."

Statement for 1960: *See* 1982 Statement

1976 Statement: "No set policy, usually second editions and second printings are indicated on copyright page."

1982 Statement: "Same policy on all books from 1910-1982.

"No indication of first edition on copyright page. However, second editions and second printings are usually indicated on copyright page."

1988 Statement: "We always state on the copyright page if a book is a second or subsequent edition. All others are first editions."

CHRISTOPHERS (ENGLAND)

1937 Statement: "We always put the date of first publication on the back of the title, thus—

    First published   1923

When the book is reprinted we alter this to—

    First published June   1923
    Reprinted September   1923
    Reprinted October   1928"

1947 Statement: *See* 1937 Statement

CHRISTOPHER'S BOOKS

1976 Statement: "Christopher's Books does not indicate 1st edition or printing; we have never done a 2nd, but would indicate a 2nd printing or edition if we were to produce one."

1981 Statement: *See* 1976 Statement

CHRONICLE BOOKS

1976 Statement: "Our first editions can be identified by the lack of any edition imprint. Subsequent editions are indicated on the copyright page.

"We specify all subsequent 'printings' after the first one. When it is a 'new edition,' we so specify. So, first printings of the first editions are the only books that do not carry a printing or edition reference."

1981 Statement: *See* 1976 Statement

1988 Statement: "First edition Chronicle Books are indicated on the copyright page. Each book is printed with the numbers 10 9 8 7 6 5 4 3 2 1. With each printing a number is removed from the list. A first edition has the complete list."

CHURCHILL LIVINGSTONE
1976, 1981 Statements: *See* 1976, 1981 Statements of Longman Inc.

CISTERCIAN PUBLICATIONS
1988 Statement: "As a specialized short-run publisher, we do not identify First Editions. Most of our books are First Editions and first printings. When a book is reprinted, the copyright page identifies it as a reprint with the date of the original publication and the reprint date."

THE CITADEL PRESS
1949 Statement. "Our first printings are sometimes marked so, and at other times are not. However, second printings are always indicated on our original books."
1976 Statement: "It is our normal practice to print the words First Edition on the copyright page."
1982 Statement: "We continue to print First Edition on the copyright page of original titles."
1988 Statement: *See* 1988 Statement of Citadel Press Publishers

CITADEL PRESS PUBLISHERS
1988 Statement: "We no longer print First Edition on the copyright page of our titles. However, second and subsequent printings are indicated by a number code, the lowest number indicating the printing."

CITIZEN PRESS, LTD. (ENGLAND)
See Skelton Robinson (England)

CITY LIGHTS BOOKS, INC.
1976 Statement: "We don't really have a method. Most of our books state second printing, third printing, etc., but sometimes a new printing has been done without a notice. Usually the absence of any identifying statement would indicate a first printing of a first edition."
1981 Statement: "All the information on City Lights that you have is still accurate. We still follow the same practices we did in 1976."
1988 Statement: *See* 1981 Statement

ARTHUR H. CLARK COMPANY
1976 Statement: "We designate first editions by using only one date on the copyright page. If the edition is a 2nd, it is so stated on the copyright page."
1981, 1988 Statements: *See* 1976 Statement

T. & T. CLARK LIMITED (SCOTLAND)
1976 Statement: "All our first editions will have simply the date of publication or 'first printed—'. All subsequent editions will have the date of first, latest and intervening editions clearly set out."
1981, 1988 Statements: *See* 1976 Statement

CLARK UNIVERSITY PRESS
1988 Statement: *See* 1988 Statement of University Press of New England

JAMES CLARKE & CO., LTD. (ENGLAND)
1988 Statement: *See* 1988 Statement of Lutterworth Press (England)

CLAY PUBLISHING CO., LTD. (CANADA)
1976 Statement: All printings after the first are designated by month and year.

CLEARWATER PUBLISHING CO., INC.
1976 Statement: "We do not mark our first editions First Edition. Subsequent editions are marked second edition and so on. If the book has no changes, the second printing is considered part of the first edition and is marked, Second Printing."

1981 Statement: *See* 1976 Statement

CLEAVER-HUME PRESS, LTD. (ENGLAND)
1947 Statement: "We inscribe on the back of the title page of the first edition of a book the date of appearance, e.g. 'First published 1948.' Reprints unaltered are recorded thereunder: 'Reprinted 19 .' We reserve the word 'Edition' for a version containing significant revisions, and the dates of successive editions are given in a similar way."

"We believe you will find this coincides with the practice of most serious British publishers."

CLEVELAND STATE UNIVERSITY
1988 Statement: "All of the books we have published have been first editions at the time they were issued. The year of publication is indicated by the copyright date. A couple of our books have gone into a second printing, unchanged, and more may do so in the future; there is no indication in the book that it is a second printing. We have also reprinted some books in an enlarged or revised edition; these editions are so indicated on the acknowledgments page, with additional copyright dates where appropriate. Some of our books have been issued simultaneously in hardcover and paperback editions; these have the same copyright date but different ISBNs on the acknowledgments page. If anyone wishes to apply to us for the particular publication history of a book, we will try to provide it."

THE CLIQUE (ENGLAND)
1989 Statement: "All printings after the first are noted on the copyright page."

CLOCK HOUSE PUBLICATIONS (CANADA)
1976 Statement: Editions and printings and their dates are designated on the copyright page.

EDWARD J. CLODE INC.
(Out of business sometime prior to 1949.)
1928 Statement: "There is no way in which it is possible to distinguish any of our first editions from later ones."
1937 Statement: *See* 1928 Statement

CLOUD, INC.
1947 Statement: "We distinguish the first printing only by an absence of the words 'second edition,' 'third edition,' etc., on the copyright page of the book."

CLYMER MOTORS
1947 Statement. "On the Historical Motor Scrapbooks, the first edition that was printed in 1944 did not have an index, and only 1,700 of these books

were printed. All subsequent printings (we have printed over 150,000) are indexed."

COACH HOUSE PRESS, INC.

1988 Statement: "Coach House Press, Inc. first editions bear no special markings, and are sometimes re-printed without designation. Since most of our books are production scripts of plays, they receive brief, heavy use and are often discarded."

THE COACH HOUSE PRESS (CANADA)

1976 Statement: "Some books the first edition was numbered by machine. None have said 'First Edition'. Some books had letterpress first editions and offset second or silkscreen and offset. 'Second Printing' and date are usually put in the colophon."

1981 Statement: " 'Second Printing' and date are usually put in the colophon."

COBBETT PRESS, LTD. (ENGLAND)

1947 Statement: "In general principle we print the date of the first printing or biblio on the verso of the title-page with dates of subsequent re-printings where relevant. While this practice has sometimes been omitted, in general it will be adhered to."

COBBLESMITH

1976 Statement: "We have no special marks."
1981, 1988 Statements: *See* 1976 Statement

R. COBDEN-SANDERSON (ENGLAND)

1928 Statement: "I do not follow any rule in regard to the designation of my first editions. I can only give you examples such as the following:—

First published 1926
Copyright 1926
First published 1925
Second impression May 1925
Third impression October 1925
Fourth impression (cheap edition) September 1927
First published October 1927
Second impression November 1927
First published 1920
Second edition 1920
New and revised edition 1926

"All the above appear on the back of the title page, but sometimes I have the year of publication printed on the title page only."

R. COBDEN-SANDERSON, LTD. (ENGLAND)

(Formerly R. Cobden-Sanderson; out of business prior to 1949.)
1937 Statement: *See* 1928 Statement of R. Cobden-Sanderson (England)

COFFEE HOUSE PRESS

1988 Statement: "Presently at Coffee House Press, we have no system of designation for the first editions of our books."

COKESBURY PRESS
(Merged with Abingdon Press August , 1940 and became Abingdon-Cokesbury Press.)

1937 Statement: "Most Cokesbury books carry an edition symbol at the bottom of the copyright page. The first edition carries a symbol 'C'; second editions, the symbol 'O,' and subsequent editions according to the following scheme:

1 2 3 4 5 6 7 8 9 0
COKESBURY P

"A few books in certain classifications carry no edition marks at all. Occasionally a first edition carries the words 'First edition' on the copyright page but this is not our general practice."

COLLEGIATE PRESS, INC.
(Became Iowa State College Press, sometime prior to 1947.)

COLLIER BOOKS
1989 Statement: *See* 1989 Statement of Macmillan Publishing Co., Inc.

REX COLLINGS LIMITED (ENGLAND)
1976 Statement: "The only information we print in the first edition of any of our publications is the year in which the book is published. This follows the name of the copyright holder (Rex Collings or the author) and appears on the title verso, as:

© REX COLLINGS 1976

"All subsequent editions or reprints carry the impression or edition number in addition to the year of original publication."

1981 Statement: "In general the information you quote is correct. What appears in a first edition is:

First published in Great Britain by Rex Collings,
6 Paddington Street, London W1
©Rex Collings 1981
ISBN.....

Reprints are shown:
©Rex Collings 1981
ISBN.....
Reprinted 1981
Second edition 1982
Reprinted 1982 (twice)
Reprinted 1984
Third edition 1985."

1988 Statement: "We still follow the practice outlined in our 1981 Statement, although a 1988 Statement would show our address as 38 King Street, London, WC2. At present we have no subsidiaries nor imprints."

WILLIAM COLLINS PTY LTD (AUSTRALIA)
1981 Statement: "For the first printing for hardbacks and paperbacks, these are designated in Cataloguing in Publication (CIP) data which is on the reverse of the title page. The line reads:

First published by William Collins Pty Ltd, 19..

This is standard practice for us.

"If the book is a paperback (takeover) the hardback data is given as well as the line

First published in Fontana (our paperback imprint) 19..

"This procedure has been followed for the last 10 years (before that the copyright line for the author would have been the only indication). The change probably came about either in response to a request from the National Library or was initiated in house."

W. COLLINS, SON & CO., LTD. (ENGLAND)

1928 Statement: *See* 1937 Statement

1937 Statement: "We do not adopt any special method of designating first editions or first impressions. All our books bear on the reverse of the title page the date of publication and the word 'copyright.'

"In case of subsequent publication of a cheaper edition, the date of the original edition and that of the cheap edition are inserted on the back of the title-page.

"We have always used this method of identifying first editions."

1947 Statement: *See* 1937 Statement

1988 Statement: *See* 1988 Statement of William Collins Sons & Co. Ltd. (United Kingdom)

WILLIAM COLLINS SONS & CO. LTD. (UNITED KINGDOM)

1988 Statement: "We still follow the practice outlined in the [1947] statement of W. Collins, Son & Co., Ltd. (England) and all imprints and subsidiaries follow this practice."

See 1947 Statement of W. Collins, Son & Co., Ltd (England)

THE COLONIAL WILLIAMSBURG FOUNDATION

1976 Statement: Currently, first printings are not designated. Subsequent printings are so designated; as well as new or revised editions. In the past, second printings, revised editions, etc., were not always designated.

1981, 1988 Statements: *See* 1976 Statement

COLORADO ASSOCIATED UNIVERSITY PRESS

1976 Statement: "We have no particular method of identifying first editions . . . we are a small operation and seldom reprint."

1981 Statement: "We have no particular method of identifying first editions, although subsequent editions are always identified by 'Revised Edition,' 'Fourth Edition,' and so on."

1988 Statement: *See* 1981 Statement

COLT PRESS
(Paterson, New Jersey)

1947 Statement: "All editions marked in fly sheets of books."

COLUMBIA UNIVERSITY PRESS

1928 Statement: "No distinction exists in regard to first and other editions except that there is printed on the title page the date of first printing for the first editions. On succeeding editions the date is removed from the title page and the second or third printing is noted on the copyright page."

1936 Statement: "The first printing of any edition is indicated by the presence of a date with the imprint on the title page. On subsequent printings the date is removed from the title page, and the information is given on the copyright page. Revised editions are so noted on the title page, and first or subsequent printings of such editions are indicated in the same way as they are indicated for the first editions."

1947 Statement: *See* 1936 Statement

See also King's Crown Press

1976 Statement: "We make a careful distinction between the terms 'printing' and 'edition'—a 'second printing' is merely a happy reprinting (with errata corrected) of a book that has sold rather well and is indicated by the disappearance of the '1' from the string of numbers on the copyright page; a 'second edition' means that the text has been extensively overhauled, perhaps even chapters added. The latter is indicated by the words 'Second Edition' on the title page and the dates of the first and second editions on the copyright page."

1988 Statement: "We are no longer putting a date on the title page of our books. The year of publication is stated in the copyright notice on the copyright page. Indication of a second (or later) printing of a book can be seen in a series of digits printed on the copyright page. We are very careful to distinguish a second edition—meaning that the text has been substantially revised or that new chapters have been added or former ones deleted."

COMMEMORATIVE EDITIONS (AUSTRALIA)

1981 Statement: *See* 1981 Statement of Widescope International Publishers Pty. Ltd. (Australia)

COMMONWEALTH PRESS

1976 Statement: "At CP first editions carry no designation. Second, third, fourth, etc., editions are so designated. We have always used this system."

1981 Statement: "You may repeat [the 1976 Statement]. Also, when we have a top selling book, we include the printing history (month and year of each reprinting)."

1988 Statement: "You may repeat the information supplied SRP in the 1976 and 1981 policy statements, but omitting 'top-selling books include month and year of each reprinting.' "

COMPASS EDITIONS

1949 Statement: *See* 1947 Statement of The Press of James A. Decker

COMSTOCK BOOKS

1988 Statement: *See* 1988 Statement of Cornell University Press

CONSTABLE & COMPANY, LIMITED (ENGLAND)

1928 Statement: "We have no standardised method of designating our first editions, but generally speaking, we put 'First published [date]' on the back of the title-page, and if this appears without any other detail, the book on which it appears is a first edition. Reprints are noted also on the back of the title-page, under the original legend. Please observe that this is merely our usual practice and not a standardised or official method."

1937, 1947 Statements: *See* 1928 Statement

Statement for 1960: *See* 1928 Statement

1982 Statement: "Our practice since 1970 has been to designate a first edition with the words 'First published in Great Britain 0000.' Any further editions have the words 'Reprinted 0000' in addition. If there is no mention of this, the book in question should be a first edition. This has been our usual practice since 1970 but is not a standardised or official method. Prior to 1970 the method indicated in our earlier statement is applicable."

1988 Statement: *See* 1982 Statement

CONTEMPORARY BOOKS INC.

1988 Statement: "Contemporary does nothing to designate first printing and never has."

LEO COOPER LTD. (ENGLAND)

1976, 1981 Statements: *See* 1976, 1981 Statements of Seeley, Service & Cooper Ltd. (England)

1989 Statement: *See* 1989 Statement of The Octopus Publishing Group PLC (England)

COPPER BEECH PRESS

1981 Statement: "Since we do paperback books exclusively (perfect bound), we almost never have more than one edition of a single title. When we do, as has happened during the past eight years only three times, I believe, we generally indicate either by a change of cover or by some note after the title page that the imprint is indeed a second printing. This practice may change in the foreseeable future, if we go into cloth-bound editions."

1989 Statement: *See* 1981 Statement

COPPER CANYON PRESS

1976 Statement: "Since all our titles to date have been first editions, we make no notice of same. When (this winter) we DO make a second printing, it will be so stated on the copyright page. We also do very limited editions signed and hand bound on most titles. These, of course, are distinguished by the poet's signature and by the binding itself"

1981 Statement: "Unless otherwise noted, all Copper Canyon Press books are first editions. When we reprint trade paperbacks from limited signed fine editions, it is so stated in the colophon. Second printings are noted on the copyright page."

1988 Statement: *See* 1981 Statement

CORK UNIVERSITY PRESS (REPUBLIC OF IRELAND)

1988 Statement: "I set out hereunder the present position of the Press in this regard:

"Our past editions and past printings carry the following wording:
    'First published 19..' on copyright page.
"If we have a subsequent printing the description used is
    'First published 19..
    Second edition 19...' "

CORNELL MARITIME PRESS

1947 Statement: "No special method of identifying first editions. Copyright date is date of first printing. Subsequent prints so stated under copyright line."

1976 Statement: "We do not use any specific method other than indicating later printings as a Second Printing, etc."

1981 Statement: "Beginning in April of 1980, we have tried to leave as clear a 'bibliographical trail' as we can, although sometimes a paucity of records has made this difficult.

"As a matter of standard practice, we do give the data about the printing history in each new printing of any book. We don't, however, make any attempt to recite all the details. If we are doing, for example, the third printing of the fourth edition of a work, we would show (on the copyright page) a notice which might read like this:

'First edition, 1960. Fourth edition, 1970;
third printing, 1981.'
"We make no effort, you will notice, to indicate when the second and third editions were issued nor the number of printings of any previous edition. But we do indicate in each printing just which one it is."
1988 Statement: *See* 1981 Statement

CORNELL UNIVERSITY PRESS
1976 Statement: "A book published by Cornell University is a first edition unless stated otherwise. It is also a first printing unless stated otherwise."
1981, 1988 Statements: *See* 1976 Statement

COSMOPOLITAN BOOK COMPANY
(Out of business prior to 1937.)
1928 Statement: "Up to the present time we have published only large editions of popular authors and there has been no cause to designate the first edition. We are changing our policy slightly now and it is possible that we may find it necessary to mark the editions. In this case we will probably print the words 'First Edition' under the copyright notice and remove it on any later printings."

COUNCIL FOR BRITISH ARCHEOLOGY (ENGLAND)
1988 Statement: We do not specify a first printing or first edition; this is implied if the copyright page simply states: 'Published 1988,' etc. A further printing will state: 'reprinted 1988.' A new edition will state, for example: '1st edition 1985,' '2nd edition 1988,' etc.
"This is the method we have always used, and we have no imprints or subsidiaries."

COUNTRY LIFE, LTD. (ENGLAND)
1937 Statement: "It is our practice not to put the date of publication on the title page but on the back of the title. In subsequent editions the Bibliographical description is added. Thus:
First Published 1934
Second Impression 1935
Second Edition 1936."
1949 Statement: *See* 1937 Statement
1989 Statement : *See* 1989 Statement of The Octopus Publishing Group PLC (England)

COUNTRYMAN PRESS
(Absorbed by A. S. Barnes and Company, Inc.)
See A. S. Barnes and Company, Inc.

THE COUNTRYMAN PRESS, INC.
1976 Statement: "The Countryman Press does nothing to indicate a first edition in the original printing. On a subsequent printing, there is noted 'second printing' with the date, or 'revised edition.' Anything other would be considered a first edition."
1981 Statement: *See* 1976 Statement
1988 Statement: "Please note that there have been some changes effected since the statement that appeared in 1976. To wit: The Countryman Press is now the parent company for two imprints, Backcountry Publications and Foul Play Press. All titles published have a full colophon on the copyright

page listing the designer, compositor, printer, et al. The printing or edition [after the first] is also listed thereon."

THE COUNTRYWOMAN'S PRESS

1988 Statement: *See* 1988 Statement of Padre Productions

COURIER OF MAINE BOOKS

1976 Statement: "Our first editions and their first printings are designated in no special way. They simply carry on the copyright page a standard copyright notice, the ISBN, and LC number. These methods do not differ from any previously used."

PASCAL COVICI
(Became Covici, Friede.)

1928 Statement: "Sometimes we print 'first edition' on the reverse of the title page, and sometimes not, but invariably we print 'second printing' on the second issue."

COVICI, FRIEDE, INC.
(Out of business. Publications bought by Crown Publishers.)

1937 Statement: "We do not identify our first editions in any way. However, when a book goes into a second printing we record on the copyright page the date of the first printing and the date of the second printing, etc. In other words, a first edition of Covici, Friede is generally identified by the fact that the copyright page does not designate the edition."

COWARD-McCANN, INC.

1937 Statement: "When we first began to publish in 1928, we used to print our colophon on the copyright page of all first editions:
"On second and subsequent editions we omitted the torch part of the colophon and used only the lower half.

"However, we did not continue with this arrangement, so that it is impossible to be certain of our first editions. What is certain though, is that any edition appearing with the colophon without the torch is not a first.
"At present our first editions bear no distinguishing marks. If a book goes into a second or third printing, a note to this effect appears on the copyright page."

1947 Statement: *See* 1937 Statement

CRAFTSMAN BOOK COMPANY

1976 Statement: "We make no effort to identify first editions."
1981, 1988 Statements: *See* 1976 Statement

CREATIVE AGE PRESS, INC.

1947 Statement: "Creative Age Press books which are first printings simply say 'Copyright—' with no reference to a printing of any kind. Subsequent printings, however, carry the legend on the copyright page, 'Second Printing,' 'Third Printing,' etc. Therefore, a rule of thumb which can safely be followed is: if there is no reference to a printing, it is a first; all others identify themselves."

CREATIVE PUBLISHING COMPANY

1988 Statement: "We have always stated the edition and printing. Our first book was published in 1978. If we reprinted a book and added or deleted material, we would indicate that it was a second edition, first printing."

CRESCENDO

1988 Statement: *See* 1988 Statement of Taplinger Publishing Co., Inc.

CRITERION BOOKS

1976 Statement: *See* 1976 Statement of Thomas Y. Crowell Company
1981, 1988 Statements: *See* 1981, 1988 Statements of Harper & Row Publishers, Inc.

F. S. CROFTS & CO., PUBLISHERS

(Merged with D. Appleton-Century Co., Inc., on January 2, 1948, to become D. Appleton-Century-Crofts, Inc.)

1947 Statement: "The verso of the title page of one of our books, *'Basic Spanish,'* will show you how we indicate the printings that are made of our books:—

Copyright, 1939, by F. S. Crofts & Co., Inc.
First printing, April, 1939
* * * * * * * * * *
* * * * * * * * * *
Twenty-first printing, September, 1947"

CROSBY LOCKWOOD STAPLES (ENGLAND)

1976, 1981, 1988 Statements: *See* 1976, 1981, 1988 Statements of Granada Publishing Limited (England)

THE CROSSING PRESS

1976 Statement: "The only way we designate 1st editions is the omission of 2nd printing, 3rd printing, so on. (or 2nd edition, 3rd edition). Am I clear? When we rerun a book, we place the date of the rerunning & the words 2nd or 3rd printing or edition."
1981, 1988 Statements: *See* 1976 Statement

CROSSROAD / CONTINUUM

1988 Statement: "Our first editions bear no special designation. If, however, a title is reprinted or reissued, that fact is set forth on the copyright page.

"Crossroad/Continuum was established in 1980 as a new, independent publishing house, continuing to publish the programs developed by Herder and Herder in the 1960s, Seabury Press in the 1970s, and The Frederick Ungar Publishing Company since 1940. Crossroad/Continuum imprints and subsidiaries follow the same practice."

CROSSROAD / CONTINUUM PUBLISHING GROUP

1988 Statement: *See* 1988 Statement of Crossroad / Continuum

THOMAS Y. CROWELL COMPANY

1928 Statement: "Our present practice is not to indicate in any way the first edition. Subsequent printings are so indicated.

"In the absence of the words, Second Printing, Third Printing, etc., it can be safely assumed that without such an inscription the book is a copy of the first edition."

1937 Statement: "Our present practice is not to indicate in any way the first edition. Subsequent printings are so indicated.

"In the absence of the words 'Second Printing,' 'Third Printing,' etc., it can be safely assumed that without such an inscription the book is a copy of the first edition.

"We began using this method about ten years ago."

1947 Statement: "The statement above is still true, although of course the statement that we began using the method about ten years ago needs bringing up to date.

"You might also mention that offset books carry a series of numbers from 1 to 10 at the bottom of the copyright page. Since additions cannot be made to offset plates, the lowest number is rubbed out with each reprinting. Thus the first printing will have all the numbers; the second printing will run from 2 to 10; the third printing from 3 to 10; the fourth from 4 to 10; and so on."

1976 Statement: "On first editions, the numbers 1 2 3 4 5 6 7 8 9 10 appear at the bottom of the page. Each time the book is reprinted, the next number is deleted, thus designating the current printing. A long time ago, I believe the previous method was to say: 'First printing,' 'Second printing,' etc."

1981, 1988 Statements: *See* 1981, 1988 Statements of Harper & Row Publishers, Inc.

CROWN PUBLISHERS

1947 Statement: "In most instances, we make no identification beyond numbering the various printings of each of our books."

Statement for 1960: "[Prior to July, 1979] a first edition, first printing, had absolutely no printing history on it. Reprints were indicated by the printing history."

1976 Statement: *See* Statement for 1960

1981 Statement: "At Crown, the first printing of a first edition is indicated by the printing number '1' (in a descending series starting with '10') and the words 'First Edition.' After the first printing, the words 'First Edition' and the number '1' are deleted. Numbers are deleted with each corresponding reprint; thus, the line '10 9 8 7 6' would indicate the sixth printing.

"The above system is used for all Crown adult, Clarkson N. Potter and Harmony titles produced in-house, and it appears on the copyright page of books published after January 1980.

"Until I joined this company in July 1979, a first edition, first printing, had absolutely no printing history on it. Reprints were indicated by the printing history."

1988 Statement: *See* 1988 Statement of Crown Publishers Inc.

CROWN PUBLISHERS INC.

1988 Statement: "First printings carry the numbers 10 9 8 7 6 5 4 3 2 1 and the words First Edition under the numbers. In subsequent printings, we eliminate each number as needed and the words First Edition are deleted as well.

"This is for Crown, Harmony Books, Clarkson N. Potter, Inc., titles."

CRUCIBLE BOOKS (ENGLAND)

1988 Statement: *See* 1988 Statement of Thorsons Publishing Group Ltd (England)

CURBSTONE PRESS

1976 Statement. "We designate a first edition by the words 'First Edition' on the copyright page. We make no distinction between 'First Edition' and 'First Printing.' If we print more copies of the same book, it is labelled 'Second Edition.'"

1981 Statement: *See* 1976 Statement

1988 Statement: "We designate a first edition by the words, 'First Edition' on the copyright page. If we print more copies of the same book, it is labelled 'Second Printing.'"

SAMUEL CURL, INC.

(A continuation of Hillman-Curl, Inc., it includes the imprints Arcadia House and Mystery House.)

1947 Statement: "First editions of our publications are distinguished by the lack of any printing notice on the copyright page. Following editions bear the date of the first printing, together with date of new printing, and which printing it is."

CURRENT BOOKS, INC.

See A. A. Wyn, Inc.

CYGNET BOOKS (AUSTRALIA)

1988 Statement: *See* 1988 Statement of the University of Western Australia Press (Australia)

D

DACRE PRESS (ENGLAND)

1976 Statement: *See* 1976 Statement of Adam and Charles Black Publishers Limited (England)

ANDREW DAKERS, LTD. (ENGLAND)

1947 Statement: "Our method of identifying first printings of our books and of differentiating subsequent printings, is that of printing on the back of the title page as follows:—
First published January 1945
Reprinted August 1946
Reprinted March 1947 and so on."

DAKOTA PRESS

See 1988 Statement of The University of South Dakota Press

DALKEY ARCHIVE

1988 Statement: "Since 1988, first printings of our books carry a 'First Edition' statement. Our earlier books (1984-87) have only a copyright date, but they can be assumed to be first printings unless a 'Second Edition' notice appears. We have no imprints or subsidiaries."

C. W. DANIEL COMPANY (ENGLAND)

1928 Statement: "Our method of designating first editions of our books is to put 'First published, etc.,' on the back of each title page, and to add to that the dates of all further editions as they are issued."

THE C. W. DANIEL COMPANY, LTD. (ENGLAND)

1937 Statement: "Our method of designating first editions of our books is to put 'First published,' etc., on the back of each title page, and to add to that the dates of all further editions as they are issued."

1948 Statement: *See* 1937 Statement

1988 Statement: "Our company and subsidiaries still follow the practice [as given in the 1937 Statement]."

JOHN DANIEL, PUBLISHER

1988 Statement: "We don't have any uniform practice of designating editions or printings."

DARTMOUTH COLLEGE

1988 Statement: *See* 1988 Statement of University Press of New England

THE DARTNELL CORPORATION

1976 Statement: "First printing of a first edition designated by copyright date only. This has always been our standard practice."

1981, 1988 Statements: *See* 1976 Statement

DAUGHTERS OF ST. PAUL

1976 Statement: "Our first editions may be designated by the copyright date on the page after the title page."

1981 Statement: "Our first editions may be designated by the earliest copyright date on the page after the title page."

JONATHAN DAVID PUBLISHERS

1988 Statement: "Our first printings are designated by the appearance of the numeral one on the copyright page. The year appears above the numeral. Subsequent printings are indicated by a change in numerals. This has been our practice since 1974."

DAVID & CHARLES (HOLDINGS) LTD. (ENGLAND)

1976 Statement: "We only identify first editions by providing the usual '© John Smith 1976' on the back of the title page; any subsequent impressions or editions would be identified as such, with their date. So the absence of any note such as 'second impression' conveys that the book is in fact a first impression."

1981 Statement: *See* 1976 Statement

1988 Statement: *See* 1988 Statement of David & Charles Publishers PLC (England)

DAVID & CHARLES PUBLISHERS PLC (ENGLAND)

1988 Statement: "Apart from the fact that we are now called David & Charles Publishers PLC, we can confirm that the [1976 Statement of David & Charles (Holdings)] still stands."

See 1976 Statement of David & Charles (Holdings) Ltd. (England)

PETER DAVIES, LTD. (ENGLAND)

1928 Statement: "I have no hard and fast method of designating a first edition.

"More often than not a bibliographical note is printed on the verso of the title-page of my publications. It reads: 'First printed in (e.g.) May, 1928.' In case a further edition or impression is issued, there will be an addition to the note, e.g. 'Reprinted, June 1928.' In the absence of any such addition, the book will be a first edition.

"If there is no bibliographical note at all, in which case the date, that is the year, will almost certainly appear on the title-page, then also the book may be taken to be a first edition."

1937, 1947 Statements: *See* 1928 Statement

Statement for 1960: "Our 1976 statement would equally have applied to the situation in 1960 and continues to reflect our current practice. If a book is a first edition it will carry the notice 'First published/First published in Great Britain 19...'

"If it is a reprint or a second or subsequent edition the original notice will be followed by 'Reprinted 19..' or 'Second edition 19..' as appropriate."

1976 Statement: "We have no means of identifying first editions other than the obvious bibliographical information provided on the verso title page of all our books."

1981 Statement: *See* 1976 Statement

DAVIS PUBLICATIONS, INC.

1988 Statement: "We do not make any designation. Essentially, we publish an anthology once. If these volumes are subsequently republished, they are done so in hardcover or in omnibus editions and are often prepared and distributed by other publishers who would apply their own policy."

DAVIS-POYNTER LIMITED (ENGLAND)

1976 Statement: "We have no particular method of identifying first editions. We use the normal international copyright line, that is the details of copyright holder and date. Any reprints have another date line."

1981 Statement: *See* 1976 Statement

DAW BOOKS, INC.

1981 Statement: "DAW Books include on the copyright page the designation 'First Printing,' and the month and year of that first release. Below this we print a sequence of numbers from 1 to 9. With each new printing, a number is deleted.

"Thus a first printing would have the number '1' lead off beneath the notice of this 'First Printing.' If the copyright date given on that page is the same as the year of our first printing, then you can be sure that it is also a First Edition.

"It should be noted that DAW Books are published by DAW Books, Inc., a separate corporate entity from New American Library, Inc, which is our co-publisher for marketing, production, and services, but which does not have any proprietary interest in us."

1988 Statement: *See* 1981 Statement

THE DAWN HORSE PRESS

1976 Statement: "We originally published in hard cover, *The Knee of Listening*, by Franklin Jones. To identify our first edition, this first publication was printed by CSA Press, Lakemont, GA 30552. This is the distinguishing characteristic of the first edition of the publication. All our other publications are duly marked, 1st edition, 2nd edition, etc."

1981, 1988 Statements: *See* 1976 Statement

DAWNE-LEIGH PUBLICATIONS

1981, 1988 Statements: *See* 1981, 1988 Statements of Celestial Arts

DAWSON'S BOOK SHOP

1976 Statement: "We do not identify first editions of our publications since we very seldom reprint our titles. In the few instances when they have been reissued, the later edition is clearly indicated."

1981, 1988 Statements: *See* 1976 Statement

THE JOHN DAY CO., INC.
(Includes Asia Books; formerly John Day & Company.)

1928 Statement: "This company has adopted the method of designating first editions on the copyright page with a line reading: First published, month, year. Subsequent printings are designated by a line below this reading: second printing, date, third printing, date, etc."

1937 Statement: "For some time now The John Day Company has adopted the following method of distinguishing first editions: On the first printing copyright page appears only the copyright notice: Copyright, 1936, by Richard Roe, and the usual printer's imprint: Printed in the United States of America by The John Smith Printing Company. Lately we have included a paragraph: All rights reserved, including the right to reproduce this book or portions thereof in any form. However, all other printings of the same book may be distinguished by: Second printing, Jan. 1936, Third printing, February, 1936, et cetera, with the proper month inserted.

"You will notice that 'John Day & Co.' is no longer used; when the book is wholly owned by The John Day Company 'The John Day Company, New York' appears on the title page.

"The same method applied to Reynal and Hitchcock; that is, no notice of first printing appears on the first edition, but notices of second, third, and fourth printings being added as is the case. In 1935, The John Day Company was associated with Reynal and Hitchcock, and on the title page of books published under this new association you will find the imprint: 'a John Day Book, Reynal and Hitchcock, New York.' This method of imprinting our books is similar to The Atlantic Monthly Press and Little, Brown & Co., with which you may be familiar. On the copyright page of books put out under the joint imprint you will find on both first printing and subsequent printings the words: 'Published by John Day in association with Reynal and Hitchcock.' However, this has no bearing on the edition printings."

See also 1937 Statement of Reynal and Hitchcock, Inc.

1947 Statement: "As of May, 1938, we ceased our relationship with Reynal and Hitchcock, and all new books published since then, and reprintings made since then of older books, have carried no mention of Reynal and Hitchcock.

"Our present title pages carry: 'The John Day Company, New York.' Our copyright pages, on first impressions, carry the following:

Copyright, 1947, by Richard Roe
All rights reserved. This book, or parts thereof, must not be reproduced in any form without permission.
Manufactured in the United States of America.

"On books for which we control the Canadian rights, the copyright page also carries a line reading: 'This book is published on the same day in the Dominion of Canada, by Longmans, Green and Company, Toronto.' In most cases, this last entry does not mean that any copies of the book have been printed in Canada; Longmans, Green and Company act as selling agents for copies of our own edition.

"If the copyright page has no reference to the number of the impression, the copy is from the first impression. On subsequent printings, we add 'second impression,' 'third impression,' etc.

"The copyright pages of Asia Books are handled in exactly the same way as John Day books. The only difference is that on certain Oriental books published by John Day, the line 'An Asia Book' is included on the title page, the binding, and the jacket."

1976 Statement: *See* 1976 Statement of Thomas Y. Crowell Company
1981, 1988 Statements: *See* 1981, 1988 Statements of Harper and Row Publishers, Inc.

STEPHEN DAYE PRESS
(Became Stephen Daye Press, Inc. Bought by Frederick Ungar Publishing Co. in 1945.)

1937 Statement: "We mark second editions and second and subsequent printings on copyright page. We do not print the words 'First Edition.' "
1949 Statement: *See* 1937 Statement

JOHN De GRAFF, INC.

1976 Statement: "We do not have an unvarying procedure to identify which of our books are first editions and which ones are reprints.

"Normally a reprint is indicated on the copyright page by 'reprinted and year' but there are occasions like book club printings and oversights when the copyright page is not changed."

1981, 1988 Statements: *See* 1976 Statement

DeVORSS & COMPANY

1988 Statement: "We have no particular system for indicating 'First Edition.' The copyright date would indicate the year of the first edition, and in almost all cases, we indicate on the copyright page the number of printings there have been since the copyright."

DEAN & SON LTD. (ENGLAND)

1976 Statement: "As we are in the mass children's book market we do not publish special first editions.

"Generally speaking, we do an initial large run and do not reprint except in special circumstances."

1981 Statement: *See* 1976 Statement
1989 Statement: *See* 1989 Statement of The Octopus Publishing Group PLC (England)

DECEMBER PRESS

1976 Statement. "We designate only those printings and/or editions after the first, and so far we haven't had any of those."

1981, 1988 Statements: *See* 1976 Statement

DELACORTE PRESS

1976, 1981 Statements: *See* 1976, 1981 Statements of Seymour Lawrence Incorporated

JAMES LADD DELKIN

1947 Statement: "No mention is made of 'Printing' in the First Edition. Following printings say 'Second Printing,' 'Third Printing,' 'Fourth

Printing'—as in the case of my 'Pacific Ocean Handbook.' Indications of 'Revision' or 'Enlargement,' when necessary, are so printed.

"As to my Fine Press Books—none are numbered—and *none have* or will be reprinted in the same format, hence the date will tell the first printing of the material (when and if). (Example: The Grabhorn Press does not reprint editions.)

"'Flavor of San Francisco' (in its four editions) is indicated only by dates—the material being revised in each issue."

DEMBNER BOOKS

1988 Statement: "Dembner Books does not designate the first printing of a first edition. When a book goes back to press, we indicate 2nd, 3rd, 4th, etc., printing."

T. S. DENISON & CO., INC.

1976 Statement. "We do very little in this regard. We do designate second, third, fourth, etc., printings on the copyright page, but usually do nothing to designate a first edition other than the standard book # and copyright date. In the publishing of special edition books we assign registration numbers. This is usually a limited printing."

1981 Statement: *See* 1976 Statement

1988 Statement: "We usually do nothing to designate a first edition other than the standard book # and copyright date. In the publishing of special edition books we assign registration numbers. This is usually a limited printing."

DENLINGER'S PUBLISHERS

1976 Statement: "We do not include a statement in our books to identify first editions. We identify second editions or other later editions through inclusion of additional dates in the copyright statement. A single copyright date in one of our books indicates that the book is a first edition.

"Second printings or other later printings are identified through inclusion of the words 'Second Printing' or other later printing on the copyright page."

1981, 1988 Statements: *See* 1976 Statement

J. M. DENT PTY LTD (AUSTRALIA)

1989 Statement: *See* 1989 Statement of Houghton Mifflin Australia Pty Ltd (Australia)

J. M. DENT & SONS, LTD. (ENGLAND)

1928 Statement: "Our usual practice is to print a date on the title page of a first edition; if a book is reprinted we put a new date on the title page and print on the reverse—'First published so-and-so. Reprinted so-and-so.' Thus you will be able to identify first editions by the absence of any such note on the reverse of the title page."

1936 Statement: "The procedure which we follow for identifying first editions is now slightly different from that of 1928, and I think the following paragraph states the present position.

"Our usual practice is to print on the back of the title page a biblio. note giving the date of publication of the edition. If a book reprints the date of the reprint is added. Thus it may be assumed that if the following line 'First published......' only appears it is a first edition. If it is a reprint of our own first edition the line 'Reprinted......' will be added underneath. If it is the first time that we have published it and it is the reprint of some earlier edition, we print 'First published in this edition......' This applies particularly to reprints of old and established books. This has been our practice since 1929."

1947 Statement: *See* 1936 Statement

Statement for 1960: *See* 1976 Statement

1976 Statement: "We do not have any set formula for identifying our first editions, but these normally carry (on the title verso) the statement 'First published 19...'

"Where a previously published title is to appear for the first time in a new format or series, we usually make the statement 'First published in this edition 19...' "

1981 Statement: *See* 1976 Statement

1989 Statement: *See* 1989 Statement of George Weidenfeld & Nicolson Limited (England)

THE DERRYDALE PRESS, INC.
(Went out of business in 1941.)

1937 Statement: "All of our publications are limited editions. This is so stated, together with the number of copies in the edition, either at the end of the book or on the back of the title page. If a second edition of one of our books is issued, it is so noted in the limit notice."

See also Windward House

DESERET BOOK COMPANY

1976 Statement: "We do not make a designation for first edition; however, if the date of publication on the title page is the same as the copyright date, it is a first edition.

"If the book is reprinted, the date of publication on the title page will be changed to correspond to the reprint date. We do not indicate a revised edition unless substantial copy changes are made."

1981 Statement: "Deseret Book company has changed the policy and we will now include the number of each edition of our publications on the title page. The reason for this is that it is very possible that we would have more than one or two reprints in a year.

"We have begun doing this as of January 1, 1981, and all of our new books reflect this new practice. We will be adding printings on older books as reprints are ordered and as information is available. Unfortunately, some of the records of the past are no longer available, so books that were published before 1975 are almost impossible to bring up to date. Books published since that year will have the printings added as we reprint them."

1988 Statement: "All of our books printed since January 1, 1981, have the month and year of each printing, including the first one, indicted on the copyright page. Thus, 'First printing March 1988' would appear in the first printing, and subsequent printings would be similarly listed below that entry. As books first printed prior to 1981 are reprinted, we try to indicate the dates of prior printings if the information is available; however, some of our records are incomplete, particularly for books published prior to 1975, and this is not always possible.

"If a book is revised, each new printing will have the original publication date as well as the month and year for each reprinting of the revision.

"If a book that has been out of print for several years is brought back into publication, we will similarly indicate both the original printing date and the date of the new printing."

DESTINY BOOKS

1988 Statement: *See* 1988 Statement of Inner Traditions International Ltd.

DETSELIG ENTERPRISES LTD. (CANADA)

1988 Statement: "We do not make any special identification of first editions—that is, all of our titles are first editions except when identified otherwise. Second and subsequent reprints are sometimes identified as such. Our company has not made any changes in this area since it was formed in 1975."

ANDRE DEUTSCH LTD. (ENGLAND)

1976 Statement: "Our normal practice is to print our copyright notice on the imprint page (i.e. the reverse of the title page). This will normally read:
    First published 19.. by
    Andre Deutsch Limited
    (etc.)
"If we do a reprint then a further line would be added saying
    Second impression 19...
"In other words, the first edition is not identified as such but merely by the absence of any reference to further printings, revised editions, etc."
1981 Statement: *See* 1976 Statement

THE DEVIN-ADAIR COMPANY

1947 Statement: "All books published by us in recent years have carried the notation *second printing* on the copyright page. Otherwise it is assumed that all books are first editions."
Statement for 1960: In 1960, a first printing was designated by the words "First Printing" on the copyright page. Printings subsequent to the first were identified as "Second Printing," etc.
1976 Statement; "In almost all instances the second and subsequent printings carry the notation *second printing* on the copyright page."
1981, 1988 Statements: *See* 1976 Statement

DHARMA PUBLISHING

1988 Statement: "In 1975 we began using registration numbers at the bottom of the copyright page. In a first printing, the number 1 appears at the end of a series of numbers. Before this date we noted 'Second edition' or 'Second Printing,' but very few books were reprinted before 1975. Since then we have kept nearly all of our books in print.
"We are a small, non-profit company dedicated to preserving the Tibetan cultural and religious heritage. We have no other imprints or subsidiaries as of this date."

MICHAEL di CAPUA BOOKS

1988 Statement: *See* 1988 Statement of Farrar, Straus & Giroux, Inc.

THE DIAL PRESS

1976 Statement: "We designate a first printing of a first edition by writing 'First printing 19..' on the copyright page."

1981 Statement: "First printings of first editions at The Dial Press are designated by the words 'First printing' on the copyright page. We add the year for later printings; for example, 'Second printing—1981.' "

DIAL PRESS, INC.
(Formerly Lincoln MacVeagh, The Dial Press.)

1937 Statement: "We wish to state that our system is to carry on the title page the year in which the edition is published and on the back of this page, merely a note as to when it was reprinted, such as is done by most publishers."

1947 Statement: *See* 1937 Statement

DIANA PRESS, INC.

1976 Statement: "We do not usually designate first editions—only second editions."

LOVAT DICKSON, LIMITED (ENGLAND)
(Taken over by Peter Davies.)

1937 Statement: "It is our practice to print bibliographical data on the reverse of the title page of all our books, in which the date of first publication and subsequent reprints is stated, as follows:

First Published 1934
Second Impression 1935
Third Impression 1936
Lovat Dickson Ltd. 38 Bedford Street London
and St. Martin's House Bond Street Toronto
set and printed in Great Britain
by Billing & Sons Limited Guildford and Esher
Paper made by John Dickson and Company Limited
Bound by G. & J. Kitcat Limited
Set in Monotype Baskerville"

DIDIER, PUBLISHERS

1947 Statement: "With our own publications second and subsequent printings are indicated as such in the front matter of the book."

THE DIETZ PRESS

1947 Statement: "Some of our earlier books contained a statement on the copyright page, 'first edition.' Other first editions of our books have not been imprinted 'first edition.' However, on all subsequent editions we use the imprint 'second printing' or 'second edition.'

"In other words all of the first editions from this press may be identified by the imprint 'first edition' or by no specific edition imprint."

DILLON PRESS, INC.

1981 Statement: "At present, Dillon Press does not use a method for indicating a first edition. Subsequent printings and revisions are indicated on our copyright page. If such information does not appear there, the book in question is a first edition."

1988 Statement: *See* 1981 Statement

DIRIGO EDITIONS

1947 Statement: *See* 1947 Statement of Falmouth Publishing House, Inc.

DISCUS

1981 Statement: *See* 1981 Statement of Avon Books

DIXIE PRESS

1988 Statement: *See* 1988 Statement of Pelican Publishing Company

DENNIS DOBSON, LTD. (ENGLAND)

1947 Statement: "Our books bear the date of their first publication in Great Britain on the verso of the title page. Style as below. Sometimes they have the publication date in Roman figures on the title page itself.

(Title page.)

DENNIS DOBSON, LTD.

LONDON—MCMXLVII

(Verso.)

FIRST PUBLISHED IN GREAT BRITAIN IN 1947 BY

DENNIS DOBSON, LIMITED

29 GREAT QUEEN STREET

KINGSWAY, LONDON W C 2"

1928 Statement: *See* 1937 Statement

1937 Statement: "We have never made a practice of labelling our books as first editions or second editions, etc., in fact, to our mind an edition is not the same thing as a printing. The first seems to us to denote some change in the contents of a book while the second is simply the number of times the book has been put to press. While we do not label our books First Edition or First Printing, we do, as soon as a second printing is ordered, add a notice on the copyright page giving the date of the publication of the book and the date of the second printing. If other printings follow, a third, etc., up to sometimes as many as fifteen, we add the date of each subsequent printing as it is ordered. This has been our practice up to the present time, and has been in use at least since 1925."

1947 Statement: *See* 1937 Statement

Statement for 1960: "I am not absolutely certain how we designated first printings in the books we published in 1960. In some cases we may have printed 'First Edition' or 'First Printing,' and in other cases we may have printed nothing in the first edition, but would print 'Second Printing,' 'Third Printing,' etc., in printings done subsequent to the first edition."

DODD, MEAD & CO.

1976 Statement. "We generally do not mark a book's first edition nor do we usually mark second and later printings, although there are exceptions to this practice and there seems to be no consistency about doing so. Naturally, if a second printing is marked, the absence of such notice would indicate a first edition. Any notice of editions would appear as such on the copyright page.

"We would only be certain to mark a second edition if there were changes extensive enough to warrant a change in the copyright notice and the second edition came out in a year different from the first.

"As of December 9, 1976, Dodd, Mead & Company, Inc. has changed its practice regarding the designation of first printings. The new practice is as follows:

"A line of numbers—1 through 10—appears on the copyright page of the first printing of a book. On the second printing, the number 1 is simply blanked out, leaving the first number of the sequence a 2, and so on for each subsequent printing.

"Dodd, Mead will begin this method of printing indication with all new books, the copyright pages for which have yet to be set into type. This includes adult and juvenile titles."

1981 Statement: *See* 1976 Statement

1988 Statement: "A line of numbers—1 through 10—appears on the copyright page of the first printing of a book. On the second printing, the number 1 is simply blanked out as well as the words First Edition, leaving the first number of the sequence a 2, and so on for each subsequent printing.

"On some occasions we delete the number line and say Second Printing, Third Printing, and so forth. This is at my discretion."

DODGE PUBLISHING COMPANY

1937 Statement: "First editions of our books carry the line:

FIRST EDITION

on the copyright page. On subsequent editions this line is eliminated and the month and year of publication is substituted; the number of subsequent printings is listed below that:

PUBLISHED, JANUARY, 1936
THIRD PRINTING. MARCH, 1936"

DOG EAR PRESS

1988 Statement: "To designate the first printing of a first edition, Dog Ear Press books have the words 'First Edition' either on the jacket flaps (earlier books) or on the copyright page (more recent books).

"In addition, the newer books have numbers 10 through 1 in descending order, and subsequent editions remove a number (second edition removes the '1,' etc.)."

THE DOLMEN PRESS LIMITED (REPUBLIC OF IRELAND)

1976 Statement: "We are publishing this autumn (1976) a bibliography of our Press in which all our first editions are identified."

1988 Statement: *See* 1988 Statement of Colin Smythe Limited, Publishers (England)

THE DOLPHIN BOOK CO., LTD. (ENGLAND)

1976 Statement: "We have no particular identifying method for defining first editions. Only when a second edition is published we state on the verso of the title page the date of the first edition. Otherwise it is understood that the book is a first edition, and we always mention the date of publication."

THE DONNING COMPANY/PUBLISHERS

1981 Statement: "We usually do not designate first editions; however, when we do, we simply print 'FIRST EDITION' on the copyright page. We also do a number of limited editions in science fiction art and regional pictorial histories that we designate by printing a signed and numbered bookplate on the end sheet."

1988 Statement: *See* 1981 Statement

M. A. DONOHUE & COMPANY

1947 Statement. "We have never made it a practice to mark our first editions and are not now doing so. Sometimes there is a little difference between the first and second editions but we have no general rule to follow. Ordinarily we print from plates and all editions are the same. Our lines today consist primarily of children's books and for that reason we operate as we do."

GEORGE H. DORAN & CO.
(Merged with Doubleday, Page, as Doubleday, Doran & Co.
on December 30th, 1927.)

1927 Statement: "The sign of a first edition of a Doran book is a small round colophon in which the initials 'G H D' appear and which is always placed directly beneath the copyright line.

"Occasionally the colophon is omitted, in which case the words 'First Printing' always appear."

DORLING KINDERSLEY LIMITED (ENGLAND)

1989 Statement: "All titles published in the U.K. by Dorling Kindersley Ltd. indicate the date of first U.K. publication on the copyright page. If nothing else appears on this page, then the volume can be taken to be the first printing of the first edition.

"Subsequent printings are indicated by 'Reprinted... (date).' New editions, for which significant revisions have been made, are indicated by 'Second edition...(date),' 'Third edition...(date),' or whatever.

"Overseas editions of our books—in both English language and foreign languages—are published all over the world by our numerous co-edition partners. They are responsible for the wording of the imprint details and printing history that appears in their editions."

DORRANCE & CO. INC.

1928 Statement: "As a usual thing, First editions are not indicated as such other than by a line giving copyright and year, but when other Editions are got out, full information is given. Take for example, the volume *Record Flights* which we have published this spring. On the Second Edition we had 'copyright 1928. First printing March—Second printing March.' In a special Limited Edition of this book there was printed 'In a limited Edition of five hundred copies, of which this is No...' In the future, in the case of unusual books and rare books, we expect to print 'First Edition' on the First Edition. [This method has been in use since 1920.]"

1937 Statement: *See* 1928 Statement

1947 Statement: "As a usual thing First Editions are not indicated as such other than by a line giving copyright and year, but when other editions follow, full information is given. For example, a Third Edition would be indicated as follows:

> Copyright 1947
> First Printing March
> Second Printing May
> Third Printing June

on the copyright page. If the year of copyright only appears, then we consider the book a First Edition book."

DORSET NATURAL HISTORY AND ARCHEOLOGICAL SOCIETY
(ENGLAND)

1988 Statement: "We do not use any designation on our first editions, copyright and date of publication only, but for our rare second editions we put 'reprinted [and date].' Think this is what DNHAS have always done."

THE DORSEY PRESS

1976 Statement: "First editions have only title & author's name on the cover. Second & subsequent editions are identified by placing appropriate designation after the title on the cover & title page.

"First printings & their dates we identify as such by a statement (example: First Printing, January 1976) which appears under the copyright declaration."

1981 Statement: "The second paragraph [of the 1976 statement], is no longer correct. We use a printers' key under the copyright declaration. It may be rendered as follows:

1 2 3 4 5 6 7 8 9 0 K 7 6 5 4 3 2 1

"The first numeral 1 stands for the first printing. When we have a second printing, this numeral 1 is opaqued on the film before plates are made so that the first numeral becomes 2, designating the second printing. The last numeral 1 stands for 1981. When a printing is ordered in 1982, the 1 will be opaqued. This continues until a new edition is published. The letter in the center stands for the printer used to manufacture this book. K is for Kingsport Press, M.V. is for Maple-Vail, etc."

DOUBLEDAY
(A division of Bantam Doubleday Dell Publishing Group, Inc.)

1988 Statement: "The words First Edition are indicated on the copyright page. On subsequent printings this is removed and the print history line indicating the current printing is added."

DOUBLEDAY (AUSTRALIA)

1988 Statement: *See* 1988 Statement of Transworld Publishers (Australia)

DOUBLEDAY & CO., INC.
(Formerly Doubleday, Doran & Co., Inc.)

1947 Statement: "Our method of indicating first editions is the printing of the words 'first edition' beneath the copyright notice which backs up the title page.

"Unfortunately there is no record of the date on which we began to follow this plan. It was many years ago."

1976 Statement. "We designate First Editions on the copyright page thus: FIRST EDITION. On subsequent printings this is removed."

1981 Statement: *See* 1976 Statement

1988 Statement: *See* 1988 Statement of Doubleday

DOUBLEDAY, DORAN & CO., INC.
(Changed name to Doubleday & Co., Inc. December 31, 1945.)

1928 Statement: "We always plan to indicate right under the copyright line on the first printing the fact that the book is the first edition."

1937 Statement: "Our method of indicating first editions is the printing of the words 'first edition' beneath the copyright notice which backs up the title page.

"Unfortunately there is no record of the date on which we began to follow this plan. It was many years ago."

DOUBLEDAY, PAGE & CO.
(Merged with George H. Doran & Co. as Doubleday, Doran & Co., Inc. on December 30th, 1927.)

1927 Statement: "Our method of indicating first editions is the printing of the words 'first edition' beneath the copyright notice which backs up the title page."

NOEL DOUGLAS, LTD. (ENGLAND)
(Out of business prior to 1949.)

1928 Statement: *See* 1937 Statement

1937 Statement: "We designate our first editions by printing the date of publication on the reverse of the title page, as 'published 1928.' Subsequent editions or reprints are added below, as,

    published 1928
    reprinted 1929
    second edition 1930

"This method was adopted about 1926 or 1927."

DOUGLAS-WEST PUBLISHERS, INC.

1976 Statement: "The first copies of a new title are normally designated 'First Printing' or 'First Edition' if we anticipate the title going into several printings. If the book carries an expensive list price and is likely to become a collector's item, we designate the first printing as 'First Edition.' Most publishers, we find, use the two terms interchangeably; in other words, First Printing or First Edition means the same thing."

1981 Statement: *See* 1976 Statement

DOVER PUBLICATIONS, INC.

1976 Statement: "We do not distinguish in any way between the first and subsequent printings of our publications."

1981, 1988 Statements: *See* 1976 Statement

DOWN EAST BOOKS

1988 Statement: "For the past 8 years or so, Down East Books has designated its editions with the number system, the lowest number shown being the current edition. Prior to that it was either First edition or no indication.

"The above applies to imprints and subsidiaries of the Book Division."

DRAMATISTS PLAY SERVICE, INC.

1988 Statement: "The Dramatists Play Service, Inc. is a play-licensing organization, and we publish our plays in acting editions so that they will be available for production by stock and amateur groups.

"Therefore we do not designate first printings or first editions in any special way. We reprint our titles as needed."

DREENAN PRESS, LTD.

1976 Statement: "All of our book printings, whether 1st editions or subsequent ones bear the 10 9 8 7 6 5 4 3 2 1 indicators on the copyright page. The last numeral that appears is the number of the printing. E.G. if the copyright page reads 10 9 8 7 6 then the copy is from the sixth printing of that edition.

"Only revised editions (not reprints) bear the info. as to edition and that is on the title page. If no info. appears on title page then it is a first edition."

1981, 1988 Statements: *See* 1976 Statement

MAXWELL DROKE, PUBLISHER

1947 Statement: "On an initial printing of a book we make no particular identification beyond the customary copyright data. As subsequent printings are ordered, these are indicated directly beneath the copyright notice.

"Where a revision of any consequence in any of our backlog texts is made, this is treated as a new edition and is noted below the copyright material."

LINDSAY DRUMMOND, LIMITED (ENGLAND)

1947 Statement. "A first edition of a book of British origin would contain, usually on the verso of the title page, the words 'First published 1947.' Owing to production delays it is difficult to put a month with any accuracy. In a second printing of the book we would add below the original line 'Second impression' etc. This would imply that there were no radical changes from the first printing. If the book was revised or brought up to date by the inclusion of new material this further printing would be registered as a second edition, with date.

"This is the usual method we adopt, which I believe is the general one, though some publishers use the word 'reprinted' instead of first, second or third impression."

GERALD DUCKWORTH & CO., LTD. (ENGLAND)

1928 Statement: *See* 1937 Statement

1937 Statement: "Our usual custom is to put on the reverse of the title page 'First published, 1928.' In some cases instead of this we put the date at the foot of the title page. In either case a second edition has a definite statement that it is a New Impression or a New Edition on the reverse of the title page.

"We are sorry it is not possible for us to give the date when we first began using this method of identifying first printings."

1947 Statement: "Our usual custom is to put on the reverse of the title page 'First published, 1928.' In some cases instead of this we put the date at the foot of the title page. Second or other revised editions are always proclaimed as such on the reverse of the title page, where the date of the most recent printing is also given."

1982 Statement: "The copyright notice on the verso of the title page includes a year date, which is the date of first publication unless the book contains previously copyrighted material in which case the date of first volume publication is also given."

1988 Statement: *See* 1982 Statement

DUELL, SLOAN AND PEARCE, INC.

1947 Statement: "We have not been altogether consistent in our method of indicating editions of our books. In general it is our practice to indicate first impressions of trade books by words 'First Edition,' or by Roman numeral 'I' on reverse of title page. In subsequent printings these are replaced by 'Second Printing' or numeral 'II' respectively, or in cases where texts are revised by 'Second Edition.' In case of a book published in another country prior to, or simultaneously with our edition, we use line 'First American Edition' to indicate this fact."

DUFFIELD & CO.

(Became Duffield & Green, now out of business. Publications purchased by Dodd, Mead & Co., in April, 1934.)

1928 Statement: "We designate our first editions by printing the copyright date on the reverse of title page. Occasionally we insert the phrase 'First edition printed such and such a date,' in cases where the first edition is assumed to be important."

JAMES DUFFY & CO., LTD. (REPUBLIC OF IRELAND)

1976 Statement: "Our only method is to print the year on the cover and inside title. For reprints we put:

First published 1976
Reprinted 1977
Reprinted 1978

"On the reprints we would omit the year on the cover and inside title."
1981 Statement: *See* 1976 Statement

DUKE UNIVERSITY PRESS

1947 Statement: "The Duke University Press is a small organization devoted almost wholly to the publication of the results of scholarly research for a limited audience, largely academic. Consequently our editions are small, and we print from type rather than plates. Any book of ours is likely to be a first edition, though it may be a second or third impression. If there are no corrections, often there is no way to tell which impression a particular book comes from. If there have been corrections, a note of this, and of the impression, is to be found on the copyright page. If a demand for a book continues after the type has been melted, we use a photo-offset process to reprint. Here a good eye for type is the only way to tell such a reprint from the original."

1976 Statement: "Although we customarily note a second or later edition or second or later printing as such, we have no particular means of noting a first edition."

1981, 1988 Statements: *See* 1976 Statement

DUNSTER HOUSE BOOKSHOP

1928 Statement. "Our own publications have always had the date in the First edition on the title page. This is the same method as that used by Messrs. Houghton Mifflin Company."

DUQUESNE UNIVERSITY PRESS

1976 Statement: "There has been no consistent method used to identify first editions of Duquesne University Press titles. For the most part, however, first editions can be identified by the notation 'first printing' which, when used, appears on the copyright page. In instances where there is no indication of the edition or number of printings, there is no doubt that the book is a first edition.

"If a book has been revised and a new edition printed, the information is always registered on the title page. The number of printings of the new edition is notated on the copyright page."

1981 Statement: "From 1978 on, the notation 'First Edition' appears on the copyright page. Prior to 1978, there had been no consistent method used to identify first editions of Duquesne University Press titles. For the most part, however, first editions can be identified by the notation 'first printing' which, when used, appears on the copyright page. In instances where there is no indication of the edition or number of printings, there is no doubt that the book is a first edition.

"If a book has been revised and a new edition printed, the information is always registered on the title page. The number of printings of the new edition is notated on the copyright page."

1988 Statement: *See* 1981 Statement

OLIVER DURRELL, INC.

1947 Statement: "Unless the copyright page bears a notice of the second or additional printings, the book is a first edition."

DUSTBOOKS

1976 Statement: "We simply print 'First Printing' on reverse of title page."

1981 Statement: "We simply put © date—author and sometimes add '1st printing—date.' Nothing more."

1988 Statement: *See* 1981 Statement

E. P. DUTTON & CO., INC.

1928 Statement: "Unfortunately we have no definite scheme for identifying First Editions. Recently a copyright notice behind a title-page, on which nothing occurs but that, is an indication it is a first, because when we begin the second printing we mark it on the back."

1936 Statement: "Since 1929 we use the words 'first edition' immediately below our copyright notice for all such books. If the book is reprinted a notice is substituted on the copyright that this is the second or third printing as the case may be.

1947 Statement: *See* 1936 Statement

Statement for 1960: First printings were not indicated.

1976 Statement: First printings are indicated on the copyright page.

1981 Statement: *(E. P. Dutton changed its name to Elsevier-Dutton in 1978. In 1981, the name was changed back to E. P. Dutton.)*

"The first printing of a first edition is designated on the copyright page. Five years ago, we didn't include this information; this is the only difference in our method of identification."

1988 Statement: "The first printing of a first edition is indicated on the copyright page by the words 'First Edition.'

"This is the policy for adult books and our Obelisk, William Abrahams, and Truman Talley subsidiaries."

E

THE EAKINS PRESS FOUNDATION

1976 Statement: "In fact Eakins publications are not intended to go into editions beyond the first, and consequently no particular mark of identification is accorded the first printing."

1981 Statement: *See* 1976 Statement

THE EAST WOODS PRESS

1981 Statement: "We designate the first printing of a first edition by simply typesetting 'first printing' underneath the copyright information. I believe we have done this with each book during our four years of publication.

"The East Woods Press is the trade name and imprint of Fast & McMillan Publishers, Inc. All books from our company follow the same practices."

1988 Statement: *"The East Woods Press merged with The Globe Pequot Press on October 1, 1986."*

See 1988 Statement of The Globe Pequot Press, Inc.

EASTMAN KODAK COMPANY

1988 Statement: "We do not designate the first printing of first editions."

THE ECCO PRESS

1976 Statement: "Starting with our spring, 1977 books, all copyright pages will run the line 'FIRST EDITION' when it is applicable. Previously, we have not run this line. However, if any of our books should go into a second printing, we will run the line 'SECOND EDITION.' "

1981 Statement: "The 1976 statement you have on file for The Ecco Press regarding our designation of first editions is still correct. The line we use to indicate that a book is a first edition is 'First published by The Ecco Press in.... (year).' Additional printings are indicated by the following line: 'Second printing.....' If any of our books should be reprinted in a new edition, we will indicate this by the line 'Second Edition.' "

1988 Statement: *See* 1981 Statement

EDEN PRESS (CANADA)

1988 Statement: "The words 'First Edition' appear on our copyright / ISBN page. This has been done since 1978. Subsequent editions and/or printings are also so marked."

EDINBURGH (SCOTLAND)

1988 Statement: *See* 1988 Statement of Edinburgh University Press (Scotland)

EDINBURGH UNIVERSITY PRESS (SCOTLAND)

1988 Statement: "Since the introduction and use of ISBNs in the late 1960s, Edinburgh University Press has adopted a style which makes use of the copyright sign followed by the name of the copyright holder (if applicable) and the year of publication, viz.: © N. Author 1988.

"Only when a book reprints is 'First edition' mentioned, viz.:
    First published 1984
    Reprinted 1986, 1988

"With reference to Edinburgh University Press books (we are the imprint 'Edinburgh'), it can be taken that no reference or mention of 'First edition' means that that particular printing *is* the first."

WM. B. EERDMANS PUBLISHING CO.

1976 Statement: "We never explicitly state the appearance of a first edition. The absence of any identifying statement would indicate the first printing of a first edition.

"All other printings of a first edition are indicated as such. Revised editions are explicitly identified."

1981, 1988 Statements: *See* 1976 Statement

ELAND BOOKS (ENGLAND)

1989 Statement: "By and large, nearly all our books are reprints. We like therefore to put 'First published by,' designating the original publisher.

"We then like to put, also on the verso page 'First issued in this edition,' giving the year of issue.

"Occasionally our books are mongrels, some of the material having been published in book form before, some of it being new. We try to indicate where this is the case and usually use the sentence 'First issued in this edition,' again giving the date.

"If we reprint our edition of the book, we like to put in 'Reprinted,' giving the year of the reprint."

ELDON PRESS, LTD. (ENGLAND)
(Controlled by Macdonald & Co.)

1937 Statement: "First Editions are marked on the back of the title page
Published by
Eldon Press Ltd.
1934

"For reprints the month of publication is added together with the date of the reprint, as follows.

Published by
Eldon Press Ltd.
December 1934
Second Impression January 1935"

1947 Statement: Publisher supplied sample title page showing present method. This bears on verso:

First published 1947
Second Impression December 1947

PAUL ELEK PUBLISHERS, LTD. (ENGLAND)

1947 Statement: "All first editions of our books are printed with copyright notes and date, whereas 'reprints' and 'second editions' always have the words 'reprinted' or 'second edition' and the date."

1976 Statement: "We have no method of identifying first editions."

ELK GROVE BOOKS

1976, 1981, 1988 Statements: *See* 1976, 1981, 1988 Statements of Childrens Press

AIDEN ELLIS (ENGLAND)

1988 Statement: "Date of edition is always indicated on the imprint page."

ELM TREE BOOKS (ENGLAND)

1988 Statement: *See* 1988 Statement of Hamish Hamilton Ltd. (England)

ELM TREE PRESS

See William Edwin Rudge

ELSEVIER

1988 Statement: *See* 1988 Statement of Elsevier Science Publishing Company, Inc.

ELSEVIER-DUTTON PUBLISHING CO., INC.

See 1981 Statement of E. P. Dutton Co., Inc.

ELSEVIER SCIENCE PUBLISHING COMPANY, INC.

1988 Statement: "Elsevier Science Publishing Co., Inc., indicates the first printing of a first (or subsequent) edition on the copyright page using the following designation.

Current printing (last digit):
10 9 8 7 6 5 4 3 2 1

"When we reprint a book, we update the copyright page by opaquing the last digit (e.g., for the second printing, we would opaque the '1'). This system was instituted in 1985 and is used for all Elsevier New York imprints (Elsevier, North-Holland, and Medical Examination Publishing Company). Prior to 1985 we did not have a method of indicating the number of the printing of a book.

"We do not state that a book is a first edition; however, subsequent editions are designated on the cover, copyright page, and title page."

EMERSON BOOKS, INC.

1976 Statement: "We make no specific identification mark on our first editions and to the best of my knowledge have never done so.

"We do identify subsequent editions marking each by the number of its printing. For example—
    2nd Printing 1943
    3rd Printing 1967
"In some instances we eliminate reference to previous printings but always identify with the current printing."
1981 Statement: *See* 1976 Statement

EMPIRE STATE BOOKS

1988 Statement: *See* 1988 Statement of Heart of the Lakes Publishing

ENCYCLOPAEDIA BRITANNICA, INC.

1988 Statement: "As publishers chiefly of encyclopedias and yearbooks, we issue very few first editions. The *Encyclopaedia Britannica* is in its 15th edition (first issued 1974, with annual revised printings); *Compton's Encyclopedia* has, since 1922, referred to each annual revised version as an edition, but they are identified by year of copyright rather than serially numbered. Our yearbooks of course, have only one printing each and one date of issue.

"Our principal book-publishing subsidiary, Merriam-Webster, Inc., of Springfield, Mass., has in recent years used the common practice of indicating serial number and year of printing by a line of type: 12345RMcN888786 indicating a first printing (in 1986), 345RMcN8887 indicating a third printing (in 1987). The imprints 'First Printing' and 'First Edition' are also found."

ENRICH BOOKS

1989 Statement: *See* 1989 Statement of Price/Stern/Sloan Publishers Inc.

ENTRADA BOOKS

1988 Statement: *See* 1988 Statement of Northland Press

ENTWHISTLE BOOKS

1981 Statement: "We say 'First Printing,' sometimes followed by the month & year."

This method of identification has not differed from any previously used. All imprints use this method.
1989 Statement: *See* 1981 Statement

EPWORTH PRESS (ENGLAND)

1937 Statement: "It is our practice to put the date of the publication of any book on the back of the title-page. If the book is reprinted, the date of the reprint appears on the back of the title-page, e.g.:

First Edition 1922

Reprinted 1923"

1947 Statement: *See* 1937 Statement

EQUATION (ENGLAND)

1988 Statement: *See* 1988 Statement of Thorsons Publishing Group Ltd (England)

EQUINOX COOPERATIVE PRESS, INC.

1937 Statement: "Most of our previous books have been limited editions and there was therefore only one printing. The only book on which we have had a second printing is 'Imperial Hearst,' by Ferdinand Lundberg. All subsequent editions carry a line to that effect on the copyright page."

PAUL S. ERIKSSON PUBLISHER

1976 Statement: "We customarily make no mention of first editions or first printings. We do make an attempt to print notices on the © page designating which printing of a particular edition it is—after the *first* printing. On new editions, we mention *revisions* only; e.g. © 1971. Revised Edition, 1976."

1981 Statement: "We also now sometimes use the numerical system 10 9 8 7 6 5 4 3 2 showing which *printing* a title is in."

1988 Statement: "We now use the numerical system 10 9 8 7 6 5 4 3 2 showing which *printing* a title is in."

THE ESSEX INSTITUTE

1928 Statement: "It is very unusual for our publications to run to more than one edition and we have not designated the first in any case except by the date. We have designated second editions as such on the title page."

1937, 1947 Statements: *See* 1928 Statement

EUROPA PUBLICATIONS LIMITED (ENGLAND)

1988 Statement: "We designate the first printing of a first edition by putting 'First Edition 1988' or 'Second Edition 1989' on the copyright page."

M. EVANS AND COMPANY, INC.

1976 Statement: "We do not designate first editions as separate from first printings. Our printing history is usually listed on the very last line of the copyright page. For example: '9 8 7 6 5 4 3 2 1' means that it is the first printing. No other use of words such as 'First Edition' is used. If the right hand digit is deleted, the final digit is the printing. For example, if the final digit is 2, it is the second printing."

1981, 1988 Statements: *See* 1976 Statement

EVANS BROTHERS LIMITED (ENGLAND)

1976 Statement: "We . . . include the year of first publication, i.e.

First published 1976 by

Evans Brothers Limited,

Montague House,

Russell Square,

London WC1B 5BX.

"For a reprint we would add the words 'reprint' and the date for the reprint under the above."

1981 Statement: "An example of our current verso copy is [as shown]. For a reprint we would add the words 'reprinted' and the date for the reprint under first published.

> Published by
> Evans Brothers Limited
> Montague House
> Russell Square, London WC1 5BX
> Text © [holder] 1981
> Illustrations © [holder] 1981
> First published 1981"

1989 Statement: *See* 1981 Statement, but note that publisher's address will now read: 2a Portman Mansions, Chiltern Street, London W1M 1LE.

HUGH EVELYN LTD. (ENGLAND)

1976 Statement: "The imprint carries the words 'first published in 19...' Any subsequent printing or new edition would carry the same statement followed by the year of the new printing."

EVERGREEN

1988 Statement: *See* 1988 Statement of Grove Press, Inc.

EYRE & SPOTTISWOODE (PUBLISHERS) LIMITED (ENGLAND)

1937 Statement: "First Edition. Year of publication printed under our name at the foot of title page.

"Second and subsequent editions are shown as follows:
Upon the reverse side of the title page:

> First published   19...
> Reprinted   19...
> Reprinted   19...

"Where two editions have been printed in the same year, the month is added, i.e.,

> First published June   19...
> Reprinted October   19..."

1947 Statement: "First Edition. Year of publication printed either under our name at the foot of the title page or included in the printer's imprint at the foot of the verso of the title page, in the form 'This book, first published 19.., is printed.......'

"Second and subsequent editions are shown as follows:
Upon the reverse side of the title page:

> First published   19...
> Reprinted   19...
> Reprinted   19...

"Where two editions have been printed in the same year, the month is added, i.e.,

> First published June   19...
> Reprinted October   19..."

EYRE METHUEN LTD. (ENGLAND)

1976 Statement: "Beyond the usual information about publisher and publication date, and the date of the copyright, we do not have any particular method of identifying first editions."

1981 Statement: *See* 1976 Statement

F

FABER & FABER, LTD. (ENGLAND)

1937 Statement: "When, in 1929, the firm became Faber and Faber, we started our present method of wording the note on the back of the title page of all our books.

FIRST PUBLISHED MAY MCMXXXIV
BY FABER AND FABER LIMITED
24 RUSSELL SQUARE LONDON W. C. I.
SECOND IMPRESSION JULY MCMXXXIV
PRINTED IN GREAT BRITAIN BY
THE CURWEN PRESS, PLAISTOW
ALL RIGHTS RESERVED

"This is a typical example, and we now adhere rigidly to this form."

1947 Statement: "Our general practice is still the same as shown above.

"During the war, however, we have made one or two modifications as follows:—

"1. We generally omit the month, and content ourselves with naming the year. This is due to production delays.

"2. Any reprint in which substantial alterations appear is called a new edition. Otherwise we call the reprint a new impression.

"3. Sometimes, when the biblio is very extensive, we say 'reprinted 1938 and 1939' instead of 'second impression,' 'third impression,' etc."

Statement for 1960: "I don't really think that there is very much to add or subtract [from the 1976 statement]. I think that we have always treated this information in a similar fashion and the only thing which was obviously different in the year 1960 was the way in which we printed the date. Up to and including the year 1967 we indicated the publication dates in Roman numerals. Thus for the year 1960 the date would have read mcmlx. This policy became less common among London publishing houses after the World War II and some people seemed not to have learned how to read these dates! The practice was therefore changed and in 1968 we began to use Arabic numerals regularly."

1976 Statement: *See* 1976 Statement of Faber and Faber Ltd., Publishers (England)

FABER AND FABER LTD., PUBLISHERS (ENGLAND)

1976 Statement: "Our practice here is to print on the back of the title page 'First Published in 19.. by Faber and Faber Ltd.' That seems quite straightforward and is in fact so for all books originating here. But there is a slight difficulty that has to be watched. We sometimes use exactly the same formula for books that have already been published in the United States by an American publisher. This may seem a little odd at first, but you will see that it is quite justifiable if you rearrange the words: that is to say, 'First Published by Faber and Faber Ltd, in 19...' Sometimes we do add 'First Published in the United States of America' which makes the situation clear.

"I have two new books in front of me at the moment which illustrate the situation. The first is *EZRA POUND: THE LAST ROWER* by C. David Heymann where you will find on the verso of the title page the following:

'First Published in Great Britain in 1976 by
Faber and Faber Ltd.'

and lower down

'First Published in United States of America 1976'

"I am not sure whether this does everything that is necessary, but at least it indicates that there is an American publication the date of which has to be checked. The second book is *NUREYEV: ASPECTS OF THE DANCER* by John Percival where we don't say that the book was first published in the United States, though in fact the first edition was published by Putnam's in 1975. There is a special reason for this because the book originated with us and we sold the rights to Putnam's, who published it very quickly. We published later and included some additional material, so the copyright notice reads: © 1975 and 1976 by John Percival.

"All I want to do in drawing attention to these points is to warn you that in cases where there is an American edition it is as well to check carefully when it was published.

"I might mention that for books by T.S. Eliot published after he became a director of this firm and published all his books through us, we always arranged that the English edition should be published at least a day before the American edition and thus the English edition becomes the real first edition.

"But as I said at the beginning of this letter, the collector must really be prepared to do a bit of work in order to make sure what he is getting hold of.

"In some ways the real question to be considered is, how are subsequent editions described? We always take care to indicate second, third impression or whatever it may be, or second, third, fourth edition if there has been an alteration in the text. I think you will find that this rule is carefully followed.

"In the case of translations, we give the title of the original and if possible the place of publication and the name of the publisher."

1981 Statement: *See* 1976 Statement

1988 Statement: "The only addition to the evolving story of Faber practice is that since the last statement on our behalf we have published very many more paperback editions simultaneously with the hard-cover edition, and this dual character is identified as such on the title page verso. Also, of course, the ISBNs for both editions are expressed in both versions. Limited editions, which we still occasionally do, usually have some extra feature which requires a different ISBN—the date of publication will usually be the same year, though it may well be that the limited edition will come out weeks or even months later than the trade edition. We regret to say that our practice is not perfect, and bibliographical niceties (on the Gallup scale) should ultimately be checked with the Faber archive."

FABER & GWYER, LTD. (ENGLAND)
(Reorganized as Faber & Faber, Ltd. in 1929.)

1928 Statement: "Our practice—and I cannot say that we have adhered to it absolutely rigidly up to the present, has been to print on the back of the title page 'First published by Faber & Gwyer, Ltd. in so and so' and with subsequent editions, or impressions, 'Second Impression...' etc. We do not as a rule print the date of publication on the title page itself."

FABIAN SOCIETY (ENGLAND)

1976 Statement: "We have no special method of identifying first editions. However, they can easily be identified as subsequent editions would contain the information that the particular pamphlet or book was reprinted."

88

1981 Statement: *See* 1976 Statement

FAIRCHILD PUBLICATIONS

1947 Statement: "We are publishers of semi-technical or business books and have no particular way of designating first printings. Obviously second or revised printings are so noted and in this way at least we do have a key to first editions by the process of elimination."

FAIRLEIGH DICKINSON UNIVERSITY PRESS

1976, 1981, 1988 Statements: *See* 1976, 1981, 1988 Statements of Associated University Presses

THE FALCON PRESS (LONDON) LIMITED (ENGLAND)

1947 Statement: "Our only method is to examine the biblio on the reverse of the title page.
"This always reads in this order:

> First published in 1947 (or other date.)
> by The Falcon Press (London) Ltd.
> 7, Crown Passage, Pall Mall
> London, S. W. 1
> Printed in Great Britain (or other country.)
> by Tonbridge Printers Limited (or other printer.)
> Tonbridge, Kent.
> All rights reserved.

"In the event of a second or subsequent impression being published that fact and the date would also be given on the reverse of the title page as follows:

> Second impression   November 1947
> Third impression   December 1947"

FALMOUTH PUBLISHING HOUSE, INC.

1947 Statement: "We would distinguish a first edition from subsequent editions by stating so, most always on the back of the title page. We would say either 2d edition, etc. or 2d printing, etc.

"However, of the 75 or so titles we have published all are first editions except *The Umbrella Bird*. The same would hold true of the Dirigo Editions and Triad Editions. Wherever they are found they are first editions.

"We do mostly small editions. In the future, however, we will be publishing on a larger scale."

FARRAR AND RINEHART, INC.

(Became Rinehart and Co., Inc. on January 1, 1946.)
1937 Statement: "Farrar & Rinehart first editions can be identified by the small oval colophon, forming the letters F and R, which appears immediately above the copyright line in all first editions of our books."

FARRAR, STRAUS AND COMPANY, INC.

("On November 21, 1945, the firm of Farrar, Straus & Company was incorporated in New York. Roger W. Straus, Jr., and John Farrar [formerly of Farrar & Rinehart] were its founders.")
1947 Statement: "If our colophon appears on the copyright page it is a first edition. It will be dropped for subsequent editions; which in most cases can also be identified because the printings are indicated."

FARRAR, STRAUS & GIROUX, INC.

("On December 14, 1950, the name of Farrar, Straus & Company was changed to Farrar, Straus & Young, to include Stanley Young, a member of the Board of Directors who was appointed Managing Director in 1949. Mr Young left the company in 1955, and the name again became Farrar, Straus & Company. On March 18, 1955, the firm became Farrar, Straus & Cudahy. Sheila Cudahy had been on the Board of Directors since the acquisition of Pelligrini and Cudahy in 1953. (Creative Age Press was acquired in 1951. Later acquisitions were: L. C. Page & Company in 1957; McMullen Books, Inc., in 1958; Noonday Press, Inc., in 1960; Octagon Books, Inc., in 1968; and Hill and Wang in 1971.) When Miss Cudahy left the company in 1962, the name was, once again, Farrar, Straus & Company.
It has been Farrar, Straus & Giroux, Inc., since September 21, 1964.")

1976 Statement: "In answer to your query, we designate first editions by saying just that, plus the year of publication, on the copyright page of our books. An earlier method was to use the words 'first printing.' "

1982 Statement: "I can amplify [the] previous statement by pointing out that we have never used an absolutely consistent method for designating first editions. I think it is safe to say, however, that virtually all of our first editions include the words 'First edition' or 'First printing,' followed by the year of publication, on the copyright page. (During the past ten years or so, 'First edition' has been used almost exclusively.) Subsequent printings sometimes include information about the first edition, sometimes not."

1988 Statement: "The [1982] statement that you enclosed is by and large the policy Farrar, Straus & Giroux employs. On occasion an editor may use a different method. Again, our imprints and subsidiaries as a rule follow this procedure. There may be exceptions from time to time."

FAWCETT BOOKS

1981 Statement: "At Fawcett Books, we designate the first printing by number on the bottom of the copyright page. We list the numbers from left to right, with 1 being the first number in the case of a first printing.

"We do not designate a first edition in our books. This method of identification does not differ from past practice, and all the imprints of Fawcett follow the same method."

FREDERICK FELL, INC.

1947 Statement: "We identify the first printings of our books by inserting on the copyright page the phrase 'First Printing, month, year.' Subsequent printings are differentiated by using the phrase 'Second Printing, month, year,' etc."

FREDERICK FELL PUBLISHERS, INC.

1976 Statement: "We use 1 2 3 4 5 6 7 8 9 0. When reprinted, we delete figure 1, etc., insert 2nd, 3rd, etc., printing on copyright page, change copyright year to Roman numerals."

1981 Statement: "We will merely revise our [1976 Statement] as follows:
"We use 1 2 3 4 5 6 7 8 9 0. When reprinted, we delete figure 1, etc. and insert 2nd, 3rd, etc., printing on copyright page."

1988 Statement: *See* 1981 Statement

THE FEMINIST PRESS

1976 Statement: "First printing of first edition just says first edition—subsequent printings say first edition, second printing, etc."

1981 Statement: "We say 'First edition, first printing,' 'First edition, second printing.'"

1988 Statement: "As of 1984, we have been listing in reverse sequence the years of printing and reprints; beside that sequence we list the number of the edition, in relative order to the year it is printed. For example:

89 88 87 86   5 4 3 2

"In this case, the second edition would have been printed in 1986. Therefore, the first edition would have been printed in 1985."

FENLAND PRESS, LTD. (ENGLAND)
(Subsidiary of Williams and Norgate, Ltd.)

1937 Statement: "It is our practice to print the year of publication on the reverse of the title page, e.g.

FIRST PUBLISHED 1934

"When the book is reprinted we then insert the month and year when it was first published and the date of the 2nd impression, e.g.

FIRST PUBLISHED MARCH 1934

SECOND IMPRESSION APRIL 1934

THIRD IMPRESSION AUGUST 1934

and so on."

1947 Statement: *See* 1937 Statement

FESTIVAL

1988 Statement: *See* 1988 Statement of Abingdon Press

FICTION COLLECTIVE

1988 Statement: "As we have from the onset, the Fiction Collective designates the first printing of the first edition with the following lines on the copyright page:

'First Edition

First Printing, 19--'

"As to imprints and subsidiaries, we have none."

FIDDLEHEAD POETRY BOOKS (CANADA)

1989 Statement: *See* 1989 Statement of Goose Lane Editions (Canada)

FIDES/CLARETIAN

1981 Statement: "Fides/Claretian is now the imprint of Claretian Publications and is the successor of Fides Publishers.

"Our present practice is to indicate: First Printing, January 1981, on the copyright page.

"Since we are just initiating a new line, we have no policy regarding reprints."

See also Fides Publishers, Inc.

FIDES PUBLISHERS, INC.

1976 Statement: "We do not identify first editions in any particular way. Revised editions are usually noted on the back cover."

1981 Statement: *See* 1981 Statement of Fides/Claretian

FIELDING TRAVEL BOOKS

1988 Statement: *See* 1988 Statement of William Morrow & Co. Inc.

THE FIGURES

1988 Statement: "First printings are not in any consistently particular way indicated. Any The Figures book is a 1st edition if it lacks the words 'Second Printing' on the copyright page."

FILTER PRESS

1976 Statement. "Generally our first printings are 500 copies, and are so identified as 'First Printing, date, 1957,' etc. on the reverse of the title page. As succeeding printings are made they are not identified in most cases. The lateness of the printing can usually be determined by the fact that on the reverse of the title page we print a list of our WILD & WOOLLY WEST SERIES in chrono order, and the imprint date of latest on it shows it was ready at the time of that printing. For internal use we also use a digit such as 512 or 608, which indicates that particular printing was done on December of 1975 or August of 1976, etc. A single digit, such as 1 or 1/2 in lower right part of reverse of title page shows the size of the press run in thousands. We're pretty small, so rarely run more than 1500 or so at a time."

1981 Statement: *See* 1976 Statement

1988 Statement: "The information on our edition designations is still correct. All of our imprints follow the same system, though on a couple we may have failed to definitely state first printing. In that case, comparison of our 3 digit date with imprint date should be helpful."

THE FINE ARTS MUSEUMS OF SAN FRANCISCO

1976 Statement: "We use no designation to indicate a first edition or a first printing. We note subsequent editions and printings as they occur."

1981, 1988 Statements: *See* 1976 Statement

FINE ARTS PRESS

1947 Statement: "So far I have not used any method except date on title page, as 'Fine Arts Press 1930' etc. I have published 23 books to date and never reprinted any. I am about to break over, however, as I am reprinting *Shadows of Old Saddleback*. So all of my books have been one printing only. The press was established in 1930."

FIRESIDE PRESS, INC.

1947 Statement: "Fireside Press has a very limited list, and in the past we have done nothing to indicate first editions. In the future, however, I believe we will put a first edition line on the copyright page."

L. B. FISCHER PUBLISHING CORPORATION
(Out of business prior to 1948.)

See A. A. Wyn, Inc.

FJORD PRESS

1988 Statement: "We designate the first printing of a first edition on the copyright page as follows:

First edition, 19XX

"A few years ago we included the month as part of the date, but we have stopped doing so. Second printings are designated as such immediately below the previous line:

Second printing, 19XX

"Sometimes we use the month here, sometimes we don't."

FLARE
1981 Statement: *See* 1981 Statement of Avon Books

RONALD FLATTEAU & CO. (ENGLAND)
1947 Statement: "Typical of the rather uninspired and unimaginative British publisher, we have the usual method of differentiating between the first and subsequent printings. Namely, 'First Edition—May 1946,' 'Second Edition—June 1946.' "

FLEET PRESS CORPORATION
1988 Statement: "We do not designate a 'first printing' or 'first edition' on copyright page."

FLORIDA A & M UNIVERSITY
(Tallahassee)
1976, 1981, 1988 Statements: *See* 1976, 1981, 1988 Statements of University Presses of Florida

FLORIDA ATLANTIC UNIVERSITY
(Boca Raton)
1976, 1981, 1988 Statements: *See* 1976, 1981, 1988 Statements of University Presses of Florida

FLORIDA INTERNATIONAL UNIVERSITY
(Miami)
1976, 1981, 1988 Statements: *See* 1976, 1981, 1988 Statements of University Presses of Florida

FLORIDA STATE UNIVERSITY
(Tallahassee)
1976, 1981, 1988 Statements: *See* 1976, 1981, 1988 Statements of University Presses of Florida

FLORIDA TECHNOLOGICAL UNIVERSITY
(Orlando)
1976 Statement: *See* 1976 Statement of University Presses of Florida

FOCAL PRESS, LTD. (ENGLAND)
1947 Statement: "Our method of indicating our first editions is as follows:—
On the page following the title page—
First published in......by Focal Press.
"Subsequent reprints have their impression number or edition number quoted on the same page."

FOLGER SHAKESPEARE LIBRARY
1988 Statement: *See* 1988 Statement of Associated University Presses

THE FOLIO SOCIETY LIMITED (ENGLAND)
1988 Statement: "The date of publication of the first edition is given on the title-page of all editions. The dates of subsequent editions are given as 'Second Impression 1988' (as applicable) on the title verso page."

FOLLETT PUBLISHING COMPANY
1981 Statement: "Our policy regarding first printings of books varies. In the case of trade publications we print the words 'First Printing' on the copyright page. In our educational titles we use a printing key on the last page of the book. It reads '123456789/8584838281,' the first numbers in-

dicating printing, the last numbers indicating year of printing. In either case the printing number changes with each subsequent printing.

"This has been our policy over the past several years."

1989 Statement: "Follett Publishing is out of business."

FONTANA PAPERBACKS (AUSTRALIA)

1981 Statement: "We designate the first printing of a first edition as follows:

Copyright: © A. B. & J. W. Smith 1975
First published in 1975 by William Collins
Publishers Pty Limited, Sydney

"This method does not differ from any previously used and all the imprints of our book follow the same practise."

FORDHAM UNIVERSITY PRESS

1976 Statement: "The first editions of books published by Fordham University Press carry the year of publication at the bottom of the imprint on the title page. This year will coincide with the year of (first) copyright. The publication and copyright information on the copyright page always carries enough information to enable the bibliographer to determine the edition or printing in his hands. A first edition is usually described as such, or no statement of edition is present; both carry equal weight. Our reprints or revisions are always designated as such: the year of first publication is either removed from the imprint on the title page or replaced by the new year of republication; the copyright information always carries a complete, if brief, printing history, specifying the years of editions, reprintings, and revisions."

1981 Statement: "Our 1976 statement is basically still accurate, and it may stand with, at most, a slight emendation. I suggest that the second sentence be rewritten to give the following version: 'This year will normally coincide with the year of first Fordham copyright.'

"The matter is a small point, but since you are concerned precisely with such questions of detail, you will probably find some background pertinent. I am speaking, of course, purely from the viewpoint of what constitutes a first-edition publication by us. On rare occasions, we bring out our first edition of a work by a member of our faculty, which was previously published elsewhere. Although the work which we publish is not necessarily the original edition of the book per se, it is the first edition which we have issued, and constitutes what some bibliographers and booksellers are wont to classify as 'first edition thus' or some similar designation."

1988 Statement: *See* 1981 Statement

THE FOREST PRESS (ENGLAND)

1937 Statement: "It is our practice to put the date of publication of any book on the title-page itself. If the book is reprinted, the date of the reprint appears on the title-page and a bibliographical description on the back of the title."

1947 Statement: *See* 1937 Statement

FOUL PLAY PRESS

1988 Statement: *See* 1988 Statement of The Countryman Press, Inc.

G. T. FOULIS & CO. LTD. (ENGLAND)

1988 Statement: *See* 1988 Statement of Haynes Publishing Group (England)

T. N. FOULIS, LTD. (ENGLAND)
(Out of business prior to 1937.)

1928 Statement: "My usual plan with regard to title pages is to print the date of publication on the back thereof, e.g.
'First published January the fifteenth 1928.
Reprinted February 1928.
Reprinted March 1928.' "

FOUR O'S PUBLISHING CO. (ENGLAND)

1949 Statement: *See* 1947 Statement of The Oakwood Press (England)

FOUR SEAS COMPANY
(Out of business before 1937.)

See 1937 Statement of Bruce Humphries, Inc.

FOUR WALLS EIGHT WINDOWS

1988 Statement: "We identify first editions by printing 'First Edition' on the copyright page. We indicate which printing the book is in by printing 'First printing,' 'Second printing' etc., and the date, on the copyright page."

THE FRANKLIN LIBRARY

1981 Statement: "The Franklin Library is the exclusive publisher of a series of limited First Editions in deluxe bindings that are selected, printed, and bound for members of The First Edition Society.

"In each book, its First Edition status is designated in the front matter on the series identification page, on the title page, copyright page, and above the author's special introduction, as well as (since September 1976) on the spine. Wording on the copyright page may vary slightly from book to book dependent on arrangements made with the trade publisher who will handle subsequent editions. No essential changes in this identification method have been made since The First Edition Society's first selection in March 1976.

"Publishers use The First Edition Society copies for registration of the work with the Copyright office. Trade first printings cannot be coded simply as 'first edition' but must indicate that a privately printed First Edition has been published by The Franklin Library."

1988 Statement: "The Franklin Library is the exclusive publisher of a series of limited first editions in leather bindings that are selected, printed, and bound for members of the Signed First Edition Society.

"Each book is designated as a Signed First Edition in the front matter (on the series imprint page, the title page, copyright page, and above the author's special introduction, which is exclusive to this edition), on the colophon page, and on the spine. Each book is signed by the author. No essential changes in the identification method have been made since the Signed First Edition Society's first selection was published in July 1983.

"Trade first printings cannot be coded simply as 'first edition' but must indicate that a privately printed Signed First Edition has been published by The Franklin Library."

GORDON FRASER GALLERY LIMITED (ENGLAND)

1976 Statement: "We designate first editions simply by having the words 'first published in 19 ' on the copyright page. Any subsequent editions or reprints would include further information, e.g. 'reprinted 19..' or 'new edition 19..' "

1981, 1988 Statements: *See* 1976 Statement

FREEDEEDS BOOKS

1988 Statement: *See* 1988 Statement of Garber Communications Inc.

W. H. FREEMAN AND COMPANY, PUBLISHERS

1976 Statement: "All editions after the first are indicated. Printings are not designated. These methods do not differ from any previously used."

1981 Statement: "All editions after first are indicated. In the early 1970's, Freeman began the practice of indicating the *printing number* of each title by means of a keyline on the copyright page, whereby the printing was indicated by the lowest digit in the keyline."

1988 Statement: *See* 1981 Statement. "Our subsidiaries and joint-venture partners follow the same rule."

SAMUEL FRENCH, INC.

1976 Statement: "There is no way that I can answer you but to say that our reprints are not marked as such and our first printings are not marked as such. There is no difference between either, and we do not indicate a difference."

1981 Statement: "The only way you can determine if a play might have some author corrections since the first printing is to look at the copyright. If changes were made in the text it will be reflected in the copyright notice as (revised & rewritten) by such and such an author and the revised copyright date. By this, naturally, you can see it is not a first printing."

1988 Statement: *See* 1981 Statement

MAURICE FRIDBERG (REPUBLIC OF IRELAND)

1947 Statement: "We differentiate between our First and Second Editions by stating on the reverse of the title page if the edition concerned is not the First."

ELEANOR FRIEDE, INC.

1976 Statement: "I am an associate publisher with Delacorte Press, and we indicate First Printing on all books published first in America."

1981 Statement: *See* 1976 Statement

FRIENDS OF THE EARTH, INC.

1976 Statement: "Briefly, we publish two main lines of picture books, the Earth's Wild Places series (eight volumes now published) and the Celebrating the Earth series (three volumes in six editions now published). Each of the CTE books (*Only a little planet, Song of the Earth Spirit* and *Of all things most yielding*) have been published in hard and paperback; there is no way to tell from colophons or other marks between the various printings, so far as I know.

"On the Earth's Wild Places Series no attempt has been made to systematically distinguish between the editions, but it is possible, by comparing colophons and spines, and by the fact that second editions do not have spot-varnished pages. By title, this is what I'd recommend a first edition seeker seek:

RETURN TO THE ALPS:
Colophon: (or publisher's note, as it is called in all FOE books) includes the phrase 'Color separations and lithography by Imprimeries Reunies SA, Lausanne,'
Spine: Friends of the Earth
Second and subsequent editions:
Colophon: says 'Lithographed and bound by Arnoldo Mondadori Editore, Verona'
Spine: Friends of the Earth, Seabury Press
Copyright page says 'This...printing contains corrections of minor errors but no substantive changes in text, photographs, or other illustrations.'
  EARTH AND THE GREAT WEATHER:
Colophon: says 'printed by Imprimeries Reunies SA, Lausanne... color separations by Gravure De Schutter NV, Antwerp.'
Spine: Friends of the Earth, McCall
Second edition:
Colophon: says 'lithography and bound by Arnoldo Mondadori Editore, Verona.'
Spine: Friends of the Earth, Seabury Press
Copyright page includes same statement as *RETURN TO THE ALPS.*
  A SENSE OF PLACE:
Colophon: 'lithography and bound by Arnoldo Mondadori, color separations by Gravure De Schutter'
Spine: Friends of the Earth, Saturday Review Press
Second and subsequent editions:
Colophon: 'lithographed and bound by Arnoldo Mondadori'
Editore, Verona
Spine: Friends of the Earth, Seabury Press
Copyright page includes the same statement as *RETURN TO THE ALPS.*
  MAUI: THE LAST HAWAIIAN PLACE:
Colophon: 'It was printed on Champion Kromekote by Barnes Press, Inc., New York City. It was double-spread collated and bound in Columbia Mills' Sampson linen by Sendor Bindery, New York City.'
Spine: Friends of the Earth, McCall
Second and Subsequent editions:
Colophon: 'lithographed and bound by Arnoldo Mondadori Editore, Verona.'
Spine: Friends of the Earth, Seabury Press
Copyright page includes the same statement as *RETURN TO THE ALPS.*
  PRIMAL ALLIANCE: EARTH AND OCEAN:
(I don't have a copy at hand to check, but believe the colophon credits the color separations to H.S. Crocker Company in Burlingame, California, and the spine probably says Friends of the Earth, Saturday Review Press.)
Second and subsequent editions:
Colophon: 'lithographed and bound by Arnoldo Mondadori Editore, Verona'
Spine: Friends of the Earth, Seabury Press
Copyright page: same statement as *RETURN TO THE ALPS;* copyright page is the same page with 'Contents.'

"On the following three titles there have been no second editions:
ERYRI: THE MOUNTAINS OF LONGING:
Colophon: 'lithographed by Arnoldo Mondadori Editore, Verona...color separated by Gravure De Schutter NV, Antwerp'
Spine: FOE, McCall, George Allen & Unwin
GUALE: THE GOLDEN COAST OF GEORGIA:
Colophon: 'lithographed and bound by Arnoldo Mondadori Editore, Verona'
Spine: Friends of the Earth, Seabury Press
MICRONESIA: ISLAND WILDERNESS:
Colophon and spine are the same as on *GUALE: THE GOLDEN COAST OF GEORGIA*
"I should point out that all books with Seabury Press on the spine also have 'A Continuum Book' on the title page.
"We will be bringing out a limited-edition called *HEADLANDS* (signed and numbered, 700 for sale) in October, 1976."
1981 Statement: *See* 1976 Statement

FULL COURT PRESS, INC.

1981 Statement: "Alas, our method varies. Our special signed limited first editions leave no doubt, including, as they do, a special colophon page."

WILFRED FUNK, INC.

1947 Statement: "First printings of books published by Wilfred Funk, Inc., carry the usual copyright line on the page following the title. When subsequent printings are issued we add the information to the copyright page, so—
First Printing, April 1945
Second Printing, May 1945
—the bottom line always designating the latest printing."

FUNK & WAGNALLS COMPANY

1937 Statement: "In February 1929 we published the first book in which we used the following line, under the copyright notice, to designate a first edition:
'First published—February, 1929.'
"A reprint of the same edition would be distinguished by a line beneath the above line such as:
'Reprinted—March, 1929.'
"A new edition would be designated by a line such as:
'Second Edition—April, 1930.'
"A book might then bear under the copyright notice,
'First published—February, 1929'
'Reprinted—March, 1929'
'Second Edition—April, 1930.' "
1947 Statement: *See* 1937 Statement

FUNK & WAGNALLS PUBLISHING COMPANY, INC.

1976 Statement: *See* 1976 Statement of Thomas Y. Crowell Company
1981 Statement: "The information you want updated was supplied in 1976 by the Funk & Wagnalls Publishing Company, an imprint at that time of the Thomas Y. Crowell Company. Crowell has since been sold to Harper & Row, Publishers, along with all of the subsidiary imprints, including Funk & Wagnalls."

See 1981 Statement of Harper & Row, Publishers, Inc.

1988 Statement: "The trade imprint 'Funk & Wagnalls,' plus the entire backlist was sold to Harper & Row in 1977; it was an imprint owned by T. Y. Crowell.

"This firm, Funk & Wagnalls, is an encyclopedia publisher and owns the trademarks 'Funk & Wagnalls' and 'F & W.' At present we do no trade publishing."

LEE FURMAN, INC.
(Out of business prior to 1949. Bought by Citadel Press.)

1937 Statement: "We make no particular attempt to distinguish first editions from subsequent printings."

G

SAML. GABRIEL SONS & COMPANY

1947 Statement: "We make no differentiation, except for certain sheets that are kept in our files. We find no need in publications such as ours (some of which have little or no text) to identify first editions from subsequent editions."

GAMBIT, INC.

1976 Statement: "We continue to identify first editions as we always have by carrying the words First Printing in a separate line above the copyright notice."

1981 Statement. "We haven't changed our policy vis-a-vis the identification of first editions.

"In your revision you will face a somewhat different problem. Here's how we solved it recently:

    Sixth Printing

    First Revised Edition."

1988 Statement: *See* 1981 Statement

GANNETT BOOKS

1988 Statement: "Every new book is identified as a First Edition on the copyright page. Future reprints are identified as Second, Third, etc. printing on the copyright page and on the cover, if appropriate for marketing purposes.

"For example, cookbooks may be so successful that they are in their Fourteenth Printing. That we feature on the cover and in all advertising.

"For some specific titles, we have and may again print and bind a limited number of Special First Editions in different color and quality cloth covers. Normally this would be no more than 1,000 copies. These are identified as Special Signed and Numbered First Editions. The author will then sign and number them and they will be featured as such in marketing and advertising. Regular hardcover cloth editions are sold through stores, but many key bookstores will order, stock and sell the signed, numbered First Editions."

GARAMOND PRESS (CANADA)

1988 Statement: "Our first editions simply indicate copyright and the year of publication.

"For second, third, or revised editions, again we indicate the copyright and year of publication, followed somewhere further down the page, by a numeric statement—e.g. '2nd. ed.' "

GARBER COMMUNICATIONS INC.

1988 Statement: "In all our books we indicate on the copyright page the year of publication as well as the edition whether it is first or whatever. This is true for reprints as well."

This method was adopted in 1959 and does not differ from any previously used. All imprints and subsidiaries follow this practice.

GARDEN WAY PUBLISHING CO.

1981 Statement: "We do very little to designate our editions as first or second (we've never had a third). What we prefer to do is to do a *revision*, which then gets a new cover, updated material, often a new design, and even a new title sometimes.

"We usually print the printing number on the copyright page starting with the second printing. If the book carries no printing notice, it presumably is a first printing of that edition. Otherwise it will state 'Second printing, March 1979' or something similar.

"Garden Way has no other imprints, and we have followed more or less these practices since our beginning in 1971."

1988 Statement: *See* 1988 Statement of Storey Communications, Inc.

WELLS GARDNER, DARTON & CO., LTD. (ENGLAND)

1928 Statement: "We have followed no strict principle in designating our first editions or first impressions. The nature of our publications, which include fiction, children's books, Religious books, and some poetry as well as miscellaneous works, has been so varied and the Trade conditions in regard to format, price, re-prints, and other details have changed so frequently during the past quarter of a century, our methods have depended very much on circumstances of the particular time, and, of course, to a certain extent also on the personal discretion of the author and the member of the firm concerned with a particular book. We are, therefore, unable to give you any definite information in general. If there is any particular book which we publish, about which you wish to make enquiry, we can probably give you the accurate facts whether they are printed in the book or not."

1937 Statement: *See* 1928 Statement

GASOGENE PRESS, LTD.

1989 Statement: "We do designate first editions but do not distinguish between printings. Our designation is by date only for first editions. A second edition is so designated. This has been our policy from the beginning."

GAY & HANCOCK, LTD. (ENGLAND)

(Purchased by A. & C. Black, Ltd., April, 1929, who continued to issue a few volumes under Gay & Hancock, Ltd. imprint at least as late as 1935.)

1928 Statement: "*First Editions* of our publications have the date on the title page; second and reprints are notified on the back of the title page."

1937 Statement: "*First Editions* of our publications have the date on the title-page only; Second and Reprints have the date of reprint on the title-page and particulars of all printings in a bibliography on the verso."

GEM GUIDES BOOK CO.

1988 Statement: "A book published by Gem Guides Book Company is a first edition unless stated otherwise. The copyright date is the date of the first edition and the first printing. Subsequent printings or revisions are indicated below the copyright line. In the case of revisions, the date of original printing and the last copyrighted revision are indicated. Thus:

First edition 1971
Second Revised Edition 1987."

GENTRY PRESS
(Out of business.)

1947 Statement: "We never reprinted any of our books when our press was alive, so they are all first editions."

GEOGRAPHICAL PUBLICATIONS LIMITED (ENGLAND)

1976 Statement: No particular methods are used.
1981 Statement: *See* 1976 Statement

GEORGIA STATE UNIVERSITY COLLEGE OF BUSINESS ADMINISTRATION BUSINESS PUBLISHING DIVISION

1981 Statement: "Our approach to designating a first edition, first printing is by the absence of a designation. Only the second and succeeding editions carry these notices. A second or third edition notice is carried on the cover and title page. We do not designate additional printings."
1988 Statement: *See* 1981 Statement

GEORGIA STATE UNIVERSITY, SCHOOL OF BUSINESS ADMINISTRATION, PUBLISHING SERVICES DIVISION

1976 Statement: "Our approach to designating a first edition, first printing is by the absence of a designation. Only the second and succeeding editions and printings carry these notices—verso title page."
1981 Statement: *See* 1976 Statement of Georgia State University College of Business, Administration Business Publishing Division.

GEORGIA STRAIGHT WRITING SERIES (CANADA)

See 1988 Statement of New Star Books (Canada)

GILL AND MACMILLAN LTD. (REPUBLIC OF IRELAND)

1976 Statement: "We do not in fact have an particular method of identifying first editions of our books. The relevant information is included on the reverse title, or imprint, page of each book we publish."
1981 Statement: *See* 1976 Statement
1988 Statement: "Date of first publication is always included on our books and is shown on reverse title or imprint page of each book."

GINN (ENGLAND)

1989 Statement: *See* 1989 Statement of The Octopus Publishing Group PLC (England)

GINN AND COMPANY

1988 Statement: *See* 1988 Statement of Silver Burdett & Ginn

GLADE HOUSE, PUBLISHERS

1947 Statement: "First editions are so marked on the copyright page, which follows or precedes the title page, depending on the design of the book. Subsequent printings are similarly identified."

GLENIFFER PRESS (SCOTLAND)

1981 Statement: "The statement 'First Edition' has always been used. All imprints use the same method."

GLIDE PUBLICATIONS

1976 Statement: "No mention is made of *any* edition unless there is a Revised Edition, which is so indicated."

THE GLOBE PEQUOT PRESS, INC.

(The Pequot Press, Inc. changed its name to The Globe Pequot Press in 1978.)
1988 Statement: "Our normal procedure is to put on the verso of the title page the words FIRST EDITION. With minimum or no changes we will list again the words FIRST EDITION and add the words, 'Second Printing.' When revisions are more than minimal, we will list SECOND EDITION.' "
See also The Pequot Press, Inc.

GNOMON PRESS

1988 Statement: "Re: first editions. None are labelled such and you'd have to know your stuff to detect one. But some have information on colophon as to limitation, etc."

DAVID R. GODINE, PUBLISHER, INC.

1988 Statement: "When we are printing a book which we acquired and produced from the manuscript, we will print 'First Edition' at the bottom of our copyright page. For subsequent printings, we will write 'first published in 19xx by David R. Godine,' and then at the bottom of the page we will print 'second printing' or 'third printing' or whatever the case may be.

"As we often produce books which were originally published at other houses, we will in such cases write 'first published by David R. Godine in 19xx' and will also include a line about where it was originally published, and when.

"As for imprints and subsidiaries, we have only one of the former and none of the latter and yes we use the same practices for our imprints."

GODINE COUNTRY CLASSICS

1988 Statement: *See* 1988 Statement of David R. Godine, Publisher, Inc.

GODINE DOUBLE DETECTIVES

1988 Statement: *See* 1988 Statement of David R. Godine, Publisher, Inc.

WILLIAM GODWIN

See Hillman-Curl, Inc.

GOLD EAGLE BOOKS (CANADA)

1989 Statement: *See* 1989 Statement of Worldwide Library (Canada)

GOLDEN BOOKS

1988 Statement: *See* 1988 Statement of Western Publishing Company, Inc.

THE GOLDEN COCKEREL PRESS (ENGLAND)

1937 Statement: "With a few exceptions all our books have been issued in a first edition only limited to between 150 and 750 copies, often signed by the author and the artist, for collectors of finely produced and illustrated books of literary worth.

"The exceptions are:

1921, *ADAM & EVE & PINCH ME* by A. E. Coppard
(of which there were three editions)

1921, *TERPSICHORE & OTHER POEMS* by H. T. Wade-Gery
(of which there were two editions)

1922, *THE PUPPET SHOW* by Martin Armstrong
(of which there were two editions)

1932, *RUNNING* by A. E. Coppard
(of which there were two editions)

1932, *CONSEQUENCES*
(of which there were two editions)

"The Press will be pleased to answer any questions which may arise about any of their books."

1948 Statement: "With a few exceptions all our books have been issued in a first edition only, limited to between 150 and 750 copies, often signed by the author and the artist, for collectors of finely produced and illustrated books of literary worth.

The exceptions are:

April 1921. *ADAM & EVE & PINCH ME* by A. E. Coppard
550 copies.
July, 1921.
500 copies
Dec., 1921.
1000 copies.

April 1921. *TERPSICHORE & OTHER POEMS* by H. T. Wade-Gery
350 copies.
2nd. edition:
350 copies.

June 1922. *THE PUPPET SHOW*: Tales and Satires.
By Martin Armstrong.
25 signed copies: 1200 unsigned copies.
1923: 2nd. edition—1500 copies.

Oct. 1932. *RUMMY*: That Noble Game Expounded in Prose, Poetry, Diagram and 15 Engravings by A. E. Coppard and Robert Gibbings with an Account of Certain Diversions into the Mountain Fastnesses of Cork and Kerry.
250 numbered and signed copies: 1000 unsigned copies.

Oct. 1932. *CONSEQUENCES*. A Complete Story in the Manner of the Old Parlour Game in Nine Chapters, each by a different author.
200 numbered and signed copies: 1000 unsigned copies.

March 1935. *THE HANSOM CAB AND THE PIGEONS* by L. A. G. Strong.
200 numbered and signed copies: and unlimited unsigned edition.

Nov. 1936. *THE EPICURE'S ANTHOLOGY*. Collected by Nancy Quennell.
150 numbered copies: and an unlimited edition.

Nov. 1936. *THE TALE OF THE GOLDEN COCKEREL* by A. S. Pushkin. Translated by Hannah Waller.
100 numbered copies: and unlimited unsigned edition.

Nov. 1936. *CHANTICLEER.* A Bibliography of the Golden Cockerel Press, April 1921-August 1936.

300 numbered and signed copies: and unlimited unsigned edition.

July 1937. *ANA THE RUNNER:* A Treatise for Princes and Generals, attributed to Prince Mahmoud Abdul. By Patrick Miller.

150 numbered and signed copies: and unlimited unsigned edition.

Aug. 1937. *HERE'S FLOWERS:* An Anthology of Flower Poems, compiled by Joan Rutter.

200 numbered copies: and unlimited unsigned edition.

Sept. 1937. *MR. CHAMBERS AND PERSEPHONE* by Christopher Whitfield.

150 numbered and signed copies: and unlimited unsigned edition.

Aug. 1937. *ANIMAL ANTICS* by Elizabeth Geddes.

Unlimited edition only.

Oct. 1937. *GOAT GREEN* of the Better Gift by T. F. Powys.

150 numbered and signed copies: and unlimited unsigned edition.

Feb. 1938. *THE WHITE LLAMA*, being La Venganza del Condor of V. G. Calderon. Translated by Richard Phibbs.

75 numbered copies: and an unlimited edition.

March 1938. *TOMORROW'S STAR* by L. Cranmer-Byng.

Unlimited edition only.

Aug. 1938. *TAPSTER'S TAPESTRY* by A. E. Coppard.

75 numbered and signed copies: and unlimited unsigned edition.

Aug. 1938. *BRIEF CANDLES* by Lawrence Binyon.

100 numbered and signed copies: and unlimited unsigned edition.

Sept. 1939. *LADY FROM YESTERDAY* by Christopher Whitfield.

50 numbered and signed copies: and unlimited unsigned edition.

Oct. 1939. *THE WISDOM OF THE CYMRY* translated from the Welsh Triads by Winifred Faraday.

60 numbered copies: and unlimited edition.

"The Press will be pleased to answer any questions which may arise about any of their books."

GOLDEN GATE JUNIOR BOOKS

1976, 1981, 1988 Statements: *See* 1976, 1981, 1988 Statements of Childrens Press

GOLDEN PRESS

1976, 1981, 1988 Statements: *See* 1976, 1981, 1988 Statements of Western Publishing Company, Inc.

GOLDEN PRESS PTY LTD. (AUSTRALIA)

1988 Statement: *See* 1988 Statement of Western Publishing Company, Inc.

GOLDEN WEST BOOKS

1976 Statement: "The first edition is the first printing of a book. It lacks any comment on the copyright page. As it receives a second printing it is noted here that this happens to be the second printing and the date. If it is revised it so states."

1988 Statement: *See* 1976 Statement

GOLDENCRAFT

1988 Statement: *See* 1988 Statement of Western Publishing Company, Inc.

VICTOR GOLLANCZ, LTD. (ENGLAND)

1928 Statement: "Our first editions are distinguished by the fact that they contain no information on them as to what edition they are. All editions other than first editions bear, at the back of the title-page, the words 'First Published—second impression (date)' and so on."

1937, 1947 Statements: *See* 1928 Statement

Statement for 1960: "The statement for identifying a Gollancz first edition between 1949 and 1976 is identical to the [1976 statement]."

1976 Statement: "The only way to identify a Gollancz first edition is the negative one of seeing that there is no reference to a second or subsequent impression or a revised edition or a reissue on the verso of the title page."

1981 Statement: *See* 1976 Statement

1988 Statement: "During 1984 Gollancz started to print 'First published in ....' on the verso of the title page."

GOMER PRESS (WALES)

1988 Statement: "We do not adopt a standardised method of designating first editions other than to record the date of publication on the reverse of the Title Page."

GONDOLA (ENGLAND)

1989 Statement: *See* 1989 Statement of The Octopus Publishing Group PLC (England)

GOOSE LANE EDITIONS (CANADA)

1989 Statement: "Goose Lane Editions does not have any method of identifying first editions. Unless one of our books is clearly designated as either a second edition or a revised edition, the reader and bibliographer may assume that they are dealing with a first edition.

"This practise has remained unchanged since the founding of the house, under the original name of Fiddlehead Poetry Books, in 1958."

GPC BOOKS (WALES)

1988 Statement: *See* 1988 Statement of University of Wales Press (Wales)

GRAFTON BOOKS (ENGLAND)

1988 Statement: "On the copyright page we state:
            'Published by Grafton Books 1988' (or other date)
"This indicates first publication in Great Britain. Reprints and subsequent editions are listed after the 'Published by' line.

"In the case of Grafton paperbacks, the first edition of a paperback original is indicated thus:
            'A Grafton paperback original 1988'
"If the book has been previously published in the USA but has not been published in hardback in the UK the following statement appears:
            'A Grafton UK paperback original 1988'
"As far as I know this has always been Grafton's (previously Granada Publishing's) practice."

See also Granada Publishing Limited (England)

GRANADA PUBLISHING LIMITED (ENGLAND)

1976 Statement: "Our first editions are identified in the copyright notice appearing in the prelims of every book which of course incorporates the year of publication. Re-issues and reprints can easily be identified by a state-

ment to this effect which would appear within the copyright notice which will also incorporate a statement as to the date the book was first published."
1981 Statement: "Granada Publishing Ltd is the parent company and the situation regarding first editions is as shown [in the 1976 statement].

"First editions of our hardcover imprints are identified on the title verso by the wording 'Published by Granada Publishing' plus the appropriate year. Reprints and new editions are listed below this statement, e.g.,

    Published by Granada Publishing 1975
    Reprinted 1976
    Second edition 1981

"In the case of paperback first edition the words 'A Granada paperback original' appear."
1988 Statement: *See* 1988 Statement of Grafton Books (England)

GRAPEVINE (ENGLAND)
1988 Statement: *See* 1988 Statement of Thorsons Publishing Group Ltd. (England)

GRAPHIC ARTS CENTER PUBLISHING COMPANY
1988 Statement: "First edition copies of all Graphic Arts Center Publishing Company (and/or Charles H. Belding) titles make no reference to edition or printing. All subsequent printings state the printing on the copyright page. From 1968 to 1977 all titles showed Charles H. Belding as publisher. From 1978 to 1981 titles showed either Charles H. Belding or Graphic Arts Center Publishing Company as publisher.

"Charles H. Belding founded the book division of Graphic Arts Center, Inc., in 1968. On November 13, 1974 Graphic Arts Center Publishing Company was incorporated in Oregon as a separate corporation."

GRAY'S PUBLISHING LTD. (CANADA)
1976 Statement: "It could be assumed that we designate only those printings and/or editions after the first. These methods of identification do not differ from any previously used."
1981 Statement: "Gray's still indicates only editions or printings after the first, on the copyright page."

GRAYSON & GRAYSON, LIMITED (ENGLAND)
(Formerly Eveleigh Nash & Grayson, Ltd.)
1937 Statement: "In all books published by us we insert bibliographical details on the *back* of the title page as follows:
For first editions

First published by
Grayson & Grayson Ltd.
1935

For reprints

First published by
Grayson & Grayson Ltd.
May 1935
Second Impression May 1935"

GRAYWOLF PRESS

1988 Statement: "Graywolf Press First Editions are specified by the following notation on the copyright page:

9 8 7 6 5 4 3 2

First Printing,____(year of publication)."

THE GREAT EASTERN BOOK CO.

1981 Statement: *See* 1981 Statement of Shambhala Publications, Inc.

1988 Statement: This imprint no longer exists.

GREAT LAKES BOOKS

1988 Statement: *See* 1988 Statement of Wayne State University Press

GREAT OCEAN PUBLISHERS

1988 Statement: "Since our beginning (1975) we have indicated edition and printing on the copyright page."

WARREN H. GREEN, INC.

1976 Statement. "First editions are not identified in any way. On the copyright page we simply put © (date), Warren H. Green, Inc.

"Then on the Title Page and on the Copyright Page, each straight reprinting is noted as 'second printing,' 'third printing" etc.

"If a printing is revised but not sufficiently to call it a new edition, on the Title Page and Copyright Page it is identified as 'Revised First Printing,' 'Revised Second Printing,' whatever applies.

"For new editions, on both the Title Page and the Copyright Page, we simply put new copyright information, i.e., © 'second edition.' "

1981, 1988 Statements: *See* 1976 Statement

GREENBERG, PUBLISHER, INC.

1928 Statement: "We do not designate first editions in any special way. But all later editions bear a notice to that effect."

1937, 1947 Statements: *See* 1928 Statement

THE STEPHEN GREENE PRESS

1976 Statement: "At the present time, we run a printing code line at the foot of the copyright page. Starting at the left, it shows printing numbers 1 through 9; and then, starting from the right it shows the current year and 5 or 6 succeeding years—as follows:

1 2 3 4 5 6 7 8 9 80 79 78 77 76

"The first printing carries the entire code line. The second printing carries the entire line minus the figure 1, and, if necessary, minus as many year figures at the end to make the line end with the current year.

"So that a third printing in 1979 would look like this:

3 4 5 6 7 8 9 80 79

"We do not now have any particular method of identifying first editions (as distinct from initial printings). We do identify subsequent editions—e.g., 'second edition,' 'first revised edition,' and the like. But for the most part our first editions are identified by the absence of any statement identifying them as anything but a first edition."

1981 Statement: "Since [1976] our practice has changed somewhat, and we are going to change it again.

"For the past year or two we have still not identified first editions in so many words, although we do identify subsequent editions. At the time of a reprint of whatever edition, we add or update a block spelling out the printing history of a title, stating when the book was first published and when its subsequent printings took place, such as:

Published October 1979

Second printing March 1980

Third printing July 1980

"We are now adding the words 'First edition' to our standard copyright page copy, and all first editions will carry these words."

1988 Statement: "Stephen Greene Press became a subsidiary of Viking Penguin in New York in 1984. Our books now follow whatever practices Viking uses."

See 1988 Statement of Viking Penguin Inc.

GREENHILL BOOKS (ENGLAND)

1988 Statement: "Our imprint pages show the year of publication of our edition. Reprints following the first edition are not identified as such and they can only be dated by means of change of address, or change of advertisements for other books. In a short time in the evolution of this new imprint we have had three addresses and this is also one means of checking whether a book has been reprinted. Initially (1984-6) we were in Hampstead High St., London NW3, then briefly in 1987 at Barham Avenue, Elstree, Hertfordshire, and now, settled for some time we trust, at Russell Gardens, London NW11. This sequence of addresses would identify the sequence of reprints."

GREENWILLOW BOOKS

1981 Statement: The copyright page will show the following information:

First Edition

1 2 3 4 5 6 7 8 9 10

"As we reprint, we drop the first number. For the second printing, cancel 1; for the third, cancel 2; etc. Also, on *reprints*, we delete 'First Edition.'

"Before 1978, we did not print the words First Edition, only the number sequence showing printings."

1988 Statement: *See* 1981 Statement

GREENWOOD PRESS, INC.

1976 Statement: The first printing of a first edition is designated by: "First published in 19..." All printings thereafter are indicated. Revised editions and editions after the first are indicated on the copyright page.

THE GRESHAM PRESS, INC.

1947 Statement: "Second, third, etc. printings are so designated beneath copyright notice, the first not being identified."

THE GREVILLE PRESS (ENGLAND)

1988 Statement: "Our current (1988) practice is to print the following on the reverse of the title page: First published in this edition (date) / by (publisher's name / address) / © (author/date).

"Previous (1982-87) practice contained a variable to the above on the reverse of the title page: © (date/author); in the same period, the number of copies per edition was printed on the back page.

"In the period 1979-81, the practice was to print (usually on the reverse of the title page): Published by (publisher's name / address) © (author/date); with, usually on the back page: This edition is limited to (number) numbered copies signed by the poet / copy number / poet's signature."

GREY FOX PRESS

1988 Statement: "We do not specially designate first editions, but we do indicate second printings with years and revised editions on the copyright page. If one of our editions has no indication of that sort it is the first."

THE GREY WALLS PRESS, LIMITED (ENGLAND)

1947 Statement: "The biblio of all GREY WALLS books appears on the reverse of the title page; first printed, followed by date of year, in the case of succeeding printings second impression and date, etc. Our firm was founded in 1939 and we have since published books interesting to collectors and dealers."

GREYSTONE PRESS

(Established 1936. Ceased publishing 1942. Bought by Book Presentations in 1943; operated in the direct mail field until August, 1947 when the Greystone Press imprint was again used for trade books.)

1947 Statement (by one of the editors of the original Greystone Press): "First printings of all Greystone Press books published before 1942 have the words 'First Printing' on the back of the title page, or else they have no reference at all to printings, which means that they are 1st. editions. In that case, subsequent printings would say 'first printing such and such a date, reprinted such and such a date.' In general, however, first printings actually say so."

1947 Statement (by one of the editors of the new Greystone Press): "As far as I can discover, there is no system used to identify printings on the current Greystone and Book Presentations titles."

GROLIER, INC.

1988 Statement: "As a general rule, we do not identify first editions or first printings of our publications. Subsequent reprintings are also not identified. Revised editions, those editions which have had significant changes made from the first editions are generally not identified by a special notice. They are, however, identifiable because they contain a copyright year for the revised edition in addition to the copyright year of the first editions. These are general practices and are not absolutely observed in all publications."

GROSSET & DUNLAP

1988 Statement: *See* 1988 Statement of The Putnam & Grosset Group (Children's)

GROSSMAN PUBLISHERS

1976 Statement: "There is no designation for the first edition of Grossman Publishers' books. Other printings are so indicated on the copyright page."
1981 Statement: "As of 1977, all [Grossman Publishers] titles were incorporated into the Viking list. Grossman Publishers no longer exist—all titles have been absorbed by Viking Penguin, Inc."

GROVE PRESS, INC.

1976 Statement: "All our books carry a printing history on their copyright page.
"The legend says 'First Printing,' 'Second Printing,' etc. This means of identification has been in use at Grove at least since 1970."
1981 Statement: "The [1976 Statement] is still accurate. We now, however, include the exact same copy on the copyright page for the first editions of

both paperback and hardcover. This way, we don't have to reset the page for the paperback edition. The way you can tell whether or not it is a first edition paperback or hardcover should be apparent from the binding. (We often issue first editions of books in paper and hardcover simultaneously.)

"Later editions say either 'First Edition 1979/Third Printing 1980' (or whatever). New editions will say something like 'First Revised Evergreen Edition 1981/First Printing 1981' (or whatever). Essentially, to tell whether or not a Grove book is a real 'first edition' is to see whether or not it says 'First Edition (Date)/First Printing (Date).' "

1988 Statement: "All our books carry a complete printing history on their copyright page. A Grove Press hardcover first edition and an Evergreen paperback first edition say 'First edition' and the year near the bottom of the page.

"When a second edition or a revised edition is published, this edition and date appear following an information line about the first edition and year. When Grove Press reprints a book from another publisher's edition, this history appears on the copyright page following the copyright holder information.

"Printings of an edition are shown by the serial numbers at the very bottom of the page. For example, 10 9 8 7 6 5 4 indicates that an edition is in its fourth printing."

THE JOHNNY GRUELLE COMPANY

1947 Statement: "There is no way of surely identifying the first printings of 'Raggedy Ann' books.

"The first title, *Raggedy Ann Stories*, was published by P. F. Volland and Co., Chicago in 1918 and the first printing was 5,000 copies with no mark designating them as the first printing. Public acceptance of this material was such that we simply put edition after edition on the press and continued to add titles to the series, each of which enjoyed unprecedented popularity. About five years after the start we began running such lines on the copyright page, as, Fifty-six Printing, etc. This, however, meant little because the size of the various printings ranged from five to fifty thousand copies.

"Under the circumstances, I think it can only be said that there is no way of being sure in this matter."

GRUNE & STRATTON, INC.

1976 Statement: "The last page of the index has a code, a lettered code. 'A' is a first printing; 2nd printing, the 'A' is deleted and the top letter is 'B', etc.

"Following editions become part of the title of the book."

1981 Statement: *See* 1976 Statement

GULF PUBLISHING COMPANY

1988 Statement: "The first printing of the first edition of a book contains no specific designation beyond the copyright notice. Subsequent printings and subsequent editions show the printing history:

First edition 1975
2nd printing 1976
3rd printing 1978
Second edition 1980."

GWASG PRIFYSGOL CYMRU (WALES)

1988 Statement: *See* 1988 Statement of University of Wales Press (Wales)

H

MICHAEL HAAG (ENGLAND)

1988 Statement: "Our first editions are identified on the reverse of the title page as 'First edition' and then the date, or possibly (when it is the same) the date of copyright. Second and subsequent editions are similarly identified, though the date of first edition might not then be mentioned.

"We have always done things thus. We have no other imprints and no subsidiaries."

PETER HALBAN PUBLISHERS LTD. (ENGLAND)

1988 Statement: "We do indeed designate the date of first publication and where a reissue or new edition of a work is brought out it is clearly marked on the copyright page. If it is a question of a translation we generally put the original title either in the English or the original language together with the copyright and date of first publication in the original language."

HALE, CUSHMAN & FLINT, INC.

(Bought in 1942 by Ralph T. Hale and Co. which was in turn succeeded by Charles T. Branford Co.)

1937 Statement: "In books published by us we give on the copyright page the information as to the edition or printing."

E. M. HALE & COMPANY

1976 Statement: "We do not identify a first edition, but we do identify subsequent printings: 'Second printing,' 'Third printing,' etc. Our books are published under the imprint of Harvey House, Publishers."

1981 Statement: *See* 1981 Statement of Harvey House, Publishers

RALPH T. HALE AND CO.

(Succeeded by Charles T. Branford Co.)

ROBERT HALE AND COMPANY (ENGLAND)

1937 Statement: "This Company was formed in February 1936, and we have not yet published any books—the first lot of titles will be issued next month (September).

"Our books may be divided into two categories—NON-FICTION and FICTION. The title-pages of the former will bear the year of issue in roman numerals beneath our imprint at the foot; and where they are first editions the title-page itself will bear no date. When the book is reprinted the bibliography will be placed at back of title.

"In the case of FICTION, the title-page will bear no date of issue, but at back of title-page will be given the month and the year when the book was first published. Any subsequent reprints will be added to that bibliography."

ROBERT HALE LIMITED (ENGLAND)

(Formerly Robert Hale and Company.)

1947 Statement: "This company was formed in February 1936.

"Our books may be divided into two categories—NON-FICTION and FICTION. The title-pages of the former bear the year of issue on the reverse of title. When the book is reprinted the bibliography is placed at back of title.

"In the case of FICTION, the title-page bears no date of issue, but on the reverse of title is given the year when the book was first published. Any subsequent reprints will be added to that bibliography."

Statement for 1960: "From 1941-56 many books have simply, for example, 'First published 1951,' though some early books have nothing at all on the imprint page. Others have copyright date and author, e.g. 'F. Bloggs copyright 1939.' Since 1958 the bibliographical line has been in the form as 'First published in Great Britain 1961.'"

1976 Statement. "There is not a great deal I can say about our method of identifying first editions. This is mainly by implication. The first bibliographical line that appears on our imprint page is, for example, 'first published in Great Britain 1976.' If there is no following bibliographical detail the book is our first edition. Publication or prior publication in another country would be noted if the book were a translation. In the case of publication in English (in America, for instance) there would not necessarily be a mention unless it originally appeared under another title.

"It is necessary to read the bibliographical details in conjunction with the copyright line which in the case of prior publication in America will have a different date from the British publication date.

"As a matter of interest a considerable number of books produced by us which appeared both in America and Britain have joint imprints on all copies."

1982, 1988 Statements: *See* 1976 Statement

HAMISH HAMILTON LTD. (ENGLAND)

1937 Statement: "When a book is first published, we print a notice at the top of the reverse of the title page reading 'First Published, 1934, 1935 or 1936,' as the case may be. When we come to a second impression, we alter this notice by inserting in the top line the month upon which the book was published, January, February, etc., and beneath it we insert a second line reading Second Impression.... (Month) 1934, 1935, 1936, as the case may be, and so on for subsequent reprints."

1947 Statement: *See* 1937 Statement

Statement for 1960: "We designated a first printing in 1960 in the same way as described in our 1976 statement."

1976 Statement: "The only method of identifying first impressions (I think this is safer nomenclature than 'editions') is to say 'first published in Great Britain 19.. by Hamish Hamilton Limited.' Any further impressions are simply along the lines of 'second impression July 1976,' etc."

1981 Statement: *See* 1976 Statement

1988 Statement: "This style was introduced during 1988 and is followed by the whole of the Penguin Group.

First published in Great Britain 1988
by Hamish Hamilton Ltd.
Copyright 1988 by Hugh Thomas
1 3 5 7 9 10 8 6 4 2"

See also 1988 Statement of Penguin Publishing Co Ltd. (England)

HAMISH HAMILTON CHILDREN'S BOOKS (ENGLAND)

1988 Statement: *See* 1988 Statement of Hamish Hamilton Ltd. (England)

JOHN HAMILTON, LTD. (ENGLAND)
(Firm was in liquidation in 1941.)

1937 Statement: "It is our practice to have no date shown on our first edition. If the book is reprinted then the date of the first edition appears together with the reprint date underneath, e.g.:
First Edition 1922.
Reprinted 1923."

HAMLYN PUBLISHING GROUP LTD. (ENGLAND)

1989 Statement: *See* 1989 Statement of The Octopus Publishing Group PLC (England)

HAMMOND, INC.

1981 Statement: "We do not designate the first printing of first editions."
1988 Statement: *See* 1981 Statement

HAMMOND, HAMMOND & COMPANY, LTD. (ENGLAND)

1947 Statement: "Our first edition of any important book is usually indicated by having the month and year of production given in Arabic figures under the imprint of the printers. Any reprint is marked on the imprint page as a reprint, with the date in full."

THE HAMPSHIRE BOOKSHOP, INC.

1947 Statement: "In the last thirty years we have published about twenty books with printings not over one thousand copies. If the designation 'second edition' does not appear on the reverse of the title page, it is a first printing."

HANCOCK HOUSE PUBLISHERS LTD. (CANADA)

1989 Statement: "We do not designate 1st editions as such. Further editions are labelled as 2nd, 3rd, etc., on the copyright page. Likewise for printings.
"This is simply the way it is at Hancock House. There are no current plans to alter the system. We do not have other imprints or subsidiaries."

HANGING LOOSE PRESS

1976 Statement: "We only started publishing books about a year ago and have yet to reprint a book. When we do, I suppose we will add 'Second Printing.' There is nothing in the original copies of the first 6 titles to indicate that they are first editions or first printings."
1981 Statement: "First Editions could be identified only by the copyright date. Second printings are clearly identified as such, with the year."
1988 Statement: "50 titles later, ditto."

HARCOURT, BRACE & CO., INC.

1928 Statement: "We have not been following any fast rule for indicating first editions. On all books for which we think there may be some demand, we indicate the first edition by placing a small figure 1 on the copyright page under our copyright notice, or by putting on a line 'Published' and then the date. Subsequent editions have either a number 2 on them or a line 'Second Printing,' and then the date."
1936 Statement: "In general it is the practice of Harcourt, Brace & Company to indicate the first impression of their general trade books by the words 'first edition' on the copyright page underneath the copyright notice. In cases where the book has been first published in another country, the

words 'first American edition' or 'first printing' are substituted. Previous to about 1930, first editions were generally indicated by placing a small figure 1 underneath the copyright notice, or by putting on a line 'Published' and then the date."

1947 Statement. *See* 1936 Statement

See also 1948 Statement of Reynal and Hitchcock, Inc.

HARCOURT BRACE JOVANOVICH, INC.

1976 Statement. "I believe our method of designating first editions is fairly standard throughout the industry. On the first printing, the words 'First edition' appear on the copyright page. On each subsequent printing, the phrase 'First edition' is dropped and the printing is identified by a letter: the second printing is identified by the letter B, the third printing is C (but the letter B is also retained, so that on the copyright page this designation appears 'BC'). This goes up to the letter J. At the 11th printing, we begin using a number identification: 11th printing, 12th printing, etc. However, in the case of *juvenile* or paperback titles, we do *not* start using numbers at the 11th printing, but instead continue with letters right through Z. If there are more than 26 printings, we start using double letters: AA, BB, and so on.

"If the material in the book is substantially changed, we will identify it as the second edition, apply for a new copyright, and begin the same numbering sequence as for a first edition."

1981 Statement: "I believe our method of designating first editions is fairly standard throughout the industry. On the first printing, the words 'First edition' appear on copyright page. On each subsequent printing, the phrase 'First edition' is dropped and the printing is identified by a letter: the second printing is identified by the letter B, the third printing is C (and the letter B is dropped). This goes up to the letter J. At the 11th printing, we begin using a number identification: 11th printing, 12th printing, etc. However, in the case of *juvenile* or paperback titles, we do *not* start using numbers at the 11th printing, but instead continue with letters right through Z. If there are more than 26 printings, we start using double letters: AA, BB, and so on.

"If the material in the book is substantially changed, we will identify it as the second edition, apply for a new copyright, and begin the same numbering sequence as for a first edition."

1988 Statement: *See* 1981 Statement

HARMONY

1981, 1988 Statements: *See* 1981, 1988 Statements of Crown Publishers Inc.

HARPER & BROTHERS

1928 Statement: "It is our custom to print on the copyright page, of all first editions the two words 'First Edition'. These are removed from the plate on all subsequent printings.

"In addition to these you will find on our copyright pages two key letters beneath the copyright.

"These give the month and year when the edition was printed. This key may be read by referring to the enclosed card."

1937 Statement: *See* 1928 Statement, plus the following statement.

"The use of the key letters on copyright pages began in 1912. The use of the words 'First Edition' began a number of years later, so that there are early copies of books by Harpers in the area between 1912 and perhaps

1920 or thereabouts (unfortunately the date is not a matter of record) which have the key letters but which do not have the words 'First Edition.' This is, of course, important."
1947 Statement: *See* 1937 Statement

Harper & Brothers Key to Editions
on Copyright Page

Months

A . . . . . January		G . . July	
B . . . . February		H . . August	
C . . . . March		I . . . September	
D . . . . April		K . . October	
E . . . . . May		L . . November	
F . . . . . June		M . . December	

Years

M 1912	Z . . . 1925	N 1938
N 1913	A . . 1926	O 1939
O 1914	B . . 1927	P 1940
P 1915	C . . 1928	Q 1941
Q 1916	D . . 1929	R 1942
R 1917	E . . 1930	S 1943
S 1918	F . . . 1931	T 1944
T 1919	G . . 1932	U 1945
U 1920	H . . 1933	V 1946
V 1921	I . . . 1934	W 1947
W 1922	K . . 1935	X 1948
X 1923	L . . 1936	Y 1949
Y 1924	M . . 1937	

HARPER & BROTHERS (ENGLAND)
(London house discontinued prior to 1937.)

1928 Statement: "Our first editions are designated by printing at the back of the title page the following words: First Edition."

HARPER & ROW, PUBLISHERS, INC.

1976 Statement: "The copyright page says 'First Edition.' Under that is a chain of numbers, 76 77 78 79 9 8 7 etc.

"As a book reprints, the First Edition line gets dropped and so do the out-dated numbers.

"A book in its third printing in 1976 would have a line that looks like:
76 77 78 79 9 8 7 6 5 4 3."

1981 Statement: "According to our Production Department we are still using the same First Edition form on the Harper & Row books.

"Thomas Y. Crowell was merged into Harper & Row after its purchase in 1977. All imprints then owned by Crowell now follow the procedures of Harper & Row.

"In 1978 Harper purchased J. B. Lippincott Company which, in 1979, they combined with Thomas Y. Crowell to form a new imprint of Lippincott & Crowell. In 1980 Harper abolished this new imprint and reabsorbed Lippincott & Crowell into the Harper & Row imprint."

1988 Statement: "The [1981] Statement is still correct. There should be no change to that statement."

HARPSWELL PRESS

1988 Statement: "Harpswell Press titles are all identified for editions on the copyright page. First editions are marked as such; subsequent printings, revised editions, etc., are noted."

GEORGE G. HARRAP & COMPANY LIMITED (ENGLAND)

1928 Statement: "Our first editions are distinguishable by the date of publication appearing on the reverse of the title-page. We print a notice in that place, running for example:

First published 1928
By........

followed by the name of the firm and the address. Should the book reprint the notice is added as follows:

Reprinted March 1928

and the month of publication is added to the original notice (the month is not put in at first because when a book goes to press the date of publication cannot conveniently be determined to a nicety). The notice in the case of a reprint, therefore, would be, for example:

First published June 1916
By........
Reprinted March 1928

"Succeeding reprints are entered thus:

Reprinted: July, 1925; January 1927
February 1928

"When a book has previously been printed in America or elsewhere abroad we omit 'First' from the notice reading:

Published 1928
By.......

"But a translation first issued by ourselves would be marked 'First published.' "

1937 Statement: *See* 1928 Statement, plus the following statement.

"When a book has been previously printed in America or elsewhere abroad we nevertheless include 'First' in the notice, implying that publication under our imprint was first made at the time referred to.

"We began using our present method at some time prior to 1924."

1947 Statement: "Our practice in regard to the bibliographical notice on the reverse of the title page follows, with temporary modifications what is laid down in your 1937 edition [1928 and 1937 Statements]. The parenthetical remark that 'when a book goes to press the date of publication cannot conveniently be determined to a nicety' has been greatly emphasized in these difficult days of production, and it applies now to reprints as well as to new books. For this reason we do not at present attempt to give the month of publication. For books that were issued during or after 1945, therefore, the bibliographical notice would read on these lines.

First published 1945
By......
Reprinted: 1946; 1947"

Statement for 1960: "The method this company uses to identify first editions is to print the publication date; any reprint dates follow this date in subsequent impressions as do the dates of any new or revised editions. This system has always been followed including for the years 1949 through to 1976."

1976 Statement: "The method which we . . . use to identify first editions, is to print the publication date; any reprint dates follow this date in subsequent impressions, as do the dates of new or revised editions."
1981 Statement: *See* 1981 Statement of Harrap Limited (England)

HARRAP LIMITED (ENGLAND)
1981 Statement: *See* 1976 Statement of George G. Harrap & Company Limited (England)
1988 Statement: *See* 1988 Statement of Harrap Publishing Group Ltd (England)

HARRAP PUBLISHING GROUP LTD (ENGLAND)
1988 Statement: "The method this Company uses to identify first editions is to print the publication date on the title-page verso; any reprint follows this date in subsequent impressions, as do the dates of any new or revised editions.
EXAMPLE:
First published 1987 by Harrap Books Ltd.,
19-23 Ludgate Hill, London EC4M 7PD
Reprinted 1988
(We do *not* include the month of publication in the reprint line.)"
The company is moving to new premises in the spring of 1989. Thus, the address on the copyright page will be different from that given in the example above.

HARRISON-HILTON BOOKS, INC.
(In 1940 changed name to Smith and Durrell, which in 1947 became Oliver Durrell, Inc.)

RUPERT HART-DAVIS, LIMITED (ENGLAND)
1948 Statement: "The principles we use to identify the various printings of our books are as follows:
"The first printing is distinguished by either (a) the date (year) on the title page, or (b) by the words 'First published 194-' on the reverse of the title page. Sometimes we use both (a) and (b).
"The second printing has the words 'Second Impression 194-' added on the reverse of the title page, leaving the original date on the title page itself. If the second printing, or any subsequent printing, contains enough alterations to merit the distinction, we should use the words 'Revised Edition 194—.' "

HART-DAVIS, MACGIBBON LIMITED (ENGLAND)
1976, 1981, 1988 Statements: *See* 1976, 1981, 1988 Statements of Granada Publishing Limited (England)

HARTSDALE HOUSE, INC.
1947 Statement: "We have made no attempt to distinguish first printings from later printings of any books which we publish."

HARVARD BUSINESS SCHOOL DIVISION OF RESEARCH
1976 Statement: "We use no unusual identification for First Editions: the date of publication on the title page. Second, Third, etc., Printings are noted on the Copyright Page.

"Date of publication is on title page of *all* printings. The absence of a 2nd printing, etc., on copyright page does not necessarily assure the reader of 1st ptg. of 1st edition."

1981 Statement: *See* 1976 Statement

HARVARD BUSINESS SCHOOL PRESS
(Formerly known as the Harvard Business School Division of Research.)

1988 Statement: "We use no unusual identification for First Editions. All printings are noted on the copyright page."

THE HARVARD COMMON PRESS

1981 Statement: "We identify the various printings of each of our books on the copyright page, by using the series of numbers '10 9 8 7 6 5 4 3 2 1.' At each subsequent printing of the book, we delete the last number on the list, so that the last number appearing indicates what printing the book is in."

1988 Statement: *See* 1981 Statement. All imprints and subsidiaries follow this practice.

HARVARD UNIVERSITY PRESS

1928 Statement: "We have no distinguishing mark which signifies that a book is a first edition. As a general thing, we put second, third, fourth impression, etc. on the reverse of the title-page whenever we make new printings."

1937 Statement: *See* 1928 Statement

1947 Statement: "May we say that a statement made some years ago still applies. Our books are not labeled 'first edition,' but if a second or later edition has been published this is stated below the copyright notice on the reverse of the title page."

Statement for 1960: "To answer your question about how we designated a first printing in 1960, we did not then have any special way of indicating a first edition—that is, if the edition was not identified as second or revised, it was a first edition."

1976 Statement: "We do not have a special way of identifying first editions. In other words, if the edition is not identified as second or revised, it is a first edition. The first printing of the first edition carries the same date on the title page as on the copyright notice. When the edition is reprinted, the printing is identified on the copyright page, as, for example, Second printing, 1976, and the date on the title page is deleted. A second edition is called that on the title page and dated. If a second edition is reprinted, the words 'second printing' refer to a reprint of the second edition."

1981 Statement: "We do not have a special way of identifying first editions. In other words, if the edition is not identified as second or revised, it is a first edition. The first printing of the first edition carries the same date on the title page as on the copyright notice. When the edition is reprinted, the printing is identified on the copyright page, as, for example, Second printing, 1976, and no date appears on the title page."

1982 Statement: "Beginning some time in 1983, we will change our way of designating second and successive *printings*. We will still delete the date on the title page, but instead of inserting on the copyright page 'Second printing, 1983' (for example), we will simply remove the '1' from a row of numbers running from 10 to 1; we will not add the date of the second printing."

1988 Statement: "The statement we made in 1982 still stands, and it applies to all books published under our imprint and that of The Belknap Press of Harvard University Press. We have no subsidiaries."

HARVEST HOUSE PUBLISHERS

1988 Statement: "We do not indicate at the present time. However, beginning in 1989 we will use the listing of numbers 1-10 on bottom of copyright page and delete a number with each printing."

THE HARVESTER PRESS LTD. (ENGLAND)

1988 Statement: "For your information, this Company, and also Wheatsheaf Books Limited, has recently been sold and is now a division of Simon & Schuster International Group.

"Our current copyright page states 'First published 1988' and below we print a series of numbers '1 2 3 4 5 92 91 90 89 88.' The first number and the last eighty-eight indicate the printing and date of the current publication. Therefore a second edition would carry the line '2 3 4 5 92 91 90 89.'

"The system of the line of numbers has been adopted since the sale of the Company. Previously, we simply added a reprint line: 'Reprinted 1988,' for instance.

"All of this also applies to Wheatsheaf Books Limited, which is another imprint of this Company."

HARVEY HOUSE, PUBLISHERS

1981 Statement: "Harvey House, Publishers does not identify a first edition or subsequent printings. At one time we identified each new printing but we have not been doing that lately. A new edition (where there are substantive changes in text) is identified as a 'second edition' etc., but we seldom do second editions. If there is a considerable change and updating of a title we are more inclined to redo the entire book with a new title."

HARVEY MILLER PUBLISHERS (ENGLAND)

1976 Statement: "We do not identify the first printing in any special way. The imprint page bears the copyright notice and date.

"Subsequent printings would bear the date of the first publication and the date of the reprint or new edition. So that, unless otherwise stated, the book would be a first edition."

1981, 1988 Statements: *See* 1976 Statement

HASTINGS HOUSE

1947 Statement: "Our books are printed by three different processes, letterpress, gravure and offset. First editions of letterpress books can be identified by the lack of any other printing notices. On both the gravure and offset books this method of marking subsequent printings is quite difficult and therefore is not done. The printing notice is frequently carried on the dust jacket of the book. This, however, is done more for the convenience of the bookseller than for the aid of the book collector."

HASTINGS HOUSE, PUBLISHERS, INC.

1976 Statement: "First printings are identified only by the copyright notice. Subsequent *printings* give date. Subsequent editions so state and give date."

1981, 1988 Statements: *See* 1976 Statement

HAWTHORN BOOKS, INC.

1976 Statement: "Although Hawthorn does not use the phrase 'First Edition' on its copyright page, we do have a method of identifying various printings of a book. At the foot of the copyright page we set Arabic numerals from one to ten. For the second printing we delete the one, etc., so that the first number indicates the number of the printing.

"According to copyright law, a specified amount of material in a book must be completely new if a book is to be considered a second edition. On any title for which these requirements are fulfilled, we print the words 'Second Edition' on the jacket, title page, and copyright page. This second edition is not, however, indicated in the Arabic numbering codes. The first printing of the second edition would simply list all the numbers from one to ten again, indicating that it was the first printing of the second edition.

"A revised or updated edition of a book will be so listed on the jacket, title page, and copyright page—just as with a second edition. But in this instance, since the work cannot legally be called a second edition, we delete another number in the code and call it a third, fourth, or whatever, printing."

HAWTHORN HOUSE
(No longer in operation in 1949.)

1947 Statement: "Perhaps to the despair of the bibliographer, Hawthorn House had no orderly plan for identifying First Editions. Publishing activities of the press were always on a small scale, and often in limited editions. The problem of what to do about repeated printings was not a very live one!

"In one instance a practice was used that might confuse bibliographers. When we published '*Notes on the Care & Cataloguing of Old Maps*' by Lloyd A. Brown, in 1940, it was apparent that production could not be completed until nearly the turn of the year. Accordingly, when the sheet that included the title page was run through the press, only 100 copies were run off with the date *1940* on the title page, and the press then stopped and the date for the remaining sheets changed to 1941—the humdrum effort of a publisher to make his wares appear as fresh as possible."

HAYNES PUBLISHING GROUP (ENGLAND)

1988 Statement: "First Editions are indicated on the copyright page for all Haynes Publishing Group publications bearing the Haynes Publishing Group imprint as follows:

1) By the absence of any acknowledgement of previous publication of the book in its entirety; or

2) By the words 'First Edition' printed on the title verso.

"Revised editions are designated on the copyright page. Printings are indicated by a line of code letters (A-Z) on the outside back cover, the highest remaining letter being deleted at each reprinting."

J. H. HAYNES & CO. LTD (ENGLAND)

1988 Statement: *See* 1988 Statement of Haynes Publishing Group (England)

J. H. HAYNES (OVERSEAS) LTD. (ENGLAND)

1988 Statement: *See* 1988 Statement of Haynes Publishing Group (England)

HEALING ARTS PRESS
1988 Statement: *See* 1988 Statement of Inner Traditions International Ltd.

HEART OF THE LAKES PUBLISHING
1988 Statement: "We have no system to indicate first printings. Most of our titles see only one printing due to the limited demand for our type of historical research materials. On some of our trade titles we have gone into multiple printings. Some are so indicated on the copyright page while others are not. Some changes may be made (typos etc corrected) between printings. Our reprints of older/antique/out-of-print type books are clearly indicated by a new title page inserted in front of the old title page. When possible CIP information is added to a title on the copyright page.

"This applies to our publications under all of our imprints at present, i.e., Heart of the Lakes Publishing, Empire State Books and Windswept Press."

HEATH CRANTON, LTD. (ENGLAND)
1937 Statement: "In the first edition of books published by us, the year of publication will be found on the Title page or on the back thereof. In the case of a reissue or further edition, we insert on the back of the Title page the year of the original publication with a note of the year when the reissue or further edition first appears."
1947 Statement: *See* 1937 Statement

HEBREW PUBLISHING COMPANY
1976 Statement: "We really have no system for indicating first editions."
1988 Statement: *See* 1976 Statement

CHESTER R. HECK, INC.
1947 Statement: "Generally we don't have any identifying marks of first printings unless we definitely indicate on the copyright page 'Second,' 'Third' and the like. On books that have a collector's appeal we would use a symbol of some sort."

W. HEFFER & SONS, LTD. (ENGLAND)
1928 Statement: "It is our custom to put the date on the title page as part of our imprint. Only in the case of later impressions or editions do we put bibliographical data on the verso of the title page. May we say that although this is our invariable practice now, we have not been strictly consistent in the past."
1936 Statement: "Our present custom is to put the date of the book and other bibliographical details on the verso of the title page. This is our invariable practice now, although we were not consistent in books published by us before 1930."
1947 Statement: *See* 1936 Statement

THE HEINEMANN GROUP (ENGLAND)
1989 Statement: *See* 1989 Statement of The Octopus Publishing Group PLC (England)

W. HEINEMANN, LTD. (ENGLAND)
(For statement of practice from 1890 through 1989, please see 1989 Statement of The Octopus Publishing Group PLC [England])
1928 Statement: *See* 1937 Statement of William Heinemann, Ltd. (England)

WILLIAM HEINEMANN, LTD. (ENGLAND)

1937 Statement: "During the early years of the history of this firm there was, I believe, no attempt made specially to designate first editions. The date of publication of a book was usually placed underneath the imprint on the title page. In some cases when further editions or further impressions were issued, the words 'second edition' third edition,' etc., appeared either on the title page or on the fly overleaf, and the absence of such a notice was the only indication of the fact that the book was a first edition. In recent years, however, we have instituted the practice of printing on the back of the title page, or on a fly, a bibliographical note in all the books we publish. That is to say, on the first edition we print 'First published such and such a date' and as each new impression or new edition is called for we add the note 'second impression such and such a date' and so on. We take great pains to get these bibliographical notes accurate and to discriminate carefully between new impressions and new editions. In the event of a book being reprinted without any alterations in the text as it originally appeared, we call the re-issue a new impression. If the text is changed in any way we call it a New Edition.

"We do not follow the American practice of printing the words 'First Edition' anywhere in our books. This I believe is quite a recent idea inspired by the interest taken by the modern American in first editions of modern books.

"I am afraid I cannot tell you the date at which we first began using this present method, but it was certainly soon after 1920."

1947 Statement: *See* 1937 Statement

Statement for 1960: "Our 1976 statement would equally have applied to the situation in 1960 and continues to reflect our current practice. If a book is a first edition it will carry the notice 'First published/First published in Great Britain 19..'

"If it is a reprint or a second or subsequent edition the original notice will be followed by 'Reprinted 19..' or 'Second edition 19..' as appropriate."

1976 Statement: "All our new books carry the line 'First published in 19..' When we reprint the date of the reprint is shown and in this way one can always tell first editions."

1981, 1988 Statements: *See* 1976 Statement

See also 1989 Statement of The Octopus Publishing Group PLC (England)

HELLMAN, WILLIAMS AND COMPANY

1947 Statement: "Herewith, our method of distinguishing between first editions and subsequent printings:

"1. Identification, if any, is on the copyright page.

"2. Actually, we have two 'first' editions. The first edition proper is marked 'First Pre-publication Printing.' This edition may be followed by a second or third pre-publication printing. The 'first' edition after pre-publication printings is unmarked unless the book was originally published in a foreign country, in which case the words 'American Edition' will be found on the copyright page.

"3. Subsequent printings are known as 'Second Edition,' 'Third Edition,' etc."

CHRISTOPHER HELM PUBLISHERS LIMITED (ENGLAND)

1988 Statement: "In answer to your enquiry: we do not have any special way of identifying first editions as such, but subsequent printings are marked thus:

Reprinted, date
Revised edition, date
Second edition, date

and so on.

"We have always adopted this form of designation as far as I can remember."

HELM PUBLISHING

1988 Statement: *See* 1988 Statement of Padre Productions

RAE D. HENKLE CO., INC.

(Established 1927. Became The Henkle-Yewdale House in early 1936.)

1928 Statement: "As to our method of marking first editions, we omit any edition reference on the first printing and on the reverse of the title page note the first, second and other printings in subsequent editions."

THE HENKLE-YEWDALE HOUSE, INC.

(Succeeded Rae D. Henkle Co., Inc, in 1936. Out of business prior to 1949.)

1937 Statement: "As to our method of marking first editions, we omit any edition reference on the first printing and on the reverse of the title page note the first, second and other printings in subsequent editions. It has been in continuous use since 1928."

HER MAJESTY'S STATIONERY OFFICE (ENGLAND)

1988 Statement: "Our first editions are distinguishable by the date of publication appearing with the Crown copyright legend, normally on the reverse of the title page. Typical examples are:

i.

© Crown copyright 1984
First published 1984

Second Impressions:

ii.

© Crown copyright 1983
First published 1983
Second impression 1984

iii.

© Crown copyright 1976
First published 1976
Third impression (with amendments) 1981

"Non Crown copyright material published by HMSO may carry a legend similar to the following:

iv.

© Royal Botanic Gardens Kew
First published by HMSO 1984

"Publications in the Parliamentary series do not carry a Crown copyright legend, and publishing history details are usually shown as part of the publisher's imprint, normally at the foot of the title page or, in the case of an Act of Parliament, at the end of the text."

HERALD PRESS

1976 Statement: "The first edition of a Herald Press book carries only the standard copyright notice.

"Herald Press reprints always carry an additional line indicating the current printing and the date of the reprint.

"I believe we have followed this pattern consistently over the years."

1981 Statement: "The first edition of Herald Press books includes the year beneath the publisher's imprint on the title page:

HERALD PRESS
Scottdale, Pennsylvania
Kitchener, Ontario
1981

The date is deleted on subsequent printings.

"Information on reprints always appears under the copyright notice. Until about 1978 this was written out (Third Printing, 1977). Then for several years we often used a code, 10 9 8 7 6 5 4, with the last number to the right indicating the printing involved (in the example, Fourth Printing). However, this code did not include information on the year of the reprint.

"Beginning in 1980 we refined the code so that the number at the left indicates the year of the reprint and the one at the right which reprint is involved. For example, 81, 82, 83, 84, 85, 10, 9, 8, 7, 6, 5 indicates Fifth Printing, 1981. Numbers can be deleted from either end of the code in the above example to identify any combination of years and printings through Tenth Printing, 1985, without needing to set new type."

HERALD PUBLISHING HOUSE

1988 Statement: "We use a code on the copyright page which shows the year each edition was printed."

THE HERBERT PRESS LIMITED (ENGLAND)

1988 Statement: "The first printing of the first edition of one of our books is indicated on the title-verso page with the words 'First published in Great Britain [date] by The Herbert Press Ltd.' Subsequent reprintings are shown by the word 'Reprinted' and the date. The company has followed this style since its first book was published in 1975.

"We have no imprints or subsidiaries."

HERDER AND HERDER

1988 Statement: *See* 1988 Statement of Crossroad / Continuum

JOHN HERITAGE, PUBLISHER (ENGLAND)
(Incorporated with Unicorn Press, Ltd.)

1937 Statement: *See* Unicorn Press (England)

HERMAN PUBLISHING, INC.

1976 Statement: "We're too new to have any single established method of identification. However, a second printing is *usually* identified as such on the copyright page."

1981 Statement: "*Newer* titles use this method to identify printings of an edition: for instance, '10 9 8 7 6 5 4' would indicate 4th printing."

HERMITAGE

1988 Statement: "When we reprint a book we indicate that it is the second or whatever printing. On the first edition we say nothing. In other words, if a book does not refer to any particular printing, you might rightly assume that it is in the first printing of the first edition."

HIGHWAY BOOK SHOP (CANADA)

1976 Statement: "We have very short press runs & no exciting system for designating first editions. Most of our books are of regional and local interest."

ADAM HILGER LTD. (ENGLAND)

1976 Statement: "The first edition of an Adam Hilger book is identified as such by its very omission of all identifying statements. The second edition is marked 'Second Edition' and so on for all later editions."
1981, 1988 Statements: *See* 1976 Statement

LAWRENCE HILL & CO. PUBLISHERS, INC.

1976 Statement: "Lawrence Hill & Company books contain on the copyright page of each title the phrase 'first edition.' It is followed by the month and year of publication."
1981 Statement: "Subsequent editions are indicated by a number system." The system employed is a line of numbers from 1 through 10, with deletion beginning at the lowest number.
1988 Statement: *See* 1981 Statement

HILL & WANG

1981 Statement: "At Hill and Wang, which is a division of Farrar, Straus, and Giroux, we try to identify our first editions by stating on the copyright page 'first edition.' We also include a line that stipulates First printing (with date). For the purposes of the collector, the first printing of the first edition is the book to be sought after.

"In subsequent printings of the first edition, we usually, but not always, include a line that indicates it is the second printing, with the date. But unless the text has been changed, the second printing is identical with the first printing.

"When an author revises a book and we reissue it, we of course stipulate that the book is a revised edition, and this revised edition notice is followed by a printing notice (first, second, third, etc.). For the bibliographer or scholar, the second edition may represent important changes he will want to know about. During the years Hill and Wang has published, we may indeed have varied from this pattern, but what I've described is the general rule."
1988 Statement: "Our 1981 statement regarding first editions still applies."

HILLMAN-CURL, INC.

(Including Arcadia House and William Godwin as additional imprints. Hillman-Curl was succeeded by Samuel Curl, Inc.)
1937 Statement: "First editions of our publications are distinguished by the lack of any printing notice on the copyright page. Following editions bear the date of the first printing, together with the date of new printing, and which printing it is."

HMSO (ENGLAND)

See Her Majesty's Stationery Office (England)

HODDER & STOUGHTON LIMITED (ENGLAND)

1928 Statement: "We are unable to help you with regard to our First Editions, as our methods vary with every book."

1937 Statement: *See* 1928 Statement

1947 Statement: "The date of every edition of every book is printed on the reverse of the title-page, where the number of the edition is usually recorded. The words 'First Printed' are usually included on all first editions."

1976 Statement: "Brockhampton Press has now changed its name to Hodder & Stoughton. The information given below was standard for Brockhampton Press and is now used by Hodder & Stoughton.

"With a Hodder & Stoughton original we state: First published in 19... The absence of any second edition information identifies this as a first edition. For subsequent editions we state: First published in 19... Second edition 19...

"For a title that has previously been published elsewhere we always state: Date, Name of original publisher, and original title. Then: This edition first published by Hodder & Stoughton 19.., and subsequently: This edition first published by Hodder & Stoughton 19.., second impression 19..."

1981 Statement: "Our methods of designating First Editions are exactly the same as were printed [in the 1976 Statement] and this is relevant for all our Publishing Divisions."

1988 Statement: "I can confirm that the statement of 1976, confirmed in 1981, is still our current policy."

THE HOGARTH PRESS (ENGLAND)

1928 Statement: *See* 1937 Statement

1937 Statement: "In first editions our custom is to have the year of publication on the title page and no other indication. In case of a second impression or edition we print 'Second Impression (or edition)' on the title page with the year of publication and on the back the dates of first and second editions.

"The method as set out has been our method since the beginning of the Press."

1947 Statement: *See* 1937 Statement

1988 Statement: *See* 1988 Statement of Chatto & Windus Ltd (England)

HOLIDAY HOUSE, INC.

1947 Statement: "We have had no particular system, consistently followed in the past. We now plan to use the words 'second printing' on the copyright pages, above or below the copyright line, for the next printings (second printings), and to number each subsequent printing."

1976 Statement: "Currently, most of the time, only the first printing has a price on the jacket."

1981 Statement: *See* 1976 Statement

1988 Statement: "Usually 'First Edition' appears on the copyright page of the first printing only of the first edition."

HOLLIS AND CARTER, LTD. (ENGLAND)

1947 Statement: "We always put on the verso of the title page, '1st published, 1947. Second Impression,' etc. The last date on this list therefore will tell the book collector which edition or printing he is buying."

HOLMES AND MEIER PUBLISHERS, INC.

1976 Statement: "Most of our books are scholarly monographs which, as yet at least, have not been issued in revised second editions. If we were to do so, however, we would identify only editions after the first.

"The first printing of a first edition is distinguished by: carrying no printing or edition number. Subsequent printings would be identified by number—Second Printing, Third Printing, etc."

HENRY HOLT AND COMPANY, INC.

1928 Statement: "We have never had a definite method of indicating a first edition in our books. Ordinarily, under the copyright line, we insert the dates of the printings so that any book which bears a single date is probably a first edition. In some cases, however, where we know there is to be only one printing, no date is inserted. Also, when sheets are imported from Europe, no special notation is made."

1937 Statement: *See* 1928 Statement

1947 Statement: "Prior to 1945 we never used a definite method of indicating a first edition in our books. Up to that time it was our general practice to insert the date of printing under the copyright notice and a book bearing but one date line of printing was usually a first edition. In some cases, however, when we knew that only one printing was to be made, the date line was omitted. Also, no date line appeared in books bound from sheets that had been printed abroad. Since 1945 it has been our custom to insert the words 'first printing,' or similar language, and first editions may be so recognized—with the exception of foreign sheets as mentioned above."

1988 Statement: "Please be advised that we are no longer part of Holt, Rinehart & Winston, but are now an independent trade book publishing company called Henry Holt and Company, Inc. Holt, Rinehart & Winston still does exist, but it is a *different* company that produces textbooks rather than trade books.

"We signify our first editions with a line stating 'First Edition' on the copyright page and a reprint code that shows numbers 10 to 1. If it is the first printing of the first edition, all 10 numbers appear. If the book is the second printing of a first edition the line 'First Edition' is deleted and so is the number 1, leaving the last in the number code as 2, or second printing. The same is done for subsequent printings.

"There was a time when we left on the words 'First Edition' but also ran a line stating 'Second printing' with the month and year, but found the above to be more efficient."

HOLT, RINEHART AND WINSTON

1976 Statement: "We signify our first editions with a line stating 'First Edition' on the copyright page and a reprint code that shows numbers 10 to 1. If it is the first printing of the first edition, all 10 numbers appear. If the book is the second printing of a first edition the line 'First Edition' is deleted and so is the number 1, leaving the last in the number code as 2, or second printing. The same is done for subsequent printings.

"There was a time when we left on the words 'First Edition' but also ran a line stating 'Second printing' with the month and year, but found the above to be more efficient."

HOME & VAN THAL, LTD.

1947 Statement: "As far as we are concerned we strictly adhere to what I have always understood to be the correct bibliographical details, viz. that an impression is simply a reprint of the first edition without any textual alterations. A second edition would be a revision of the text of the first edition."

HOOVER INSTITUTION PRESS

1976 Statement: "Our Press does not have a particular method of identifying first editions. Subsequent editions of a book are identified by the entry on the copyright page as second edition, third edition, etc."

1981 Statement: "First editions are not identified as such. Subsequent editions are identified by entries on the title and copyright pages.

"First printings carry only our standard copyright notice.

"Second printings would be marked 'Second Printing, (date).' "

1988 Statement: "The Hoover Institution Press has not changed its designation of first editions since your guide was published in 1984. We have no subsidiaries or special imprints."

MARTIN HOPKINSON, LTD. (ENGLAND)

(Out of business prior to 1949; publications taken over by John Lane [England].)

1928 Statement: *See* 1937 Statement

1937 Statement: "Our practice is to put the date of publication on the title page. When a reprint takes place we place on the back of the title page the usual bibliographical information 'First Printed' with date—and date of reprint.

"If material alterations are made in the text or format we should call the reprint a new edition.

"We have followed our present practice since 1928."

HORIZON PRESS PUBLISHERS

1976 Statement: "We do not designate first editions."

1981 Statement: *See* 1976 Statement

THE HORN BOOK, INC.

("The Horn Book Magazine was founded in 1924 by Bertha Mahony who ran The Bookshop for Boys and Girls for The Women's Educational and Industrial Union in Boston. The Union published the magazine until 1936 when the Bookshop was closed and Bertha Mahony founded The Horn Book, Inc. which published The Horn Book Magazine from then on and still does.")

1947 Statement: "We follow the plan of making a statement on one of the back fly leaves of our books, such as that given here, to note our first editions:

ILLUSTRATORS OF CHILDREN'S BOOKS

This book issued in a first edition of 5,000 copies, etc.

"Such a note together with the year of publication on the title page gives the necessary data.

"On the third edition of *Books, Children and Men* we have given on the back fly leaf publication dates, size of editions for each printing.

"On our books, too, we always give all typographical information and wish all other publishers would do so."

Statement for 1960: All printings and editions after the first are so designated. A first printing, first edition will have no identifying notice. There are no imprints.

1976, 1982, and 1988 Statements: *See* Statement for 1960

HORWITZ GRAHAME BOOKS PTY LTD. (AUSTRALIA)

1981 Statement: "In response to your inquiry, we do not usually indicate the first edition of trade books and paperback novels as 'First Edition.' However, when we reprint the books we always give the publishing history, e.g., 'First published.... This edition.....'

"In our Educational books, since these are likely to be reprinted over a number of years, we usually do have symbols at the foot of the imprint page giving the year of first publication. As each edition is reprinted the early symbols are dropped so that at any time we can always see at a glance which edition it is."

1989 Statement: *See* 1981 Statement

HOUGHTON MIFFLIN AUSTRALIA PTY LTD (AUSTRALIA)

1989 Statement: "J. M. Dent Pty Ltd (commonly known as Dent Australia) was purchased by Houghton Mifflin Company of Boston in October 1988 and is a subsidiary of that company, under the name of Houghton Mifflin Australia. J. M. Dent & Sons is now an imprint of Weidenfeld and Nicolson in the UK and no longer exists as an independent company.

"Practice at Dent Australia was to indicate first editions and first printings by noting 'First Published....'. Houghton Mifflin Australia will continue this practice. Subsequent printings are indicated by the words 'Reprinted....'

"New or revised editions will be shown as such on the imprint page, and there may be a banner or notice on the title page and/or cover also. New editions of our own titles will normally be numbered (e.g. second edition). Titles originally published by another publisher and reissued in the same or a new edition by Houghton Mifflin Australia will have the publishing history set out on the imprint page."

HOUGHTON MIFFLIN COMPANY

1928 Statement: "It is our general custom to place the date on the title page of the first edition of all of our books and to drop this date on all subsequent editions. Perhaps we have not invariably followed this custom, but it is our intention to do so.

"The copyright page after the first printing sometimes bears the legend 'second impression,' 'third impression,' 'fourth impression' etc. This, however, is not the general practice.

"There are very likely instances where the date has not been removed from the title, after the printing of the first edition, and therefore it would not be an infallible rule to look for a date on the title page, but you may be sure that if the date is omitted it is not a first edition."

1937 Statement: "We endeavor to make a clear distinction between 'edition' and 'printing'.

"It is our general custom to place the date on the title page of the first printing of all of our books and to drop this date on all subsequent printings. There have been cases when for special reasons this rule has not been followed, but the custom so far as this House is concerned is almost invariable.

"When a new edition—meaning a revision on which new copyright is taken—is printed, the same procedure is followed: that is, the date appears on the first printing of the new edition and is omitted from the second and subsequent printings.

"The copyright page after the first printing sometimes bears the legend 'second impression,' 'third impression,' 'fourth impression,' etc. This, however, is not the general practice.

"There are very likely instances where the date has not been removed from the title, after the first printing, and therefore it would not be an infallible rule to look for a date on the title page, but you may be sure that if the date is omitted, it is not a first edition.

"We are sorry that we can't tell you just when the custom of omitting the date from the title page of later impressions of the book was instituted. It was a good many years ago. Our best impression is that it was about 1891."

1947 Statement: *See* 1937 Statement

1976 Statement: "Please let me define two words first: 'edition' and 'printing' In times past a book was set in type every time it was printed and the type was redistributed after the printing was complete. This meant that each printing was a new edition and there could be variations caused by error from the typesetter or alterations made in the text by the author or publisher. Therefore, a first edition could often be different from subsequent editions. Most modern publishers now print from permanent plates which are photographed or cast in plastic or metal, so the content of the book should be identical from printing to printing without change. A new edition of a book in present day terminology, must contain at least 6% new material if it is to be registered with the copyright office and have the words 'revised edition' or 'second edition' printed on the title page. Of course there can be limited editions or paperbound editions in which the only difference is the style of binding and possibly an author's signature or some other added item like special illustrations.

"On our fiction, all of our title pages have the year of publication in Arabic numerals on the first printing only. This is removed for all subsequent printings. Occasionally a printer fails to remove this number in spite of our instructions so that it does appear in about one title out of two years' publications on the second printing.

"On the copyright page we place a line on every book which has the digits 10 9 8 7 6 5 4 3 2 1 and the last number is removed for every subsequent printing. There is a code letter after these words which indicates which of our manufacturers (we have several) has produced the book, as we return faulty books to the manufacturer for credit. From time to time we change manufacturers so we need to know where a particular book is made.

"If we are publishing the novels of an author who has published other books earlier with another publisher and we release the earlier work, our title page and copyright page would indicate that this was a reissue but we would start out with first printing for our publication."

1981 Statement: *See* 1976 Statement

1988 Statement: *See* 1988 Statement of Ticknor & Fields

HOUSE OF ANANSI PRESS LIMITED (CANADA)

1976 Statement: "I'm sorry to say that we never specifically identify first editions or first printings of books. So it's only when the book goes into a second printing that you can tell for sure.

"We usually include a line on the back of the title page, toward the bottom, which is changed with succeeding printings. The line usually takes the form:

2 3 4 5 6 78 77 76 75 74

"If our third printing was in 1976, then the line would read:

3 4 5 6 78 77 76

for example. Unfortunately, once or twice we've forgotten to erase the numbers on the plate for a particular printing, so that we will have two printings showing the same numbers.

"We know that this sort of slip is the bane of bibliographers and collectors, but it occasionally happens to us, and, I'm sure, to many other publishers too. With a staff as small as ours, it's all too easy for one small detail to be forgotten.

"Rarely, we have made the indication:

First printing *date*
Second printing *date* etc.

But we try not to do this, as it necessitates a plate change for each printing, and since plates are good for about five printings, this is unnecessary expense."

1981 Statement: "The above is still generally correct, except that our printing line now normally includes the '1' in the sequence 1 2 3 etc. and the year of first printing at the end of the year sequence. I'm not sure when we started doing that. Unfortunately, we still slip occasionally on reprints."

1988 Statement: *See* 1981 Statement

HOWARD UNIVERSITY PRESS

1976 Statement: "Our books carry the usual data on the copyright page indicating the date of publication. If we were to reprint a title this would be added to the information already appearing."

1988 Statement: "We do not designate the first printing of a first edition. Therefore, please use our [1976] statement.

"Our books carry the usual data on the copyright page indicating the date of publication. If we were to reprint a title this would be added to the information already appearing."

HOWE BROTHERS

1988 Statement: "We do not designate a first printing or first edition by any special wording on the copyright page. However, subsequent printings and editions are identified: for example, Second printing 1988.

"The first printing of the first edition, therefore, can be identified by the absence of such a statement. This is the method that we have always used on our Howe Brothers and Westwater Press imprints."

GERALD HOWE, LTD. (ENGLAND)

(Out of business prior to 1949; publications taken over by John Lane.)

1937 Statement: "In our first editions the top of the title-page verso either contains the statement 'first published' with the date or is left blank, and in subsequent printings the dates of the first edition and of reprints and new editions are given in this place. This has been our practice since 1926 when we began business."

HOWELL-NORTH BOOKS

1976 Statement: "We have no special designation, except that subsequent editions (usually subsequent printings) are so stated on reverse of title page—our limited editions (now all O.P.) are so stated."

1988 Statement: *See* 1976 Statement

HOWELL, SOSKIN, PUBLISHERS, INC.

1947 Statement. "Unless books are specifically designated as second or third printings, our editions may be regarded as first editions."

HUDSON HILLS PRESS, INC.

1988 Statement: "The words 'First Edition' appear as the first line on the copyright page of the first edition/first printing of each of our books. These words are removed from any subsequent printings of the first editions, but no further identification is added specifying which printing it is. Any further editions which incorporate modest corrections are not specifically identified, but any further edition that involves substantial revision is usually identified as a revised edition."

B. W. HUEBSCH, INC.

(Merged in August, 1925 with The Viking Press, to become The Viking Press Inc.)

See 1937 Statement of The Viking Press Inc.

HULL UNIVERSITY PRESS (ENGLAND)

1989 Statement: First editions are not identified in any way. On the title page and on the copyright page, straight reprints are noted as "second printing," "third printing," etc.

If a printing has been revised—but not sufficiently to call it a new edition—it is identified on the title page and copyright page as "Revised First Printing," or whatever applies.

New editions are identified on the title page and copyright page. For example, the copyright page would note new copyright information, i.e., © second edition.

HUMANITIES PRESS, INC.

1976 Statement: "We do not stipulate any special designation to indicate that our books are first editions. All subsequent editions carry the notation 'second edition' or any other numbered edition which may be the case."

1981 Statement: "A first printing carries the message 'First published in the USA by Humanities Press Inc.' Subsequent editions would simply read 'Reprinted (year),' and if additional reprints were made they would also read 'Reprinted (year).' "

1988 Statement: *See* 1988 Statement of Humanities Press International, Inc.

HUMANITIES PRESS INTERNATIONAL, INC.

1988 Statement: "First printings read 'First published in the USA by Humanities Press International, Inc.' Subsequent printings read 'Reprinted (year).' New editions and subsequent editions would carry the legend 'Second edition (year).' Subsequent printings of subsequent editions would read 'Reprinted (year)' starting with new numbering for each edition.

"You should also note that this Company changed its name in 1985 [to Humanities Press International, Inc.]."

BRUCE HUMPHRIES, INC.

1937 Statement: "Books published by Bruce Humphries, Inc., if limited editions, contain a colophon giving the details of the edition, and when these books are reissued the colophon is dropped. Other books generally contain no special marking in the first edition, but second printings are almost invariably so marked on the copyright page.

"Bruce Humphries, Inc., took over many, but not all, of the publications of the Four Seas Company in 1930. In books published by the Four Seas Company there was apparently no uniform system for indicating first editions, but generally first editions were not marked, but second printings were so marked on the copyright page."

1947 Statement: *See* 1937 Statement

HENRY E. HUNTINGTON LIBRARY AND ART GALLERY

1947 Statement: "We do not identify the first printings of our books. A second printing is called either 'second printing' or 'second impression.' If there are revisions it is called 'second edition,' 'third edition,' etc.

"The books published by the Friends of the Huntington Library as souvenirs for the members, and some of which we have for sale, have a note to the effect that 'This edition consists of 1000 copies specially printed for the Friends of the Huntington Library. This copy is No....' and the copies which go to Friends are numbered by hand; those for sale are not numbered.

"The Library published books beginning in 1929 in cooperation with the Harvard University Press; since 1936 it has published its own books."

Statement for 1960: *See* 1976 Statement of Huntington Library Publications

HUNTINGTON LIBRARY PUBLICATIONS

1976 Statement: "We do not have any specific way of indicating first editions, except on the copyright page. Actually, although a number of our titles have gone through several printings, it is seldom that we bring out a book in a new edition.

"We do not indicate the number of a printing until it is second or more, at which time we give the date of the first printing, and that of, say, the fourth printing."

1981 Statement: "First editions are not indicated as such. Subsequent editions are identified by printing the number and date on the copyright page. Additional printings of an edition are so labelled."

1988 Statement: *See* 1981 Statement

HURST & BLACKETT (ENGLAND)

1928, 1937 Statements: *See* 1928, 1937 Statements of Hutchinson & Co., Ltd. (Publishers) (England)

HURTIG PUBLISHERS (CANADA)

1976 Statement: We have no method of designating a first edition. Only those printings and/or editions after the first are designated. These methods of designation do not differ from any previously used.

HUTCHINSON (ENGLAND)

1988 Statement: *See* 1988 Statement of Century Hutchinson Publishing Group Limited (England)

HUTCHINSON & CO., LTD. (PUBLISHERS) (ENGLAND)

1928 Statement: "We do not mark First Editions in any way. This may be taken to apply also to those firms which have amalgamated with Messrs. Hutchinson."

1937 Statement: *See* 1928 Statement

HUTCHINSON CHILDREN'S BOOKS (ENGLAND)

1988 Statement: *See* 1988 Statement of Century Hutchinson Publishing Group Limited (England)

HUTCHINSON PUBLISHING GROUP LTD. (ENGLAND)

1976 Statement: "We indicate the time of first publication on the fourth page of the prelims of a book with the statement: First published month year (i.e. December 1976)."

1981 Statement: "On checking through books published before 1976 it seems that Hutchinson has never included the month in the relevant statement.

"The normal form is: 'First published year (i.e. 1976)'

"However, we sometimes include 'in Great Britain' in the statement, thus: 'First published in Great Britain year (i.e. 1976)'

"This implies that the book has been published somewhere other than in Great Britain in a different year. However, if the overseas edition and our edition are published in the same year, then we use the first version. The edition in question could either be an entirely reset version, or offset from (usually) the US or sometimes the Australian edition with new prelims prepared here, or it could be bought in from the overseas publisher with our prelims substituted in the country of origin. Unfortunately, it is not obvious from the prelims how the book has been produced, although one could probably distinguish an offset or bought-in edition by looking at the text (points of house style, etc.).

"So far as I know all our imprints use this form, certainly those of the General Books division."

1988 Statement: *See* 1988 Statement of Century Hutchinson Publishing Group Limited (England)

THE HYPERION PRESS, INC.

1947 Statement: "In all our books we indicate on the colophon page the date of our first publication. In case of re-prints, we indicate also the date of the re-prints."

1988 Statement: "There has been no change in our reprint procedures."

I

ICARUS PRESS, INC.

1981 Statement: "Quite frankly, we have a rather mixed-up way of so designating them. We state nothing at all on the first edition, but we always designate a second printing or second edition on the copyright page.

"I am thinking of using a system of markings on the bottom of the page— below our CIP Date—which would designate printing number and year— i.e.,

84 83 82 81 9 8 7 6 5 4 3 2

"Then we could merely opaque out the indicated year and number upon a new printing. But we haven't yet instituted this."

1988 Statement: Icarus Press is now out of business.

IMPRINT (AUSTRALIA)

1988 Statement: *See* 1988 Statement of William Collins Pty Ltd (Australia)

INDEPENDENCE PRESS

1976 Statement: "Any books that we think will be in production through more than one printing we identify on the copyright page with the system used by many publishers. It is made up of two lines of numbers. One line is numbered one through six or seven. The second line is a listing of the next seven or eight years (the last two numbers of each year). With each new printing we erase from our offset press the appropriate number so that the first number in the first row represents the present edition and the first number in the second row represents the year of its printing.

"Sometimes this varies a bit. All numbers may be placed in one row, the edition identification on the left hand side and the year on the right hand side, numbering from gutter toward the center of the page. Then numbers are erased from each end to secure the proper identification of edition and year of printing."

1981, 1988 Statements: *See* 1976 Statement

INDIANA UNIVERSITY PRESS

1976 Statement: "Our only definition of editions is essentially a negative one: there is no marking on the copyright or title page indicating whether it is a first or second edition. However, if we ever issue second editions of any book, we announce that fact in the book."

A first printing of a first edition may be distinguished from later printings of the same edition by the fact that later printings are indicated on the copyright page as second printing, etc.

1981, 1988 Statements: *See* 1976 Statement

INNER TRADITIONS INTERNATIONAL LTD.

1988 Statement: "We began using a rub-out line in 1978, or earlier, and now use this device consistently to indicate the edition of a book. Earlier books may say 'First edition,' or nothing except the copyright date, for 1st edition.

"However, subsequent editions will always say '2nd edition,' '3rd printing,' or have rub-out."

INTERCULTURE ASSOCIATES

1976 Statement: "We do nothing to identify first editions."

INTERMEDIA PRESS (CANADA)

1976 Statement: "Our current process is to include on the back of the title page the number of the edition, i.e.

'Printed in a limited edition of 1000 copies
of which 950 are paperbound and 50 are
hardbound and signed by the author.'

"If we do a second edition we print on the back of the title page i.e.

First edition, 1975
Second edition, 1978.

"I am, of course, interested in your findings. I suppose it depends upon the book or the conception of a book that the publisher has. Is it a good policy to put the words 'First Edition' on the back of the title page? Only on books you expect to go to a second edition?"

1981 Statement: "Our policy is still essentially the same."

INTERNATIONAL ARTS AND SCIENCES PRESS, INC.

1976 Statement: "In response to your query about identifying first editions, it is not the practice of this house to do so. We have recently begun, however, to identify second printings with that phrase appearing on the copyright page.

"If the bibliographic history of the work is complicated, a revision for republication, it is usually made clear either in the author's introduction or on the copyright page.

INTERNATIONAL PUBLISHERS CO., INC.

1988 Statement: "We designate all new titles (on the verso of the title page) as

'1st printing, 19—'

and continue to number each printing (we number the printings up to 12 or 13, after which sometimes we simply enter 'this printing, 19-').

"A new edition (content of a book has been added to or altered in some way) [is designated] as

'2nd edition, 1st printing, 19—'

and thereafter as '2nd edition, 2nd printing,' etc., unless there is a 3rd edition."

INTERNATIONAL RESOURCES

1988 Statement: *See* 1988 Statement of Padre Productions

INTERNATIONAL UNIVERSITIES PRESS, INC.

1976 Statement: "Unless otherwise stated on the copyright page, the first date of copyright is the date of the first edition.

"A first printing of a first edition may be distinguished from later printings of the same edition by the fact that it either says 'first printing' or nothing at all. Subsequent printings are marked 'second printing,' etc."

1981, 1988 Statements: *See* 1976 Statement

INTER-VARSITY PRESS (ENGLAND)

1976 Statement: "Our usual practice is simply to state 'First Edition October 1976.' On reprints we usually omit the month, giving just the year date, 'Reprinted 1977, 1979.' "

1981 Statement: "We have indeed changed our method of designating the first printing of a first edition since we corresponded with you in 1976. The change took effect from May 1978, when we dropped the inclusion of the month of publication.

"Our current practice is simply to state: First published 1980 with reprints also giving just the year date: Reprinted 1981."

THE IOWA STATE COLLEGE PRESS

(Formerly Collegiate Press, Inc.)

1947 Statement: "When we publish a first edition, we merely list the date of publication and date of copyright in the copyright notice.

"When the book is reprinted with little or no revision, we may or may not specify that it is a 'second printing.'

"When the book is revised sufficiently that it can be called a new edition, we label it 'Second edition,' or 'Third edition,' etc."

IOWA STATE UNIVERSITY PRESS

1976 Statement: "The only identification of first edition that we make for our books is the identification 'First edition, date' that appears on the verso

(copyright page) of the title page. I believe this method of identification does not differ from that always previously used by this press."
The first printing of a first edition is indicated by the fact that it does not carry the designation "Second printing, date."
1981, 1988 Statements: *See* 1976 Statement

IRIS I O PUBLISHING
1988 Statement: *See* 1988 Statement of Strawberry Hill Press

IRISH ACADEMIC PRESS, LIMITED (REPUBLIC OF IRELAND)
1981 Statement: "We don't formally designate the first printing of a first edition. We usually just say on the title verso:
> This book was printed in the
> Republic of Ireland by [name of printer]
> for Irish Academic Press Limited,
> Kill Lane, Blackrock, County Dublin
> ©[author] 1981 (This is the only indication of date).

"It is only later printings that carry any sort of printing history e.g.
> First edition May 1981
> Second impression July 1981
> Second edition January 1982."

1988 Statement: *See* 1981 Statement

ISLAND PRESS (AUSTRALIA)
1988 Statement: "All bibliographical information is given on the back of the title page. [This method was] adopted in 1970 [and there has been] no change. The imprints and subsidiaries follow this practice."

ISLAND PRESS COOPERATIVE, INC.
1947 Statement: "Island Press Cooperative, Inc., is the same as Island Workshop Press. We merely dropped the Workshop from our name because the name was too long and unwieldy, and we had long ago outgrown the Workshop aspect, and were concentrating primarily on book publishing.

"In regard to first printings, we have no special way of indicating them other than the fact that they carry no printing notice whatsoever. In other words, when we print a second or third edition, this fact is noted on the copyright page, but when we print a first edition, no mention is made to single it out as a first edition. This sounds pretty involved but in practice it is very simple."

ISLAND WORKSHOP PRESS
1947 Statement: *See* 1947 Statement of Island Press Cooperative, Inc.

ITASCA PRESS
1947 Statement: *See* 1947 Statement of The Webb Publishing Company

ITHACA HOUSE
1976 Statement: "First printings of first editions carry only the copyright notice."
1981 Statement: *See* 1976 Statement
1988 Statement: "Our imprints and subsidiaries follow the practice as outlined in the 1976 Statement for Ithaca House."

J

THE JACARANDA PRESS (AUSTRALIA)
1976 Statement: "It is the policy of the Jacaranda Press to list on the imprint page the date of first publication (which also indicates first edition). Each reprinting is also listed and subsequent editions are noted accordingly. This particular method of identification has been used throughout the history of the Jacaranda Press."
1981 Statement: *See* 1976 Statement

JAMESON BOOKS, INC.
1988 Statement: To designate a first edition the words First Edition are used on the copyright page. The first printing of an edition is indicated as follows on the copyright page:
76 77 78   10 9 8 7 6 5 4 3 2 1
The second printing is indicated like this:
76 77 78   10 9 8 7 6 5 4 3 2
The numbers before 10 indicate years.

JANUS PRESS
(West Burke, Vermont)
1981 Statement: "Copyright is same year as publication year." This system of designation does not differ from any previously used.

THE JARGON SOCIETY, INC.
1981 Statement: "The books of the *Jargon Society* do not designate first printing or first edition, simply because the books are all first editions and we do not re-print. The only exception has been *The Appalachian Photographs of Doris Ulmann* (#50 in the series) which had nary a poem in it to scare away the post-literate."
1988 Statement: "The books of *The Jargon Society* do not designate first printing or first edition, simply because the books are all first editions and we do not reprint. Two exceptions to this rule are *The Appalachian Photographs of Doris Ulmann* which was reprinted once and *White Trash Cooking*. The latter, with 400,000 copies now in print, was printed in a First Printing of 5,000 copies, but the First Printing is not so marked because a second printing seemed unimaginable. After 100 titles of 2,500 or less copies, we are glad to have been wrong once."

JARROLDS PUBLISHERS (LONDON), LTD. (ENGLAND)
1937 Statement: "In the case of first editions of all our non-fiction books, the year of issue is placed in roman numerals below our imprint on the title page. There is no reference anywhere else in the book to the fact that it is the first edition. In the event of further reprint(s) being called for, the bibliography is set up on back of title, thus, for example:
First Published	May 1934
Second Impression	June 1934
Third Impression	August 1934

"In the case of fiction, the month and year of first publication in this country are set up at back of title page, thus, for example:
First Published in Great Britain May 1934
"In the event of subsequent reprint(s) the dates are set forth as in the example for non-fiction given above."

1948 Statement: "It is not our present practice to include dates in our publications. In cases where books are reprinted, we state 'Second impression,' and so on, as appropriate."

JAVELIN BOOKS (ENGLAND)

1988 Statement: *See* 1988 Statement of Cassell PLC (England)

JEFFERSON HOUSE

1947 Statement: "First printings of our books carry only the copyright notice, except in a few instances the line 'FIRST PRINTING (month, year)' below the copyright notice.

"All subsequent printings are marked 'SECOND PRINTING, THIRD PRINTING, FOURTH PRINTING,' as the case may be, and any new editions of the book are clearly marked. A distinction should be made between an edition and a printing, an edition always having some material change in either the text or format of the publication."

HERBERT JENKINS, LTD. (ENGLAND)

1928 Statement: *See* 1937 Statement
1937 Statement: "It is now our custom to put the date of our publications on the back of the title page, and if a reprint is called for we show the date of the reprint also on the back of the title page. If, however, we produce a cheap edition of the work we omit the date therefrom.

"We began using our present method about 1924."
1948 Statement: "At present and during the war, owing to existing conditions and the very considerable delays in production, we are omitting the dates of publication from our books and are using the term 'First Printing.' This is a temporary measure only and we hope later to be able to revert to our normal practice which is mentioned in our previous statement."

JEWISH CHRONICLE PUBLICATIONS (ENGLAND)

1976 Statement: "We have no particular method of identifying first editions of our books."

THE JEWISH PUBLICATION SOCIETY OF AMERICA

1947 Statement: "The first printings of our books contain the year in which the book was published on the title page, and on the copyright page the same information. Subsequent editions carry the year in which the book was reprinted on the title page, and on the copyright page, we state whatever printing it is plus the date."
1976 Statement: A first edition will carry the designation "First Edition" on the copyright page. This method of designation does not differ from any previously used.
1981, 1988 Statements: *See* 1976 Statement

THE JOHNS HOPKINS PRESS

1937 Statement: "We seldom publish but one edition of the work, endeavoring to estimate the number of copies that will be required for some time in the future. There have been, however, several instances in which another edition was published and these are indicated as a second edition or a second impression. The latter reference is used if no change is made from the original edition."
1947 Statement: "When it is not so stated in the description of the book, it is considered as the first edition or printing. We mention it if a second printing is made."

THE JOHNS HOPKINS UNIVERSITY PRESS

1976 Statement: "First editions are only designated by their copyright date. Subsequent editions are noted accordingly."

"The first printing of the first edition is designated only by the copyright date. Later printings are designated as follows.

Originally published, date
Second Printing, date
Third Printing, date
Paperback edition, date."

1982 Statement: "First editions are designated only by copyright date. First printings are not designated separately. Second, third, and subsequent printings are designated by date of manufacture. Revised editions are also designated by copyright date, and subsequent printings of revised editions are designated by date of manufacture. Thus, the printing history of a long-lived book might typically show the following sequence on the copyright page:

Originally published, date
Second printing, date
Third printing, date
Second edition, date
Second printing, date
Paperback edition, date."

1988 Statement: "We have not changed our practice in designating editions for some years. My only question is whether the item 'Second edition, date' is accurate. We would normally indicate a second edition by a new copyright line and make mention of the date of the original edition, but we would not specifically note 'Second edition, date.' "

CHRISTOPHER JOHNSON PUBLISHERS LIMITED (ENGLAND)

1947 Statement: "All bibliographical information is printed on the reverse of the title page. The formula used is: 'First published in 19..' for the first edition, and subsequent impressions and editions are printed below this."

JOHNSON PUBLISHING COMPANY, INC.

1976 Statement: "We have no particular method of identifying first editions other than copyright data for first editions."

1981 Statement: *See* 1976 Statement

1988 Statement: "Designation of printings: numbers 1 through 9. The first number indicates the printing, e.g.. for the second printing, the 1 is dropped; for the third, the 2 is dropped, etc. We began using this method in 1987. Our Spring Creek Press imprint uses the same method."

MARSHALL JONES COMPANY

1928 Statement: "It is our custom to print on the copyright page the date of printing, i.e., Printed April 1927, but we do not always do this. When we reprint we usually put on the date just below the other."

1936 Statement. "Since our practice has changed somewhat since the first edition of your book appeared, I think it would be best to substitute the following:

"We make a practice of giving the date of the second and subsequent printings or editions on the copyright page. In nearly all cases, if the copyright date alone appears, the book is of the first printing. The words FIRST EDI-

TION on the copyright page, although we do not always use them, invariably designate the first printing."

1947 Statement: *See* 1936 Statement

MICHAEL JOSEPH LTD. (ENGLAND)

1937 Statement: "It is our custom to print the year of publication of our books on the reverse of the title page.

"If the book is reprinted the arrangement indicated below is followed:

First published May, 1936

Second Impression June, 1936

"The word 'edition' is only used in the event of a cheaper reprint or when textual alterations have been effected."

1947 Statement: *See* 1937 Statement

1976 Statement: "Attached is a form of bibliography which appears in all our first editions. We have no other method of identification. If a title is re-printed, the date of the impression is inserted beneath the date of the first edition."

First printings carry the designation "First published in Great Britain by Michael Joseph Ltd. date."

1981, 1988 Statements: *See* 1976 Statement

(In late 1988, the Penguin Group changed its method of designating a first edition. For a book published in the latter part of 1988, see 1988 Statement of Penguin Publishing Co Ltd [England].)

THE JOURNEYMAN PRESS, LTD. (ENGLAND)

1988 Statement: "We designate first editions by printing on the reverse of the title page the following:

'First published by the Journeyman Press Ltd, 19..'

and further down the page

'First edition 19...'

"New impressions are designated by eliminating the last number from the sequence:

'10 9 8 7 6 5 4 3 2 1 printing'

"Reprints with corrections, or revised editions are specified as they occur, together with the relevant year of printing.

"This method was adopted in 1986, but prior to that we did not identify the first edition separately, and we always noted new impressions as reprints followed by the year of printing (unless of course there were corrections, etc.)."

JUDSON PRESS

1976 Statement: "Our first edition is that which bears the original copyright date and no further information about its being a subsequent printing. When we reprint a book, we add the number of the reprinting and the date of the reprinting. If there is any substantial editorial revision, there will be some note made of that as well on the copyright page."

1981, 1988 Statements: *See* 1976 Statement

JUNIPER PRESS
(LaCrosse, Wisconsin)

1976 Statement: "Juniper Books have the number of the printing indicated on the reverse of each title page. As of this date some are in as many as their 6th printing.

"The William N. Judson series of fine printed books by contemporary American poets are all in first edition, except the first, *Ash is the Candle's Wick*, which is in its second printing. We do all printings after the first by offset from the original letter press books. All first editions are hand set and by letter press. This information may be found on the last page of any book of a later than first edition."

1981 Statement: "There are some changes to be made. The paragraph should read:

"Juniper Books have the number of the printing indicated on the reverse of each title page. As of this date some are in as many as their 6th printing.

"Many of the William N. Judson series of fine printed books by contemporary American poets have gone into the 4th printing. It is best to contact the printer for more information.

"We do all printings after the first by offset from the original letter press books. All first editions are hand set and by letter press. This information may be found on the last page of any book of a later than first edition."

1989 Statement: "Juniper Press of LaCrosse, Wisconsin has four series of books to offer, plus the literary magazine *NORTHEAST*. The *Juniper Books Series* are all 1st editions, but some have gone through as many as 6 printings. Juniper Books are in offset printing. The *William N. Judson Series* of fine printed books by contemporary American poets are all 1st editions, and some have gone into 4th printings. These are letterpress printing in the 1st printing. The *Voyages to the Inland Seas Series* began in 1981 with Juniper Press and publishes larger works of poetry, prose or anthologies. All are 1st editions and several have gone into 3rd printings and all are offset press printed. The *Haiku-short poem Series* are all 1st editions and no other printings are made, and most of these are letterpress printed. We have recently begun to use the laser printing techniques and many of our newer books will reflect this in order to bring more quality work to our readers. Please contact the publisher for more information as we begin our 26th year of publication."

K

KALIMAT PRESS

1988 Statement: "Our first editions are identified by the words 'First Edition' printed on the copyright page. This designation is removed from subsequent printings. Sometimes, we have added the designation 'Second Printing,' 'Third Printing,' etc., to subsequent printings.

"Occasionally, we have left off the 'First Edition' designation by accident. Occasionally, a book has been reprinted with 'First Edition' left on the copyright page by accident. In such cases one can only identify the first edition by careful comparison with other books. Typos are always corrected in second printings."

KALMBACH PUBLISHING COMPANY

1947 Statement: "Most of our books are marked with 'second edition,' 'third edition,' etc. These are on the title page or the page following it when the book is not a first edition. Some books have gone into a second printing without making any such mark; however, the only changes between the first and second printing, if any, would have been minor typographical errors. We would have no way ourselves of knowing which of these were from the first printing without having to go over the book word by word to find where such errors might have been. Most of our books have gone into printings of about 3,000 on the first edition with no additional printing until the second edition of another 3,000 is made."

1976 Statement: "Our firm publishes a line of hardcover books devoted to railroading and a line of softcover how-to-do-it books devoted to hobbies, especially model railroading. We have retained all of our hardcover books in print as they were originally published and have not labeled them 'first edition.' We have never updated them or otherwise done anything to create a 'second edition.' We have done this out of consideration for buyers of an original edition, who would later either find the book they own made obsolete or face a large expenditure for material they already own to gain the small percentage of new material. We do, of course, list the various printings in the book and enter necessary corrections.

"Out of some 23 softcover titles, about 5 or 6 are in a second edition. On the title pages of these books, our usual procedure is to list the various printings by year (sometimes by month if two printings occur within the same year). If a book is in a second edition, we'll then preface the printings by placing FIRST EDITION: before the list or corresponding years and SECOND EDITION: before the list of corresponding years.

"In summary, then, note that first editions are never identified as such within the first edition book. Only second editions are identified within the book, at which time the original book 'retroactively' becomes a first edition."

1981 Statement: "In summary, first editions are never identified; only second editions are identified within the book."

1988 Statement: *See* 1981 Statement

KANCHENJUNGA PRESS

1976 Statement: "All Kanchenjunga first editions are identified as such on the copyright page. The usual form is an announcement such as, 'This first edition is limited to X copies,' or simply the statement, 'First Edition.' Second or later printings are identified as such and do not carry the 'first edition' designation. Therefore any Kanchenjunga book marked 'first edition' is from the first printing of the first edition. (This information applies to all titles published 1972 through 1976. The fact that we've done it this way in the past doesn't prevent our adopting some other method in the future.)"

1981 Statement: *See* 1976 Statement

WILLIAM KAUFMANN, INC.

1981 Statement: "I'm sorry to say we've been somewhat inconsistent in designating first editions. Sometimes we have put the 11 10 9 8 7 6 5 4 3 2 1 sequence of numbers on our copyright pages, removing the digits in ascending order as new printings are done. On the other hand, we have designated some of our 'firsts' as 'Experimental' editions."

1988 Statement: *See* 1981 Statement

KAYAK BOOKS

1976 Statement: "I use no particular sign to designate either a first edition or a first printing. I know this makes it hard on bibliographers but it also encourages them in their detective talents."

1981 Statement: *See* 1976 Statement

CLAUDE KENDALL, INC.
(Out of business prior to 1949.)

1937 Statement: "It is our custom to identify first editions by printing the legend 'First Printing' on the copyright page."

CLAUDE KENDALL & WILLOUGHBY SHARP, INC.

See Claude Kendall, Inc.

KENNEDY BROTHERS

See Yachting

KENNIKAT PRESS CORPORATION

1976 Statement: "Kennikat Press does not designate a First Edition. Subsequent printings may or may not be designated 2nd, 3rd, etc.

"A bonafide second *edition* will no doubt have some sort of designation as such on the title page and will carry a copyright date differing from that of the first edition."

1981 Statement: *See* 1976 Statement

THE KENT STATE UNIVERSITY PRESS

1976 Statement: "The absence of the words 'First Edition,' would indicate a first edition."

1981 Statement: "Second and additional printings are identified. Otherwise, no change."

1988 Statement: *See* 1981 Statement

KEYSTONE BOOKS

1988 Statement: *See* 1988 Statement of The Pennsylvania State University Press

KILLALY PRESS (CANADA)

1976 Statement: "As my publications are published to further the writing careers of the authors and not to make a profit, there is no thought of a second printing, edition, etc., and consequently the edition is not designated. There never has been any change in policy since we began publishing in 1972.

"All publications contain the following statement:

Publication is limited
to 100 copies of which
the 1st 15 are signed.
This is copy number...."

1981 Statement: *See* 1976 Statement

WILLIAM KIMBER & CO. LIMITED (ENGLAND)

1976 Statement: "Set out below is an actual example of our method of identifying first editions and the same method we have always used. (The book in question is *British Political Crises*.)

First published in 1976 by
WILLIAM KIMBER & CO LIMITED
Godolphin House, 22a Queen Anne's Gate,
London SW1H 9AE
©Sir Dingle Foot, 1976
ISBN 0 7183 0194 3."

1981 Statement: *See* 1976 Statement

1988 Statement: *See* 1976 Statement. Note, however, that the publisher's address will now read 100 Jermyn Street, London, SW1Y 6EE.

ALFRED H. KING, INC.
(Acquired by Julian Messner, Inc., prior to 1949.)

KING'S CROWN PRESS
(A Division of Columbia University Press.)
1947 Statement: "The King's Crown Press identifies its first printing by the date at the foot of the title page; on subsequent printings that date is removed and on the title page verso the dates of the various printings are given in chronological order."

KINGSWOOD BOOKS
1988 Statement: *See* 1988 Statement of Abingdon Press

H. C. KINSEY & COMPANY, INC.
(Bought by G. P. Putnam's Sons in 1943.)
1937 Statement. "Our system is very simple—if there is no printing date under the copyright notice then that is the first edition. The second printing is always indicated by a line giving the date and all subsequent editions in the same way:
    First Editions—November 1949
    Second Edition—December, etc.
"The Mary Pickford books were the only exception to this rule and we included 'First Edition' on the copyright page of the small first order for *Why Not Try God.*"

ROBERT R. KNAPP, PUBLISHER
1976 Statement: "We label edition on the verso and include printing information for each successive printing."

CHARLES KNIGHT & COMPANY (ENGLAND)
1976 Statement: "In new books we use the phrase 'First published (date)', and this is how our first editions may be identified. Information about subsequent impressions or editions is listed underneath the original statement, and this information is generally to be found on the reverse of the title page of a book . . . . Charles Knight and Company have been publishing books since 1833, and I am fairly certain that it is not possible to generalize about previous methods. I know from reference to our library shelves that many books are undated. The method I have described dates from 1974. From about 1969 onwards, any editions subsequent to first editions are described as such on our title pages."
1981 Statement: *See* 1976 Statement

KNIGHTS PRESS
1988 Statement: "Sorry, but we do not differentiate 1st Editions."

ALFRED A. KNOPF, INC.
1928 Statement: "It is our practice to indicate on the copyright page with a line thus: 'Second Printing, Third Printing,' etc. This note does not appear on the first edition."
1936 Statement: "Up until 2 1/2 or 3 years ago, the first editions of our books bore no note on the copyright page. When a book was reprinted, however, a notice of the printing was added to the copyright page. If a book was reprinted before publication date a note reading 'First and second

printings before publication' was added to the copyright page and this indicated that the particular book belonged to the second printing.

"About 2 1/2 or 3 years ago, however, we changed our practice only in the matter of first printings. On the copyright page of any one of our books issued since then we carry the note 'First Edition' or 'First American Edition.' The latter term is used only where the English edition precedes or is simultaneously published with ours."

1947 Statement: "Our present practice is to print on the copyright page of the first printing of any book we publish either the words 'first American edition' or 'first edition.' We use 'first American edition' in the case of a book which has already been published abroad, whether in English or another language."

1976 Statement: "Knopf identifies a book's edition on the copyright page. We do not indicate that a particular work is part of a first printing, but for second or subsequent printings, the information is also carried on the copyright page.

"We have been using these methods of identification for a great many years."

1981 Statement: "We have made no changes in our method of identifying editions and printings on the copyright pages of our books."

1988 Statement: *See* 1981 Statement

See also 1976, 1981, and 1988 Statements of Random House, Inc.

ALFRED A. KNOPF, INC. (ENGLAND)
(English house discontinued December 1930.)

1928 Statement: "Our practice of designating our first editions is to place on the verso of the title page the legend 'first published' followed by the month and year. The further impressions are designated by the number of the impression, and further editions by the number of the edition. In both cases the dates are shown."

KNOW, INC.

1976 Statement: "Our first editions are identified as first printings on the copyright page of each book. Later editions are also identified. This is the only identification we have ever used."

1981 Statement: *See* 1976 Statement

JOHN KNOX PRESS

1976 Statement: "We do not have a special method for designating a first edition. The copyright © 1976 John Knox Press designates both a first edition and a first printing. If subsequent editions or printings are needed, these are identified by the addition of 'Second edition' or 'Second printing' to the copyright notice. A hardback reissued in paper carries in addition to the copyright line the notice: 'Paperback edition, 19...' "

1981 Statement: "Below is an example of a first edition, first printing copyright notice:

©copyright John Knox Press 1981
10 9 8 7 6 5 4 3 2 1
Printed in the United States of America
John Knox Press
Atlanta, Georgia 30365

"Any subsequent printings would be acknowledged by the dropping of a number. For example, the second printing would drop the 1, the third, the 2, etc.

"A second edition would be acknowledged on the cover and title page as 'new, revised edition' and on copyright page as 'second edition' under the copyright notice; the numbering would return to original: 10 9 8 7 6 5 4 3 2 1.

"The first paperback of a hardback edition, somewhere, probably after copyright notice, will have a notice to that effect: 'First paperback edition (date).' If the original edition had a different title, there will be a notice to that effect: 'Originally published as (original title).' This will be placed under copyright notice.

"John Knox Press began using the 'drop number' system for reprints in late 1979. The imprints follow the same procedure."

1988 Statement: *See* 1988 Statement of Westminster/John Knox Press

KODANSHA INTERNATIONAL / USA, LTD.

1976 Statement: First editions are indicated by the words "First Edition" and the date of publication. The number and date of subsequent printings and editions are indicated.

1988 Statement: *See* 1976 Statement

A. KROCH AND SON, PUBLISHERS

1947 Statement: "We usually indicate the second edition of our publications under the copyright notice."

L

LADYBIRD BOOKS LTD. (ENGLAND)

1976 Statement: There is no method whatsoever of identifying a first edition of a Ladybird book. The year of publication is printed by the side of their name on the title page, but then this same date is repeated in subsequent printings in following years. It serves more to indicate copyright protection than a method to designate a first edition.

1981, 1988 Statements: *See* 1976 Statement

LANDMARK EDITIONS

1988 Statement: *See* 1988 Statement of University of Nebraska Press

LANE PUBLISHING CO.

1947 Statement: "If first printing, this fact and date of same is stated on back of title page, i.e.,

FIRST PRINTING, JULY, 1947

"The same is true for subsequent printings, i.e.,

TENTH PRINTING OCTOBER, 1947

"If a revised and/or enlarged edition, this fact is so stated, i.e.,

FIRST EDITION, 14 printings
REVISED (and/or enlarged) EDITION,
FIRST PRINTING, JANUARY, 1947"

Statement for 1960: The printing information is given on the copyright page. Occasionally the words "First Edition" will be omitted, but this is not the usual policy. The first printing will always be identified as such, however. Subsequent printings are also noted.

1981 Statement: "Sunset does not have any specific means of identifying first printings—all printings are handled in the same manner. For instance, our current *Casseroles* book states 'First Printing September 1980'; our *Favorite Recipes* book says 'Seventeenth Printing December 1979.' "

1988 Statement: "If first printing, this fact and date of same is stated on back of title page, i.e.,

FIRST PRINTING, JULY, 1988

"The same is true for subsequent printings. Sunset does not have any specific means of identifying first printings—all printings are handled in the same manner."

JOHN LANE THE BODLEY HEAD, LTD. (ENGLAND)

1928 Statement: "With regard to first editions, the practice here has varied in the course of time. Originally first editions had simply the date on the title page; further printings had the words 'Second' or 'Third Edition' as the case might be, and also the date, though there may have been cases in which the practice was varied slightly. Nowadays we print on the back of the title page the words 'First Published in' followed by either the date of the year or the month and the year. In event of reprints the words are added 'Second Impression' with the month and the year. In no case have we ever printed the words 'First edition' on a book."

1937, 1949 Statements: *See* 1928 Statement

1976, 1981 Statements: *See* The Bodley Head Limited (England)

LANGHAM PRESS (ENGLAND)

1989 Statement: *See* 1989 Statement of The Octopus Publishing Group PLC (England)

LANSDOWNE PRESS (AUSTRALIA)

1976 Statement: "Our imprint page identifies editions in the following format:

Lansdowne Editions
(a division of Paul Hamlyn Pty Ltd)
37 Little Bourke Street, Melbourne 3000
©(Author)
First published 1974

"If there are reprints on subsequent editions we would run under:

First published 1974
Reprinted 1975 (twice)
Reprinted 1976
Reprinted 1976

"With limited editions we state this on the imprint page and on a recto page of the prelims, usually after the title page.

"We will probably move any certificate of limitations to the final verso page in the future."

1981 Statement: "We no longer use the Ure Smith imprint, publishing now under the imprints—Lansdowne Press, Landsowne Editions and Summit Books.

"We indicate that a book is a first edition by the words 'First published 19..' or occasionally 'First Edition.' Sample imprint data follows:

Published by Lansdowne Press, Sydney,
176 South Creek Road, Dee Why West, N.S.W.

Australia, 2099.
First published 1981
©Author
"The same format is used for Summit Books, which are also published in Sydney, and for Lansdowne Editions. However, these are published in Melbourne."
1988 Statement: *See* 1988 Statement of Kevin Weldon & Associates Pty Ltd (Australia)

LANTERN PRESS, INC.

1947 Statement: "First printings are not identified in any way, but subsequent printings are identified with the month and year of printing.

"Thus if no notation appears on the copyright page of our books, the reader will know that it is a First Printing."

LARLIN CORPORATION

1988 Statement: "We have not been consistent with our identifications of first editions, but we normally use the term 'First Edition' and the coding device as shown on the enclosed sample.

"First Edition
ISBN 0-87797-1144-7
91 90 89 88   10 9 8 7 6 5 4 3 2 1"

LATIMER HOUSE, LTD. (ENGLAND)

1947 Statement: "In the case of a first edition of a book the words 'First Published 1947' appear on the verso of the title page. Subsequent printings bear the words 'Second Impression October 1948,' 'Third Impression January 1949' and so on."

LAUGHTER LIBRARY

1989 Statement: *See* 1989 Statement of Price/Stern/Sloan Publishers, Inc.

T. WERNER LAURIE, LTD. (ENGLAND)

1928 Statement: *See* 1937 Statement
1937 Statement: "We follow the custom laid down by the Publishers' Association; namely, we print on the *back of the title*, the words:

First Published in 1926
Second Impression—1926
Third Edition—1928

"An impression is an exact reprint of a former edition. An edition is where some alterations have been made.

"We cannot tell you the exact date we first issued the form but we believe it was sometime in 1925."
1947 Statement: *See* 1937 Statement

SEYMOUR LAWRENCE INCORPORATED

1976 Statement: "First editions of Delacorte Press/Seymour Lawrence titles are identified by the words 'first printing' on the copyright page. In the case of translations, we use the designation 'first American edition' or 'first American printing.' "
1981 Statement: *See* 1976 Statement

LAWRENCE AND WISHART, LTD. (ENGLAND)

1948 Statement: "In recent years we simply put the *year* of publication at the bottom of the title page—usually in this style:

London
Lawrence and Wishart
1948

"It is quite impractical to put the month of publication in the verso title page because production is still so difficult here that we never know when a book will arrive."

1976 Statement: "We have no special way of designating first editions, except that on any subsequent printing, or new editions, the previous history is always given on the verso of the title page. Therefore it is, in fact, possible to identify if a particular copy is of the first edition."

1981 Statement: *See* 1976 Statement

LEA & FEBIGER

1988 Statement: "We have been publishers since 1785 and as far as I know, we have never indicated on the title page or copyright page that a book is a 'First Edition.' Subsequent editions of the same book are indicated as 'Second, Third, etc. Editions.' Reprints are indicated by numerical symbols 1, 2, 3, 4, etc. Deleting whatever print number the reprint might be indicates the number of prints.

"We usually list editions after the first on the copyright page.

"We have no imprints or subsidiaries."

LEHIGH UNIVERSITY PRESS

1988 Statement: *See* 1988 Statement of Associated University Presses

LEICESTER UNIVERSITY PRESS (ENGLAND)

1976 Statement: "We print 'First published in 1976 by Leicester University Press' on the reverse of the title page of the first edition of our books, with the appropriate date, of course. This is the procedure we have followed for many years."

1981, 1988 Statements: *See* 1976 Statement

LERNER PUBLICATIONS COMPANY

1976 Statement: "In our publications, 'first edition' and 'first printing' are usually synonymous. A first printing is identified by either the words 'First Printing, 1977' on the copyright page or by the following code:

1 2 3 4 5 6 7 8 9 10 85 84 83 82 81 80 79 78 77

"When the book is reprinted, the appropriate printing number and year of reprint are removed. (That is, a second printing done in 1978 will have the '1' and the '77' omitted.)"

1981, 1988 Statements: *See* 1976 Statement

LES FEMMES PUBLISHING

See Celestial Arts

LIBERTY FUND, INC.

1988 Statement: "Our publishing imprints are Liberty*Press* and Liberty-*Classics* and we bring back into print works which are not available from any commercial publisher. We sometimes do collections of previously published or new material but do not identify our books as 1st editions. We do use a printing line to identify subsequent printings."

LIBERTY*CLASSICS*

1988 Statement: *See* 1988 Statement of Liberty Fund, Inc.

150

LIBERTY*PRESS*
1988 Statement: *See* 1988 Statement of Liberty Fund, Inc.

LIBRA PUBLISHERS, INC.
1976 Statement: "We use no identifying method."
1981 Statement: *See* 1976 Statement
1988 Statement: "We print 'First Edition' on the copyright page of our books. We have been doing this for several years."

THE LIBRARY OF AMERICA
1988 Statement: "Since 1983, all titles published by The Library of America have stated the printing on the copyright page (p. iv), as follows: 'First Printing,' 'Second Printing,' etc. If a second edition is published, it will be indicated on the copyright page as 'Second Edition.'

"In 1982, our first year of publications, we did not indicate the printings, but the following titles that appear with no indication on the copyright page are first printings: Herman Melville, *Typee, Omoo, Mardi,* Nathaniel Hawthorne, *Tales and Sketches,* Mark Twain, *Mississippi Writings,* Jack London, *Novels and Stories,* Jack London, *Novels and Social Writings,* and William Dean Howells, *Novels 1875-1886.*

"Two titles from 1982 had multiple printings in that year, and they may be distinguished as follows:
Walt Whitman, *Poetry and Prose*
> First Printing: no indication on copyright page.
> Second Printing: no indication on copyright page *and* the second line of the Contents page (p. ix) reads: 'Each section has its own table of contents.'
> All subsequent printings are indicated on copyright page.
Harriet Beecher Stowe, *Three Novels*
> First Printing: no indication on copyright page *and* 'Three Novels' *does not* appear on the title page (p. iii).
> Second Printing: the copyright page reads 'June 1982'.
> All subsequent printings are indicated on copyright page."

THE LIGHTNING TREE
1976 Statement: "It took me some time to decide how to indicate first editions of TLT books. I have started including a FIRST PRINTING line on the copyright page to satisfy that need. Subsequent printings are appropriately marked by the number of the printing.

"For the books published with no indication, one can be sure they are first editions. We drop in the second printing, etc., line if they are reprinted.

"But I must add the caveat that there is no way of telling which binding of which edition one might have. As do many small publishers, we frequently print larger quantities of books than we may bind. Since we print most of our own books in house, but have all binding jobbed out, it is to our economic advantage to print larger editions, and have them bound depending on sales."
1981, 1988 Statements: *See* 1976 Statement

THE LINCOLN RECORD SOCIETY (ENGLAND)
1988 Statement: *See* 1988 Statement of Boydell & Brewer, Ltd. (England)

J. B. LIPPINCOTT CO.

1928 Statement: "For the last two or three years only we have been putting First Edition on the copyright page of our important books only, such as *Hawkers and Walkers, The Practical Series,* etc. Before that, and at present on general works including fiction, we have not indicated the first edition, but we indicate all subsequent printings by placing on the bastard title the words 'Second Impression' and so on.

"Twenty years or so ago it used to be the habit, we think, of most publishers to date the first edition of Fall books the following year so that for instance a book might bear the date 1901 when it was copyrighted and first published in the Fall of 1900."

1937 Statement: *See* 1928 Statement

1947 Statement: "We now put the words First Edition on the copyright page of all of our trade publications and we still indicate all subsequent printings by using the words Second Impression, etc."

1976 Statement: "For trade books, first editions are designated by 'First Edition' printed on copyright page, with or without the number sequence '9 8 7 6 5 4 3 2 1.' Second printings of first editions are designated in one of two ways: Either 'Second Printing' is substituted for 'First Edition' or 'First Edition' is retained with the number sequence '9 8 7 6 5 4 3 2' (the 1 being omitted)."

1981 Statement. *See* 1981 Statement of Harper & Row, Publishers, Inc.

1988 Statement: *See* 1988 Statement of J. B. Lippincott Company

J. B. LIPPINCOTT COMPANY

1988 Statement: "We do not use 'First Edition' in our books. If, however, a book has been successful and warrants subsequent editions, they will be marked with edition numbers.

"The printing number sequence is shown as '9 8 7 6 5 4 3 2 1' for a flush left layout and '1 3 5 7 9 8 6 4 2' for a centered layout. The copyright notice will include references to the copyright dates of previous editions, if there are any.

"J. B. Lippincott Company is today a publisher of books in the health sciences and all titles previously published in other areas are now incorporated with the Harper & Row publishing programs."

See also 1981 Statement of Harper & Row, Publishers, Inc.

J. B. LIPPINCOTT COMPANY (ENGLAND)

1928 Statement: *See* 1937 Statement

1937 Statement: "Our books are usually designated as follows: Copyright notice followed by the date and the name of author or this Company on the back of the title, followed by the words 'First Edition' on important books. The date also sometimes appears on the front. In any case subsequent impressions are so noted on the copyright page or the bastard.

"With regard to limited editions, we usually state the words 'Limited edition printed from type and type distributed.' This information appears as a rule on the half title; copyright notice, name of author, date, or our name also appearing on the back of the title.

"We began using our present method many years ago."

1947 Statement: "So far as we are aware this Company has not changed in any way its method of identifying first editions of our publications, and first printings are still based on the information which we supplied in 1937.

152

"However, all our publications are printed in America and we do not make special printings of them for sale in this country. Therefore the information given [for American printings] should be exactly similar to that [supplied for English printings]."

LIPPINCOTT & CROWELL
1981 Statement: *See* 1981 Statement of Harper & Row, Publishers, Inc.

ALAN R. LISS
1988 Statement: "We do not identify first editions as such. We do identify second and subsequent printings."

LITTLE, BROWN & COMPANY
1928 Statement: "With few exceptions we make no attempt to designate first editions.

"Where we have brought out limited editions as well as trade editions of the same book we have sometimes indicated the first trade edition."

1936 Statement. "A Little, Brown or Atlantic Monthly Press first edition can for the most part be identified by a single line on the copyright page giving the month and year of first publication. Each new printing of a book carries an additional line on the title page also giving the month and year."

1947 Statement: *See* 1936 Statement

See also The Atlantic Monthly Press, Inc.

1988 Statement: "The edition (e.g., First Edition or First American Edition) is shown on the copyright page. Also, the first printing of a first edition is indicated by our printing line (10 9 8 . . . 3 2 1); the '1' indicates this is the first printing.

"Also . . . we have deleted the cross reference to Atlantic Monthly Press, Inc. because Atlantic Monthly Press books are published under the Atlantic Monthly Press imprint and are no longer published under the Atlantic Monthly Press / Little, Brown joint imprint."

LITTLEBURY & COMPANY, LTD. (ENGLAND)
1947 Statement: "Post-war production has been so erratic that to insert the actual date of publication of a book has been impractical. Publications issued on any one date in the year have been as late as eighteen months in production, owing to shortage of materials and labour in the Binding and other Departments.

"For this reason alone publication dates have been omitted and they will not be inserted until a more settled state in the Industry can be assured."

LITTLE HILLS PRESS PTY LTD (ENGLAND)
1988 Statement: "Although no strict rule is followed, in general it will be found that unless books are marked 'Reprinted, date' they are first editions."

LITTMAN FOUNDATION
1981 Statement: *See* 1981 Statement of Associated University Presses

HORACE LIVERIGHT, INC.
(Became Liveright Publishing Corporation.)
See Liveright Publishing Corporation

LIVERIGHT PUBLISHING CORPORATION
1937 Statement: "As a general rule we have no marking on the copyright page of our publications to show our first edition although on subsequent

editions we print Second, Third, Fourth, Fifth, Sixth edition, etc. We have had one or two books with first edition marked on the copyright page but this is not our general practice."

1947 Statement: *See* 1937 Statement

1976 Statement: "Liveright Publishing Corporation is now a wholly owned subsidiary of W. W. Norton & Company, Inc. For both Liveright and Norton books we currently indicate first editions with a series of numbers 1 through 9 on the copyright page. A first edition has all of the numbers. The second printing is indicated by the deletion of the number 1. The third by the deletion of number 2, and so on. An actual new edition is indicated either by the words 'revised edition,' or 'second edition.' . . . From house to house the practice varies and we ourselves in years past have indicated first editions with the words 'first edition.' "

1981 Statement: "Liveright Publishing Corporation is now a wholly owned subsidiary of W. W. Norton & Company, Inc. For both Liveright and Norton books we currently indicate first editions with a series of numbers 1 through 9 on the copyright page. A first edition has all of the numbers plus the words 'First Edition.' The second printing is indicated by the deletion of the number 1 and the words 'First Edition.' The third by the deletion of number 2, and so on. An actual new edition is indicated either by the words 'revised edition,' or 'second edition.' . . . From house to house the practice varies and we ourselves in years past have indicated first editions with the words 'first edition.' "

1988 Statement: *See* 1981 Statement

LIVERPOOL UNIVERSITY PRESS (ENGLAND)

1976 Statement: "We do not have any particular method of identification for first editions. We publish books for use in University teaching and research and normally we are not concerned with identifying first publication, other than by mentioning this and listing subsequent printings or editions in the usual way on the copyright page, which is the verso of the title page."

1981 Statement: *See* 1976 Statement

1988 Statement: "The current practice of Liverpool University Press is to identify, on the title verso page, the original publisher of a book if other than ourselves. Where a book is first published by ourselves, this is also stated; in this case the book is a first edition unless otherwise stated. Reprints and new editions are always identified and the year in which they were issued is given."

LLEWELLYN PUBLICATIONS

1976 Statement: "On the copyright page we put 'First Edition, date.' If it is a second printing of a first edition, we add under 'First Edition' 'Second Printing, date.' We also change the date on the title page of successive printings of a book, so that discrepancy between the date on the title page and that on the copyright page would be a clue that the book is a subsequent printing of an edition. In the past, we have not been careful to distinguish between new printings and new editions, and so the copyright page might list first, second, third, etc, editions, when what is meant is first edition, second printing, third printing. Whenever we move to a second edition, that fact is indicated on the title page, so that if there is no statement on the title page that the book is a second or third edition, then it can be assumed that it is a first edition."

1981, 1988 Statements: *See* 1976 Statement

LONDON LIMITED EDITIONS (ENGLAND)

1988 Statement: *See* 1988 Statement of Bertram Rota (Publishing) Ltd (England)

LONELY PLANET PUBLICATIONS (AUSTRALIA)

1988 Statement: "We do not designate print runs on any edition. Nearly every one of our books manages to go through more than one print run in an edition and we'd find it tedious indicating each print run.

"On the imprint page we specify the edition of the title, the first publication date of the title, and the publication date of the current edition, i.e:

India—a travel survival kit
3rd edition
First published
October 1981
This edition
June 1987

"In addition the edition number is specified on the back cover below the prices, i.e.

Australia $9.95   USA $7.95
UK £4.95   New Zealand $11.95
Canada $9.95   India Rs 80
4th edition."

JOHN LONG, LIMITED (ENGLAND)

1928 Statement: "New books published by us are printed with year date of Copyright on back of Title Page in the first edition and subsequent editions are marked 2nd Edition, etc., on title page. This applies to novels published at 7s.6d., the cheaper editions being issued later."

1935 Statement: "Actually, though we put the date in our General Books, this practice does not apply to novels. In cases, however, where 7/6 novels are reprinted at the same price, we put Second or Third Impression, as the case may be.

"We would also mention that the same procedure also applies to our affiliated company, Messrs. Andrew Melrose, Ltd."

1948 Statement: "It is not our present practice to include dates in our publications. In cases where books are reprinted, we state 2nd impression, and so on, as required."

LONGMAN INC.

1976 Statement: "Normally we make it a practice to include the legend 'First Published In...' on the verso of the title page of all first editions. This is definitely true of all books published under the Longman imprint. It is true for most books published under our Churchill Livingstone imprint (medical), but it is not the case with Oliver & Boyd publications.

"However, with all three imprints all subsequent printings or editions are clearly identified."

1981 Statement: *See* 1976 Statement

LONGMAN CHESHIRE PTY LIMITED (AUSTRALIA)

1988 Statement: "The way we normally identify the First Edition is by printing on the verso of the title page 'first published 1981.' When the same edition is reprinted we add underneath first published 1981 'reprinted 1982.'

After a further Edition is subsequently published we would again add 'second edition published 1984' and we would continue to identify additional reprints in the same way as they were identified for the first edition."

LONGMANS, GREEN & CO.

1928 Statement: "With regard to the identification of our first editions, we would say that at the present time we are printing 'First Edition' on the reverse of the title page of our general literary works.

"To distinguish between first editions and others of those books printed previous to the adoption of the present method, one may compare the date used on the title page with that of the copyright date to appear. If the date appearing at the foot of the title page and that of the copyright are the same, the volume is a first edition."

1936 Statement: "We are identifying 'First Editions' by printing the words 'First Edition' on the reverse of the title page of all works printed in the U. S. A.

"In the case of a reprint, we give a notation of the month and year in which the first edition was published and the month and year of each reprint.

"In case of a 'Revised Edition' (where there have been major changes made in the text of a new printing) we indicate that it is a new edition and not merely a reprint."

1947 Statement: *See* 1936 Statement

LONGMANS, GREEN & CO., LTD. (ENGLAND)

1928 Statement: "We always date the title page of our books, and unless the book is marked '.... Impression' or '.... Edition' it is a first edition."

1936 Statement: "Since 1928 we have modified our practice, in that we do not now put the bibliographical information regarding edition, impression or date on the title page. It is all, however, given on the back of the title."

1948 Statement: "We still follow the same arrangement as in our statement of 1936, i.e.: all bibliographical information is given on back of title page."

LORD JOHN PRESS

1988 Statement: "We print 'first edition' on the verso of the title page. On our limited editions we also state that the book is a first edition on the colophon page.

"We have used this practice from the first publication."

LORING & MUSSEY, INC.

(Became Barrows Mussey, Inc, and is now out of business.)

1937 Statement: "We have not followed a consistent practice in regard to first printings. One or two of our books contain the words 'First Edition' with the printer's colophon. In general we would probably print 'Second printing' on the copyright page when reprinting a book.

"The name of this firm will very shortly be changed to Barrows Mussey, Inc."

LOTHROP, LEE & SHEPARD BOOKS

1981 Statement: "The only change is that Lothrop has changed its name to Lothrop, Lee & Shepard Books, which is an imprint of William Morrow & Company, Inc. All imprints in William Morrow would follow the same practice.

"I have checked with our production department about our designation of printings, and they tell me that we continue to use the same method, except we no longer substitute the years.

"We print a strip of code numbers on the copyright page to designate the printing. For a first printing it reads:

1 2 3 4 5 6 7 8 9 10

"For the second printing, the number '1' is knocked off, and so on.

"There is only one printing of each edition; there rarely are any changes, such as corrections, to be made, so except for the code strip each edition is exactly like the previous ones."

1988 Statement: "We print a strip of code numbers on the copyright page to designate the printing. For a first printing it reads:

1 2 3 4 5 6 7 8 9 10

"For the second printing, the number '1' is knocked off, and so on. Prior to 1976, we included the years, as:

1 2 3 4 5 80 79 78 77 76

"In this case, the two end numbers (indicating the printing and the year) were knocked off each time.

"There is only one printing of each edition; there rarely are any changes, such as corrections, to be made, so except for the code strip each edition is exactly like the previous ones."

LOTHROP, LEE & SHEPARD CO., INC.

1948 Statement: "First editions published by our company have no markings. Subsequent editions are marked with the proper edition number on the copyright page.

1976 Statement. "We print a strip of code numbers on the copyright page to designate the printing. For a first printing it reads:

1 2 3 4 5 6 7 8 9 10

"For the second printing, the number '1' is knocked off, and so on. Heretofore we have had a different designation including the year, as:

1 2 3 4 5 80 79 78 77 76

"In this case, the two end numbers (indicating the printing and the year) are knocked off each time.

"There is only one printing of each edition; there rarely are any changes, such as corrections, to be made, so except for the code strip each edition is exactly like the previous ones."

1981 Statement: *See* 1981 Statement of Lothrop, Lee & Shepard Books

LOTUS PRESS, INC.

1976 Statement: "We are still a very small company and so far have published only first editions, with the exception of *Star by Star* which originally came out as a hard cover first edition with another company. We have no immediate plans for issuing other than first editions at this time."

1981 Statement: "We have not changed our policy regarding first editions. In addition to *Star by Star*, which we mentioned in our first report, we have made another exception in the publication of a second edition (first U.S. edition) of *Rufus*, by Ronald Fair. The first edition was published in West Germany in 1977 by Peter Schlack Verlag, Stuttgart, West Germany, and was not available to American audiences. We agreed to handle individual orders for that first edition ($12.00), but at the same time made an agreement with the original publisher whereby a cheaper edition could be made available in this country ($4.00).

"We do not plan to publish any further reprints or publications of anything other than first editions except perhaps a limited edition (about 250 copies) of the first two out-of-print books of Naomi Long Madgett in one volume which will include a number of unpublished juvenile poems. We are not yet certain about this possibility, but we are considering it.

"All of which is to say that our policy has not changed, but we are willing to consider exceptions once in a while."

1988 Statement: "1976 Statement: Essentially correct except that we have recently reprinted *Halfway to the Sun* by May Miller, originally published by another company.

"1981 Statement: OK as is. We decided not to reprint the early volumes of Naomi Long Madgett.

"The company's policy has not changed."

LOUISIANA STATE UNIVERSITY PRESS

1976 Statement: "We do not use any method of identifying our books as first editions. The only thing we do is indicate subsequent printings or editions by date or the words 'Revised edition,' if such is the case, or 'Second edition,' if there has been no substantial revision of the first edition. The assumption regarding our books, thus, would be that they are first editions, unless otherwise described."

1981 Statement: *See* 1976 Statement

1988 Statement: "We do not use any method of identifying our books as first editions. On the copyright page, we indicate subsequent printings by date and number, and we spell out 'Revised edition' and, in the case of a new edition with no substantial changes, 'Second edition.' Thus the assumption regarding our books would be that they are first editions unless otherwise described.

"We began using this system in 1986. We have no subsidiaries."

SAMPSON LOW, MARSTON & CO., LTD. (ENGLAND)

1937 Statement: "We beg to say we have no settled rule with regard to stating on the title page or elsewhere, the date of first publication or reprints."

1949 Statement: *See* 1937 Statement

LOYOLA UNIVERSITY PRESS

1976 Statement: "The absence of any identifying statement does indicate a first edition. However, reprinting without revision is not indicated. So a 'first edition' may go through a number of reprintings. When a book is revised or substantially changed, the fact is noted, and a new copyright year is printed."

1981, 1988 Statements: *See* 1976 Statement

JOHN W. LUCE & COMPANY
(Merged with Manthorne and Burak prior to 1949.)

1937 Statement: "We have never made a practice of specifically designating the different editions of the works of our authors. Had we done so with the books of Mencken, Lord Dunsany, Synge and certain of Wilde's work which we published for the first time, it would have been a distinct convenience. In the case of *George Bernard Shaw; his Plays* by Mencken, which was his first published book, we made but one printing. His other books ran into a number of editions which we can identify but which would not be easily recognized by a casual collector. The same holds true of other authors, though there was but one printing in separate form of the com-

plete *A Florentine Tragedy* by Wilde and one printing of *Pan and Desespoir*, previously unpublished poems by the same author."
1949 Statement: *See* 1937 Statement

LUTTERWORTH PRESS (ENGLAND)
1976 Statement: "Our only method of identifying first editions is by stating the fact, though the wording does vary depending on the circumstances. For instance the bibliography might read:
    First published 19..
    First paperback edition 19..
    First published in Great Britain 19..
    First published in this collected form 19.. etc."
1981 Statement: "I see no reason for changing the entry which you have provided from the previous edition of your publication, but I could add the following examples:
    Second impression 19..
    New Revised Edition 19..."
1988 Statement: *See* 1981 Statement

NICK LYONS BOOKS, INC.
1988 Statement: "On all our books a first edition can be identified by the printing code on the copyright page. This is a series of numbers which, for the first printing, proceeds in descending order from 10 to 1. On subsequent printings the 1 is deleted, then the 2, and so on. Thus the printing number is represented by the lowest number in that sequence.
"Our books have used this system since we started business in 1978."

M

THE MACAULAY COMPANY
(Out of business. Publications issued through 1939 bought by Citadel Press.)
1928 Statement: "We have not been marking our first editions in any particular way. Usually, when second and further editions are issued of the same title, they are so marked."
1937 Statement: *See* 1928 Statement

ROBERT M. McBRIDE & CO.
1928 Statement: "Our designation of the first edition is usually the line reading either First Published April 1927 or Published April 1927. This line is retained in all subsequent editions but the number of the printing is added below it in the second line such as Second Printing, June, 1927, changed on the next printing to Third Printing, etc.
"Our practice, of course, in the past has not been uniformly thus, but we are among the few houses which has consistently printed the number of the edition on the back of the title page."
1937 Statement: *See* 1928 Statement
1947 Statement: "Our designation of the first edition is the line stating First Edition. The date of the first edition, of course, appears above this designation in the copyright notice. In the case of second and subsequent printings, we use the line Second Printing, March 1948. You can see from this that only those volumes that are actually first editions carry the designa-

tion of first editions. All following editions are marked with the number of the printing."

McCLELLAND AND STEWART LIMITED (CANADA)

1976 Statement: McClelland and Stewart has no specific designation for a first edition. All reprintings or editions are indicated on the copyright page. While this practice is usually consistent, there are exceptions.

1981 Statement: *See* 1976 Statement

MACDONALD & CO., (PUBLISHERS) LTD. (ENGLAND)

1947 Statement: *Furnished sample title page showing method. This bears on verso*:
First published 1947
Second Impression December 1947

McFARLAND & COMPANY, INC., PUBLISHERS

1988 Statement: "We do not designate first *editions* or first *printings*; we rarely designate *reprintings* except that if corrections are made we say so near the C.I.P./copyright page (e.g., 'second printing with corrections and revisions').

"All subsequent *editions* are clearly marked."

McGRAW-HILL RYERSON LIMITED (CANADA)

1988 Statement: "First and subsequent editions of our books are designated in the copyright notice, indicating the copyright year of the first edition and each subsequent edition. This method has been used since we started publishing in Canada around 1954.

"Printings are indicated in a reprint line on the copyright page showing the number of the printing and the year in which the reprint was made. This style has been used since 1965. We had previously listed the number of printings made.

"We follow the style used by our parent company, McGraw-Hill Publishing Company."

McGRAW-HILL PUBLISHING COMPANY

1988 Statement: *See* 1988 Statement of McGraw-Hill Ryerson Limited (Canada)

DAVID McKAY CO.

1928 Statement: "There isn't any way you could identify the first editions of our books."

1937, 1947 Statements: *See* 1928 Statement

1988 Statement: " 'First Printing' will appear on copyright page of a first edition book."

See also 1988 Statement of Random House, Inc.

MACLAY & ASSOCIATES

1988 Statement: "On our local-interest titles, we do not designate a first edition, since there is only one printing. On our nationally-distributed fiction titles, the words FIRST EDITION appear on the copyright page of such, and are dropped on any succeeding printings.

"We have no other imprints or subsidiaries.

"This has been our only method since we began in 1981."

ALEXANDER MACLEHOSE & CO. (ENGLAND)
(Out of business prior to 1947.)

1937 Statement: "It is our general practice to put the date of the publication of any book on the title page itself. If the book is reprinted, the date of the reprint appears on the title page and a bibliographical description on the back of the title."

THE MACMILLAN COMPANY

1928 Statement: "On the reverse of the title page of our books, just below the copyright notice always appears a notice to the following effect: 'Set up and electrotyped. Published.....' or 'Set up and printed. Published.....' Usually any reprintings or new editions are listed below. If there are no such reprintings or new editions listed and if the date above our imprint on the title page and the publishing date as given above coincide, the book is a first edition. In cases where the reprintings are listed on the back of the title page, a comparison of this imprint date and the publishing date is usually sufficient to identify the book."

1937 Statement: "On the reverse of the title page of our books, just below the copyright notice, always appears a notice to the following effect: 'Set up and electrotyped. Published.....' or 'Set up and printed. Published.....' Usually any reprintings or new editions are listed below. If there are no such reprintings or new editions listed and if the date above our imprint on the title page and the publishing date as given above coincide, the book is a first edition. In cases where the reprintings are listed on the back of the title page, a comparison of this imprint date and the publishing date is usually sufficient to identify the book.

"From now on (April 24, 1936), however, we propose to place the words 'First Printing' under the copyright of all trade books which we print here in America, these words to be deleted with the second printing.

"We are unable to tell you just when we used our present method of identifying first printings. In checking up renewal of copyright notices, we find that books reprinted since 1894 as a rule have had their imprint date corrected with each printing, but the words 'Reprinted,' etc., do not always appear"

1947 Statement: "The Macmillan practice concerning the edition notice has now changed and we no longer include a statement to the following effect: 'Set up and electrotyped. Published.... ' or 'Set up and printed. Published.....'

"The words *first printing* always appear on the back of the title page of a first edition. Should the book go into a second edition either the word *second* is substituted for *first* or the statement *second printing* listed below *first printing*."

See also Macmillan Publishing Co., Inc.

MACMILLAN & CO., LTD. (ENGLAND)

1928 Statement: *See* 1937 Statement

1937 Statement: "Our first editions carry the date of publication on the title page. If the book is reprinted a statement is put on the back of the title page, saying: 'First edition (say) 1900 Reprinted 1902.' Any subsequent reprints are indicated in the same way. We do not call a book 'second edition' unless (1) the type has been reset, or (2) very substantial alterations have been made, In that case instead of 'Reprinted,' 'Second Edition' would be printed on the back of the title page and occasionally on the title page itself, though there is no special rule about this. The date appearing on the title page itself is the date of printing in every case.

"To give a concrete example, a book that was first published in 1900 and then reprinted without much alteration in 1902, and of which a second edition appeared in 1908, would be designated as follows: On the title page the date 1908 would appear, and on the back of the title page the words.

First Edition 1900
Reprinted 1902
Second Edition 1908

"We are sorry to say that it is impossible for us to give the date when we first adopted this practice."

1947 Statement: *See* 1937 Statement
See also Macmillan Publishers Limited (England)

MACMILLAN OF CANADA (CANADA)

1989 Statement: "Macmillan of Canada does not designate first editions."

MACMILLAN PUBLISHERS LIMITED (ENGLAND)

Statement for 1960: *See* 1982 Statement
1976 Statement: *See* 1982 Statement
1982 Statement: "Until 1968/9 our first editions carried the date of publication on the title page. If the book was reprinted or a new edition was produced, a statement was added to the back of the title page saying 'First edition (say) 1900/Reprinted 1902/Second edition 1908/Reprinted 1910'; the date of the latest printing then appeared on the title page.

"Since 1968/9 our practice has been to omit the date from the title page. Instead, the words 'First published (say) 1972 by.....' now appear on the back of the title page of all first editions. Subsequent reprints and new editions replace this with the wording 'Published by.....' and a statement similar to that used before 1968/9 to show the bibliographical history of the book.

"During 1968 and 1969 either practice may have been used."

MACMILLAN PUBLISHING CO., INC.

1976 Statement: "If I understand your use of the term 'first impressions' as meaning what we would call the first 'printing' of a new title, the answer to your question is simple.

"On the reverse side of the title page where all the copyright information is recorded you will find, in all Macmillan titles (for books published in 1976 for example) the statement 'First Printing 1976.' This has been and will continue to be our method of identification of first printings on new titles."

1981 Statement: "We have noted the reply sent you in 1976 in answer to your question concerning the designation of a 'first edition' published by Macmillan Publishing Co., Inc., or its divisions.

"In December 1979 it was decided that the policy of placing the printing line on the copyright page would be changed. Instead of printing a line, e.g. 'First Printing 1979' or 'Tenth Printing 1978' etc., [it was decided] that a numbering system would be used. When a new title (manuscript) is published the following is added to the copyright page:

10 9 8 7 6 5 4 3 2 1

and whenever the title is reprinted, the previous number is removed before it is sent to the press. Thus, the second printing would begin the print line at the right with '2,' the '1' having been removed. (For back list titles the numbers will start with the current printing number and ascend as high as the space will allow.) This procedure had been used by the Children's Books Department at Macmillan since 1971-72, being an informal adaption of some other publisher's method.

"It was decided that the indications of First Collier Books Edition (date) would be retained, but other divisions and imprints adopted the new system in 1979."

1989 Statement: *See* 1981 Statement

THE DECLAN X. McMULLEN COMPANY, INC.

1947 Statement: "Only two of our books have gone into second printings. As a temporary measure we have indicated this fact on the jacket.

"Should our later publications go into additional printings, and we expect that they will, we shall probably include the fact on the copyright page. No decision has been made as yet, however, on this point.

"Several books published in England, to which we have the American rights and which have been issued under our imprint, announce this fact also only on the jacket."

McNALLY & LOFTIN, PUBLISHERS

1976 Statement: "We've never paid any heed to this aspect of our work. Some of our books are now in their l7th or l8th printing. I'd have to spend a week in trying to figure out my own first editions."

1981 Statement: *See* McNally & Loftin, West

1989 Statement: "Our first printings are now noted as 'First Edition' on the © page. It is removed on subsequent printings."

McNALLY & LOFTIN, WEST

1981 Statement: "We still reprint books with little regard for exactly which edition is involved. I myself have found that the first edition is likely to have typos that are corrected in subsequent reprints."

See also McNally & Loftin, Publishers

WAYNE L. McNAUGHTON, PUBLISHER

1947 Statement: "We use three figures separated by periods, thus: 1.1.1. The first designates the stock number of the title, the second the edition, and the third, the printing. 10.2.4, for instance, would mean title #10, second edition, and 4th. printing of the 2d. edition."

McPHEE GRIBBLE PUBLISHERS PTY LTD (AUSTRALIA)

1988 Statement: "McPhee Gribble began publishing in 1975.

"Our company indicates first printings on all our publications.

"Since 1983 marketing and distribution has been handled by Penguin Books and all our paperback publications carry a joint imprint to maximize sales, We are, however, the intitiating publisher."

Sample imprint pages supplied show hardback first printings identified on copyright page by:

"First published 19—."

Paperback first printings are identified by:

"First published by McPhee Gribble Publishers
in association with Penguin Books Australia 1986"

McPHERSON & COMPANY

1988 Statement: "McPherson & Company was developed in 1983 from Treacle Press (founded in 1973) and Documentext (an imprint added in

1979). No Treacle Press books were reprinted, aside from a second edition of *Shamp of the City-Solo* in 1980.

"In most cases for all books of our imprints the copyright page will state 'first edition,' which is removed in subsequent printings. Often a series of numbers also appears on the copyright page, the lowest number being the printing.

"Special edition notices are dropped from second and subsequent printings, and often we provide a publishing history if we are presenting a new edition of a book originated elsewhere. It should be noted that simultaneous hardcover, paperback, and/or deluxe signed hardcover versions are often released together as the first edition of a book."

MACRAE SMITH & CO.

1928 Statement: "On the copyright page, which is the back of the title page on our books the first edition contains only the copyright notice. Following editions give a record of the number of printings and the dates."

1937 Statement: "Prior to 1930, the copyright page of our books contained only the copyright notice. Subsequent printings were identified with the number of the printing and occasionally the date. Since 1930 the copyright page has contained either of the following to indicate a first edition: 'First Edition' or 'First Printing.' "

1947 Statement: *See* 1937 Statement

LINCOLN MACVEAGH, THE DIAL PRESS

1928 Statement: "We wish to state that our system is to carry on the title page the year in which the edition is published and on the back of this page, merely a note as to when it was reprinted, such as is done by most publishers."

See also Dial Press, Inc.

MACY-MASIUS
(Combined with Vanguard Press.)

1928 Statement: "On the page backing the title page, we place invariably this legend on the first editions of our books:

Published (with the date of publication).

"We don't refer to further printings as editions, since they obviously aren't in the true sense of the word. But we list the date of each further printing within the first edition. We call a printing a second edition only if there is something different in it from the first."

MADISON BOOKS

1988 Statement: "Our first editions have no designation on the copyright page. However, near the bottom of the page, we indicate subsequent printings:

Second Printing
Third Printing, etc."

MADRONA PRESS, INC.

1976 Statement: "Our first editions carry the notation 'First Edition' on the copyright page. Any subsequent printings carry the notation 'Second Printing 1975' or 'Third Printing 1976' etc. also on the copyright page. We have only done second and third printings, and no further editions on any of our books."

1981 Statement: *See* 1976 Statement

164

THE MAIN STREET PRESS

1976 Statement: "No, we have no particular manner in which to indicate first editions, other than the usual 'FIRST PRINTING' on the copyright page."

1981 Statement. "No, we have no particular manner in which to indicate first editions, other than the usual 'FIRST EDITION' on the copyright page."

1988 Statement: "Our general copyright notice carries the year of first publication. Subsequent printings or editions are indicated as such on the copyright page."

MANCHESTER UNIVERSITY PRESS (ENGLAND)

1976 Statement: "As a matter of fact we don't really have anything to identify our first editions: it is only reprints or subsequent editions that are identified by some such statement as 'reprinted 1976' or 'Second edition 1976', or 'Second, revised, edition 1976'."

1981 Statement: "The Press goes on the assumption that a book is a first edition unless otherwise indicated: a new MUP book will include no specific statement that it is a first edition, but a new impression or edition will always be designated as such on the back of the title page."

1988 Statement: "The absence of any indication on the reverse of the title page that the book is a new impression or a new edition indicates that the book is published for the first time. A new impression or new edition will always be designated as such."

MANSELL PUBLISHING LIMITED (ENGLAND)

1988 Statement: "Mansell use the following legend on the reverse title page of all books:
    First published 1988 (or whatever year)
    by Mansell Publishing Limited (followed by address).
"If there is a second printing, the above would be followed by the following:
    Reprinted 1989.
"And:
    Second reprinting 1990.
"If we have limited territories, the first line might read:
    First published in the United Kingdom 1988
    by Mansell Publishing Limited"

RICHARD MAREK PUBLISHERS, INC.

1981 Statement: "Our first printing, as it always has, goes unmarked; however subsequent printings are identified by '(the number) impression,' i.e., first impression, second impression, etc., on the copyright page."

MARGENT PRESS

1947 Statement: *See* 1947 Statement of Richard R. Smith

PETER MARTIN ASSOCIATES LIMITED (CANADA)

1976 Statement: "Our practice here is to designate only editions after the first (*second edition*, etc.); we do not designate printings."

1981 Statement: Since 1976, a new system was initiated. Besides the copyright date, the numbers 1 through 10 are printed in a line at the right side of the page. A first printing would show all of the numbers.

"In subsequent printings one of the numbers for the string of numbers (1-10) at the right side of the page would be dropped; e.g. for a second printing the '1' would be dropped so that the first number appearing would be '2.' A second edition would be designated as such with a string of numbers 1-10 for that edition."

MARTIN BRIAN & O'KEEFFE LTD. (ENGLAND)
1976 Statement: "Our first editions are identified quite simply, by the words 'First published in (year) by Martin Brian & O'Keeffe Ltd. 37 Museum Street London WCI,' followed by 'Copyright (©) (author's name) (year).'"

ELKIN MATHEWS & MARROT, LTD. (ENGLAND)
(Succeeded prior to 1937 by Ivor Nicholson & Watson, Ltd.)
1928 Statement: "In the case of a first impression we make no special mention; subsequent printings are noted on verso of title-page. In the case of Limited Editions we insert an explanatory note. All our books without exception we date on the title page. Such has in former years been the usual practice it is now invariable."
1937 Statement: "In the case of a first impression we make no special mention, subsequent printings are noted on verso of title-page. In the case of Limited Editions we insert an explanatory note. All our books without exception we date on the title page. Such has in former years been the usual practice: it is now invariable.
"Since 1933, when the policy of the firm changed and only educational text books have been issued, no indication whatsoever of a first edition or subsequent edition is given."

MATSON'S PUBLICATIONS (ENGLAND)
1947 Statement: "All our editions bear the date of publication. Thus the first edition might be—
    'First published November 1947'
"The next edition would carry the lines—
    'First published November 1947
    Reprinted December 1947,' and so on."

MEDICAL EXAMINATION PUBLISHING COMPANY
1988 Statement: *See* 1988 Statement of Elsevier Science Publishing Company, Inc.

MEDICI SOCIETY, LTD. (ENGLAND)
1937 Statement: "As you are probably aware, we are publishers of both the Riccardi Press books, which are set by hand, and also books produced in the normal manner from machine set type. All the Riccardi Press books are published in limited editions and not reprinted, the editions being limited to the number stated on the certificate which faces the half-title. Date on title page. With our ordinary books it is usual to put the publication date:
1. On the foot of the title page, or
2. On the reverse of the title page below the line 'Printed in Great Britain.'
"On reprints we do not usually put the date on the title page, but on the reverse, printing a bibliographical note as—
FIRST PUBLISHED (or FIRST PRINTED) 1930
REPRINTED (or 2d. EDITION) 1931
the difference being that if the book is printed from standing type we state REPRINTED or if the book is revised to any extent then we use the words, 2d. EDITION."

1947 Statement: *See* 1937 Statement

THE MEDICI SOCIETY LIMITED (ENGLAND)

1976 Statement. "In answer to your query: no, we do not identify first editions of our children's books and art books. The Publisher's copyright line carries the year of first publication and is repeated unchanged in subsequent impressions. If we make any revisions in a particular title, we would print, for instance, *Revised, 1976*."

1981, 1988 Statements: *See* 1976 Statement

MELBOURNE UNIVERSITY PRESS (AUSTRALIA)

1976 Statement: "Our method of identifying first editions is quite simply to place upon the imprint page (the title page verso) the words 'First published 1976' (or whatever year the publication first appeared)."

1981, 1988 Statements: *See* 1976 Statement

ANDREW MELROSE, LTD. (ENGLAND)

1935 Statement: *See* 1935 Statement of John Long, Limited (England)

MEMPHIS STATE UNIVERSITY PRESS

1976 Statement: "We do not indicate 'first editions' as such but do indicate subsequent 'printings' and editions and revisions as they occur."

1981 Statement: "Our policy on the designation of first printing has not changed. Therefore, 1976 statement is accurate for all our publications including imprints."

1988 Statement: *See* 1981 Statement

MENTOR

1988 Statement: *See* 1988 Statement of New American Library

MERCER UNIVERSITY PRESS

1988 Statement: "First editions are not designated as such on our copyrights page; however, any succeeding edition—revised, second, and so forth—is so designated."

THE MERCIER PRESS, LIMITED (CORK, REPUBLIC OF IRELAND)

1947 Statement: "There is an announcement, usually on the back of the title page of all our publications, indicating the year of issue, and all subsequent printings carry similar announcements giving full particulars of all previous printings. Where two or more reprints are issued in any one year it is usual to give the month of issue."

1988 Statement: *See* 1988 Statement of The Mercier Press Ltd (Republic of Ireland)

THE MERCIER PRESS LTD (REPUBLIC OF IRELAND)

1988 Statement: "The statement regarding Mercier Press published in your first edition still holds good."

MERIDIAN

1988 Statement: *See* 1988 Statement of New American Library

MERIDIAN BOOKS, LTD. (ENGLAND)

1947 Statement: "It is not the policy of this firm to identify first printings of our books by any particular system. In the event of a second edition of a book it is our practice to insert:—

FIRST PUBLISHED (followed by month and year)
SECOND EDITION (date)."

MERIWETHER PUBLISHING LTD.

1988 Statement: "Since 1983, when we began publishing books in addition to plays, we put 'First Edition' under our copyright notice. When we do a second printing we indicate this under the edition designation. If we do a second edition revision we so indicate. We have no subsidiaries."

MERLIN BOOKS LTD PUBLISHERS (ENGLAND)

1988 Statement: "Our first editions are identified by the words:
First published in Great Britain—followed by the date.
"Reprints are identified by:
Reprinted—followed by the date.
"Subsequent impressions are not identified."

THE MERLIN PRESS LTD. (ENGLAND)

1988 Statement: "We endeavour to follow best British bibliographical practice, but Homer (and Merlin) frequently nods."

MERRIAM-WEBSTER INC.

1989 Statement: "Since the mid-1970's, the copyright pages of all of our books have included a printing key near the bottom of the page. The number that is farthest to the left is the printing number. Hence, the first printing can be identified by a '1' in the first position. (Note, of course, that the sequence of numbers would have to be '1234'; '121314' would indicate the twelfth printing.)

"Before the mid-1970's, the title pages of many of our books (but probably not all) included a boxed number that indicated the printing number. The first printing of *Webster's Third* includes no number on its copyright page, but I believe all subsequent printings do.

"First printings of the eighth edition of *Webster's New Collegiate Dictionary* and of *Webster's Ninth New Collegiate Dictionary* include the note 'First printing' on the title page."

See also 1988 Statement of Encyclopaedia Britannica, Inc.

JULIAN MESSNER, INC.

1937 Statement: "We have, up to now, made no differentiation between our first and subsequent editions of books other than the conventional copyright page revision."

1947 Statement: "Our first editions bear only the copyright date; subsequent editions bear the further legend of second printing, third printing, etc. as the case may be. This appears on the copyright page."

1976 Statement: "We do not identify a first edition. Subsequent reprintings bear the notation Second printing, 1977 or whatever, etc."

1981 Statement: *See* 1976 Statement

METHUEN, INC.

1988 Statement: *See* 1988 Statement of Routledge, Chapman and Hall, Inc.

METHUEN & CO. LTD. (ENGLAND)

(For statement of practice from 1889 through 1989 see 1989 Statement of
The Octopus Publishing Group PLC [England])

1928 Statement: "For some years past all first editions of books we have published have had on the back of the title page 'First Published in....' As and when the book is reprinted so a further note is added.

"This does not apply to Limited Editions, which bear on the back of the title page a note to the effect that 'This Edition is Limited to.... copies of which this is No.....' "

1937 Statement: "Since 1905 all first editions of books we have published have had on the back of the title page 'First Published in.....' As and when the book is reprinted so a further note is added.

"In the case of books first published in the U.S.A. the words 'First published in Great Britain in....' are used.

"Limited Editions bear on the back of the title page a note to the effect that 'This Edition is Limited to.... copies of which this is No.....'

"Translations of foreign books published by us bear on the back of the title page 'First published in (French) under the title of ..... This translation first published in Great Britain in....' "

1947 Statement: *See* 1937 Statement

Statement for 1960: The copyright page of a book in its first printing would carry the statement "First published in 1960."

1976, 1982 Statements: *See* Statement for 1960

1988 Statement: *See* 1988 Statement of Routledge, Chapman and Hall (England)

See also 1989 Statement of The Octopus Publishing Group PLC (England)

METHUEN CHILDREN'S (ENGLAND)

1989 Statement: *See* the Methuen entry in the 1989 Statement of The Octopus Publishing Group PLC (England)

METHUEN LONDON (ENGLAND)

1989 Statement: *See* the Methuen entry in the 1989 Statement of The Octopus Publishing Group PLC (England)

THE METROPOLITAN MUSEUM OF ART

1976 Statement: "This institution rarely produces a second edition, but often produces second and third printings of a first edition. In a second printing...we ordinarily make corrections in text or illustrations, whether minor or major, without calling attention to same. It would be routine, therefore, to expect some differences between first and second printings. In a current instance, our second printing of a book involves issuing copies in dust jackets, whereas the same book when first published, was put jacketless into a slipcase. In another instance, illustrations printed originally in one black (one pass through the press), are printed in two blacks (a second press pass) in the second printing to improve the quality of the reproduction. In any of these cases, the original copyright date (or printing date, if the book was produced for us abroad) will tell the scholar that he is holding the first edition in hand. We routinely print the year and 'second printing,' etc., on the copyright page or in the colophon notice when we reprint." This method of identification does not differ from any previously used.

1981 Statement: *See* 1976 Statement

1988 Statement: "This institution rarely produces a second edition, but often produces second and third printings of a first edition. In a second printing . . . we ordinarily make corrections in text or illustrations, whether minor or major, without calling attention to same. It would be routine, therefore, to expect some differences between first and second printings. In any case, the original copyright date will tell the scholar that he is holding the first edition in hand. We routinely print the year and 'second printing,' etc., on the copyright page when we reprint."

This method of identification does not differ from any previously used.

METROPOLITAN PRESS

1976 Statement: *See* 1976 Statement of Binford & Mort

MEYERBOOKS PUBLISHER

1988 Statement: "First editions are *not* designated.

"Second, third and later printings are usually, but not always, designated by simple statement: 'Second printing.' No date of later printing is given.

"Revised editions are noted: 'This edition, with additions and modifications, copyright [year].'

"Price changes and new ad copy on back covers appears on later printings of every work."

MICHIGAN STATE UNIVERSITY PRESS

1988 Statement: "Unless designated otherwise, assume that it is 1st printing."

MICROSOFT PRESS

1988 Statement: "We do not designate a first edition, but we do indicate editions 2, 3, 4, etc. Printings are designated by a print line on the copyright page (1 2 3 4 5 6 7 8 9), with each number being omitted as the book is reprinted. We also use the print line to show when a title is printed or reprinted, using the same number method:

<pre>
1 2 3 4 5 6 7 8 9   FGFG   3 2 1 0 9 8
   (printing)   (printer)   (year completed)."
</pre>

THE MIDDLE ATLANTIC PRESS, INC.

1988 Statement: "We designate first printings on the copyright page by the notation, 'First Middle Atlantic Press printing, (month, year).'

"Subsequent printings are sometimes (but not always) indicated by the notation, 'Second printing, (date).'

"This method of designation is the one we are currently using. Previously, we did not always indicate the month of publication."

MIDLAND HOUSE

1947 Statement: *See* 1947 Statement of The Webb Publishing Company

THE MILITARY SERVICE PUBLISHING CO.

1947 Statement: "All of the books which we print are marked either with the edition number in the case of texts, or with the number of printings."

M. S. MILL CO., INC.

1947 Statement: "The method the M. S. Mill Company uses to identify first printings of its books is actually by omission of any reference to the edition on the copyright page. Subsequent editions will indicate the number of the edition and date of publication, so therefore a book not having this information on the copyright page can be assumed to be one of the first printing."

J. GARNET MILLER LTD. (ENGLAND)

1976 Statement: "What we put in first editions is 'First published by J. Garnet Miller Ltd. in 19..'

"A subsequent printing would retain this and have '2nd Impression', or '2nd Edition' added. This material appears on the back of the title page.

"We have another firm at this address called The Actinic Press, Ltd., which is a medical publisher, and has done books since 1955 in this way. But it is possible that some titles published earlier had a different wording."

1981 Statement: "There is no change in our method of designating first editions in this firm or in The Actinic Press Ltd. The information on your print out is correct for your new edition."

MILLS & BOON, LTD. (ENGLAND)

1928 Statement: *See* 1936 Statement

1936 Statement: "We place on the back of the title page the month and the year that we publish our books; as for instance one published in January of this year would be as follows:

Published January 1936

"We have used this method since we first started publishing in 1909."

1947 Statement: "We have been compelled to revise that statement on the back of our title pages, owing to the difficulties of production. Our present method is that we omit the month of publication, and merely state:

First Published 1947 etc."

1976 Statement: First impressions are designated by the words "First published 19.. " on the copyright page.

1981 Statement: *See* 1976 Statement

MINNESOTA HISTORICAL SOCIETY PRESS

1976 Statement: "First editions carry only the copyright date. Revised editions are clearly identified on the title page and in the copyright statement. Subsequent printings of each edition are specified, by date, following the copyright statement."

1981 Statement: *See* 1976 Statement

1988 Statement: "First editions carry the copyright date and the digits 1 through 10, in descending order. Subsequent printings of each edition are indicated by the last number shown; no date is specified. Revised editions are clearly identified on the title page and in the copyright statement.

"We have no separate imprints or subsidiaries."

MINTON BALCH & CO.

1928 Statement: "All first editions of our books contain the date on the title page and the copyright date following. Subsequent printings are indicated by the words (under the copyright notice) 'second printing' with the month and year in which this printing is made."

1937, 1947 Statements: *See* 1928 Statement

MISSISSIPPI VALLEY PRESS

1947 Statement: "We only publish one edition."

THE MIT PRESS

1976 Statement: "All first editions at the MIT Press include a copyright page (generally page iv of the front matter) to indicate that the material in the book has not been published before. Revised or subsequent editions of a book also have their own copyright date (through the Library of Congress). Any time material is added or changed in a book, it must receive a new copyright. Later editions of a book will often list the publication year of first, second, third printings, etc."

1981 Statement: "All first editions at The MIT Press include a copyright page (generally page iv of the front matter) to supply proper copyright notice, which includes copyright symbol, date and copyright owner. If the material has been previously published by a different press, then 'First MIT Press edition' is specified above the copyright notice. A revised edition of a book requires an additional copyrights notice for new material. Later editions of a book will often list the year of first, second, third printings, etc."

MITCHELL BEAZLEY (ENGLAND)
1989 Statement: *See* 1989 Statement of The Octopus Publishing Group PLC (England)

MOCKINGBIRD BOOKS INC.
1976 Statement: "At the present time Mockingbird Books publishes only paperback books. We identify the first and each subsequent printing by date on the copyright page, e.g.
    First Printing: January, 1976
    Second Printing: June, 1976
and so on."
1981, 1988 Statements: *See* 1976 Statement

MODERN LANGUAGE ASSOCIATION OF AMERICA
1981 Statement: "The Modern Language Association of America does not employ any uniform codes or other designations of first editions or first printings. In the absence of any statement of indication to the contrary, any book may be assumed to be the first printing of the first edition, as the Association publishes most of its books in only one edition with only one printing. With but few exceptions (and those only in small pamphlets), any edition or printing other than the first is clearly indicated on the verso of the title page."
1988 Statement: *See* 1981 Statement

MODERN LIBRARY
1988 Statement: *See* 1988 Statement of Random House, Inc.

THE MODERN PILGRIM PRESS
1947 Statement: "The Modern Pilgrim Press publishes primarily pamphlet guides to Cape Cod, and probably has very little material that would be of interest to first edition collectors. Our *Modern Pilgrim's Guide to Provincetown*, *Modern Pilgrims Bayshore Guide*, and *Modern Pilgrim's Oceanside Guide*, did not differentiate between first and subsequent editions. However, first editions of these guides could be spotted by the fact that they carried no illustrations other than linoleum initial pieces by Saul Yalkert. Subsequent editions carried photographic illustrations, or yellow overprinting on the initial spots. Our *Cape Cod Pilot*, by Jeremiah Digges (American Guide Series), carries only our own imprint on the first edition, whereas subsequent editions were brought out under the joint imprint of the Modern Pilgrim press and the Viking Press. Our *Vittles for the Captain*, a pamphlet cook book, does not differentiate between the first and subsequent editions. However, the paper covers on the first edition were varnished, while the second edition has unvarnished covers."

MOJAVE BOOKS
1976 Statement: "All information as to the printing history of our books is contained on the copyright pages of our books. The distinguishing characteristics are as follows
    a. All first editions bear only the copyright date.

b. All subsequent printings and impressions of that edition are described in the printing history which follows the copyright date.

c. Editions subsequent to the first are explicitly stated on the title page and are followed by the history of previous editions."

1981, 1989 Statements: *See* 1976 Statement

MONAD PRESS OF THE ANCHOR FOUNDATION, INC.

1976 Statement: "First editions of Monad Press books generally say: 'First edition, (year).' In some cases a book will be labeled 'First U.S. edition, (year)' or 'Monad Press edition, (year),' and the year of previous publication will be given: 'First French edition, 1939' or 'copyright 1936 by—.' If no printing number is given, the printing is the first."

1981 Statement: *See* 1976 Statement

MONARCH LINE (REPUBLIC OF IRELAND)

1988 Statement: *See* 1988 Statement of Wolfhound Press (Republic of Ireland)

MOODY PRESS

1947 Statement: "We do not follow a definite plan of marking the various editions of the books we publish. Only on a few of our books are we indicating whether it is first, second or a subsequent edition. This is a matter which we are studying."

Statement for 1960: "Our hardbacks normally indicate 2nd, 3rd printings, etc. Thus one without that identification in cloth (hardback) could be assumed to be a first printing.

"The same appears to be true on trade (quality) paperbacks.

"However, on mass paperbacks we give the number of printings only on a select number of fastselling titles—and this is only a recent policy, so earlier editions probably do not have the printing indicated."

This practice was followed for books published from 1949 through 1981.

1976 Statement: *See* Statement for 1960

1982 Statement: "Beginning in 1982, *all* books published will indicate printing and year printed, regardless of type of book."

1989 Statement: *See* 1982 Statement

MORAVIAN MUSIC FOUNDATION

1988 Statement: *See* 1988 Statement of Associated University Presses

THE THOMAS MORE ASSOCIATION (PRESS)

1976 Statement: "No designation is used."

1981 Statement: "[Any of our books] can be presumed to be a first printing unless otherwise indicated on the copyright page."

1988 Statement: *See* 1981 Statement

MOREHOUSE

See 1976 Statement of Morehouse-Barlow Co., Inc.

MOREHOUSE-BARLOW CO., INC.

1976 Statement: "Most Morehouse-Barlow volumes are first editions and are not identified as such. However, subsequent printings and editions are usually denoted as 'Revised Edition' or 'Second Printing' or 'nth printing' on the cover, title page or copyright page. It is safe to assume that in most, though not quite all, cases, books bearing the Morehouse (pre-1935)

Morehouse-Gorham (1935-1958) or Morehouse-Barlow (1958-present) imprint are first editions unless otherwise noted."
1981, 1988 Statements: *See* 1976 Statement

MOREHOUSE-GORHAM
See 1976 Statement of Morehouse-Barlow Co., Inc.

MORGAN & LESTER
1988 Statement: *See* 1988 Statement of Morgan & Morgan Inc.

MORGAN & MORGAN INC.
1988 Statement: "Relevant information is given on copyright page, 'First Edition' is rarely used but '2nd (3rd, 4th etc.) printing' and/or 'Revised Edition' is used.

"[First Edition] was used in earlier publications, 1930s through early 60s, first [as] MORGAN & LESTER, then [as] MORGAN & MORGAN.

WILLIAM MORROW AND CO. INC.
1928 Statement: "The first printing of our books either carry on the page following the title page the line

First Printing......

or in some cases merely the copyright notice without anything further.

"Subsequent printings are always designated as 'Second Printing' or 'Third Printing,' as the case may be.

"A new edition of the book is also clearly marked.

"You will note that we distinguish between editions and printing. An edition with us is where some material change has been made in the copy or the make up of the book."

1937 Statement: *See* 1928 Statement
1947 Statement: "First printings of Morrow books carry only the copyright notice, except in a few instances the line 'FIRST PRINTING (month—year)' below the copyright notice. All subsequent printings are marked 'SECOND PRINTING, THIRD PRINTING, FOURTH PRINTING,' as the case may be, and any new editions of the book are clearly marked. A distinction should be made between an edition and a printing, edition having some material change in the text or format of the publication."

1976 Statement: First editions are designated by the lack of any reference to the edition on the copyright page. Revised editions are designated on the copyright page.

Printings are indicated by a line of code numbers on the copyright page. The following line indicates a first printing, 1976:

1 2 3 4 5 80 79 78 77 76

The "1" would be deleted for a second printing.
1981 Statement: "First Editions are indicated on the copyright page for all William Morrow and Company, Inc. publications bearing the William Morrow and Company, Inc. imprint as follows:

1) By the absence of any acknowledgment of previous publication of the book in its entirety;

2) By the words 'First Edition' printed on the line directly above the line of code numbers indicating the printing; and

3) By the fact that the line of code numbers indicating the printing begins with the numeral '1.'

The line of code numbers and the 'First Edition' line appear on the copyright page of a first printing as follows:
First Edition
1 2 3 4 5 6 7 8 9 10
"A William Morrow and Company, Inc. publication that is a first edition published in the U.S.A. but which has been previously published in some other country is indicated on the copyright page as follows:

1) By the words 'First U.S. Edition' printed on the line directly above the line of code numbers indicating the printing and

2) By the fact that the line of code numbers indicating the printing begins with the numeral '1' (see above).

"A William Morrow and Company, Inc. Publication that is published under the Morrow Quill Paperbacks imprint as a first edition under that imprint (but which has previously been published in a William Morrow and Company, Inc. hardcover edition or is being simultaneously published in a William Morrow and Company, Inc. hardcover edition) is indicated on the copyright page as follows:

1) By the absence of any acknowledgment of previous publication of the book in its entirety;

2) By the words 'First Morrow Quill Paperback Edition' printed on the line directly above the line of code numbers indicating the printing; and

3) By the fact that the line of code numbers indicating the printing begins with the numeral '1.'

The line of code numbers and the 'First Morrow Quill Paperback Edition' line are indicated on the copyright page as follows:
First Morrow Quill Paperback Edition
1 2 3 4 5 6 7 8 9 10
"If, however, a First Morrow Quill Paperback Edition has been previously published in a Morrow paperback imprint no longer in existence, then the line 'First Morrow Quill Paperback Edition' will not be printed; the fact that it is a First Morrow Quill Paperback Edition will be indicated by the fact that the line of code numbers indicating the printing begins with the numeral '1' (see above)."

1988 Statement: "William Morrow and Company, and all of its imprints and divisions, place the following information on the copyright page of first editions:
First Edition
1 2 3 4 5 6 7 8 9 10
"On subsequent printings, the number corresponding to the previous edition is deleted as is the edition statement, so that the second printing of the above books would read:
2 3 4 5 6 7 8 9 10
"We designate the first printing as the actual number of copies that have been ordered from the printer when the book is first produced. Should we ask for more copies, those copies become the second printing."

MORROW JUNIOR BOOKS

1988 Statement: *See* 1988 Statement of William Morrow and Co. Inc.

MORROW QUILL PAPERBACKS

1981, 1988 Statements: *See* 1981, 1988 Statements of William Morrow and Co. Inc.

MOSAIC PRESS (CANADA)

1988 Statement: "First printings are always noted as Copyright....and year. Second and subsequent printings are noted as 'x printing, year.' "

THE C. V. MOSBY COMPANY

1976 Statement: "No designation is used for the first edition. All editions after the first are indicated by stating '2nd edition', '3rd edition', etc., after the title."

1981 Statement: *See* 1976 Statement

1988 Statement: "Mosby still follows the practice outlined in our 1976 Statement. All Mosby subsidiaries follow this practice."

MOUNTAIN PRESS PUBLISHING CO.

1976 Statement: "First editions are not designated as such; it can be assumed that we indicate only those printings or editions after the first."

1981, 1988 Statements: *See* 1976 Statement

THE MOUNTAINEERS BOOKS

1988 Statement: "Since we started publishing books in 1961, first editions of our titles have sometimes been identifiable by the words 'First Edition,' and sometimes by the *absence* of printing histories on the copyright pages. Subsequent printings, however, will usually be marked, for example: First printing September 1984, second printing November 1986.

"An illustration of copyright-page printing information for second and succeeding editions is the following:

First edition May 1980, second printing January 1981
Second edition September 1982, second printing November 1983, third printing January 1985
Third edition May 1986

"Since 1986 or 7, we have been using for many (but not all) titles the following alternative numerical symbols:

0 9 8 7   the last number on the right on this line represents the year of printing (e.g. 1987)
5 4 3 2 1   the last number on the right on this line represents the number of the printing; the first, in this example."

A. R. MOWBRAY & CO. LTD. (ENGLAND)

1976 Statement: "A book is a first edition (first printing) unless otherwise stated."

1981 Statement: *See* 1976 Statement

JOHN MUIR PUBLICATIONS

1976 Statement: "We designate a first edition by printing 'First Edition, 19.. '. Then we say 'Second Printing' if the book has not been changed. If the book is substantially revised, we say the above plus 'Second Edition & date.' "

1981, 1988 Statements: *See* 1976 Statement

MULLER (ENGLAND)

1988 Statement: *See* 1988 Statement of Century Hutchinson Publishing Group Limited (England)

FREDERICK MULLER, LTD. (ENGLAND)

1937 Statement: "On the back of the title pages of our books is a bibliographical note which reads: 'First published by Frederick Muller Ltd. (here follows the year in which the book was published).'

"When a second edition is published we add the words: 'Second Edition,' and the year. We then also add the month when the first edition was published."

1947 Statement: *See* 1937 Statement

1988 Statement: *See* 1988 Statement of Muller (England)

MULTI-MEDIA PUBLISHING, INC.

1988 Statement: *See* 1988 Statement of The C. V. Mosby Company

MULTIMEDIA PUBLISHING CORPORATION

1976 Statement: "1. We put in a new book—First Edition.

2. If we print more we put—Second printing, Third Printing, etc.

3. Only if we change content, introduction etc. do we note —2nd Revised Edition, etc.—and this we put on copyright page."

1981 Statement: *See* 1976 Statement

JOHN MURRAY (ENGLAND)

1928 Statement: *See* 1937 Statement

1937 Statement: "The practice we have followed for many years is to omit the date from the title page and to insert at the back of the title page the words 'First Edition' together with the year of issue.

"In the case of certain books, chiefly those printed for private circulation, the date appears at the foot of the title page with no biblio on the reverse."

1947 Statement: *See* 1937 Statement

1982 Statement: "We now very rarely print the date of publication on the title page. Even in those rare cases we always print 'First published' or 'First Edition' with the date, as well as the copyright notice on the reverse of the title page."

1988 Statement: *See* 1982 Statement

MURRAY & GEE, INC.

1947 Statement: "We have no set rule in this respect. In general, however, the first editions carry only the copyright line and subsequent editions list the printing: second, third, etc."

THE MUSEUM OF MODERN ART

1981 Statement: "First editions of our books are identified negatively. That is, we do nothing to say 'first edition' but we try to be quite careful about indicating on the copyright page 'Second printing', 'Third printing,' 'Revised Second Edition,' or whatever."

1988 Statement: *See* 1981 Statement

THE MUSEUM OF NEW MEXICO PRESS

1976 Statement: "Our title page imprint has the date of publication. The c/r page has the year of c/r & only second printings are indicated. '2nd ptg...., etc.' We don't have a steadfast rule as yet."

1981 Statement: "Our title page imprint does not include the date of publication. The c/r page has the year of c/r & only second printings are indicated."

1988 Statement: "Our title page imprint does not include the date of publication. The c/r page has the year (indicating year of publication) of c/r & only second printings (and thereafter) are indicated."

MUSEUM PRESS, LTD. (ENGLAND)
1947 Statement: "In the case of first editions of all our books, the year of issue is placed under our imprint on the title page. In the case of subsequent editions the bibliography appears on the reverse of title."

BARROWS MUSSEY, INC.
1937 Statement: *See* 1937 Statement of Loring & Mussey, Inc.

MYCROFT AND MORAN
1947 Statement: *See* 1947 Statement of Arkham House

MYSTERIOUS PRESS
1988 Statement: "The Mysterious Press had its first book published in 1976 and it, as well as all subsequent books, identified its first printing on the copyright page, employing the term 'First Edition' or 'First Printing.' The terms were used interchangeably, depending upon the typesetter. When second and later printings were called for, the words 'Second Printing' (or third, etc.) were added to the copyright page. In 1986, we adopted the policy of running numbers from 1 to 10 in addition to using the words 'First Edition' or 'First Printing.' The first printing begins the number sequence with number '1,' the second printing retains the phrase 'First Edition' but the number sequence begins with the number '2' and so on.

"My only subsidiary is Penzler Books and the same practice pertains."

MYSTERY HOUSE
1947 Statement: *See* 1947 Statement of Samuel Curl, Inc

MYSTIC SEAPORT MUSEUM
1988 Statement: "We normally designate the first edition of a work with a 'First Edition' line on the copyright page. Second editions are either so designated on the copyright page, or else implied with a multiple copyright date. We do not distinguish the different printings of an edition."

THE MYTHOLOGY COMPANY
1947 Statement: "The first edition of *This Was My Newport* may be recognized by a strange error occurring on page 160 line 20. The reading should be: 'The son of Dr. Parkman murdered by Dr. Webster.' "

N

THE NAIAD PRESS, INC.
1981 Statement: "We use FIRST EDITION as our mark. When we go into other printings we add SECOND PRINTING and so on. Thus, absence of any other marking is indication that it is first edition, first printing. We have always done this."
1988 Statement: "Everything is the same . . . . We try very hard to be very uniform about our habits on the verso of the title page recognizing that nothing in a book is so vital as that page of information."

NAL
See New American Library

NAL BOOKS
1988 Statement: *See* 1988 Statement of New American Library

EVELEIGH NASH AND GRAYSON, LTD. (ENGLAND)
(Became Grayson & Grayson, Ltd [England].)
1928 Statement: "On the reverse of the title page:
First published in....
Second printing........."

NATIONAL AERONAUTICS & SPACE ADMINISTRATION (NASA)
1988 Statement: "All NASA publications are printed through the U. S. Government Printing Office, and are offered for sale by the U. S. Superintendent of Documents, Washington, DC. NASA publications are not protected by copyright and are in the public domain. The year of publication is most often not indicated in a NASA publication. Reprints are not differentiated from original printings. No indication is ever given of first or subsequent editions."

NATIONAL FOUNDATION PRESS
1947 Statement: "The National Foundation Press, a division of National Foundation for Education in American Citizenship, usually does not expressly identify first printings as such. Subsequent printings are identified as 'second printing,' and so on. Second editions are expressly identified. The first edition can in actuality be identified by the absence of any reference at all to the printing or edition."

NATIONAL GEOGRAPHIC SOCIETY
1976 Statement: "The Society has no particular symbol or identification mark to indicate first printings. Most of our larger books contain a notice on the copyright page indicating whether the work is a first edition or a later printing. On some of the Society's other publications, the original copyright date, which coincides with the original publication date, and the dates of subsequent copyright registration and printings are marked on the copyright page.

"There is no simple way to ascertain whether early editions of the National Geographic Magazine are original editions or reprints. The best information relating to identification of original editions of the Magazine appears in Edwin Buxbaum's book 'The Collector's Guide to the National Geographic Magazine.'

"In the late 1950's the Society reprinted the first 20 years of National Geographic Magazines. The word 'reprint' appears on the covers of these reprints."
1981, 1988 Statements: *See* 1976 Statement

NATIONAL LIBRARY OF AUSTRALIA (AUSTRALIA)
1988 Statement: "As a government authority the National Library follows guidelines set by the Australian Government Publishing Service.
First editions are identified by:
© (date) National Library of Australia
Subsequent editions are identified by:
© (date) National Library of Australia
First published (date)

Reprinted (date)
"We do not have any additional imprints and subsidiaries."

NATUREGRAPH PUBLISHERS, INC.

1976 Statement: "Many of the early Naturegraph titles have been revised, sometimes 2 or 3 times. First editions are not designated as such, rather, revised editions are—e.g., 'Second revised and enlarged edition' accompanies copyright dates."

1981 Statement: "As we do not identify our books by designating them as a 'first printing,' 'second printing,' etc., all of our books are first editions until, if necessary, they are revised. A revised edition is always identified as such. The previous statement submitted by our company remains valid."

1988 Statement: "Our company hasn't changed practices in the way of identifying printings, and we are a small publisher without imprints and subsidiaries."

THE NAUTICAL & AVIATION PUBLISHING CO.

1988 Statement: "We don't make a point of designating first printings, but on second, third, etc., we mark the month and year.

E.g., *South to Java*:

Second printing, December 1987
Third printing, January 1988

"The information is included on the copyright page."

NAVAL INSTITUTE PRESS

1976 Statement: "The U.S. Naval Institute does not make a practice of identifying books as first editions. Most books don't go beyond a first edition. Those that do are identified as 'Second Edition,' or whatever. So if there is nothing to indicate otherwise, one can be sure the book in hand is a first edition."

1981 Statement: "Like most publishers, the U.S. Naval Institute does not identify books as first editions, only second and succeeding editions. Similarly, the Institute does not identify first printings of first editions, only second and succeeding printings. Hence, if there is no mention of the edition on the title page, and there is also no mention of the printing on the copyright page, then the book is among the first printing of the first edition.

"Books published prior to 1971 carry the imprint of the U.S. Naval Institute; a few published since then do also. Most books published since 1971 carry the imprint of the Naval Institute Press. The U.S. Naval Institute and the Naval Institute Press are one and the same."

1988 Statement: "The [1981] statement is still correct. We do not identify first editions, only subsequent ones."

THE NAYLOR COMPANY

1976 Statement: "Only one date will appear on the copyright page and if it is a second or later edition it should be so stated."

THOMAS NELSON & SONS, LTD. (ENGLAND)

1928 Statement: "We have used the following three phrases on the reverse of the title page in a number of our General and Fiction publications:

First Printed....
First Published....
First Impression....

"When a second impression or a reprint is issued, we usually put the following in the same position:
First Impression....
Second Impression....
First Published....
Reprinted....
1936 Statement: "We may say that the method we now use on the title page of our books is as follows:
First Published ....
Reprinted ...."
1947 Statement: *See* 1936 Statement

NELSON CANADA (CANADA)

1989 Statement: "Until the late 1970's, Nelson Canada had no established method for identifying first editions or printings. Usually the new edition of a book would be denoted on the cover, copyright page and title page as follows: *Nelson Math Second Edition.*

"The printing number would be indicated whether at the front or the back of the book by a print line which would also show the year of printing (see below).

"A standard was established in the late 1970's which now appears on the copyright page of all Nelson Canada titles. This information usually appears at the front of the book. However, occasionally it will appear at the back.

"The standard statement reads:
© Nelson Canada, A Division of International Thomson Limited, YEAR.
Published in YEAR by
Nelson Canada
A Division of International Thomson Limited
1120 Birchmount Road
Scarborough, Ontario"

NELSON, FOSTER & SCOTT, LTD. (CANADA)

1976 Statement: "In reply to the above request we practice the following:
© The Author's name 1976
First edition 1976
Reprinted 1977."

NELSON-HALL PUBLISHERS

1976 Statement: Only those printings and/or editions after the first are indicated.

"Additional printings (or 'impressions') of the first edition are numbered and so identified on the copyright page.

"Subsequent editions (after the first) carry additional copyrights and are clearly identified on the copyright page. We have no secret codes."
These methods of designation do not differ from any previously used.
1981, 1988 Statements: *See* 1976 Statement

NETHERLANDIC PRESS (CANADA)

1989 Statement: "The Netherlandic Press of Windsor, Ontario has no method for identifying first editions. We list all information on the copyright page. However when a book would be reprinted we would indicate this by adding the information 'Second Printing,' and the dates of both the first and second printing."

NEW AMERICAN LIBRARY

1988 Statement: "New American Library clearly designates on the copyright page first printings of first editions in the imprints Signet, Signet Classic, Mentor, Onyx, Plume, Meridian, and NAL Books by the words:

First Printing, (date)

1 2 3 4 5 6 7 8 9

"Subsequent prints are denoted by the numbers on the above printing line.

"A revised edition would contain the words:

First Printing, Revised Edition, (date)

1 2 3 4 5 6 7 8 9

"When we reprint a book we indicate that it has been previously published by another publisher or by New American Library in another imprint by the following:

First (current imprint name) Printing, (date)

1 2 3 4 5 6 7 8 9"

NEW AMSTERDAM BOOKS

1989 Statement: "Usually, we say 'First Printing.' Sometimes the hand of the potter shakes."

NEW DIRECTIONS

1947 Statement: "Unfortunately for any collector, there is no standard way to tell a first printing of our books. The points vary in each case; they mainly consist of the use of a different color or type of cloth, and sometimes the absence of color printing, the use of offset printing, varying bulk of paper, etc., in later editions."

Statement for 1960: "Starting in 1970 a 'First published' line appears on the copyright page of New Directions books. In earlier years, the absence of a copyright page notice as to second, third etc. printing indicates that the book in hand is most likely a first printing. In the days when it was feasible to store sheets, there were second bindings, not always identical to the true first edition. Very few clothbound editions of New Directions books have ever gone into second printings."

1976 Statement: "There is no way to tell first printings of the early ND books . . . a few years ago, we began putting SECOND PRINTING etc. on the copyright page of reprints."

1981 Statement: "The first editions of the early ND books were not identified in any way but since many of the books did not go into second printings most early ND books are first editions. In recent years all reprints are identifiable since 'Second Printing' and any further reprinting is noted on the copyright page.

1988 Statement: *See* 1981 Statement

NEW ENGLAND PRESS INC.

1988 Statement: "As of about 18 months ago I started using the words 'First Edition' on all initial printings of new works. After the first printing runs out, I simply delete those words and identify which printing it is and give the date, e.g., 'Second printing, October 1988.'

"Previously we had not designated first editions except by the lack of reprint information."

NEW ENGLISH LIBRARY LIMITED (ENGLAND)

1976 Statement: "When we first publish a book, we include on the copyright line the year of publication, and beneath 'first published by New English Library in 1976' and this date will coincide with the copyright notice. If, on the other hand, we buy a book from the American publisher we will mention on the copyright page when and where it was first published. In this instance the year on the copyright line may differ from the English publishing date."

1981 Statement: *See* 1976 Statement

1989 Statement: "Our usual copyright page . . . is slightly different from our previous practice. The line 'First published in Great Britain 19—' shows when our company would first have published a book (it is, I think, unlikely for us to reissue a book in hardcover that has been previously published by another hardback company).

"The second half of our 1976 statement is still valid."

NEW GLIDE PUBLICATIONS

1981 Statement: "We don't usually make a distinction."

THE NEW REPUBLIC BOOK CO., INC.

1976 Statement: "We have not—so far—designated our first editions or first printings in any special way.

"We would note a second or revised edition on the jacket and on the title page."

1981 Statement: "NRB (New Republic Books) became an 'imprint' (actually, it's a co-publishing arrangement) of Holt, Rinehart, & Winston in December, 1980. Their method of first edition designation will be ours, as they produce and publish all our books."

NEW SCIENCE LIBRARY

1988 Statement: *See* 1988 Statement of Shambhala Publications, Inc.

THE NEW SOUTH COMPANY

1981 Statement: A first printing is not identified as such. However, all printings or editions after the first are indicated on the copyright page.

1988 Statement: *See* 1981 Statement

THE NEW SOUTH WALES UNIVERSITY PRESS LIMITED (AUSTRALIA)

1988 Statement: "We generally do not specify the first printing of a first edition—we simply append the year to the copyright convention e.g. © Keith Amos 1988. However, if the book is subsequently revised or reprinted more than once we sometimes provide more detail though we rarely include the month of publication."

NEW STAR BOOKS (CANADA)

1988 Statement: "Since 1982, the usual form in which information regarding the edition and form of one of our titles has appeared on our copyright pages is as follows:

'Copyright © 1989 [for example] by [name of copyright holder]
'First Printing [month and year of first printing of first edition]
'1 2 3 4 5 93 92 91 90 89'

"When we reprint a book we opaque the lowest number on the left side of this bottom line. The lowest remaining number would indicate the printing number of a given book. Similarly, the number furthest right on that last line would be opaqued as necessary so that the right-hand number would be the year in which the copy of the book that you hold was printed.

"This convention was not generally used by us before 1982, but in almost all cases where a book was reprinted, this information was made known on the copyright page of the reprint.

"Previous to but not including 1989, no titles originated by New Star Books were reissued by us or by any other press in a revised edition.

"Previous to 1974, when the press's name was changed to New Star Books, titles published by the same press were issued under the imprint of 'Vancouver Community Press' or 'VCP,' and 'Georgia Straight Writing Series' or 'GSWS.' To my knowledge, none of the titles bearing these imprints was ever reprinted or issued by us in a new edition."

NEW YORK CULTURE REVIEW PRESS
1976 Statement:
" 'First Edition'
"Thereafter:
2nd Printing, Date
3rd Printing (Revised), Date
4th Printing, Date
5th Printing, # Copies in Print, Date."

NEW YORK GRAPHIC SOCIETY
1976 Statement: "We are now a part of Little, Brown and Company so we follow their style:
'First Edition' is printed on the copyright page, followed by a code, e.g.
'T 10/76' (Trade, October, 1976).
Alternatively the words 'First Printing' are used.
"Prior to our affiliation with Little, Brown we generally used the words 'First printing,' or in the case of books imported from foreign publishers, 'First published by.....' If the edition or printing is not specified it generally means the first edition, as subsequent printings are identified as 'Second printing,' etc."
1981 Statement: "We are now a part of Little, Brown and Company so we follow their style:
'First Edition' is printed on the copyright page.
Alternatively the words 'First Printing' are used.
"Prior to our affiliation with Little, Brown we generally used the words 'First printing,' or in the case of books imported from foreign publishers, 'First published by....' 'First U.S. edition.' If the edition or printing is not specified it generally means the first edition, as subsequent printings are identified as 'Second printing, 19..,' etc."
1988 Statement: *See* 1988 Statement of New York Graphic Society Books/Little, Brown

NEW YORK GRAPHIC SOCIETY BOOKS / LITTLE, BROWN
1988 Statement: " 'First Edition' is printed on the copyright page. Alternatively the words 'First Printing' are used.
"In the case of books imported from foreign publishers, 'First published by ...,' 'First U.S. edition' is used. If the edition or printing is not specified it generally means the first edition, as subsequent printings are identified as 'Second printing, 19..,' etc."

NEW YORK ZOETROPE

1989 Statement: "We designate our first editions by printing a statement on the copyright page, such as, 'First Edition' or 'First Printing' followed by the month and year. First and subsequent editions bear a '5 4 3 2 1' indicator, also on the copyright page."

GEORGE NEWNES, LTD. (ENGLAND)

1928 Statement: "So far as this firm is concerned we have no fixed rule. It so happens that the greater part of our Book publishing work is concerned with the re-issue of books that have already appeared in library editions.

"In cases where we do publish original work ourselves, we do not mark our first editions in any way. On our second and subsequent editions or impressions we generally state on the page facing the title page the number of editions that have been published with the date of their publication, thus: 'First Impression May, 1928, Second Impression July 1928,' and so on."

1937 Statement: "We have no fixed rule. The greater part of our Book publishing work is concerned with the re-issue of books that have already appeared in library editions.

"In cases where we do publish original work ourselves, we usually print the word 'copyright' and the date of issue on the back of the title page of the first edition of a book. On our second and subsequent editions or impressions we generally state under this the number of editions that have been published with the date of their publication, thus: 'First Impression May, 1936, Second Impression July, 1936' and so on."

1947 Statement: "Our usual rule now is to insert on the back of the title page of every new book the date of publication, for example, 'First published...........October 1947,' or sometimes the year only, as 'First published......1947.'

"Subsequent reprints or editions are noted as 'Second Edition....... December 1947,' or again, the year only.

"Also, on the back of the title page, we include the words 'copyright' and 'All rights Reserved.'

"The previous note which we sent to you does not now apply, as at that time we dealt chiefly with cheap reprints of novels.

"With the exception of two special Series, namely the 'WILLIAM' books and the 'SUDDEN' titles, we have now discontinued the issue of Fiction, and our Catalogue is devoted almost entirely to Technical works, dealing with Engineering, Electrical, Building, Radio, Automobile, etc. publications; also Children's Books.

"We publish too, a small number of General Books dealing with Literature, Art, etc."

IVOR NICHOLSON & WATSON, LTD. (ENGLAND)
(Successors to Elkin Mathews & Marrot, Ltd. [England])

1936 Statement: "Our first editions are indicated by the words 'First published in 1936' on the title page verso. Subsequent issues and impressions are added below and the month of original publication is also included, i.e.:

First Edition......................May 1936
Reprinted.........................May 1936
Reprinted........................June 1936

"This is now our invariable practice, although since the firm started in 1931 various methods have been used."
1947 Statement: *See* 1936 Statement

NIGHTWOOD EDITIONS (CANADA)
1989 Statement: "None of our editions are reprinted—unless indicated on the copyright page as a second or subsequent printing."

JAMES NISBET & CO., LTD. (ENGLAND)
1928 Statement: *See* 1937 Statement
1937 Statement: "It is our practice to insert the date of our First and subsequent Editions of general books on the reverse of the title page.
"We much regret that we cannot tell you when this practice commenced, but we have dated our editions over a considerable period."
1947 Statement: *See* 1937 Statement

THE NONESUCH PRESS, LTD. (ENGLAND)
1928 Statement: *See* 1937 Statement
1937 Statement: "Our practice is to date our books, whether they be first or subsequent editions, upon the title page; and to record upon the back of the title page or elsewhere the particular impression to which the copy belongs.
"This has been our practice since the publication of our first book in 1923.
1948 Statement: "Our practice nowadays and since the early 1940's is to date the particular impression to which the copy belongs on the title page, and to record the date of the first edition on the title verso."

NONPAREIL BOOKS
1988 Statement: *See* 1988 Statement of David R. Godine, Publisher, Inc.

NOONDAY PRESS
1988 Statement: *See* 1988 Statement of Farrar, Straus & Giroux, Inc.

NORTH ATLANTIC BOOKS
1976 Statement: "No particular method is used to designate first editions. Second editions, of which we have not had any so far, will be marked as such. In the case of *Io*, it is more difficult, and a different system is needed for almost every issue. For instance, in number 7, only a small difference on the last page distinguishes first from second edition. Other *Io*'s like 1, 2, 3, 4, 5 state second edition. 6 is also difficult to tell. 8 is an enlarged edition. But if you are just asking about North Atlantic, there are none so far."
1981 Statement: "There is no special method of designating first editions for either North Atlantic Books or *Io*. Those issues of *Io* that have second editions are: 1, 2, 3, 4, 5, 6, 7, 8, 11, 24, and 25. In all cases except #7, there is some sort of double-dating or redating on the copyright page. Issue #4 also has a third edition, enlarged and revised.
"The North Atlantic Books that have second editions are: *Selected Poems* by Diane di Prima (enlarged, with different cover color and different dates on the cover) and *Ranger Volume I*, by Theodore Enslin, the second edition of which is pink instead of blue and extensively revised. *Essence of T'ai Chi Ch'uan*, the verse translation of the t'ai chi classics, has three going on four editions, and each of the later editions is marked by the edition number on the copyright page."
1988 Statement: "We often run second, third, etc., editions without any indication."

NORTH POINT PRESS

1981 Statement: "We do not designate first printings. However we will designate subsequent printings, with a new slug on the copyright page indicating 'Second Printing,' 'Third Printing,' etc. This has not yet been necessary."

1988 Statement: "We do not designate first printings. However we will designate subsequent printings, with a new slug on the copyright page indicating 'Second Printing,' 'Third Printing,' etc.

NORTHEASTERN UNIVERSITY PRESS

1988 Statement: "We print, below the line 'Manufactured in the United States of America,' a line of numbers showing the year of publication preceded by the next four or five years in descending order and followed by the numbers 5 through 1. For example:

94 93 92 91 90 89 5 4 3 2 1

"This shows that the book was first printed in 1989. When it is reprinted in, say, two years, the 90 and the 89 will be deleted by the printer, and the line will read:

94 93 92 91 5 4 3 2

—showing that the 2d printing was in 1991.

"A revised edition (very rare) is so noted by a new copyright notice: 'Revised edition © 1985 by Joe Doe.' (The row of numbers at this point would return to the full row, with '1' at the far right showing first printing of the revised edition)."

This method was adopted around 1984.

NORTHERN ILLINOIS UNIVERSITY PRESS

1976 Statement: "In answer to your questions, we have—so far—no second editions, so we haven't faced the problem of identifying subsequent editions. All books published by NIU Press, unless otherwise noted on the copyright page, are first editions. Second printings (not editions) are usually noted on the copyright page.

"The preceding paragraph does not constitute a formal statement of our policy; it is merely a description of our method of identifying editions and printings."

1981, 1988 Statements: *See* 1976 Statement

NORTH-HOLLAND

1988 Statement: *See* 1988 Statement of Elsevier Science Publishing Company, Inc.

NORTHLAND PRESS

1976 Statement: "We have, since August, 1972, labeled all our books as first editions on the copyright page of each volume.

"Prior to August 1972 there was no such pattern. Some first editions were identified as such. Others were not.

"However, I know of no Northland Press title which when reprinted did not indicate such on the copyright page."

1981 Statement: *See* 1976 Statement

1988 Statement: "We do still follow the practice outlined in the 1981 statement, and all imprints bear the same sort of designation."

NORTH-SOUTH BOOKS (UNITED KINGDOM)

1988 Statement: *See* 1988 Statement of Blackie and Son Limited (United Kingdom)

NORTHWESTERN UNIVERSITY PRESS

1981 Statement. "The first editions of our books generally carry only the copyright date and notice on the copyright page. Subsequent reprints will carry the first printing and second printing, etc., notices and their respective dates. Although the Press has no official policy on this matter, I find this to be the case with almost all of our publications.

"Our Press has no other imprints; we do, however, sometimes distribute books which originate in other University departments, and we do import books from foreign publishers which will carry our imprint."

1988 Statement: "The first editions of our books carry the copyright date and notice on the copyright page. Subsequent editions include all printing notices and their respective dates. We have no other imprints."

NORTHWOODS PRESS

1988 Statement: "We do not designate first editions or first printings, but we do designate successive editions or printings."

W. W. NORTON & COMPANY, INC.

1937 Statement: "On books when first published by us, we run a legend on the copyright page reading 'First edition.' On subsequent printings this legend is deleted, but we do not indicate second, third, etc., printings in the books."

1947 Statement: *See* 1937 Statement

1976 Statement: "Our method of identifying first impressions is shown by . . . the line of numbers across the bottom of the copyright page. When the second impression is made the number 1 will be dropped from the line; when the third impression is made the number 2 will be dropped, and so on."

1981, 1988 Statements: *See* 1976 Statement

NUNAGA PUBLISHING CO., LTD. (CANADA)

1976 Statement: *See* 1976 Statement of Antonson Publishing Ltd. (Canada)

O

THE OAKWOOD PRESS (ENGLAND)

1947 Statement: "All our first editions simply bear the imprint 'Published by' and the date, whereas further editions or reprints carry the imprint 'First published..... Second editions (or reprint).....' Thus as far as our books are concerned the absence of a statement to the contrary in the front-papers stamps it as a first edition.

"This company has been in existence since 1936; before that date it was known as the Four O's Publishing Co. (1931)."

OASIS BOOKS (ENGLAND)

1976 Statement: "Oasis Books first editions are identified by the statement 'First published in (year) by Oasis Books, (address)' to be found on the reverse of the title page, or by the statement beginning 'First published in

(month) (year) by Oasis Books (address)...' to be found beneath our logotype on the page immediately following the last page of the book."
1981 Statement: "[The 1976 statement] is still an accurate description of the method by which Oasis Books designates its first editions. Perhaps the only rider to add to it is that the method used in Paragraph 1 is the most frequently used in the books produced since 1976.

"But this does not mean that the second method will never be used again, so that statement should stand as well. No other methods of designating first editions are likely to be used. Second editions always have the words 'second edition' and the date appended after the first statement."

OBELISK
1988 Statement: *See* 1988 Statement of E. P. Dutton & Co., Inc.

O'BRIEN EDUCATIONAL (REPUBLIC OF IRELAND)
1981, 1988 Statements: *See* 1981, 1988 Statements of The O'Brien Press (Republic of Ireland)

THE O'BRIEN PRESS (REPUBLIC OF IRELAND)
1981 Statement: "Normally we would do the following:
First published 1981
by The O'Brien Press
20 Victoria Road
Dublin 6, Ireland.
"You will note our new address. Previously it will have read 11 Clare Street, Dublin 2.
"Our other imprint, O'Brien Educational, is done in the same way except with the different imprint name."
1988 Statement: *See* 1981 Statement

OCEANA PUBLICATIONS, INC.
1976 Statement: "We make no distinction at the outset, either with regard to editions, or with regard to printings. If a book goes to a second printing (rare), we will sometimes indicate 'second printing' on the copyright page. If it goes to a second edition, we will usually indicate with 'second edition' on either the copyright or title pages, or both."
1981 Statement: "The [1976] statement which is printed in *A First Edition?* concerning Oceana's method of designating the first printing of a first edition is still accurate. We have made no changes in our method."
1988 Statement: *See* 1981 Statement

THE OCTOPUS PUBLISHING GROUP PLC (ENGLAND)
1989 Statement: "I apologise for the delay in responding; the Group's archive library is still in the process of being developed and until recently we did not have all the books relevant to your query.

"The Octopus Group comprises a number of publishers, the major ones being: the Heinemann Group; Secker & Warburg; Methuen; Octopus; and the Hamlyn Group. Smaller publishers coming under the Octopus umbrella include: Mitchell Beazley; Leo Cooper; Ginn; Brimax; Eyre & Spottiswoode; George Philip; and Osprey."
BRIMAX: "First printings have the statement 'published by Brimax Books .... 19--'. The absence of any note indicating subsequent printings will indicate first printing."

LEO COOPER: "Leo Cooper is an independent imprint of the Octopus Publishing Group. After leaving Warne, he became associated first with Secker & Warburg, then William Heinemann (both now part of the Octopus Group). First printings are indicated by the statement 'first published in 19--' and the absence of any note of subsequent printings."

COUNTRY LIFE: "Our archive copies only go back to 1903; from this date up to and including 1925 first printings are indicated by the date on the title page and no additional information on the title verso. From 1928 up to and including 1967 the statement on the title verso reads 'first published 19--' or 'first published in England 19--' (if previously published in another country). The absence of information about subsequent or earlier printings should indicate a first printing. From 1968 when Country Life became part of the Hamlyn Publishing Group, first printings follow the Hamlyn practice."

GINN: "First publication is indicated by the date in the copyright statement. Information about later editions or impressions is always included. Therefore, the absence of such information would indicate a first edition."

THE HAMLYN GROUP: "1960's, 70's and early 80's publications contain only a copyright line to indicate date of publication and first printing. From 1983 the statement on the title verso reads 'first published 19—.' For both periods the absence of additional information (earlier copyright dates as well as reprint or foreign printing details) should indicate a first printing. Other imprints such as Gondola, Spring and Rainbow follow the same practice. (Gondola and Spring are in fact almost totally reprint imprints.) Acquired companies such as Dean and Son usually follow the same practice from the date of acquisition. The Dean publishing company began at the turn of the nineteenth century. However first printings of the publications before the late 1960's will be extremely hard to identify as neither date of publication nor copyright line was included."

THE HEINEMANN GROUP: "From William Heinemann's first publication in 1890 up to and including 1921, first printings have just the year on the title page. Subsequent printings and editions would be indicated on the title verso. From 1923 to date the statement on the title verso reads 'first published, 19—' or 'first published in Great Britain 19—' (when it has previously been published in another country). In the absence of any note of subsequent reprintings or editions, it may be assumed that the book is a first printing. However, I have noticed that impressions in the same year as first publication were—very occasionally—not indicated."

METHUEN: "From the first publications in 1889 up to and including 1903, first printings have just the year on the title page. Subsequent editions are listed on the title verso or occasionally indicated on the title page. However, if words such as '43rd Thousand' appear on the title page the book is going to be a later edition despite no statement to that effect. From 1904 to the 1970's the statement on the title verso reads: 'first published in 19—.' 1980's publications (excepting children's) have the statement 'first published in Great Britain 198-' regardless of whether the work has been previously published in another country. If the work has been published previously by another company or in another language this will be indicated. In conclusion, the absence of printing history notes should indicate a first printing, however I have noticed that reprints and even different editions issued in the first year of publication are not always indicated in any way in the book itself.

"Methuen and Co. (the academic division of Methuen) was amalgamated with Routledge in 1986 when Associated Book Publishers bought Routledge. At the end of 1987, International Thomson bought out ABP and sold on Methuen London, Methuen Children's, Pitkin Pictorial, and Eyre & Spottiswoode to the Octopus Group. Methuen and Co. remained but lost the Methuen name (now with Octopus) and became absorbed into Routledge."

MITCHELL BEAZLEY: "First printings have a copyright statement and date; no statement as to 'first published'. Subsequent editions will be indicated but reprints are not always noted so identification of a first printing would be difficult."

OCTOPUS: "From the earliest books in 1972 to date, first printings are indicated by the statement 'first published (in) 19—.' An absence of any notes about subsequent printings or an earlier copyright will confirm first printing."

OSPREY: "First printings have the statement 'published in 19--.' The absence of any additional printing notes will indicate a first printing."

SECKER & WARBURG: "Our archive is incomplete for Secker & Warburg. Up to 1937, the date of publication appears on the title page. Note of subsequent printings is made on the title verso. During the 1940's and 1950's the statement appears on the title verso. It reads 'first published 19—.' From the early 1960's to date the statement reads 'first published in England [latterly 'Great Britain'] 19—' regardless of whether the work has been previously published in another country. Printing history notes are always included on the title verso, therefore their absence will indicate a first printing."

THE ODYSSEY PRESS, INC.

1947 Statement: "We indicate every first edition of one of our books by printing the line, 'First Edition' just beneath the copyright notice of the book. In subsequent printings we change the line to read 'Second Printing,' 'Third Printing,' and so on. If the book is revised, the first edition of it is, in the same manner, called 'First Printing of Revised Edition,' and subsequent printings are labeled 'Second Printing of Revised Edition,' and so on."

OHARA PUBLICATIONS, INCORPORATED

1976 Statement: "We do not use any particular identifying statement to identify first editions. As the books move into second, third, etc. printings that is designated on the title page.

"If a book is a reprint that is explained in the publisher's foreword."

1981, 1988 Statements: *See* 1976 Statement

OHIO STATE UNIVERSITY PRESS

1976 Statement: "The Ohio State University Press does not identify in any special way the first editions of the books that it publishes."

All printings of a first edition are indicated except for the very first. The absence of any statement would indicate the first printing of a first edition.

1981, 1988 Statements: *See* 1976 Statement

OHIO UNIVERSITY PRESS

1988 Statement: "Ohio University Press does not designate its first printings in any way, but we note subsequent printings by printing number

('Second Printing') and date ('December 1999'). This has been our standard practice since 1965."
See also The Swallow Press, Inc.

OLIVER & BOYD
1976, 1981 Statements: *See* 1976, 1981 Statements of Longman Inc.

OLIVER & BOYD, LTD. (SCOTLAND)
1937 Statement: "It is our practice to put the date of publication of any book on the title page itself. If the book is reprinted, the date of the reprint appears on the title page and a bibliographical description on the back of the title, e.g.

First Edition 1922
Reprinted 1923
Second Edition 1924"

1947 Statement: "Our first editions are indicated by the words on the title page verso—'First Published—' or 'First Edition—' depending on whether the matter is completely new or whether it has appeared, or in part appeared, in some previous publication.

"It may or may not also appear on the title page, this being decided on the basis of appropriateness to the title page layout. Subsequent editions are added below on title page verso thus:

First Published	September 1944
Second Edition—Revised	May 1945
Reprinted	November 1945

"This is our current practice but there have naturally been many variations since our first publication in 1778."

101 PRODUCTIONS
1976 Statement: "We state the printing date of reprints on our copyright page. Thus, any book without a printing date, only the copyright date, would be a first edition."
1981 Statement: *See* 1976 Statement
1988 Statement: "We are no longer publishing."

ONTARIO FILM INSTITUTE (CANADA)
1981, 1988 Statements: *See* 1981, 1988 Statements of Associated University Presses

OPEN COURT PUBLISHING COMPANY
1981 Statement: "Open Court does not have fixed rules to apply to first editions. When a publication carries the copyright date only on its copyright page, it is an indication of a first edition. We usually designate second printings, second editions, etc."
1988 Statement: "Open Court does not have fixed rules that apply to first editions. When a publication carries the copyright date only on its copyright page, it is an indication of a first edition. Recently we have begun to include the words 'first printing' and the date of publication on the copyright page, where appropriate. We usually designate second printings, second editions, etc."

ORBIS BOOKS
1976 Statement: "We do not designate first editions. We indicate only those printings and/or editions after the first printing. This method is the only one we use and have ever used."

1981, 1988 Statements: *See* 1976 Statement

OREGON HISTORICAL SOCIETY PRESS

1988 Statement: "No specific designation is made for first editions, although numbers 1 through 5 are often listed on the copyright page in anticipation of additional printings. Otherwise each new printing (e.g. 'second printing') or edition (e.g. 'second edition, revised') is listed on the copyright page."

OREGON STATE UNIVERSITY PRESS

1976 Statement: "We use no special means of identifying first impressions, except that second printings and second editions are so indicated."
1981 Statement: *See* 1976 Statement
1988 Statement: "We use no special means of identifying first impressions, except that second and subsequent editions are so indicated."

ORIEL PRESS LTD. (ENGLAND)

1976 Statement: "Our practice is to state the date of first publication on the verso of the title page along with the date of copyright. Any reprintings, or subsequent editions are noted as such on the verso of the title page."
1981 Statement: *See* 1976 Statement
1988 Statement: "We are no longer publishing under the Oriel imprint, but the name is still with us."
See 1988 Statement of Associated Book Publishers (UK) Ltd. (England)

OSPREY (ENGLAND)

1989 Statement: *See* 1989 Statement of The Octopus Publishing Group PLC (England)

OUTDOOR PUBLISHERS

1988 Statement: *See* 1988 Statement of Cobblesmith

OUTPOSTS PUBLICATIONS (ENGLAND)

1976 Statement: "All our publications are 'first editions' in your sense of the term, and all are collections of poetry. We do not make any identifying statements. We do give each title a number in the *OUTPOSTS MODERN POETS SERIES*."
1981 Statement: *See* 1976 Statement

GEORGE OVER (RUGBY), LTD. (ENGLAND)

1928 Statement: "Our practice is to print date of publication only, and in case of later editions to state which."
1937, 1947 Statements: *See* 1928 Statement

THE OVERLOOK PRESS

1976 Statement: "We write 'first printing' on the copyright page. We've been doing this since we started five years ago."
1981 Statement: "Shortly after we wrote you, in 1976, we changed our policy; we no longer write 'first printing.' We write 'first published' or 'first edition' until we go back to press; we then add 'second printing' on the copyright page. On some books, we are happy to report, we add 'fifth printing.' "
1988 Statement: "We now print 'First published in (year) by The Overlook Press' and, as stated in our 1981 Statement, we add designations for each subsequent printing. On some books, we are happy to report, we add 'twenty-second printing.' "

PETER OWEN LTD. PUBLISHERS (ENGLAND)

1976 Statement: "On all our first editions on the reverse of the title page there is marked 'first published by Peter Owen, followed by the year of publication.' If we reprint we state this below."

1981, 1988 Statements: *See* 1976 Statement

OXFORD ILLUSTRATED PRESS (ENGLAND)

1988 Statement: *See* 1988 Statement of Haynes Publishing Group (England)

OXFORD PUBLISHING COMPANY (ENGLAND)

1988 Statement: *See* 1988 Statement of Haynes Publishing Group (England)

OXFORD UNIVERSITY PRESS (ENGLAND)

1928 Statement: "We never, I think, print *first edition* on any first edition. All our title pages are dated. For the information of the public we distinguish 'second edition' i.e. an issue embodying substantial alterations (whether reset or not) from 'second impression' i.e. an issue substantially (though not always identically) the same as the first. I know that this is not quite sound from a bibliographical point of view; but I think publishers in our position are bound to put the convenience of the public first. It is often important for a student to be sure he has the latest edition of a book; but it would be unfair to cause him to buy a mere reprint by calling it 'nth edition' simply."

1937 Statement: "We never, I think, print *first edition* on any first edition. All our title pages of first editions are dated, and so are the title pages of the first printing of editions which we distinguish as 'second,' 'third,' etc. For the information of the public we distinguish 'second edition,' i.e., an issue embodying substantial alterations (whether reset or not) from 'second impression,' i.e., an issue substantially (though not always identically) the same as the first. I know that this is not quite sound from a bibliographical point of view; but I think publishers in our position are bound to put the convenience of the public first. It is often important for a student to be sure he has the latest edition of a book; but it would be unfair to cause him to buy a mere reprint by calling it 'nth edition' simply.

"It is probably unnecessary to explain in this note our regular practice, when we produce an unaltered or corrected 'impression,' of taking the date off the title page and giving the necessary bibliographical information opposite the title page: with us, the absence of the date from the title page is a sign that the issue is not the first printing of an 'edition' in our sense of the term.

"We are afraid we cannot give you the date when we began using our present method of identifying first editions, but it was a good many years ago."

1947 Statement: *See* 1937 Statement

Statement for 1960: "As far as we know, the practice described to you in 1976 was already being followed in previous years, and it is still our practice."

1976 Statement: "Our normal practice is to give the date on the title page for the first edition of a book. On subsequent printings the date is transferred to the verso of the title page, where the dates of the succeeding impressions are given. If there is a new edition, the date is normally given on the title page and then for subsequent impressions transferred to the verso in the same manner as before."

1981, 1989 Statements: *See* 1976 Statement

OXFORD UNIVERSITY PRESS (NEW YORK)

1937 Statement: "In regard to the indicating of First and subsequent printings of books we use in general the system followed by our home office [in England]."

1947 Statement: "We now use in general the following procedure:

"The first edition of a book carries a single copyright line, bearing the date of the first printing. The dates of later printings and editions are given in additional lines under the original copyright line, and in the case of a new edition, the date is also added to the original copyright line. The imprint may then read:

Copyright 1945, 1947, by Oxford University Press,
New York, Inc.
Second printing, 1946
Second edition, revised and/or enlarged, 1947

"However, if the book is a first American edition of one that has been previously published in England or elsewhere, the copyright line bears the date of the original publication, and may read:

Copyright 1945 by the Oxford University Press,
New York, Inc.
First American edition, 1947
First published in England, 1945"

1988 Statement: "The first edition of a book carries a single copyright line, bearing the date of first publication. The dates of later editions are added to the original copyright line as appropriate.

"The current printing of the current edition is listed on a separate line near the foot of the copyright page:

Printing (last digit): 9 8 7 6 5 4 3 2 1

"For each subsequent reprint, the final digit is deleted. We began this designation in December 1980.

"Oxford University Press, Inc. has no subsidiaries."

OXFORD UNIVERSITY PRESS CANADA (CANADA)

1988 Statement: "On the verso of the title page of the books we published in 1988 the following numbers appear: 1234 1098.

"The number 1 at the extreme left indicates this is a first impression and the number 8 at the extreme right indicates the first impression was published in 1988. If a second impression were produced in 1989 then this line would be changed to read: 234 109.

"This practice is followed by the Canadian division of Oxford University Press; I cannot speak with confidence of the policy followed by our other offices around the world.

"I don't know when we started using this method to designate first and subsequent impressions but I believe it's been in practice for some time."

OXMOOR HOUSE, INC.

1976 Statement: "In answer to your query: Oxmoor House does not identify a first edition or a first printing of a first edition of our ordinary books (cookbooks, quilt books, etc.). Our first printings are our first editions. Then we identify second printings as second editions on the copyright page.

"Now in our art books: *Jericho, The American Cowboy, A Southern Album, Southern Antiques and Folk Art,* we not only identify the first edition, we actually number each book of the first edition. Later editions are not numbered and are identified as later editions."

1981 Statement: *See* 1976 Statement

1988 Statement: "Oxmoor House does not now normally number its art books as we once did for first editions. Nothing else has changed."

P

PACIFIC BOOKS

1947 Statement: "Thus far I have made no special indication in a book that it is a first edition. It shows only the copyright date. But for future printings or second editions I have clearly indicated that fact by recording the date of the first printing or first edition and giving the dates of subsequent printings or editions."

1988 Statement: "The statement we supplied previously still is valid."

PACIFIC SEARCH PRESS

1981 Statement: "The copyright notice is the only indication of a first printing of a first edition. This is the only method that we have ever used."

1988 Statement: *See* 1981 Statement

PADRE PRODUCTIONS

1988 Statement: "Padre Productions is a publishing company which includes the following imprints: Bear Flag Books, The Countrywoman's Press, Helm Publishing, International Resources, The Press of MacDonald & Reinecke, as well as Padre Productions.

"Our first editions simply bear the copyright data, usually on the verso of the title page, but occasionally on the title page itself. Subsequent printings and editions (meaning printings with significant revisions), are so noted adjacent to the original copyright notice."

L. C. PAGE & CO.

1928 Statement: "We use practically the same method as Doubleday, Page & Co., to designate our first editions. We print 'first impression' with the month and the year on the reverse of the title page. We do not, however, add the date on the title page."

1937 Statement: "We print 'first impression' with the month and the year on the reverse of the title page. We do not, however, add the date on the title page."

1947 Statement: *See* 1937 Statement

CECIL PALMER (ENGLAND)
(Out of business prior to 1937.)

1928 Statement: "The plan we have always adopted is to print on the back of the title page 'First Edition' and then the year of publication. In the event of further editions, we add to this information the following example:

First Edition	June 1927
Second Edition	September 1927
Third Edition	January 1928"

PAN (ENGLAND)

1988 Statement: *See* 1988 Statement of Pan Books Ltd. (England)

PAN BOOKS LTD. (ENGLAND)

1988 Statement: "I should like to point out to you that Pan Books is still predominantly a reprint house, issuing in paperback form books that have already been published in hard covers. At the moment, about fifteen per cent of our output is original material.

Pan Books Ltd, London
(including Pavanne, Picador, Piccolo and Piper)

"There are four sources for our books, each of which makes a small but significant difference to the way we set out the bibliographical details.

(a) Books first published in Great Britain as hard cover editions;

(b) Books first published elsewhere, then in Great Britain as hard cover editions;

(c) Books first published outside Great Britain, then by Pan Books directly;

(d) Original works.

"These are identified and printed as follows:

(a) First published 19.. by (name of British publisher)

(b) First published in Great Britain 19.. by (name of British publisher) This edition published 19.. by Pan Books Ltd

(c) First published (elsewhere) 19.. by (name of publisher) This edition first published in Great Britain 19.. by Pan Books Ltd

(d) First published 19.. by Pan Books Ltd"

"In each there then follows this information:

(i) Pan Books Address

(ii) A numerical indication of the impression number

(iii) The copyright symbol and the name of the copyright owner

(iv) The ISBN

"A note on (ii): up to about six years ago second and subsequent printings were designated as such by the addition of the legend '2nd printing,' '3rd Printing' and so on. Since then all printings have been indicated by a row of figures—9 down to 1, 19 to 10—with the lowest figure showing the current impression number.

"As far as I can ascertain from looking at books published by Pan in the late 1940s and early 1950s, Pan Books has always followed this pattern of designating the first and subsequent printings.

"A new edition of a book is shown as such, preferably with actual edition number—2nd, 3rd or whatever it is. A reprint with corrections is also specified, usually in cases where the changes are not sufficient to warrant its being called a new edition but with, possibly, a note from the author or publisher drawing the attention of the reader to the fact that advantage has been taken of the reprint to make minor but important changes.

"All the imprints in the Pan stable follow the same procedure."

PANJANDRUM BOOKS

1976 Statement: "On copyright page, it says 1st edition. Used to use a colophon in first 5-6 books I published, but dropped it. Also have poets/writers sign 25 copies, numbered, of first edition, for future collectors."

1981 Statement: "Books published 1971-5: On copyright page, it would state First Edition. Books published after 1975: On copyright page, it states First Printing. Subsequent printings are so stated.

"Colophon: Contained in poetry books published by us between 1971-4. Twenty-five copies of all poetry books published are signed and numbered by the author."

1988 Statement: *See* 1981 Statement

PANTHEON BOOKS, INC.

1947 Statement: "We *always* differentiate subsequent printings of a book by inserting '2nd printing' (or third, or fourth, as the case may be) on the copyright page.

"First printings are either specifically identified by inserting 'First Printing' on the copyright page, or *no mention* of printing or edition is made on copyright page. Whenever nothing to the contrary is mentioned, the edition is the first printing of the title."

1976, 1981 Statements: *See* 1976, 1981 Statements of Random House, Inc.

1988 Statement: *See* 1988 Statement of Schocken Books

PARENT AND CHILD (ENGLAND)

1989 Statement: *See* 1989 Statement of The Octopus Publishing Group PLC (England)

PARENTS' MAGAZINE PRESS

1976 Statement: "Up to the present time, we have not had any method of designating first editions of the books we publish through our book publishing division, Parents' Magazine Press.

"However, beginning with our fall list (1977), we will be designating first and subsequent editions of our books with a line at the end of the copyright information (and preceding the Library of Congress Cataloging in Publication data) as follows:

10 9 8 7 6 5 4 3 2 1

and with each additional printing, one number at the right drops off to indicate edition."

1981, 1988 Statements: *See* 1976 Statement

PARNASSUS IMPRINTS

1988 Statement: "We print 'first edition' on the copyright page. Subsequent printings are designated as 2nd printing, 3rd printing, etc."

ERIC PARTRIDGE, LTD. (SCHOLARTIS PRESS) (ENGLAND)
(Out of business prior to 1949. Oxford University Press took over some publications.)

1937 Statement: "It is our practice to put the date of the publication of any book on the title page itself. If the book is reprinted, the date of the reprint appears on the title page and a bibliographical description on the back of the title page, e.g.

First Edition	1922
Reprinted	1923
Second Edition	1924"

S. W. PARTRIDGE & CO. (ENGLAND)

1947 Statement: *See* 1947 Statement of A. & C. Black, Ltd. (England)

THE PATERNOSTER PRESS LTD. (ENGLAND)

1976 Statement: "There is no difficulty about identifying first editions of our publications since a full bibliographical account appears on the verso of every book that we publish.

"In the absence of any indication to the contrary, it may be safely assumed that a book is a first edition."

1981, 1988 Statements: *See* 1976 Statement

PATHFINDER PRESS

1976 Statement: "Pathfinder Press uses the following form on the data pages of its books:

Copyright © 1976 by Pathfinder Press
All rights reserved
Library of Congress Catalog Card Number
00-00000
ISBN: 0-87348-000-0
Manufactured in the United States of America
First Edition, 1975

"Subsequent printings and editions are listed under the First Edition line, which is retained in all later printings and editions. In earlier years we did not list printings or editions and used only the copyright notice and year. We changed our practice after renewal of copyrights eliminated reference to the original year of publication."

1981, 1989 Statements: *See* 1976 Statement

KEGAN PAUL, TRENCH, TRUBNER & CO., LTD. (ENGLAND)

1947 Statement: "If there is no statement at all as to a second or later edition or impression, the assumption, of course, is that the book is a first edition. In the case of reprints, or new editions, we state this on the reverse of the title page.

"We regret we cannot tell you the date on which this method was started but it has been going on now for a very long period."

1976, 1981 Statements: *See* 1976, 1981 Statements of Routledge & Kegan Paul Ltd. (England)

PAULIST PRESS

1981 Statement: "Paulist Press does not designate first editions."

1988 Statement: *See* 1981 Statement

PAVANNE (ENGLAND)

1988 Statement: *See* 1988 Statement of Pan Books Ltd. (England)

PAYSON & CLARKE, LTD.

(Became Brewer & Warren on Jan. 1, 1930, which later became Brewer, Warren & Putnam, Inc.; all three firms out of business prior to 1937.)

1928 Statement: "We do not put the actual words 'first edition' on the reverse of the title page for the first edition but when we go into the second printing we say 'first printing such and such a date,' 'second printing such and such a date,' therefore, all copies of a book which do not carry such designation may be taken as being 'firsts.' "

PEERAGE (ENGLAND)

1989 Statement: *See* 1989 Statement of The Octopus Publishing Group PLC (England)

PEGASUS (PUBLISHING)

1976 Statement: "First editions are designated on copyright page as first printing, second printing, etc."
1981 Statement: *See* 1981 Statement of Bobbs-Merrill Company, Inc.

PEGASUS PRESS LTD. (NEW ZEALAND)

1976 Statement: "Our usual method of identifying a first edition of our books is to state on the verso of the title page—First Published—and giving the year. In other cases if no date of a second printing or new edition is shown it can be taken that it is a first edition."
1981 Statement: "First editions of our books can be identified from the note normally printed on the verso of the title-page; this carries the words First Published, followed by the date. If no mention is made of a later edition or printing the book can be taken to be a first edition."

PELICAN BOOKS (ENGLAND)

1988 Statement: *See* 1988 Statement of Penguin Publishing Co Ltd. (England)

PELICAN PUBLISHING COMPANY

1976 Statement: "Pelican has no standard method of identifying first editions. First edition may have no designation on copyright page, or it may read first printing. All subsequent editions or printings are so stated on the copyright page."
1981 Statement: *See* 1976 Statement
1988 Statement: "All Pelican first editions carry the copyright date only. Additional printings or editions are so designated.
"Our imprints and subsidiaries do follow our practices."

PELLEGRINI & CUDAHY

1947 Statement: "Our first books came out this spring and to date we have not specified the first printing as such. Our subsequent printings have been so indicated, as:
    1st printing August, 1947
    2nd printing September, 1947
and so forth."

PENDULUM PUBLICATIONS, LTD. (ENGLAND)

1947 Statement: "No method is at present employed by us to identify first printings of our books, although most of them bear a date and when a second edition is produced, this fact is usually imprinted on the verso of the title page."

PENGUIN

1988 Statement: *See* 1988 Statement of Penguin Publishing Co Ltd. (England)

PENGUIN BOOKS LTD (ENGLAND)

1988 Statement: *See* 1988 Statement of Penguin Publishing Co Ltd. (England)

PENGUIN BOOKS AUSTRALIA LTD. (AUSTRALIA)

1988 Statement: *See* 1988 Statement of Penguin Publishing Co Ltd. (England)

PENGUIN BOOKS CANADA LTD. (CANADA)
1988 Statement: *See* 1988 Statement of Penguin Publishing Co Ltd. (England)

PENGUIN BOOKS (NZ) LTD (NEW ZEALAND)
1988 Statement: *See* 1988 Statement of Penguin Publishing Co Ltd. (England)

PENGUIN OVERSEAS LTD (ENGLAND)
1988 Statement: *See* 1988 Statement of Penguin Publishing Co Ltd. (England)

PENGUIN PUBLISHING CO LTD (ENGLAND)
1988 Statement: "Since we last corresponded the Penguin Group has introduced a new standard system for indicating the current impression of a book. This is now standard practice for all our imprints worldwide including Frederick Warne. I enclose a photocopy of an imprint page of one of our autumn titles from which you can see that we simply put the year of first publication followed by a row of numbers from 1 to 9 which indicates the impression number. As we reprint we knock off one number so that the lowest number shown is the number of the current impression. There is a slight variation according to whether the prelims are centred or ranged left. If they are centred the numbers are as in the enclosed sample. If it is ranged left style then they are consecutive in descending order."

The sample provided shows:

First published 1988
1 3 5 7 9 8 6 4 2

PENMAEN PRESS
1988 Statement: "Penmaen Press does not publish, and hasn't since 1985. Nevertheless, we designated our first editions by simply printing 'First Edition' on the copyright page next to the copyright material."

THE PENN PUBLISHING COMPANY
(Succeeded by The William Penn Publishing Corporation.)
1928 Statement: "As we indicate first editions in none of our books, we are unable to give you any information regarding the subject about which you inquire."
1936 Statement: "The only way they can be distinguished from subsequent editions is by the fact that in later editions the words second, third, or fourth printing, with the date, will be found on the copyright page."

WILLIAM PENN PUBLISHING CORPORATION
1947 Statement: "We use no special mark to indicate first printings of new books. All our first printings merely bear the copyright information."

PENN STATE STUDIES
1988 Statement: *See* 1988 Statement of The Pennsylvania State University Press

THE PENNSYLVANIA STATE UNIVERSITY PRESS
1976 Statement: "This press identifies first editions only in the sense that the absence of a legend on the title page such as 'Revised and Enlarged Edition' or 'Third Edition' clearly implies that a book is in its original edition. The same is true of printings, since all printings after the first are so identified on the copyright page."

1981, 1988 Statements: *See* 1976 Statement

THE PENNYWORTH PRESS (CANADA)

1976 Statement: " 1. 1st printings of 1st editions are not so marked—subsequent printings are, e.g. 'second printing' etc.

"2. 1st editions are so marked either on the title page or in the colophon on the last page."

PENTAGRAM PRESS

1976 Statement: "Thus far most Pentagram 'first editions'—all we've had so far—have been more or less labeled as such by the wording of the colophon, usually to the effect of 'this edition is limited to 626 copies, 26 of which are lettered and signed by the author.' Because I usually am content to let the first printings sell out, there has been thus far no need to designate a book as either 2nd edition or 2nd printing. To my mind, tho, (& the way I'd do it shd I need to) the 2nd printing of a book would exactly reproduce the contents of the first, while a 2nd edition would have the original contents either expanded, reduced, or otherwise edited. . . .

"Where I've included neither colophon nor the words 'first edition,' I do assume that people automatically take the book to be a first edition."

1981 Statement: "Only one Pentagram Press publication has gone into a second printing, due to confusion on the size of the initial pressrun. That second printing is so indicated on reverse of the title page, '700 copies July 1976/480 copies January 1978.'

"Pentagram is now issuing handset letterpressed books; each colophon states 'this edition is limited to 242 copies,' for example. I've no desire to re-issue a title once it's gone OP; the energy and spirit that went into the 1st edition could not be duplicated. Except for the offset-printed book noted above, all Pentagram books are first editions."

1988 Statement: *See* 1981 Statement

PENZLER BOOKS

1988 Statement: *See* 1988 Statement of Mysterious Press

THE PEQUOT PRESS, INC.

1976 Statement: "Our normal procedure is to put on the verso of the title page the words FIRST EDITION. With minimum or no changes we will list again the words FIRST EDITION and add the words, 'Second Printing.'

"When revisions are more than minimal we will list SECOND EDITION."

1988 Statement: *See* 1988 Statement of The Globe Pequot Press, Inc.

PEREGRINE BOOKS (ENGLAND)

1988 Statement: *See* 1988 Statement of Penguin Publishing Co Ltd. (England)

PERFORMANCE PUBLISHING
(Elgin, Illinois)

1976 Statement: "We do not maintain a system of identifying first editions of our publications."

1981 Statement: *See* 1976 Statement

PERGAMON PRESS LTD. (ENGLAND)

1976 Statement: "The only way in which we identify the first edition is the printing of the words 'First Edition 1976' on the verso of the title page along with the remainder of the copyright and bibliographic information.

"This has been our practice since 1965, prior to which the first edition was not identified in any way."

1981 Statement: "The statement as given in your letter describing how we designate the first printing of a first edition is still correct. However, we would like to add the following:

"In our school books, published under the imprint of Wheaton, we print 'First Published 1976' and subsequently add reprint notices with dates."

1988 Statement: "I confirm that the 1976 statement is still correct, but that the 1981 addition is no longer relevant."

PERIGEE BOOKS

1989 Statement: Printings are indicated by a sequence of numbers ranging from left to right on the copyright page:

$$1\ 2\ 3\ 4\ 5\ 6\ 7\ 8\ 9\ 10$$

The last number on the left indicates the number of the printing. In the example above, a first printing is indicated.

A Perigee edition of a book previously published in another edition is identified as the First Perigee Edition.

PERIGORD PRESS

1981 Statement: *See* 1981 Statement of William Morrow and Co. Inc.

THE PERISHABLE PRESS LIMITED

1981 Statement: "There is no designation because, being a sort of glorified hobby press, doing small editions of usually 200, there is only one edition. We have never printed anything but as first edition."

1989 Statement: "As far as the 1981 statement goes, it is essentially still true. Since I have never re-printed anything, every edition from this press remains as the only edition."

PERIVALE PRESS

1981 Statement: "We use the designation 'First published in 19..' followed by 'Second printing,' etc. In one case we used 'Second printing corrected' instead of 'Second edition.' We have not yet gone into a second edition for any of our titles, nor has the method first used been changed. The imprints of our company, therefore, follow standard form."

1988 Statement: *See* 1981 Statement

THE PERMANENT PRESS

1981 Statement: "All Permanent Press books have a colophon at the back of the book which includes the words 'first edition,' and which gives the number of copies printed in both clothbound and paperback editions."

1988 Statement: "We do not designate first editions. We do designate as such all subsequent printings and editions."

PERSEA BOOKS, INC.

1976 Statement: "We print 'First Edition' on the copyright page. We had been using 'First Printing.' As soon as the book goes into a new printing, the designation becomes 'Second printing,' whether or not the book is the first edition of the work."

1981, 1988 Statements: *See* 1976 Statement

PETER PAUPER PRESS INC.

1947 Statement: "With one or two exceptions, any book of ours with a 'limitation notice' (i.e. number of copies printed) is a first edition or first printing. But in a large number of cases—in fact in all books of recent years—there has not appeared such a limitation notice. The absence of such a notice is therefore *not* an indication of a later edition or printing. In general there is not any such indication."

1988 Statement: *See* 1947 Statement

PHAIDON PRESS LIMITED (ENGLAND)

1947 Statement: "The second and following editions of our books are always marked: Second Edition or Third Edition and so on, whilst our first editions have no note at all to this effect."

Statement for 1960: "In [1960] we simply added the date of publication to the copyright notice, without any indication that it was a first edition. In general, we used the terminology:

© PHAIDON PRESS LTD. LONDON 1960"

1976 Statement: "I enclose a copy of our official copyright page which states that a book is first published in such and such a year. For reprints we always state 'second impression 19xx' and for a new edition we put 'first published 19xx' followed by 'second edition 19xx.' This is standard form for all Phaidon books."

1981 Statement: *See* 1976 Statement

1988 Statement: "Our company still follows the practice outlined in our last statement, and this applies to our other imprints."

PHILADELPHIA ART ALLIANCE PRESS

1976, 1981 Statements: *See* 1976, 1981 Statements of Associated University Presses

GEORGE PHILIP LIMITED (ENGLAND)

(George Philip & Son Limited changed its name to George Philip Limited in April of 1988.)

1988 Statement: *See* 1976 Statement of George Philip & Son Limited (England). Imprints of George Philip & Son Limited follow similar practices to those of the cartographic publishing.

GEORGE PHILIP & SON LIMITED (ENGLAND)

1976 Statement: "I can reply only about cartographic publications.

"We have no particular method of identifying first editions other than the biblio and the copyright date but these we have always taken considerable care to make and keep accurate. A second printing of a first edition is rare because we almost invariably make some corrections at every printing of an atlas and thus change the edition number. If there were to be a second printing without correction we would state this in the biblio thus 'reprinted, date.' "

1981 Statement: *See* 1976 Statement

1988 Statement: *See* 1988 Statement of George Philip Limited (England)

PHILIPSBURG MANOR

1981 Statement: *See* 1981 Statement of Sleepy Hollow Press

S. G. PHILLIPS, INC.

1976 Statement: "Usually there is no designation of first editions. Later printings indicate number of printings and date."

PHILOMEL BOOKS
1988 Statement: *See* 1988 Statement of The Putnam & Grosset Group (Children's)

PHILOSOPHICAL LIBRARY, INC.
1947 Statement: "All subsequent editions are marked as such, 2nd., 3rd. edition, etc."

PHOENIX PRESS
1947 Statement: "Printings are listed as first, second, etc."

PHOENIX PUBLISHING
(Canaan, New Hampshire)
1976 Statement: "We do not identify first editions as such but merely include the Copyright date, statement of rights and limited reproduction permitted, LC number, ISBN number, and names of printer, binder and designer. On subsequent reprintings or revisions we indicate first and second printings, etc."

1981 Statement: "We do not identify first editions as such but merely include the Copyright date, statement of rights and limited reproduction permitted, Library of Congress CIP data which includes LC number, ISBN number, and names of printer, binder and designer. On subsequent reprintings or revisions we indicate first and second printings, etc."

PICA PRESS
1988 Statement: *See* 1988 Statement of Universe Books

PICADOR (ENGLAND)
1988 Statement: *See* 1988 Statement of Pan Books Ltd. (England)

PICCOLO (ENGLAND)
1988 Statement: *See* 1988 Statement of Pan Books Ltd. (England)

PICKERING & INGLIS LTD. (SCOTLAND)
1976 Statement: "Our system is that in a first edition the date appears directly under our imprint on the title page, while on any reprints further editions appear on the reverse side of the title page."

1981 Statement: "Our present system is that any such information regarding editions is now printed on the reverse side of the title page. On the first edition we state 'First Printing' followed by the year and on any reprints we state 'First Published' followed by the year, and then 'Reprinted' followed by the year.

"We changed to this new method approximately four years ago."

1988 Statement: "Our current system is much the same as that used in 1981.

"All imprint information appears on the reverse of the title page. On the first edition, we state:
'First published in' followed by (year)
and on any reprints we state
'Reprinted: Impression number
88 89 90:   10 9 8 7 6 5 4 3 2
and delete as applicable.
"The above is standard to all our imprints."

PILOT PRESS, PUBLISHERS, INC.
1947 Statement: "We have not adopted any system of identifying the first printings of our books."

PINEAPPLE PRESS, INC.

1988 Statement: "We began publishing in 1982 in Englewood, Florida. Our first books do not indicate edition. Beginning in 1985, 'first edition' is printed on the copyright page of each first edition along with the numbers going backward from 10 to 1. At each subsequent printing a number is dropped so that the printing will be the last number appearing. Or some books just say 'third printing' or whichever.

"From 1988, place of publication is Sarasota, Florida."

PIPER (ENGLAND)

1988 Statement: *See* 1988 Statement of Pan Books Ltd. (England)

PITKIN PICTORIAL (ENGLAND)

1989 Statement: *See* the Methuen entry in the 1989 Statement of The Octopus Publishing Group PLC (England)

PITMAN LEARNING, INC.

1981 Statement: *See* 1976 Statement of Pitman Publishing Corporation

PITMAN PUBLISHING CORPORATION

1976 Statement: "Pitman uses a printing line on the copyright page as follows.

10 9 8 7 6 5 4 3 2 1

"This is the way the line would appear on a first printing of the first edition. For each successive printing, one number would be removed at the right. Normally, after nine printings, we revise or substitute a new line with higher numbers."

1981 Statement: Pitman Publishing Corporation has changed its name to Pitman Learning, Inc.

See 1981 Statement of Pitman Learning, Inc.

PLATT & MUNK

1976 Statement: *See* 1976 Statement of Questor Educational Products Company

1988 Statement: *See* 1988 Statement of The Putnam & Grosset Group (Children's)

PLAYERS PRESS, INC.

1988 Statement: "No mention is made of any edition unless there is a Revised Edition, which is so indicated."

PLAYLAND BOOKS

1988 Statement: *See* 1988 Statement of The Putnam & Grosset Group (Children's)

PLAYS, INC., PUBLISHERS

1976 Statement: "We don't designate first editions—second and others are stated second printing or second edition, etc."

1981 Statement: "The answer as typed is correct. We designate only editions after the first; the first edition simply bears the date of copyright.

"The only exception to this is an *import*, which may read:

First U.S. edition published by PLAYS, INC. 1981.

Formerly published by.... Ltd... London in 19..

"This information is also true for our other company, THE WRITER, INC."

1988 Statement: *See* 1981 Statement

PLAYTIME PRESS (ENGLAND)

1989 Statement: *See* 1989 Statement of The Octopus Publishing Group PLC (England)

PLAYWRIGHTS CANADA (CANADA)

1988 Statement: "The Playwrights Union of Canada, under the imprint PLAYWRIGHTS CANADA, designates a first edition or first printing on the copyright page. A second printing will be designated as such, a printing and not an edition. Each subsequent printing will also be listed. A second edition will be listed only if the work has been revised or re-edited. Style is as follows:

First Edition: October 1988
Second Printing: November 1988
Third Printing: December 1988

(Or in the case of a revision of the work)

First Edition: October 1988
Second Printing: November 1988
Second Edition: December 1988
Second Printing: January 1989"

PLEIADES BOOKS, LTD. (ENGLAND)

1947 Statement: "Our present practice is as follows: In the case of the first edition we include in the prelims a statement to the effect that the book was 'First published 19...' In the case of a reprint: 'First published 19.., reprinted 19...' In the event of a second reprint: 'First published 19.., Reprinted 19 ., Reprinted 19..,' and so on."

PLENUM PUBLISHING CORPORATION

1981 Statement: "Plenum Publishing company does not identify first editions or first printings in any positive way; however, editions other than the first will have an identifying statement on the title page, and printings other than the first will have an identifying statement on the copyright page. As far as I know this has always been our policy, and it applies to all the imprints under which we publish."

THE PLOUGH PUBLISHING HOUSE

1989 Statement: "We do not indicate in any way that a book is a first edition. In the absence of '2nd edition' etc., this can be assumed."

PLUME

1988 Statement: *See* 1988 Statement of New American Library

POETRY AUSTRALIA (AUSTRALIA)

1988 Statement: *See* 1988 Statement of South Head Press (Australia)

POETRY BOOKSHOP (ENGLAND)
(Out of business prior to 1937.)

1928 Statement: "The First Editions of the Poetry Bookshop are generally designated by the words *on the back of title-page*: Published: month: year.

"For second and subsequent editions the words Reprinted or 2nd Impression, etc., are *added*.

"We would mention that this has only been a general rule heretofore, but it is certainly one we would be prepared to adopt in the case of future publications."

THE POMEGRANATE PRESS

1976 Statement: "We designate a first edition usually in the traditional colophon following the text of the book or broadside. We generally limit our publications to one printing."

1981 Statement: "We designate a first edition usually on the masthead (copyright) page and also in the colophon on a separate page at the end of the text. Here the explanation of paper, handprinting, graphic illustration and no. of copies are described. The books are numbered and limited number usually signed. Editions range from 200-900 copies."

THE POND-EKBERG COMPANY

1947 Statement: "There is no mark of identification on the first edition of any of the books we have published.

"We now have in process the first reprint of three of our books which will be so indicated on either the title page or the page immediately back of the title."

POOLBEG PRESS LIMITED (REPUBLIC OF IRELAND)

1981 Statement: "Poolbeg Press's only method of designating first editions is in the printing of the preliminary pages. There we list the edition and the year and our own position, and when one of our own books goes into another edition we also list this in the same manner."

1988 Statement: "The Ward River Press is no more. Poolbeg now has no other imprints.

"Poolbeg designates first editions in the printing of the copyright page. We say '*First published [date]*' and add '*Reprinted [date]*' and so on (or '*New Edition/Revised Edition [date]*' and so on."

PORCEPIC BOOKS (CANADA)

1989 Statement: *See* 1989 Statement of Press Porcepic Ltd. (Canada)

THE PORPOISE PRESS (SCOTLAND)
(Out of business prior to 1949.)

1928 Statement: "The first impressions of our ordinary issues bear on the back of the title, to which all bibliographical matter is relegated: 'First published in (date of year) by The Porpoise Press, 133a George Street, Edinburgh.' On the second and subsequent impressions, there is stated 'First impression (month and year); Second impression (month and year),' etc.

"Where special editions have also been issued, this fact is stated on the ordinary edition, and on the special edition itself there appears a statement as to the size of the edition, etc.: e.g., 'This edition, on hand-made paper, is limited to fifty signed and numbered copies. This copy is Number...' "

1937 Statement: *See* 1928 Statement

BERN PORTER BOOKS

1976 Statement: "All publications are marked first edition, second edition, etc. as reprinted.

"All publications being a first, second, third printing of a first edition are marked as such.

"As the oldest and largest small press in the world we have found it useful to be complete, consistent, accurate and non-changing in marks throughout the years.

note: should a later edition be revised over an earlier we also mark that.

note: all markings are on the back of the title page.
note: all signed numbered editions are dated firsts."—Bern Porter, Chairman of the Board, Bern Porter Books.
1981, 1989 Statements: *See* 1976 Statement

POTOMAC BOOKS, INC.
1976 Statement: Only those editions after the first are indicated. Printings of the first edition are indicated only after the first printing.
1981 Statement: *See* 1976 Statement

CLARKSON N. POTTER, INC.
1976 Statement: "Every printing after the first is listed with the edition on the copyright page (i.e. on the first edition, first printing, the c/r page says only first edition; on 2nd printing, '2nd printing' is added to first edition)."
1981, 1988 Statements: *See* 1981, 1988 Statements of Crown Publishers Inc.

PRACTICAL PRESS, LTD. (ENGLAND)
1947 Statement: *See* 1947 Statement of Rockliff Publishing Corporation, Limited (England)

PRAJNA PRESS
1981 Statement: *See* 1981 Statement of Shambhala Publications, Inc.
1988 Statement: This imprint no longer exists.

PRENTICE-HALL, INC.
1947 Statement: "Prentice-Hall is a very large organization, publishing both trade books and text books. The practice differs depending upon the division publishing the books involved.

"With trade books, we indicate the first edition by printing the words 'First Edition' on the copyright page of the book. On subsequent printings we delete that edition imprint, and substitute the number of the printing. We list all printings subsequent to the first on the copyright page, giving the month in which the printing was available for sale.

"When we publish a new textbook, the copyright page simply carries the year date of copyright and nothing else. When that book is reprinted, we generally include a statement below the copyright line reading:

    First printing, January, 1947
    Second printing, September, 1947

or whatever the case may be, and so on for subsequent printings.

"When we bring out new editions of both trade and textbooks, we indicate Second Edition, Third Edition, and so forth on both the title page and the cover of the book. And, of course, the copyright page carries the year date of all revisions. For instance, copyright, 1935, 1940, 1945, by Prentice-Hall, Inc.

"Of course, there are always exceptions to every rule, but the foregoing procedure is pretty much our general practice in both Trade and Textbook divisions."
1976 Statement: "We have no specific method of identifying first editions. We use a printing line of arabic numbers to designate how many printings a book has had:

"10 9 8 7 6 5 4 3 2 1 would be the line in the first printing of a first edition. Subsequent printings would drop a digit from the right. A revised edition would be so indicated either in the title or on the copyright page of a book.

"Before using the numeral printing line we used the words 'First print-ing,' 'Second printing,' etc."
1981 Statement: *See* 1976 Statement

THE PRESERVATION PRESS
1976 Statement: "The Preservation Press has never identified first editions as such; subsequent editions (which are rare for us) are identified as 'second revised editions,' etc., as appropriate."
1981 Statement: "The Preservation Press has never identified first editions as such; subsequent reprintings are designated as such on the copyright page with the year of reprinting (e.g., Fourth printing, 1981). The few revised editions published are identified clearly on at least the title page."
1988 Statement: "We now use a numerical system, e.g.:
92 91 90 89 88   5 4 3 2 1."

PRESIDIO PRESS
1981 Statement: "Unless a book states on the copyright page that it is a second printing or second edition—or whatever number it may be—we as-sume that it will be recognized as a first edition.
"In other words, no special note is made of first editions."
1988 Statement: *See* 1981 Statement

THE PRESS OF JAMES A. DECKER
(Including Compass Editions, Village Press, and Black Farm Press.)
1947 Statement: "We have not had second editions of our books due to the nature of the copy (poetry). Very rarely does an edition of poetry sell out, hence we have had no occasion to mark editions."

THE PRESS OF MacDONALD & REINECKE
1988 Statement: *See* 1988 Statement of Padre Productions

PRESS PORCEPIC LTD. (CANADA)
1976 Statement: "We designate only those printings and/or editions after the first, and this method of identification does not differ from any pre-viously used."
1981 Statement: "We designate only those printings and/or editions after the first, and this method of identification does not differ from any pre-viously used.
"On books which we expect to reprint or revise we now print the follow-ing: 81 82 83 84 85 5 4 3 2 1 and opaque out the relevant numbers in sub-sequent printings."
1989 Statement: "Porcepic Books, or Press Porcepic Ltd., has never desig-nated first printings or first editions."

PRESSWORKS PUBLISHING INC.
1988 Statement: "It is our practice to print the words First Edition on the copyright page. We adopted this method of designation in 1980 and it does not vary from any previous method of designation."

PRICE MILBURN AND COMPANY LIMITED (NEW ZEALAND)
1976 Statement: "We simply start with
First published 1967
on our first edition, and we continue to add
Reprinted 1968
or

New edition 1968

and so on, each time the book is printed again (on the back of the title page).

"I enclose a title page with verso from one of our books, and it proves me wrong—we often don't identify a first edition at all. But we add a publication history when it reprints."

1981 Statement: "My original answer still stands, though we have made a change in the light of offset litho printing from plates—where it is difficult and expensive to change the bibliographic information between printings. For our junior educational books we put

First published 1980. Reprinted regularly.

on all copies, so that a reader cannot tell whether the book in his hand is a first edition or not.

"When the printing plate that prints the verso of the title page wears out and has to be replaced, we bring the information up to date for the next printing."

PRICE/STERN/SLOAN PUBLISHERS, INC.

1976 Statement: "Our form is to put FIRST PRINTING on the copyright page of the book."

1981 Statement: *See* 1976 Statement

1989 Statement: "Yes, we are still following the practice of putting the first printing of the first edition on the copyright page. However, we do it differently now: as you see by the xerox enclosed, [9 8 7 6 5 4 3 2], the descending numbers go down to 2 . . . this means this is the first edition. When we print the second edition, the number 2 will be omitted . . . the third edition, the number 3 will be omitted, and so on.

"Our imprints and subsidiaries do follow our practices."

THE PRIMAVERA PRESS, INC.
(Out of business prior to 1949.)

1937 Statement: "Printings of our books following the first editions are so marked, i.e., 'Second Printing,' etc. This is true with one exception—the second printing of *Who Loves a Garden* is distinguished by the date on the title page '1935' being one year later than the date of copyright '1934.' "

PRINCETON UNIVERSITY PRESS

1928 Statement: *See* 1937 Statement

1937 Statement: "Our only way of designating first editions is by negative implication. In other words, our first editions bear no special designation. If, however, a title is reprinted or reissued that fact is set forth on the copyright page.

"We have apparently always used our present method of designating first printings from subsequent ones. 'Always' in this case means for the approximate quarter of a century that we have been publishing."

1947 Statement: "Our only way of designating first editions is by negative implication. In other words, our first editions bear no special designation. If, however, a title is reprinted or reissued that fact is set forth on the copyright page.

"We seek to distinguish between a new edition and a new printing; a new edition implying a substantive change in the text, a new printing referring to a reissue of a book.

"We have apparently always used our present method of designating first printings from subsequent ones. 'Always' in this case means for the approximate three and a half decades that we have been publishing."

1976 Statement: "We do not identify first editions, but only subsequent editions."

1981 Statement: "We do not identify first printings, but only subsequent printings. Interested collectors may contact the Press for a more detailed printing history of Princeton University Press titles."

1988 Statement: *See* 1981 Statement

PRINTED EDITIONS

1981 Statement: "Since we seldom intend to reprint an edition (like most very small presses), we don't identify our first editions as such."

PRISM PRESS

1988 Statement: "Our policy is to not make any special identification of first editions. However we do identify reprints and new editions so anything not identified as a reprint or new edition is a first edition."

PROGRESS PRESS

1947 Statement: *See* 1947 Statement of Public Affairs Press

PROSCENIUM PUBLISHERS INC

1988 Statement: "First printings of our books are all identified on the copyright page as 'First Limelight Edition' followed by the month and year of publication. Second printings are identified as 'Second Limelight Edition,' etc. It should be pointed out that since almost all of our books are paperback reprints, with hardcover reprints in a few cases, information about the original publication of a particular title also appears on the copyright page."

PRUETT PUBLISHING CO.

1976 Statement: "The only method that Pruett uses in designating first editions is by placing on the copyright page the following words:

First Edition

1 2 3 4 5 6 7 8 9

"Sometimes we do not even use the words 'First Edition,' and the numbers we use indicate the number of times an edition has been printed. For instance, if it is a second printing, the numbers will read '2 3 4 5...' "

1981 Statement: *See* 1976 Statement

1988 Statement: "We usually identify a First Edition as such on the copyright page, followed by the string of numbers, used to indicate the number of times an edition has been printed. For instance, if it is a second printing, the numbers will read '2 3 4 5...' "

PUBLIC AFFAIRS PRESS
(Includes Progress Press.)

1947 Statement: "We haven't any differentiation."

PUCKERBRUSH PRESS

1976 Statement: "I use no designation for a 1st edition. I indicate only those printings/editions after the 1st. I've used no other methods of identification."

1988 Statement: *See* 1976 Statement

PUFFIN

1988 Statement: *See* 1988 Statement of Penguin Publishing Co Ltd. (England)

PUFFIN BOOKS (ENGLAND)

1988 Statement: *See* 1988 Statement of Penguin Publishing Co Ltd. (England)

PULP PRESS (CANADA)

1981 Statement: "Our first editions do not carry any notations. However, subsequent printings/editions carry the printing history on the © page."
All imprints use the same method.

PULSE-FINGER PRESS

1976 Statement: "We usually identify first editions and/or printings on the copyright page. Where no designation is used at the outset, subsequent editions/printings are identified.
"The methods of identification do not differ from those previously used."
1988 Statement: *See* 1976 Statement

PUSHCART PRESS

1981 Statement: "[A first printing] says so on the title page verso."
1988 Statement: *See* 1981 Statement

PUTNAM & COMPANY, LTD. (ENGLAND)
(Formerly G. P. Putnam's Sons, Ltd.)

1937, 1947 Statements: *See* 1928 Statement of G. P. Putnam's Sons, Ltd. (England)

THE PUTNAM & GROSSET GROUP (CHILDREN'S)

1988 Statement: "Grosset & Dunlap is a division of The Putnam Publishing Group and now publishes juvenile titles under the imprint: The Putnam & Grosset Group.

"First editions are not identified in our books except that the copyright notice gives the year of publication. If a book is reprinted, there is no indication of which printing it is. Some of our books do carry a code in letters or numbers. For instance, under the copyright notice and other information (ISBN, LC number, manufacturing place) there may be the letters C D E F G H. It is obvious to those who are familiar with production codes that the book is in its third printing, because A and B are missing.

"If a second or third printing of a book contains new copyrightable material (new illustrations, editorial revisions, condensation) there will be a new copyright year in the notice, but the original copyright year must be included. There may or may not be a clue as to which printing it is.

"There are instances, in the case of classics (not public domain titles, but juvenile books that are in copyright and because of their popularity have never gone out of print) a line is included to show which printing it is. Our *LITTLE TOOT*, copyright 1939, © 1967 by Hardie Gramatky, states in a separate line: Twenty-seventh Impression. However, it does not give the year of the twenty-seventh impression.

"Many of our juvenile titles are imported from the countries in which they were published. In such cases, the original copyright year appears, and the copyright notice also indicates the year of the first United States edition. This is for copyright protection in the United States, not for first edition information, although the copyright year reveals the year of first printing.

"All of the imprints and subsidiaries of The Putnam & Grosset Group follow the practice mentioned."

G. P. PUTNAM'S SONS

1928 Statement: "Our system as to new publications does not usually include printing any entry on the back of the title page or otherwise indicating first edition.

"When a book is printed a second time, as a rule we print under the copyright notice the words 'First printed March 1927. Second printing April 1927, etc.' Where there is no note of this kind it may be assumed that the work is the first printing.

"It is always our intention not to use the word 'second edition' unless there is some distinct addition or change from the first edition. When that is the case, usually on the title page is the line 'second edition revised, or second edition corrected, or second edition revised, corrected and enlarged' or some such expression. A similar entry is often printed under the copyright notice.

"As to the date on the title page. This is supposed to be the date when the particular copy was printed. Reprints without change would generally have that title page, and when such reprint is made it would be the copyright entry which would tell by comparison that it was not first edition.

"For staple items that had been reprinted from year to year, as a rule that date is omitted from the title-page."

1937, 1947 Statements: *See* 1928 Statement

Statement for 1960: *See* 1976 Statement

1976 Statement: "Putnam's method of designating first editions is as follows: All editions other than the first one are distinguished by the words 'second (or third or fourth, etc.) impression' which appear on the copyright page. The first edition has no such designation."

1981 Statement: *See* 1976 Statement

1989 Statement: The printing is indicated by a sequence of numbers ranging from left to right on the copyright page:

$$1\ 2\ 3\ 4\ 5\ 6\ 7\ 8\ 9\ 10$$

The last number on the left indicates the printing. In the example above, a first printing is indicated.

A Putnam edition of a title previously published abroad is identified as the First American Edition on the copyright page.

G. P. PUTNAM'S SONS, LTD. (ENGLAND)

1928 Statement: "Our English procedure for indicating first editions is as follows:

"On the reverse of the title page, we print the line

First published.......

followed by the month and year.

"When the book is reprinted, we retain the line, adding underneath it:

Reprinted........

followed by the month and year.

"Further impressions are indicated in the same way. If, however, there is any definite alteration in matter or style, we indicate this by the words:

Second edition........

followed by the month and year.

"The same procedure would apply for subsequent editions."

THE PYNE PRESS

1976 Statement: "We have no special or unusual way of listing first editions. We merely state somewhere on the page listing copyright, ISBN number, etc., that it is the first edition."

Q

QUADRANGLE / THE NEW YORK TIMES BOOK CO., INC.

1976 Statement: "Our method of identifying editions is as follows:

"We put no identification on the first edition/first printing. Subsequent printings are marked second, third, etc.

"A second edition will usually be identified as 'revised edition' and will not have a printing identification, as with first editions."

1981 Statement: *See* 1976 Statement

THE QUAIL STREET PUBLISHING COMPANY

1976 Statement: "No designation = first printing, first edition. Other printings & editions are designated thusly:

2nd printing = 2nd printing of first edition

2nd edition, 2nd printing = the obvious."

QUERIDO, PUBLISHERS

1947 Statement: "No special identification."

QUEST

1988 Statement: *See* 1988 Statement of The Theosophical Publishing House

QUESTOR EDUCATIONAL PRODUCTS COMPANY

1976 Statement: "Thank you for contacting us re our method of identifying first editions. Unfortunately, we have none at this time. We plan to institute one, however, for our 1977 list and all future books."

QUICK FOX

1981 Statement: "We make no notation of printings—first or second, or whatever."

QUIXOTE

1976 Statement: "We indicate second and third printings of first editions and second editions, but not first edition or first printing. Also everything we print we try to have as an issue of our magazine *QUIXOTE*, so volume number and issue number usually show something about the time/edition. For something we really like, too, we do a preface or second preface as the case may be, but we have only had a few second or third printings and only two I think second editions so far."

1981 Statement: "We have made no essential changes in our indications of first editions—they are indicated by default, since we only indicate 2d editions, second printings, or revised editions. I have now had about eight second editions or revisions and several third editions and printings. Since I have talked to you about it, I have been thinking about indicating first edition at the bottom of the title page of all our work."

QUOTA PRESS (NORTHERN IRELAND)

1947 Statement: "In the case of first edition the date is usually put on title page or the book is described:

First Published ....
"In the case of a new impression or edition this is stated below, e.g.

First Published........................November 1930

Second Impression........................December 1930
"This practice was not always adhered to during the war years."

R

RADIUS (ENGLAND)

1988 Statement: *See* 1988 Statement of Century Hutchinson Publishing Group Limited (England)

RAINBIRD (ENGLAND)

1988 Statement: *See* 1988 Statement of Penguin Publishing Co Ltd. (England)

RAINBOW (ENGLAND)

1989 Statement: *See* 1989 Statement of The Octopus Publishing Group PLC (England)

RAINTREE PUBLISHERS INC.

1976 Statement: "Printings are designated by a line of numbers on the copyright page. One-digit numbers indicate the printing; two-digit numbers indicate the year of the printing.

1 2 3 4 5 6 7 8 9 0 85 84 83 82 81
"On the first printing of a first edition, the number 1 will appear on the left, and the two-digit number will agree with the last two digits of the copyright year. There will be no reference to first edition."

1981 Statement: *See* 1976 Statement

RAMPARTS PRESS, INC.

1976 Statement: "Ramparts Press now prints 'First Edition' on the copyright page of the first printing of each of our books."

1981 Statement: *See* 1976 Statement

1988 Statement: "We usually follow the practice of printing 'First Edition' on the copyright page of the first printing of our new books."

RAND McNALLY & COMPANY

1937 Statement: "We are sorry to tell you that the first editions of our publications have no marks to distinguish them from later editions, except in a few cases you will find the letters 'MA' in the lower righthand corner of the copyright page. The 'M' before the 'A' has no connection with the edition, but the 'A' does signify that the book is a first edition. Sometimes this 'A' is omitted on the first edition, but 'B' appears on the second edition, 'C' on the third edition, etc."

1947 Statement: "It has been our practice in recent years to use the letter 'A' on the copyright page, or on the last page of text to indicate the first printing. Subsequent printings are marked 'B,' 'C,' 'D' to identify them. In our earlier Rand McNally publications, however, this system was not consistently used, and very often there is nothing to identify a first printing except the copyright date."

1976 Statement: "As to how Rand McNally trade books are identified, the copyright page carries all pertinent information, including the line 'First printing,' 'First paperback printing,' or whatever appropriate wording is necessary, followed by the month and year of the edition. Previously, Rand McNally used letter identification for various editions, with 'A' being the first."

1981 Statement: "As to how Rand McNally trade books are identified, the copyright page carries all pertinent information, including the line 'First printing' 'First paperback printing,' or whatever appropriate wording is necessary, followed by the year of the edition. The month is not indicated unless two editions are printed within the same calendar year."

1988 Statement: "Rand McNally's principal publications are world atlases and maps; educational atlases, wall maps, and globes; road atlases, and state and city maps; and marketing and banking atlases and directories. These publications are identified on the copyright page which carries all pertinent information. The first printing of a new edition carrying a new copyright will not include the line, 'First Printing' or 'First Edition.'

"Subsequent printings of the unrevised publication will carry the line, 'Second Printing,' etc. If revisions have been made, but not sufficient to warrant a new copyright, the statement will be, 'Revised Edition' or 'Revised Printing.' These statements will be preceded or followed by the year. The month is not indicated unless there are more than two printings within the same calendar year.

"This practice is followed by all of our divisions."

RANDOM HOUSE, INC.

1928 Statement: "Since Random House only publishes limited editions, all of the necessary information that you require is contained in the colophon, i.e., as far as we are concerned, there is only one edition, the first."

1936 Statement: "As far as Random House first editions are concerned, with the exception of limited editions where all the necessary information is contained in the colophon, all books are plainly marked 'first edition' on the copyright page."

1947 Statement: *See* 1936 Statement

1976 Statement: "All of the first editions of Random House, Pantheon, and A. A. Knopf books carry the words 'FIRST EDITION' in small caps on the copyright page. These first editions are by our definition also first printings. This practice has not been uniformly adhered to during the entire history of all these imprints, but in recent years it has."

1981, 1988 Statements: *See* 1976 Statement

RAVAN PRESS (PTY) LTD (REPUBLIC OF SOUTH AFRICA)

1981 Statement: "We designate a first edition by the words 'first impression,' followed by the date. Books published 1978-79 often cite the month as well as the year, whereas books from 1980 onwards cite only the year. Collectors are warned that our imprint practices have not been consistent."

RAWSON, WADE PUBLISHERS, INC.

1981 Statement: "We identify the first printing of a first edition with the words 'First Edition' on the copyright page. In subsequent printings this is replaced with, for instance, 'Second Printing' and the date of the printing, month and year. That's how we've always done it."

READER'S DIGEST ASSOCIATION, INC.

1988 Statement: "The Reader's Digest Association, Inc. (the imprint of titles published by the General books division) does not identify first printings as such. We do, however, identify subsequent printings by stating, at the bottom of the copyright page, the number of the printing and the month and year of its publication. And if there are later editions (as distinguished from printings) we state that fact in a line that runs above the copyright information for the new edition.

READER'S DIGEST CONDENSED BOOKS

1988 Statement: "As a rule, Reader's Digest Condensed Books are only published and printed once and are designated 'First Edition' on the copyright page."

THE REAL COMET PRESS

1988 Statement: "Regarding the manner we designate the first printing of a first edition: We have adopted a standard formula for identifying first printings which easily identifies subsequent printings as well as the first;

First Edition 1987 (year optional)

87 88 89 90   10 9 8 7 6 5 4 3 2 1

"Thus, this reads that the first printing was in 1987. If there are two printings in the same year we would only drop the number 1, to read that the second printing was in 1987."

REAL PEOPLE PRESS

1976 Statement: "So far, none of our books has been altered in subsequent printings. The first printing is indicated on the © page thusly:

1 2 3 4 5 6 Printing 76 75 74

"The second printing has the '1' deleted:

2 3 4 5 6 Printing 76 75 74."

1981 Statement: The 1976 statement is still accurate. However, not all of their books have remained unaltered in subsequent printings.

1988 Statement: *See* 1981 Statement

RED DUST, INC.

1976 Statement: "Every Red Dust Book is a first edition. We have no special way of designating it—if it ran to a second edition—we would say second possibly on copyright page."

1981 Statement: "We have recently reprinted *The Libera Me Domine* and *Passacaglia*, Pinget 500 copies each and also *The Park*, Sollers. We did not mark these new editions 2nd edition. Otherwise all our other books are still in their first edition. Next time we reprint I will try to remember to put 2nd edition in."

1988 Statement: "We reprinted *The Third Wedding*. In it we put:

Paperback edition: 1986 (First edition 1971)."

A. H. & A. W. REED PTY., LTD. (AUSTRALIA)

1981 Statement: "This company designates the first edition of any book simply by giving the date of publication on the Imprint Page. Any subsequent reprinting or revised edition is notified by adding further date(s) in the same place."

1989 Statement: *See* 1989 Statement of Reed Books Pty., Ltd. (Australia)

REED BOOKS PTY., LTD. (AUSTRALIA)

1989 Statement: "The company you have listed as A. H. & A. W. Reed Pty. Ltd. is now the holding company, the operating company being Reed Books Pty. Ltd.

"Our designation of first printings has not changed and all imprints follow this practice."

See 1981 Statement of A. H. & A. W. Reed Pty., Ltd. (Australia)

REGENT HOUSE, PUBLISHERS, INC.

1947 Statement: "All titles carry the statement on the title page:
FIRST EDITION."

THE REGENTS PRESS OF KANSAS

1976 Statement: "The first printing does not say 'First printing.' The later printings are so labeled on © page.

"We label a second printing as 'Second printing (date).' It is not considered a new edition, even if a few corrections have been made."

1981 Statement: *See* 1976 Statement

1988 Statement: *See* 1988 Statement of University Press of Kansas

HENRY REGNERY COMPANY

1976 Statement: "The Henry Regnery Company does not have a method of designating first editions or first printings of first editions.

"A few Regnery books carried a printing code in 1974:
1 2 3 4 5 6 7 ← PY → 9 8 7 6 5 4. The '1' in the printing row would be deleted in the second printing 2 3 4 5 6 7 ← PY → 9 8 7 6 5 4. The code has been dropped and we do not intend to use it again."

1988 Statement: *See* 1988 Statement of Regnery Gateway, Inc.

REGNERY GATEWAY, INC.

1988 Statement: "We do not identify 'first editions' when we print them, although we will identify subsequent printings.

"Regnery Gateway, Inc. was formerly named Henry Regnery Co. The name change occurred in 1976."

THE REILLY & LEE CO., INC.

1937 Statement: "In the future we intend to put 'First Printing' on the copyright page and when that edition is exhausted the 'First Printing' will be removed and no other mark will be put in its place."

1947 Statement: "We put 'First Printing' on the copyright page and when that edition is exhausted the 'First Printing' will be removed and no other mark will be put in its place."

MAX REINHARDT (ENGLAND)

1988 Statement: *See* 1988 Statement of The Bodley Head Limited (England)

RELEASE PRESS

1976 Statement: "We distinguish our first editions with the statement 'first printing' on the verso of the title page. We have not had occasion to go into any printings or editions beyond the first, so anyone obtaining any of our 11 books is assured of a first ed."

RENAISSANCE HOUSE PUBLISHERS

1988 Statement: "Renaissance House Publishers makes no specific statement of first edition status unless the book is published as a limited edition. In that event, we state on the copyright page:
> This edition limited to XXXX (signed and numbered)
> copies, of which this is number XXXX.

"It can be assumed that our books are first editions unless noted otherwise on the copyright page. Subsequent editions are always noted by an addition to the copyright page that reads in the manner of this example:
> First printing February, 1985
> Second printing April, 1985
> Third printing March, 1988

"The above example refers to subsequent printings where the text is substantially unaltered. Should there be extensive revisions, we would indicate (e.g.): Revised edition April, 1988."

RESEARCH PUBLISHING COMPANY

1947 Statement: "We have not given the matter any consideration whatsoever and there is nothing in any of our publications to indicate whether first or other printing. We, ourselves, identify the various printings by color of cloth or some such matter."

FLEMING H. REVELL COMPANY

1947 Statement: "Formerly, we identified first editions of our books, but more recently we have not done so, except that the jacket of the second and subsequent editions are so indicated so that around the office and generally through the trade, a Revell Company book that has no edition indicated is a first edition."

Statement for 1960: First printings are not so marked.

1976 Statement: "We do not indicate on a First Edition that it is the first edition."

1981 Statement: *See* 1976 Statement

REYNAL AND HITCHCOCK, INC.

(Merged with Harcourt, Brace and, Co., Inc., January 2, 1948.)

1937 Statement: "For some time now The John Day Company has adopted the following method of distinguishing first editions: On the first printing copyright page appears only the copyright notice: Copyright, 1936, by John Doe, and the usual printer's imprint: Printed in the United States of America by The John Smith Printing Company. Lately we have included a paragraph: All rights reserved, including the right to reproduce this book or portions thereof in any form. However, all other printings of the same book may be distinguished by: Second printing, Jan. 1936. Third printing, February, 1936, et cetera, with the proper month inserted.

"You will notice that 'John Day & Co.' is no longer used; when the book is wholly owned by The John Day Company 'The John Day Company, New York' appears on the title page.

"The same method applies to Reynal and Hitchcock; that is, no notice of first printing appears on the first edition, but notices of second, third, and fourth printings being added as is the case. In 1935, The John Day Company was associated with Reynal and Hitchcock, and on the title page of books published under this new association you will find the imprint: 'a John Day Book, Reynal and Hitchcock, New York.' This method of imprinting our books is similar to The Atlantic Monthly Press and Little, Brown & Co., with which you may be familiar. On the copyright page of books put out under the joint imprint you will find on both first printing and subsequent printings the words: Published by John Day in association with Reynal and Hitchcock. However, this has no bearing on the edition printings."

1947 Statement: "On a first printing we carry only the copyright line (Copyright, author or Reynal & Hitchcock, as the case may be, date) and the usual short paragraph about 'all rights reserved, etc.'

"On a second printing we add a line saying simply 'Second Printing.' And on subsequent printings we change this line each time to read 'Third Printing' or 'Fourth Printing' and so on.

"John Day Company books are no longer published in association with Reynal & Hitchcock."

1948 Statement: "Reynal and Hitchcock books will from time to time appear under that imprint and will carry a Reynal and Hitchcock copyright line and a Reynal and Hitchcock title page with the sometime exception of a book appearing with a Harcourt, Brace title page but with the following annotation: A Reynal and Hitchcock book.

"Reynal and Hitchcock books will no longer be identified with respect to their first printings according to the method formerly used. Both Reynal and Hitchcock books and Harcourt, Brace books will be identified with respect to first printings according to Harcourt, Brace's 1947 statement."

RICCARDI PRESS (ENGLAND)

1937 Statement: *See* 1937 Statement of Medici Society, Limited (England)

RICE UNIVERSITY PRESS

1988 Statement: "First editions are indicated as such on the copyright page along with the year of publication, as are subsequent printings. Sometimes additional numeric sequence appears on the copyright page to indicate impressions."

RICH & COWAN, LIMITED (ENGLAND)

1937 Statement: "It is our custom now to put 'first printing 1936' 'second printing—such and such a date.' In special occasions, as with H. V. Morton, we put the number printed of the first edition.

"Our early system was to include the month of publication."

1947 Statement: "Owing to war-time production conditions we have had to omit dating our books and we are not yet reverting to the pre-war practice. The system shown on our previous statement was, of course, in use up to 1940."

RICHARDS PRESS, LTD. (ENGLAND)

1928 Statement: "It may be taken that any book published by us is the first edition unless there appears a note on the back of the title page indicating more than one printing. It is possible that in a few cases the fact that the book is not a first edition may be indicated by the words 'cheap edition' or 'new edition' on the title page itself."

1937 and 1947 Statements: *See* 1928 Statement

RIDER (ENGLAND)

1988 Statement: *See* 1988 Statement of Century Hutchinson Publishing Group Limited (England)

THE RIDGE PRESS, INC.

1976 Statement: Ridge Press does not designate first editions and never has.

RIGBY LIMITED (AUSTRALIA)

1976 Statement: "In answer to your question, we do not have any particular method of identifying first editions apart from a line on the imprint page reading 'First published in Australia 19..'. If the book is reprinted, this line would be followed by others giving the year of reprint. We have not used any method apart from this."

1981 Statement: *See* 1981 Statement of Rigby Publishers Limited (Australia)

RIGBY PUBLISHERS LIMITED (AUSTRALIA)

1981 Statement: "In answer to your question, we have not changed our method of indicating first impressions and editions of a book."

See 1976 Statement of Rigby Limited (Australia)

1988 Statement: *See* 1988 Statement of Kevin Weldon & Associates Pty. Ltd. (Australia)

RINEHART & COMPANY, INC.

1947 Statement: "Rinehart first printings can be identified by the colophon of an 'R' enclosed in a circle which appears immediately above the copyright line in all first printings of our books. On subsequent printings the colophon does not appear. The present colophon was adopted when our name was changed from Farrar and Rinehart, Inc., to Rinehart and Co., Inc., on January 1st, 1946."

THE RIO GRANDE PRESS, INC.

1976 Statement: "Our books are all reprints of rare or scarce books.

"We identify all of our first editions (all of our EDITIONS, really) by a comment just above our logo on the title page—on The Rio Grande Press title page. We indicate whether this is a first printing, a second printing, third, fourth etc.

"Where we have NOT done this, as in the very beginning (1962), there would be an indication of a subsequent printing. For instance, in some of our very first reprints, we indicated the year of the reprint, but after a year or so of business, we began inserting the print designation. So if there is NO indication other than the date, it is one of our first editions. Since the latter part of 1963, all of our editions have referred to the 'printing' by its chronology."

1981 Statement: "From 1962 (when The Rio Grande Press, Inc., started in business), thru 1963, we designated the year of publication just above our logo on the copyright page of our edition. During those two years, we did not identify the edition any further than that, so any of our editions that read 1962 or 1963 above our logo on the copyright page would be a 'first edition' of TRGP.

"However, commencing in 1964, we began to identify an edition by indicating 'First Printing 1964,' or 'Second Printing 1971,' etc. Any title we published after (including) 1964 would indicate what printing it was, i.e., second, third, fourth, etc.

"But not many of our titles go into subsequent printings. Our title *Turquois*, for instance, did go into 10 printings. *Black Range Tales* has had several printings, as have *Navajo Weaving, Hopi Katcinas, Navajo Shepherd and Weaver*, and others.

"But if the imprint above the logo on the title page says 1963 or 1964, then yes, it is one of our 'first editions.' "

1988 Statement: "All editions since 1963 are identified on the title page above our logo—

1st, 2nd, 3rd, 4th, etc."

RIZZOLI INTERNATIONAL PUBLICATIONS, INC.

1981 Statement: "On copyright page:

First edition:

First published in the United States of America in 1981 by

Rizzoli International Publications, Inc.

712 Fifth Avenue, New York, NY 10019

"Any subsequent edition:

First published in the United States of America in 1981 by

Rizzoli International Publications, Inc.

712 Fifth Avenue, New York, NY 10019

Second impression (or second edition) 1982

Third impression (or third revised (if so) edition) 1983

etc."

1988 Statement: *See* 1981 Statement. Note that publisher's address will now read 597 Fifth Avenue, New York, NY 10017.

SKELTON ROBINSON (ENGLAND)
(Formerly Citizen Press, Ltd.)

1947 Statement: "Not marked on first editions, but in cases of second impressions and editions, printed on reverse of bastard title-page."

ROCKLIFF PUBLISHING CORPORATION, LIMITED (ENGLAND)
(Practical Press, Ltd. and Art Trade Press, Ltd., associates.)

1947 Statement: "We follow the custom as given in *Rules for Compositors and Readers* of the Oxford University Press, namely the edition is indicated on the reverse of the title page. The first edition includes the date of the copyright only. All subsequent editions and impressions are indicated under the copyright line."

ROCKPORT PRESS, INC.

1947 Statement: "The words FIRST EDITION appear on the copyright page of all first editions, in small caps.

"Subsequent printings of first editions will bear proper identification in italics on the copyright page, i.e. 'Second Printing,' etc."

RODALE PRESS
(Successor to Rodale Publications, Inc.)

1947 Statement: "At the present time we have no way of identifying the first printings of our books."

1976 Statement: "We here at Rodale Press identify our first editions by indicating on the copyright page what printing that particular edition is. Obviously if the book has 'First Printing', it is the first edition. If it has 'Second Printing', Third Printing', etc. it is a later printing. Also if a book is a first edition, we sometimes make no note at all on the copyright page as to what printing the book is in."

1981 Statement: "We don't use the system described to you in 1976, but I really can't pinpoint exactly when we changed. On the copyright page, our books have a line of numbers, which we call the reprint line. It looks like this:

2 4 6 8 10 9 7 5 3 1

"The lowest number represents the number of the printing. If the number 1 is there, you have a copy from the first printing, if the line is:

6 8 10 9 7 5

you have a copy from the fifth printing.

"I don't know how pertinent this is for a book about first editions, but we have many books that go through multiple—10 or 20 or 30—printings. So after the tenth printing, a new reprint line is used:

12 14 16 18 20 19 17 15 13 11

"And so on into higher and higher numbers of printings."

1988 Statement: *See* 1981 Statement

BERTRAM ROTA (PUBLISHING) LTD (ENGLAND)

1989 Statement: "With one solitary exception all the books we have published have been first editions and we have never reprinted them. The solitary new edition bore its own date *and* the date of the original edition on the verso of the title-page.

"London Limited Editions, by definition, publishes only first printings."

THE ROUNDWOOD PRESS (1978) LIMITED (ENGLAND)

1981 Statement: "The Roundwood Press (Publishers) Limited ceased to trade in April 1978 and a new company, The Roundwood Press (1978) Limited, took over all the responsibilities of the old company including the publishing side.

"Our method of designating the first printing of a first edition is unchanged [since the 1976 statement of The Roundwood Press (Publishers), Ltd.]."

See also 1976 Statement of The Roundwood Press (Publishers), Ltd. (England)

THE ROUNDWOOD PRESS (PUBLISHERS), LTD. (ENGLAND)

1976 Statement: "Our practice is as follows: The imprint on the verso of the title page, with the copyright symbol, will show whether the book is a first edition. If the book has been reprinted it will say as much on this page, i.e. 'second impression' or similar. If there is nothing else on this page, then it may be safely assumed that it is the first printing of a first edition.

"Actually, our books are usually the first printing of a first edition, or alternatively an updated edition of a work long out of print, and we always give the most explicit information to this effect."

1981 Statement: *See* 1981 Statement of The Roundwood Press (1978) Limited (England)

ROUTLEDGE

1988 Statement: *See* 1988 Statement of Routledge, Chapman and Hall, Inc.

ROUTLEDGE (ENGLAND)

1988 Statement: *See* 1988 Statement of Associated Book Publishers (UK) Ltd. (England)

ROUTLEDGE, CHAPMAN AND HALL, INC.

1988 Statement: "Methuen, Inc. has changed its name to Routledge, Chapman and Hall, Inc. and now publishes under the two imprints of Routledge, and of Chapman and Hall.

"New editions are identified by the statement 'first published 1988/first published in the USA 1988.' Subsequent printings are designated either by 'reprinted 1987, 1988' or 'second impression 1988.' "

ROUTLEDGE, CHAPMAN, AND HALL (ENGLAND)
1988 Statement: *See* 1988 Statement of Associated Book Publishers (UK) Ltd. (England)

ROUTLEDGE & KEGAN PAUL LTD. (ENGLAND)
1976 Statement: "Our present practice is to put on the back of the title page the words 'First published 1977 by Routledge & Kegan Paul Ltd.' and any reprint would have, lower down, the words 'Reprinted in 1978'.

"Previously, our methods were more slovenly, particularly in the last century, where finding the date of an impression is a matter of guesswork and comparing our London and American addresses.

"This information applies equally to George Routledge & Sons Ltd., and Kegan Paul, Trench, Trubner."
1981 Statement: *See* 1976 Statement

ROUTLEDGE & KEGAN PAUL OF AMERICA LTD.
1981 Statement: "For books printed in the USA, the phrase: 'first published (date)' will appear on the copyright page. For a first edition, the date will correspond to the copyright date.

"Any subsequent printings are indicated on [the copyright] page as reprints. This procedure is the same for all our imprints."

GEORGE ROUTLEDGE & SONS, LTD. (ENGLAND)
1947 Statement: "If there is no statement at all as to a second or later edition or impression, the assumption, of course, is that the book is a first edition. In the case of reprints, or new editions, we state this on the reverse of the title page.

"We regret we cannot tell you the date on which this method was started but it has been going on now for a very long period."
1976 Statement: *See* 1976 Statement of Routledge & Kegan Paul Ltd. (England)

GEORGE ROUTLEDGE & SONS, LTD., KEGAN PAUL, TRENCH, TRUBNER & CO., LTD. (ENGLAND)
1928 Statement: *See* 1937 Statement
1937 Statement: "If there is no statement at all as to a second or later edition or impression, the assumption, of course, is that the book is a first edition. In the case of reprints, or new editions, we state this on the reverse of the title page.

"We regret we cannot tell you the date on which this method was started but it has been going on now for a very long period."

ROWLAND WARD LIMITED (ENGLAND)
1976 Statement: "As far as Rowland Ward's publications is concerned we publish only our own work on Big Game, and as this is rather a limited field we only handle one printing of each edition which is now published every two years.

"The work you are probably interested in is Rowland Ward's Records of Big Game of which the first edition was published in 1892 and the latest, the XVI Edition published last year."
1981 Statement: *See* 1976 Statement

ROY PUBLISHERS

1947 Statement: "Our procedure has varied in the past, but we have now determined on the following course. First editions will not be marked in any way. Second editions will have the phrase 'Second Printing' under the author's name on the title page, and, on the back of the title page, the phrases 'First Printing, date' and 'Second Printing, date' will appear under the copyright statement."

ROYAL HISTORICAL SOCIETY (ENGLAND)

1988 Statement: *See* 1988 Statement of Boydell & Brewer, Ltd. (England)

WILLIAM EDWIN RUDGE

1928 Statement: "Up to the present time we have never included anything in these limited editions of ours that would indicate that they were first editions though ninety per cent of the books we issue are first editions.

"In the future we will carry this information on the copyright page."

1948 Statement (by William Edwin Rudge, Jr.): "As in the case of my father, I can state that most books bearing my name are first editions but no effort has been made so far in thus identifying them. In the future, I will endeavor to identify first editions bearing my name as William Edwin Rudge, Publisher at The Elm Tree Press, Woodstock, Vermont."

THE RUNA PRESS (REPUBLIC OF IRELAND)

1976 Statement: "We have no method of identifying first editions."

1988 Statement: *See* 1976 Statement

RUNNING PRESS

1976 Statement: "Running Press has had no particular method of identifying first editions. We list our printings and their dates on the copyright page."

1981 Statement: Running Press indicates its printings by the use of both the copyright date and by a string of numbers from 1 through 9. A first printing would have both the copyright date and the number 1 present.

RUTGERS UNIVERSITY PRESS

1976 Statement: "The first edition of a Rutgers University Press book is identifiable as such when the edition is not indicated on the copyright page. If we have a second or succeeding editions, we indicate 'second', 'third', etc."

1981, 1988 Statements: *See* 1976 Statement

S

SAGE BOOKS, INC.

1947 Statement: "The policy of this firm is as follows:

1) First printings of any title are not numbered.

2) Subsequent printings identical in matter with the first printing (that is, printings from the same type or plates as the first printing, or printings by photo offset from the original printing) will be numbered on the copyright page, as second printing, third printing, etc.

3) Any book re-set or the matter changed in some way so that subsequent printings would not be identical matter with the first printing, will at that time be designated a subsequent edition, as second edition, third edition, etc.

4) Printings will be numbered within editions, as second edition, second printing, etc."

RUSSELL SAGE FOUNDATION

1937 Statement: "The Russell Sage Foundation has been issuing books and pamphlets in the general social field since 1908. In general our practice has been to indicate on the copyright page the year of first publication and the copyright. If nothing else appears on this page the volume concerned is a first printing of a first edition. Subsequent printings and subsequent editions are all entered on this page in clear form with the inclusion of the date of the first edition or printing. We distinguish between printings and editions on the basis of textual changes. If they are very numerous, the edition is called a new edition. If they are slight, or if no changes are made, the new issue is called a new printing."

1947 Statement: *See* 1937 Statement

1976 Statement: "Unless the word 'Reprinted' and the date appear on the copyright page, the buyer may assume the Russell Sage Foundation book in question is a first edition."

1981 Statement: *See* 1976 Statement

THE SAINT ANDREW PRESS (SCOTLAND)

1976 Statement: "The Saint Andrew Press uses 'First published 1975 by,' followed by our name and address, the copyright notice, and the International Standard Book Number. Supposing that this particular book sells out by 1980 and we decide to reprint it, without an alteration of any kind, then at the new printing the phrase 'reprinted 1980' is added.

"In a second or revised edition, the date is omitted from the opening line which now simply reads 'Published by' and the edition details and dates are given below the copyright line.

"In all honesty I cannot say that any utterly consistent method has been followed since the foundation of The Saint Andrew Press in its present form in 1954 but the scheme outlined above is certainly the one currently followed."

1981, 1989 Statements: *See* 1976 Statement

ST. BOTOLPH PUBLISHING CO., LTD. (ENGLAND)

1947 Statement: "We have so far, as a new Company, not had occasion to have second printings of any of our books. Should we do so, however, we propose to indicate the number of the printing on the back of the title page in the place usually adopted for naming series of printings and editions."

ST. JAMES PRESS

1988 Statement: "A St. James Press publication is a first edition unless stated otherwise. It is also a first printing unless stated otherwise."

ST. MARTIN'S PRESS, INCORPORATED

1976 Statement: "We very rarely designate first editions *per se*. A *revised* version of a book can be 'second' or 'third' edition, and *sometimes* we will add 'fifth printing' etc. on the copyright page. But not always."

1988 Statement: *See* 1976 Statement

ST. MARY'S COLLEGE PRESS
(As of 1980, the name was changed to Saint Mary's Press.)
1976 Statement: "We use nothing to designate a first edition in our publication. We do, however, indicate on the copyright page printings other than the first.
"Earlier we did not indicate subsequent printings."
1981 Statement: *See* 1981 Statement of Saint Mary's Press

SAINT MARY'S PRESS
1981, 1988 Statements: *See* 1976 Statement of St. Mary's College Press

SALEM HOUSE PUBLISHERS LTD.
1988 Statement: "Salem House does not identify the first edition of a publication; subsequent editions are identified as such.
"The method of designation has not changed since Salem House was founded."

THE SALTIRE SOCIETY (SCOTLAND)
1988 Statement: "Up until about 1982 publications of the Saltire Society were described as First Edition 1947, Reprinted 1974 or First Published 1951, Enlarged Edition 1983 or First Published 1951, Reprinted 1974. On one occasion, we have Fourth Edition (1977), Reprinted 1982.
"Since 1982, the year of publication appears on the title page below the name of the publisher (The Saltire Society). The year of publication is also recorded in the copyright note, usually on the verso of the title page."

SANDCASTLE BOOKS
1988 Statement: *See* 1988 Statement of The Putnam & Grosset Group (Children's)

SAMISDAT
1976 Statement: "Normally SAMISDAT does not designate first printings of first editions. We do make an exception, however, when we expect one of our books to be subsequently reprinted by someone else. Then the title page of our first printing, first edition, includes the words 'First Edition,' usually near our logo & copyright notice. I think we've done this twice, maybe three times, in our 55 publications to date.
"We do designate all printings & editions after the first, again on the title page.
"Most of our first editions do exist in several states, since we often run covers in several different colors of paper, and since we usually use paper plates, which tend to break down during long or difficult runs. (We make new plates for second & third printings, & haven't yet printed anything a 4th time.)"
1981 Statement: "Normally SAMISDAT does not designate first printings of first editions. We do make an exception, however, when we expect one of our books to be subsequently reprinted by someone else. Then the title page of our first printing, first edition, includes the words 'First Edition,' usually near our logo & copyright notice. I think we've done this twice, maybe three times, in our 115 publications to date.
"We do designate most printings & editions after the first, again on the title page. We missed once, with the 2nd printing of Dorothea Condry's poetry collection *The Latter Days*, where we used the same plates as for the

228

first printing. The first printing bore yellow covers, however, while the 2nd bears gold.

"Most of our first editions do exist in several states, since we often run covers in several different colors of paper, and since we usually use paper plates, which tend to break down during long or difficult runs. (We make new plates for second & third printings, & haven't yet printed anything a 4th time.)

"We might note that the Avon paperback edition of Tom Suddick's novel *A Few Good Men* purports to be a first; in fact, we published the first edition, long out of print, during November, 1974, 4 full years earlier, and the original title page notes 'first edition' along with the copyright information."

1988 Statement: *See* 1981 Statement

SAN FRANCISCO BOOK COMPANY, INC.

1976 Statement: "Our method of designating first editions is to print the numbers from 10 backwards to 1 on the copyright page, as follows: 10 9 8 7 6 5 4 3 2 1. If all the numbers from 10 to 1 are there, that edition is a first edition. If the number 1 is deleted, it is a second edition; if the number 2 is gone, a third edition; and so on up to 10 editions. Naturally, if the book were to go into multiple editions, a further explanation might be included."

1981 Statement: *See* 1976 Statement

SAN FRANCISCO PRESS, INC.

1988 Statement: "We specifically designate a first edition only when we publish a preliminary version of the book (such as our *ELECTRON MICROSCOPY SAFETY HANDBOOK*), of which the definitive version will be identified as a second edition and will have a similar format but in a different color. The First Edition imprint is on the cover and on the title page."

SAVOYARD

1988 Statement: *See* 1988 Statement of Wayne State University Press

THE SCARECROW PRESS, INC.

1976 Statement: "We do not designate first editions in any special manner, nor do we designate subsequent printings of first editions. All revised or other editions are noted as such on the title page."

1981, 1988 Statements: *See* 1976 Statement

SCHOCKEN BOOKS, INC.

1947 Statement: "First printings of our books are not designated in any way. Second printings, and all subsequent printings, are so noted on the copyright pages of our publications."

1976 Statement: "We do not specifically indicate that any book is a first edition. We do indicate on the copyright page of books for which we have purchased the rights from other publishers, either domestic or foreign, the year in which the book was first published by Schocken Books. We also give the printing number after the first printing."

1981 Statement: "Our practice has changed since 1976. We indicate on the copyright page of every book we publish—whether it originates with us or we have purchased rights from another publisher (either domestic or foreign)—the year in which the book was first published by Schocken Books. We also give the printing number, beginning with the first printing.

"These changes were initiated in 1978; Schocken Books has no imprints."
1988 Statement: "Schocken Books was purchased by Random House in 1987 and is now publishing in coordination with Pantheon Books, a division of Random House. It is the policy of both Pantheon and Schocken to designate books First Edition, First Paperback Edition, or First American Edition where appropriate. Reprint editions are designated using a system of numbers. Pantheon and Schocken are two separate houses and have no imprints."

SCHOLARS PRESS

1988 Statement: "Scholars Press does not normally designate either first editions or first, and subsequent, printings. If, however, the Press reprints a title that was originally published by another company, we will indicate the year in which the Scholars Press edition was originally published on the copyright page."

SCHOLARTIS PRESS (ENGLAND)

See Eric Partridge, Ltd. (Scholartis Press) (England)

SCHOLASTIC MAGAZINES, INC.

1981 Statement: "Attached is a Xerox of a copyright page from a recently published textbook, at the bottom of which appears our Printing History code and beneath which I have explained the code.

12 11 10 9 8 7 6 5 4 3 2 1   1 1 2 3 4 5 6/8
Printed in U.S.A.
[The numbers on the left (1 through 12) indicate the printings.]
Number of printings, reading from right to left.
This example represents First Printing.
(For Second Printing, the '1' would be deleted—
and so on up to Twelfth Printing—without plate change)
[The number in the middle (1) indicates the month of first printing.]
Month of First Printing. This example is January. Appears only on First Printing.
(At Second Printing it is deleted—without plate change)
[The numbers on the right (1 through 6/8) indicate the year of printing.]
Year of Printing.
This example is 1981
(Numbers are deleted from the left for subsequent printings—without plate change)
  "We have been using this code since 1975. Prior to that we used a number code (e.g., 1/811, meaning January 1981, First Printing), which meant resetting for each printing, patching the film, and remaking the plate.
  "The current code enables us to do twelve printings over a six-year period by simply deleting numbers and without any remaking of plates.
  "We use this method of identification on all our [Textbook Division and] Book Club titles."

HENRY SCHUMAN, INC.

1947 Statement: "We do not make any special identification for a first edition of our publications. The means of identification would be the usual one of the copyright date on the manufacturing notice page. On further printings of our books (we are just now issuing our first 'trade list') we would doubtless follow the usual practice of naming the number of the printing and the date. For example,

Copyright 1947 by Henry Schuman, Inc.
First Printing, November, 1947
Second Printing, January, 1948

"In the case of an entirely new edition we would, of course, follow what I believe to be the customary practice of citing the fact that sufficient changes have been made in the text of the first edition of any work to warrant the inscription of a Second or Third Edition to be carried on the title page of a new edition and on the manufacturing page."

SCM PRESS LTD (ENGLAND)

1988 Statement: "Our policy is broadly similar to that of OUP, as can be seen by a study of our biblio pages. Our main aim is to make the publishing history of the book quite clear."

Sample pages provided show the following:

First published 1988
by SCM Press Ltd
26-30 Tottenham Road, London N1

First published 1977
by SCM Press Ltd
26-30 Tottenham Road London N1 4BZ
Second Edition 1981
Second impression 1984

First published in English 1982
by SCM Press Ltd, 26-30 Tottenham Road, London, N1 4BZ
Sixth impression 1988

First published 1957
by The University of Chicago Press, Chicago 60637
First published in Great Britain 1957
by James Nisbet & Co Ltd
This edition first published 1978
by SCM Press Ltd
26-30 Tottenham Road, London N1 4BZ
Second impression 1984

WILLIAM R. SCOTT, INC.

1937 Statement: "Our policy will be to mark seconds, thirds, etc., clearly on the copyright page; marking firsts or not as the spirit moves us."

1947 Statement: "Since sending you information regarding our policy on First Editions, back in 1937, we have had to change, due to manufacturing difficulties.

"All our books are printed by offset. To indicate a first or subsequent printing, the entire black plate for the whole book would have to be made over. Therefore, our books are not marked at all, and won't be, until such time as we print by letter press, if we ever do."

SCOTTISH ACADEMIC PRESS LIMITED (SCOTLAND)

1988 Statement: "We do not specially indicate the first printing of the first edition on that edition. Subsequent printings or new editions are always indicated together with a note of the date of the first edition."

CHARLES SCRIBNER'S SONS

1928 Statement: "We have no fixed plan for designating our first editions of general publications. If a book runs to more than one printing we usually print somewhere in the 'front matter' Second Printing, Third Printing, Fourth Printing, whatever it might be. From this it might be assumed that a copy containing no such printing notice might be considered the first edition."

1937 Statement: "There is no sure way of telling in most cases what is a first edition of a book printed previously to 1930 except that in most cases in the front matter a second printing or any later printing is usually so indicated in the front matter. On books published since 1930 first editions are indicated with a capital 'A' on the copyright page."

1947 Statement: *See* 1937 Statement

1976 Statement:

"E - 9.66 [H]

"E is the fifth printing, 9.66 the date of that printing, H the manufacturer.

1 3 5 7 9 11 13 15 17 19 H/C 20 18 16 14 12 10 8 6 4 2

"After 1972 the keyline was changed to the above system where the lowest number indicates which printing, the first letter in the center, the manufacturer, and the second letter the edition (i.e. cloth or paper)."

1981 Statement: *See* 1976 Statement

1989 Statement: "In 1984, Scribner's became part of Macmillan and now follows Macmillan's procedure of indicating printings at the bottom of the copyright page: the *lowest numeral* in the sequence generally indicates the printing for that copy."

See also 1989 Statement of Macmillan Publishing Co., Inc.

CHARLES SCRIBNER'S SONS, LTD. (ENGLAND)

1928 Statement: "In response to your inquiry as to the method followed by my firm distinguishing first editions, I do not think that there is any absolute hard and fast rule laid down which would apply in every case. The rule generally followed is to note on the reverse of the title page under the copyright notice the dates when the book has been reprinted. The words 'First Edition' or 'First Printing' do not usually appear on first editions, but if the copyright date and the date on the title page are in agreement, and there is no further note, the assumption is that the copy is a first edition. Taking half a dozen books at random I note the following details:

Edward Bok. The Americanization of Edward Bok.

New York
Charles Scribner's Sons
1927

on the reverse—Copyright 1920, 1922 by Charles Scribner's Sons. First Edition September 1920, Second Edition November 1920, Third Edition December 1920, and so on down to 24th Edition August 1923, 25th Edition (Popular Edition) August 1923, and so on down to 34th Edition (Popular Edition) March 1924. In the meantime a different edition known as the Library Edition was published in February 1924 which goes down to the 40th Edition March 1927.

Will James. Smoky
Charles Scribner's Sons
New York—London
1927

Copyright 1926 by Charles Scribner's Sons. Published September 1926. Reprinted September, October, twice in November, five times in December, 1926, once in February 1927; August 1927. Popular Edition published August 1927.

Pupin. *From Immigrant to Inventor*
Charles Scribner's Sons
New York—London
1924

Copyright 1922, 1923 by Charles Scribner's Sons. Published September 1923, Reprinted November 1923, January, March, July, October 1924. In this case the copyright notice of 1922 indicates prior publication of part of the book in the Magazine, but here the actual publication date is mentioned.

"The assumption is that unless otherwise stated on the reverse of the title page the book may be considered as a first edition. Of course it does not take into account such questions as issues. A mistake might be discovered while the presses were running and an alteration made in later copies. There would naturally be nothing on the book to indicate such a change." 1936 Statement: "Charles Scribner's Sons, Ltd., are associated, as you doubtless understand, with Charles Scribner's Sons, New York. As far as editions which we import from America are concerned, the rule for distinguishing first editions is naturally the same as that adopted by the New York house of Charles Scribner's Sons. In future any books published separately here will bear on the title page 'First Published in....,' and if this coincides with the date on the title page, and there is no reprint notice, the book may be assumed to be a first edition."
1947 Statement: *See* 1936 Statement

THE SCRIMSHAW PRESS (CALIFORNIA)

1976 Statement: "To the best of my recollection, we have never indicated an edition as being the first. We have, in fact, generally assumed that the first would be the last.

"On the other hand, we have been quite consistent, I think, in indicating second and subsequent printings and even to the point of resetting some of our colophons when the printer or some other major supplier changed between one printing and another. I am reasonably sure that the verso of the title page, at least, will tell the true story: no indication of printing means first edition; any subsequent printings are named as such. Anyone who wishes may verify this with us on specific titles."

THE SEA HORSE PRESS
(New York, New York)

1981 Statement: "Sea Horse Press doesn't in any way note a first edition. Because we are a small press with rather large first printings—i.e. 2000-3000; we only note a printing if it is beyond a first printing. Then we note the months and year of the printings as follows:

First printing March, 1978
Second printing September 1978
Third Printing June 1980 etc.

which is taken from the only one of our books to have received a smaller (1000 copy) first printing: and subsequently received two more.

"This is standard for us since we began publishing. Thus every Sea Horse book is a first printing unless it says otherwise."

SEABURY PRESS
1988 Statement: *See* 1988 Statement of Crossroad / Continuum

SEAGULL BOOKS (ENGLAND)
1988 Statement: *See* 1988 Statement of The Book Guild Limited (England)

SEAL BOOKS (CANADA)
1989 Statement: Seal hardcover first editions are not designated in any particular manner.

SEAL PRESS
1989 Statement: "Our books designate the printing number by a series of numbers: 10 9 8 7 6 5 4 3 2 1. The current printing is indicated by the final number to the right.

"The first printing of a first edition also indicates the month and year: First edition, March 1989."

MARTIN SECKER, LTD. (ENGLAND)
1928 Statement: "Bibliographical entry on the reverse of the title page."
See also Martin Secker & Warburg, Ltd. (England)
See also 1989 Statement of The Octopus Publishing Group PLC (England)

MARTIN SECKER & WARBURG, LTD. (ENGLAND)
(Formerly Martin Secker, Ltd.)

For statement of practice from 1937 through 1989, see 1989 Statement of The Octopus Publishing Group PLC (England).
1937 Statement: "Bibliographical entry on the reverse of the title page.
"Above is the new style of the firm. No alteration in policy of differentiating reprints, which has been in existence since the business began."
1947 Statement: "We still continue to differentiate between new editions, reprints and first editions in the bibliographical information given on the verso of the title page of our books."
1976 Statement: "Our first editions, and indeed first printings, bear:

First published in England 19.. by
Martin Secker & Warburg Limited
14 Carlisle Street, London W1V 6NN

"Second and further impressions add below:

Reprinted 19..
Reprinted 19..

"Occasionally older books carry the words 'Second impression 19..,' but this convention is no longer followed.

"Re-issues are similarly treated (by a re-issue we mean a reprint of a book which has been out of print a sufficiently long time—a year or more; it is not a new edition, there is no new material):

Re-issued 19..

"Second and further editions follow in the same vein with the addition of
Second edition 19.."
1981 Statement: The 1976 statement is still correct. However, Martin Secker & Warburg Limited have moved. The address on the copyright page will now read:

54 Poland Street, London W1V 3DF

and not:

14 Carlisle Street, London W1V 6NN

1988 Statement: "The information on Martin Secker & Warburg still stands, and our practice is as described. However, we have moved again. Volumes published since January 1988 bear the following address on the copyright page: Michelin House, 81 Fulham Road, London SW3 6RB."
See also 1989 Statement of The Octopus Publishing Group PLC (England)

SECOND CHANCE PRESS
1988 Statement: See 1988 Statement of The Permanent Press

SECOND COMING PRESS, INC.
1981 Statement: "SECOND COMING PRESS, despite its many titles, remains a SMALL PRESS publisher, and therefore 100% of our book line is a FIRST EDITION, ranging in print runs of 500 to 2000 copies. A second edition, would be a reprinting of the first print run, something we have never done, though tempted to on two of our best sellers."
1988 Statement: *See* 1988 Statement of The Permanent Press

SEELEY, SERVICE & CO., LTD. (ENGLAND)
1937 Statement: "The following has been and is our present practice: We used to put the date on the title page of the first edition, and generally altered it, in the same position, to the date of any reprint which might follow.

"Now we sometimes follow the above practice and if not, we insert the date of printing after the printer's name at the end of the book."
1947 Statement: *See* 1937 Statement
See also Seeley, Service & Cooper Ltd. (England)

SEELEY, SERVICE & COOPER LTD. (ENGLAND)
1976 Statement: "The Leo Cooper imprint has existed only since 1969 and I think it can be safely said that the bibliographical details given on the verso title provide all the information necessary.

"Our sister company, Seeley, Service & Co. were in the past exceedingly lax about including such information in their publications, and I can say no more than if you have any specific queries regarding books published under this imprint we would be happy to let you have whatever information we can find from such files as remain."
1981 Statement: "Since you last wrote to us there has been a change in ownership and we are now owned by Frederick Warne Ltd. Leo Cooper & Seeley Service books are still published under those imprints by Frederick Warne and I see no reason to alter what we said in the first edition of your book except to say that on the spine and title page of the books it now says either a Leo Cooper book or a Seeley Service book published by Warne."

SELWYN & BLOUNT, LTD. (ENGLAND)
1928 Statement: "We always show our first editions by the words 'First Printed ..' and the date. On all further editions the words 'Reprinted....' and the date, are added. These words are printed on the back of the half title page."
1936 Statement: "The system as originally stated has not been adhered to during the past two or three years."
1947 Statement: "As a rule, we adhere to the procedure outlined in our 1928 statement, but there may have been some unfortunate occasions during the War when the rule was not strictly kept.

"This also applies to our Associate Company, Messrs. Denis Archer."

SEPHER-HERMON PRESS, INC.

1976 Statement: "We do not put any designation on our first editions designating them as such.

"Subsequent editions are designated as 'second edition,' 'third edition' etc."

1981, 1988 Statements: *See* 1976 Statement

SEREN BOOKS (WALES)

1988 Statement: "We show second impression on the title verso. New editions have always been revised and expanded in the past, so we make this clear on the book cover. This is the practice which we have always followed."

SERENDIPITY

1989 Statement: *See* 1989 Statement of Price/Stern/Sloan Publishers, Inc.

SERIF BOOKS (ENGLAND)

1949 Statement: "The first edition of each book which we publish carries the words 'First Published in 19..,' usually on the reverse of the title page. Subsequent printings have added below this 'Second Printing, Third Printing, etc.,' and the appropriate date. In the event of a new edition being produced this is stated in some such formula as 'New And Revised Edition' or simply 'New Edition' again with the appropriate date.

"We have standardised on this method since our first book. This firm was founded in 1947."

SHAKESPEARE HEAD PRESS (ENGLAND)

1988 Statement: *See* 1988 Statement of Basil Blackwell Limited (England)

SHAMBHALA PUBLICATIONS, INC.

1976 Statement: "Early Shambhala titles were marked first printing or first edition on the copyright page, later printings being marked second, third, etc.

"For the past two-three years we have stopped making marks in our books to distinguish first editions or printings. However, subsequent editions are marked so if any substantial changes have been made in the text or if a book has been changed from cloth to paper."

1981 Statement: "Our statement of designating editions and printings is still accurate with our current practices. Therefore, I suggest you leave the entry as it stands. This procedure does also apply to our subsidiary, the Great Eastern Book Co., and its imprints: Great Eastern and Prajna Press."

1988 Statement: "Early Shambhala titles were marked 'first printing' or 'first edition' on the copyright page, with subsequent printings marked numerically as second, third, etc. Current titles are marked 'first edition' on the copyright page, with subsequent editions identified numerically.

"Great Eastern Book Company and Prajna Press titles are governed by the same designation guidelines. (However, these imprints no longer exist.) New Science Library is presently the only imprint of Shambhala Publications and follows the same guidelines.

"These guidelines went into effect in approximately January of 1988."

SHEED AND WARD, INC.

1937 Statement: "Whenever we reprint a book we note this fact on the reverse of the title page. If this is not indicated, the reader is generally safe in assuming that the book is a first edition. Occasionally we explicitly state the fact that the book is a first edition, but more often we do not indicate it."

1947 Statement: *See* 1949 Statement

SHEED & WARD, INC.

1976 Statement: *See* 1976 Statement of Sheed Andrews and McMeel, Inc.

SHEED AND WARD, LIMITED (ENGLAND)

1937 Statement: "Our usual method of indicating first editions from subsequent printings, is to add to the bibliographical note on the reverse of the title-page, the number and date of the impression. For instance the bibliographical note of the first edition will have the name and address of the printer, our name and address, and 'first published September 1936,' and reprints will have '2nd impression September 1936' added beneath first published.' In the case of a new *edition* '2nd edition October 1936.'

"This method applies only to books published by us in England."

1947 Statement: *See* 1937 Statement

SHEED ANDREWS AND McMEEL, INC.

1976 Statement: "Although we have, this year, once issued a book in a thoroughly revised edition which was identified as 'Second edition, revised,' in the normal course of things we do not consider minor changes sufficient to refer to a new printing as a new edition. Thus, I will refer to first printings and second printings rather than first editions and second editions.

"We have no special identifying mark for a first printing. It has become the practice of some publishers to run the numbers one to ten on their copyright page and knock off the initial number on subsequent printings. We have not adopted this policy as yet, although it might be a good one for us to follow. The only way one could tell a first printing would be the absence of information on subsequent printings and even this can be misleading because until this year Sheed and Ward had no consistent policy of introducing a line on the copyright page indicating that the book was in a second printing, third printing, etc. Our present policy is as follows: When a book goes into a second printing we then introduce on to the copyright page the words 'First printing' and the date and 'Second printing' and the date. A new line is added for each subsequent printing. Thus, as I said, a first printing is actually identified by the lack of such a line. Because our company has a rather complicated history, having changed management a few years ago, changed location given on our title page last year, and changed our name this year, production records on some of the old Sheed and Ward books have gone astray and it is not possible even for us to identify what printing a very old book might be in. In such cases, new printings are being identified as 'A Sheed and Ward Classic' and the logo of Sheed Andrews and McMeel and our Kansas City address is being carried on the title page, to identify the book from previous printings."

1981 Statement: *See* 1981 Statement of Andrews and McMeel, Inc.

SHELDON PRESS (ENGLAND)

1937, 1947 Statements: *See* 1937 Statement of Society for Promoting Christian Knowledge (England)

1976 Statement: "We identify first editions by the following statement:
First Published in Great Britain in 19.. by Sheldon
Press Marylebone Road, London, NW1 4DU

"Subsequent printings are always identified as such."
1981 Statement: "SPCK [Society for Promoting Christian Knowledge], our parent company, incorporated from January, 1980. All imprints mention SPCK." *See* 1976 Statement
See also Society for Promoting Christian Knowledge (England)

SHENGOLD PUBLISHERS, INC.
1976 Statement: "With regard to designating a first edition, we do not use any. We do designate subsequent editions (e.g. Second Edition) which appears on the title pages and in some instances, such as our Encyclopedia, also on the copyright page. This is the same method we have always used."
1981 Statement: *See* 1976 Statement

SHEPHEARD-WALWYN (PUBLISHERS) LIMITED (ENGLAND)
1976 Statement: "Our normal wording on a first edition is:—
'First published 19.. by Shepheard-Walwyn (Publishers) Limited.' We do not at this stage identify it as the first printing. However, where the same edition is re-printed we would state 'Reprinted 19..' and we would build up the printing history, as we went into other printings of the same edition.

"Although we have published new editions of works previously published by other houses, we have not yet published second editions of works we originally published. It is therefore a little difficult to give you firm information as to how we would designate second editions, but I think it is safe to assume that we would simply say 'First published 19... Second edition published 19...' "
1981 Statement: *See* 1976 Statement

SHERIDAN HOUSE, INC.
1947 Statement: "Ordinarily when the first edition is printed, it carries nothing but the usual copyright notice. Should there be a second, third and fourth printing, we generally mark these printings on the copyright page. On the other hand, when a book sells very rapidly, it is not always practical to change the printings and we leave it without any further identification other than that which appears in the original edition. Unless there are changes made in the book, we don't see that it would make any difference whether the book is first, second or third printing."
Statement for 1960: *See* 1947 Statement
1976 Statement: "No new publishing."
1982 Statement: "Same as 1947. Also, books first published in the U.S. are clearly marked 'First published in the United States 1982.' Reprints of books long out of print are marked 'Reprinted 1982.' "
1988 Statement: *See* 1982 Statement

SHOAL CREEK PUBLISHERS, INC.
1976 Statemen: "We prefer no designation for first editions, but have on several occasions at authors request put 'First Edition' on the copyright page.
"For all subsequent editions we do put date of first and subsequent editions."
1981 Statement: *See* 1976 Statement
1988 Statement: "Shoal Creek Publishers Inc. is no longer actively publishing."

THE SHOE STRING PRESS, INC.

1976 Statement: "Although we try to be exceedingly careful when we do reprints as to who did the original edition or the edition used for reprinting, we have not had a special policy with respect to identifying first editions of original works.

"We do, however, identify subsequent editions although not necessarily impressions if there have been no changes."

1981 Statement: *See* 1976 Statement

1988 Statement: "We no longer publish reprints, as a general rule, but the 1976 statement is valid to the extent any policy applies."

GEORGE SHUMWAY, PUBLISHER

1976 Statement: "Usually we provide a statement on the back of the title page such as:

1500 copies this First Edition October 1976

2000 copies this Second Edition January 1978."

1981 Statement: "You have my permission to use my previous reply about how we designate a first edition of our books.

"In practice, however, we have not always followed this format. Our most recent publication, *Rifles of Colonia*, carries the following:

Published 1980

2800 copies casebound, standard edition

200 copies specially casebound and numbered, deluxe edition

"This of course is not so specific, and there is no particular reason for it—I just didn't think about first editions when making up the copyright page. Now that you have jogged my memory, I suppose I should be more specific on future books."

1988 Statement: *See* 1976 Statement

SIDGWICK AND JACKSON, LTD. (ENGLAND)

1928 Statement: "We do not designate our first editions at all, except by the negative method of there being no second or later edition or impression indicated on the back of the title page. Occasionally we state 'Second Impression,' or so on, on the front of the title page."

1935 Statement: "If there is no indication, either on the front or the back of the title-page of any of our publications, that the issue is a second or later edition or impression, it must be taken to be the only, and therefore the first, edition or impression.

"We have employed this method from the start of this business in 1909."

SIDGWICK & JACKSON LIMITED (ENGLAND)

1976 Statement: "In answer to your query about whether we have any particular method of identifying first editions, we can say that if the book does not bear a reprint line, then it is of the first printing."

1981, 1988 Statements: *See* 1976 Statement

ELISABETH SIFTON BOOKS

1988 Statement: *See* 1988 Statement of Penguin Publishing Co Ltd. (England)

SIGMA BOOKS, LTD. (ENGLAND)

1947 Statement: "We always identify the first edition of a new book published by ourselves by the words 'first published....' on the verso of the title page. Reprints are distinguished by having the words 'reprinted....' or 'new edition....' followed by the date, in addition to the date of the first publication."

SIGNET
1988 Statement: *See* 1988 Statement of New American Library

SIGNET CLASSICS
1988 Statement: *See* 1988 Statement of New American Library

SILVER BURDETT & GINN
1988 Statement: "Recently Ginn and Company has been joined by Silver Burdett into a new company, Silver, Burdett & Ginn. We are generally following the most recent copyright notification practices of Ginn and Company.

"First editions of Ginn publications could usually be detected by a single line on the last page of each publication that would begin by a series of letters (e.g., ABCDEFGH). If 'A' was the first letter, the book was a first impression; if 'B' were the first letter, the book was a second impression, etc.

"The copyright notice provides information about revisions. If only one year appears, the book is not a revision of an earlier copyright. If two years appear (e.g., Copyright 1985, 1982) the book is a revision of the earlier copyright.

"In the past, Ginn and Company inserted a number following the copyright notice. An example is 840.1 which indicated that the book was published in August (the eighth month) in the year 1940. The number after the decimal indicated that the book was a first impression.

"There is no date when the system changed from one to the other. In fact, for many years both systems were used on a seemingly arbitrary basis."

SIMMONS-BOARDMAN PUBLISHING CORPORATION
1937 Statement: "We print on the copyright page the date of each revised edition of our books. Each revised edition is copyrighted as to its new material."

1947 Statement: "Our entry is unchanged. You might add that the number of the reprint of an edition is also added on the copyright page."

SIMON AND SCHUSTER
1928 Statement: "Our first editions are marked by the fact that the copyright page bears *no* printing or edition notice, whereas in subsequent editions the dates, and sometimes even the quantity of the printings appear, as

    First Printing, April 1927
    Second Printing, May 1927, etc."

1937 Statement: "Our first editions are marked by the fact that the copyright page bears *no* printing or edition notices whereas in subsequent editions the dates, and sometimes even the quantity of the printings, appear, as

    First Printing, April 1936
    Second Printing, May 1936, etc.

"The date is not always used nor is the phrase 'First Printing' but second and subsequent editions are always marked."

1947 Statement: *See* 1937 Statement

1976 Statement: "Simon and Schuster indicates which printing a book is in by a string of numbers on the copyright page, which appears just below the line that reads, 'Manufactured in....' If you look at the first number on the *left*, you will know which printing you have in hand. Thus if the first number you see is 1, you have a first printing; if the first number you see is 3, you have a third printing. This system of indicating the printing is fairly common in the industry. The only difference of opinion seems to be whether to run the numbers from left to right or vice versa.

"The number system was adopted here over three years ago. We do, however, make an occasional exception to this style and go back to our earlier custom of spelling out: First Printing. Some of our books have carried the date of the printing: First Printing, 1964. The custom of spelling out the printing was, as far as I have been able to determine, the only method of identifying printings prior to mid-1973.

"It should be noted that we use the word 'edition' two ways: (1) to distinguish the style of binding, i.e. a book may be available in both a case-bound edition and a paperback edition; (2) to indicate the version of the text. We do not use 'edition' to mean 'impression' or 'printing.' Therefore one may find certain books in which the first number of the string is 1, but the title page and/or the copyright page indicates that the book is a revised (or second, or third, etc.) edition."

1981 Statement: "The entry you enclosed for Simon and Schuster is still accurate, with one exception. We continue to indicate the number of the printing on the copyright page, but it isn't always the first number on the left. We sometimes will print the numbers like this:

1 3 5 7 9 10 8 6 4 2

Regardless of which system we use, the correct printing is always the *lowest* number shown."

1989 Statement: "Simon and Schuster indicates which printing a book is in by a string of numbers on the copyright page, which appears just below the line that reads, 'Manufactured in....' If you look at the lowest number, you will know which printing you have in hand. Thus if the lowest number you see is 1, you have a first printing; if the lowest number you see is 3, you have a third printing. This system of indicating the printing is fairly common in the industry. The only difference of opinion seems to be whether to run the numbers from left to right, vice versa, or centered as in 1 3 5 7 9 10 8 6 4 2."

SKEFFINGTON & SON, LTD. (ENGLAND)

1937 Statement: "It is not our practice to insert the date of publication on the title page of our new books. In cases where they are reprinted, second, third, or fourth impressions, are printed on the title page and where new editions are issued, the words 'New Edition' are also printed.

"Our first editions are therefore quite easy to identify as the title page appears without date and no reference to any edition."

1948 Statement: "It is not our present practice to include dates in our publications. In the case of books which are reprinted, we state 'Second Impression,' 'Third Impression' and so on, as appropriate."

SLEEPY HOLLOW PRESS

1981 Statement: *See* 1976 Statement of Sleepy Hollow Restorations

SLEEPY HOLLOW RESTORATIONS

1976 Statement: "First editions of books published by Sleepy Hollow Restorations may be identified by the appearance of the words 'First Printing' on the copyright page of the book.

"Reprints of the first edition of one of our books will be identified by the words 'Second Printing,' 'Third Printing,' etc., with the date of the printing, on the copyright page of the book.

"Subsequent or revised editions will be identified by the words 'Revised Edition,' 'Second Edition,' etc., on the copyright page of the book."

1981 Statement: *See* 1981 Statement of Sleepy Hollow Press

WILLIAM SLOANE ASSOCIATES, INC.

1947 Statement: "The only distinguishing marks are carried on the copyright notice. First editions are marked 'First Printing' and subsequent printings carry the number of that particular printing: second, third, and so on."

THE SMITH

1976 Statement: "We simply print, on the copyright page, 'First Edition,' followed by the month and the year."

1981 Statement: *See* 1976 Statement

1988 Statement: "We use the same method of reporting First Editions that we have always used, though we do not indicate month of publication—only the year of copyright."

GIBBS SMITH, PUBLISHER

1988 Statement: "First editions are so designated on the copyright page. Subsequent printings of the first edition are so noted.

"We print as the first words of the copyright page 'First Edition.' Following that comes the line of numbers, then the copyright notice. As far as I know, this is the way we have always done it.

"Please note that the current and correct name of our company is Gibbs Smith, Publisher. Our books all carry the Peregrine Smith Books imprint. In the future there may be other imprints published by Gibbs Smith, Publisher."

HARRISON SMITH, INC.

(Became Harrison Smith & Robert Haas, Inc., in March, 1932.)

1937 Statement: "Although no strict rule was followed, in general it will be found that unless books are marked 'Second printing,' they are first editions."

HARRISON SMITH & ROBERT HAAS, INC.

(Organized in March, 1932. Out of business.
Merged with Random House, Inc. on April 1, 1936.)

1937 Statement: "Although no strict rule was followed, in general it will be found that unless books published by us are marked 'Second printing,' they are first editions."

PEREGRINE SMITH, INC.

1976 Statement: "Peregrine Smith, Inc. does not have a particular or unique method of identifying first editions at this time. We do note second (and subsequent) or revised editions on the copyright page of the edition so designated, however; this notation being used when there have been textual changes, additions or alterations in the book. Printing runs have seldom (if ever) been noted on Peregrine Smith, Inc. books."

1981 Statement: "Until 1980 first editions had no distinguishing mark or imprint. The date on the title page and copyright page correspond to the first publication of the book. If the book was reprinted, this would usually be noted by either a date change on the title page or the notation '2nd printing' etc. on the copyright page. Any revisions or alterations would be acknowledged by the notation 'Revised.' Since 1980, our policy has been to print 'First edition' on the copyright page of the book, this to be replaced by '2nd printing'.. etc., if the book returned to press."

1988 Statement: *See* 1988 Statement of Gibbs Smith, Publisher

PETER SMITH, INC.

1937 Statement: "Date of edition is always indicated on title page."

1947 Statement: *See* 1937 Statement

RICHARD R. SMITH
(Including Margent Press.)

1947 Statement: "Since I have been publishing under my sole individual imprint, which was in December 1935, I have placed the date of publication both on the title page and on the copyright page which backs it up. In the event that a book is reprinted, I change the date on the title page but not, of course, on the copyright. I also add to the copyright page the dates of the various reprints. It is true, however, that if a reprint happened to be required very hurriedly as was the case with some of my books during the war, we may have failed to change the date on the title page.

"Margent Press is a subsidiary imprint of mine and is used primarily for fiction, poetry, and books in the occult field."

URE SMITH (AUSTRALIA)

1976 Statement: "In answer to your question regarding the method of identifying first editions, in the majority of cases since 1960 a first edition can be identified by the words FIRST EDITION *or* First published in (date)..."

1981 Statement: *See* Lansdowne Press (Australia)

1988 Statement: *See* 1988 Statement of Kevin Weldon & Associates Pty. Ltd. (Australia)

SMITH AND DURRELL, INC.
(October 1, 1947, name changed to Oliver Durrell, Inc.)

1947 Statement: *See* Oliver Durrell, Inc.

SMITHSONIAN INSTITUTION PRESS

1976 Statement: "We do not designate first editions. Yes, we indicate only those printings or editions after the first. Thus, it may be safely assumed that any book bearing the Smithsonian Institution Press imprint is a first edition, unless otherwise indicated."

1981 Statement: *See* 1976 Statement

1988 Statement: "This year we began designating editions by means of a range of numbers listed on the copyright page. The last number on the right-hand side designates the edition, so that a first edition would bear the numerals ten, or in some cases five, through one. In some cases we follow the same format for year dates, e.g.: 93 92 91 90 89   5 4 3 2 1."

COLIN SMYTHE LIMITED, PUBLISHERS (ENGLAND)

1976 Statement: "First editions normally have the statement 'First published in....' Reprints always are indicated 'Reprinted....' If ours is not the first publication, we normally give as much bibliographical information as possible."

1981 Statement: "I think the [1976] entry could possibly be expanded to read:

"First editions normally have the statement
   'First published in....,
   second edition published in....'
"Reprints are indicated by a statement to that effect. If ours is not the first publication, we normally give as much bibliographical information as possible.

"By second edition, I mean the bibliographical second edition, where new material has been added, the old revised, or when the book has been reset, not just the CIP definition of a rewrite. If a book is a photographic reproduction of an earlier edition from a different publisher, such information is normally indicated in the book. Normally we only issue straight photographic reprints in paperback format. Regrettably I am not as consistent in my descriptions as I should be. When I started publishing I tried to give even the publication day in my description, but printers' delays so often made a nonsense of this that I had to give it up."
1988 Statement: "My 1976 statement remains unchanged. I have not found any reason for making changes.

"As to Dolmen Press, we bought the books but not the imprint or logo. We have made new contracts with many of the authors and should we reprint any of the titles, they will appear with our imprint. The Dolmen ISBN prefix 0-85105 will continue to be used for those publications for the foreseeable future. I will of course also use our own system of providing bibliographical information for Dolmen titles in future."

SOCIETY FOR PROMOTING CHRISTIAN KNOWLEDGE (ENGLAND)

1937 Statement: "It is our practice to put the date of the publication of any book on the title-page itself. If the book is reprinted, the date of the reprint appears on the title-page and a bibliographical description on the back of the title-page, e.g.
   First Edition 1922
   Reprinted 1923
   Second Edition 1924
"If only slight corrections are made we put Second Impression: and Second Edition when changes in the text are important."
1947 Statement: *See* 1937 Statement
1989 Statement: *See* 1937 Statement

THE SOHO BOOK COMPANY LTD. (ENGLAND)

1988 Statement: "Our first editions carry the statement
   'Published by the Soho Book Company Ltd,
   1/3 Brewer Street, London W1
   19...'
"Later editions add: '2nd Edition 19...'
"Later impressions add: '2nd impression 19...' "

SOHO PRESS INC.

1988 Statement: "We carry the term 'FIRST EDITION' on the copyright page of every book and have done so consistently. Additional printings are likewise noted as they occur."

SOUTH HEAD PRESS (AUSTRALIA)

1988 Statement: "South Head Press does not particularly identify First Edition printings. The date of printing set forth in each book is the way Editions are identified.

"The same applies to books published as issues of Poetry Australia."

SOUTHERN ILLINOIS UNIVERSITY PRESS

1976 Statement: "We do not indicate first printing of a first edition, but do indicate number—and give date—of subsequent printing(s). We note revised edition on title page and on copyright page."

1981 Statement: "Southern Illinois University Press has made only one change in designating printings and editions, a change effective just this month [January, 1981]. In printings after the first, we indicate the printing and date of the most recent printing and no longer indicate the date of printings prior to the current one. For example, the Fifth Printing of a book will say only 'Fifth Printing (date)' and will not list dates of printings one through four, as we used to do."

1988 Statement: "We now indicate printing and year by numbers on [the] © page:

91 90 89 88   4 3 2 1

"This is a first printing in 1988.

"Subsequent printings [are] similarly indicated by removing [the] number

91 90 89   4 3

"[This is a] third printing in 1989."

SOUTHERN METHODIST UNIVERSITY PRESS

1976 Statement: "We do not designate a first edition, but we do designate each subsequent printing and edition. Therefore it may be assumed that if any one of our books has simply the copyright date it is a first edition. A subsequent printing will have below that line on the copyright page 'Second Printing 1975' or whatever the year may be. And this will continue with each subsequent printing. A second edition carries a similar line. For example, *John C. Duval, First Texas Man of Letters* by J. Frank Dobie has the copyright date 1939 and then below it 'Second Edition, 1965.' We have used these methods of identification from the earliest days of our press."

1981 Statement: *See* 1976 Statement

1988 Statement: "In May 1987 we began to designate first editions 'First Edition 1987' or whatever the year may be, and we continue to designate each subsequent printing or edition ('Second Printing 1988' or 'Second Edition 1988').

"For books published prior to May 1987, see 1976 Statement."

SOUTHWEST PRESS
(Succeeded by Turner Company in 1935.)

THE SOUTHWORTH PRESS

1947 Statement: *See* 1947 Statement of The Anthoensen Press

SOUTHWORTH-ANTHOENSEN PRESS
(Name changed to The Anthoensen Press, in 1947.)

1947 Statement: *See* 1947 Statement of The Anthoensen Press

SOUVENIR PRESS LIMITED (ENGLAND)

1976 Statement: "We do not differentiate specifically on our various editions except to have the words, 'this edition first published by Souvenir Press Limited in the year of publication it is.' I hope this gives you sufficient information. We tend to put in the next reprint underneath whenever such a happy event occurs, which actually with our books is quite often."

1981 Statement: *See* 1976 Statement

1988 Statement: "I am astonished at how pertinent the statement we made in 1976 still is today. We do continue to have many reprints happily."

SPARROW PRESS

1988 Statement: *See* 1988 Statement of Vagrom Chap Books

ROBERT SPELLER PUBLISHING CO.

(The 1949 edition of Boutell's "First Editions of Today and How to Tell Them" incorrectly identified this company as being "out of business.")

1937 Statement: "Each book published by us carries, on the copyright page, the words FIRST EDITION. Subsequent editions are marked thus: Second Printing, Third Printing, etc."

See Statement for 1960 of Robert Speller & Sons, Publishers, Inc.

ROBERT SPELLER & SONS, PUBLISHERS, INC.

Statement for 1960: "Robert Speller Publishing Co. did not go out of business in 1938. Book sales distribution were handled by Elliott Publishing Co. in 1938-39. Elliott is out of business as far as we know.

"Robert Speller Publishing Co. changed its name to Robert Speller & Sons, Publishers, Inc. in 1957. All books are distributed by us. We have been in business since 1930.

"First impressions were identified by the words, 'First edition, 2nd printing, etc.' "

1976, 1982 Statements: *See* Statement for 1960

SPHERE BOOKS LIMITED (ENGLAND)

1988 Statement: "The publication date and record of each new impression and new edition is entered on the copyright page. This has been the practice since Sphere Books Ltd was formed twenty-one years ago in 1967. Our Abacus and Cardinal imprints use the same method."

(In late 1988, the Penguin Group changed its method of designating a first edition. For a book published in the latter part of 1988, see 1988 Statement of Penguin Publishing Co Ltd [England].)

SPINSTERS/AUNT LUTE BOOK CO.

1988 Statement: We indicate a first edition on the copyright page by indicating printings as follows:

10 - 9 - 8 - 7 - 6 - 5 - 4 - 3 - 2 - 1

"Each subsequent printing has one number deleted. 'Second Editions' are so named with a new number sequence.

"1982 was the year we adopted this method. It differs from previous years when we did nothing. We have no imprints or subsidiaries."

SPIRITUAL SCIENCE LIBRARY

1988 Statement: *See* 1988 Statement of Garber Communications Inc.

E. & F. N. SPON LTD. (ENGLAND)

1976 Statement: "We do not use any particular method to identify first editions of our books. There is a simple statement on the biblio page of when the book was first published. If there is no additional information on either reprints or new editions then the book is a first edition."

1981 Statement: "It remains true to say that we make no special announcement in the first edition of any of our titles. The absence of any information about re-printing or revision can be taken as an indication that the book in question is indeed a first edition."

1988 Statement: *See* 1988 Statement of Associated Book Publishers (UK) Ltd. (Scientific and Technical Division) (England)

THE SPOON RIVER PRESS

1977 Statement: "All books published by The Spoon River Press bear the publishing history on the title page verso. First printings are designated by the phrase 'First published (month) (year)'. Later printings are noted below this line. We have always followed this practice."

1983, 1989 Statements: *See* 1977 Statement

SPRING (ENGLAND)

1989 Statement: *See* 1989 Statement of The Octopus Publishing Group PLC (England)

SPRING CREEK PRESS

1988 Statement: *See* 1988 Statement of Johnson Publishing Company. Inc.

STACKPOLE BOOKS

1976 Statement: "I'm sorry to say that we don't have any method of identifying first editions. Generally, our books do not contain this information, since many of our publications are quality paperback titles. We may, however, put printing and edition information in the front matter of a select few of our titles in the near future."

1981 Statement: "Stackpole now identifies its second, third, fourth, etc., editions. We do not identify first editions. Thus, if one of our books is without an edition designation in the front matter, that book may be assumed to be a first edition.

"This, I understand has been our policy for a couple of years or so now."

1988 Statement: "Stackpole identifies its second, third, fourth, and subsequent editions. We have been identifying our first editions in some books and expect to do so in most of our future books. If one of our books is without an edition designation in the front matter, that book may be assumed to be a first edition.

"In 1987 we began designating the number of the printing within each edition by a row of numbers on the copyright page: 10 9 8 7 6 5 4 3 2 1. In copies from the first printing of any edition, all the numbers appear. For each successive printing, one number is removed. So, if the farthest-right number is 2, that copy of the book is from the second printing of the designated edition."

STACKPOLE SONS

1937 Statement: "The lack of notice of additional printings shows a Stackpole Sons first edition. There is one exception—*Caleb Catlum's America*. The first printing of this book is marked 'First Edition' at the bottom of the verso of the title page. "The Telegraph Press has adhered to no strict policy in the past, though usually its first printings have been marked 'First Edition'; but hereafter it will follow the same method as that used by Stackpole Sons, and its first printings will be identified by the lack of notice of subsequent reprintings."

1947 Statement: "The lack of notice of additional printings shows a Stackpole Sons first edition. There is one exception—*Caleb Catlum's America*. The first printing of this book is marked 'First Edition' at the bottom of the verso of the title page."

STAINER & BELL LTD. (ENGLAND)

1976 Statement: "We as publishers have no particular method of identifying first editions. Unless it states otherwise (i.e. 'second revised edition') then our book is a first edition—but not necessarily a 'first printing' of a first edition.

"I'm afraid we have no other more definite method of identification."

1981, 1988 Statements: *See* 1976 Statement

STANFORD MARITIME (ENGLAND)

1988 Statement: *See* 1988 Statement of George Philip Limited (England)

STANFORD UNIVERSITY PRESS

1928 Statement: *See* 1937 Statement

1937 Statement: "Our method of indicating our first editions is the negative one of not mentioning reprinting or revision. Editions or printings subsequent to the first edition or printing carry on the copyright page both

'First published, 19—'

and

'Second Printing, 19—'

or

'Second (Revised) Edition'

"We believe we have followed this practice since we issued our first books in 1925."

1947 Statement: *See* 1937 Statement

Statement for 1960: "The [1976] statement for Stanford University Press holds for all Stanford University Press books from 1928 to the present."

1976 Statement: "We do not have any particular method of identifying first editions. I believe it is correct to say, however, that a Stanford book is unquestionably a first edition if its copyright page (1) does not specify 'Second printing' or the like, and (2) does not carry a line reading 'Last figure below indicates year of this printing,' followed by a line of two-digit numbers."

1981 Statement: "Your current write-up for Stanford University Press still accurately describes our practice. I may add that it is also our practice to include the year of publication on the title page in a first printing, and to eliminate it in second and subsequent printings. This practice has been unvarying since 1956, to the best of my knowledge."

1988 Statement: "Your current write-up for Stanford University Press still accurately describes our practice. I may add that it is also usually our practice to include the year of publication on the title page in a first printing and to eliminate it in second and subsequent printings."

STANTON AND LEE

1947 Statement: *See* 1947 Statement of Arkham House

STANTON & LEE PUBLISHERS, INC.

1981 Statement: "The first printing of any book we publish carries the notice 'First Edition' on the copyright page; any subsequent printing carries the number of that printing only: second printing, October 1980; or third printing, January 1981 and so on. Our imprints use the same procedure."

STANWIX HOUSE INCORPORATED

1976 Statement: "Stanwix House does not mark First Editions in any way. In the area of our professional books, we do mark each printing after the first. Subsequent editions can be distinguished by their newer copyright."

1981 Statement: *See* 1976 Statement

STAR PUBLISHING

1988 Statement: "Currently first editions are not especially designated. However, the terms 'revised edition,' 'second edition,' etc., appear when appropriate. Indications of which printing are usually not coded in the book."

STATE HISTORICAL SOCIETY OF WISCONSIN
(THE SOCIETY PRESS)

1976 Statement: The absence of any identifying statement would indicate the first printing of a first edition.

"Subsequent printings of an edition are indicated on the copyright page."

1981, 1988 Statements: *See* 1976 Statement

STATE UNIVERSITY OF NEW YORK PRESS

1976 Statement: "In response to your inquiry, any book published by this Press may be considered a first edition, first printing, unless otherwise indicated on the verso of the title leaf.

"Our books seldom require recomposition and, hence, nearly all of them are 'first editions.' Second and third printings, first paperback printings, etc. are so indicated as noted above."

1988 Statement: *See* 1976 Statement

STEAM PRESS

1988 Statement: "First editions bear no identification. Subsequent editions are marked 'second printing 19..' or 'revised edition...' on the copyright page. We do not note reprints on subsequent editions on our Vinyl Shower books."

STEIN AND DAY, PUBLISHERS

1976 Statement: "If the copyright page does not say 'second printing,' then the book is a first edition. There are no special marks identifying first or second editions."

1981 Statement: "The [1976] information on Stein and Day is still correct." Stein and Day does indicate first printings of a first edition by the notation "First published in (date)". Second printings will also have the notation SECOND PRINTING, (date).

First printings of a book first published abroad have the notation "First published in the United States of America in (date)."

1988 Statement: Stein and Day was not publishing in 1988.

STEINER BOOKS

1988 Statement: *See* 1988 Statement of Garber Communications Inc.

RUDOLF STEINER PUBLICATIONS
1988 Statement: *See* 1988 Statement of Garber Communications Inc.

STEMMER HOUSE
1981 Statement: The practice we follow with respect to designating first editions is as follows:

"The first printing of a book originated by Stemmer House is designated First Edition on the copyright page. If the book was originally published by a foreign publisher, our own book bears the words First American Edition.

"When we go back to press for a new printing, unrevised, we delete the words First Edition and substitute Second Printing, along with the month and year of this printing. Subsequent printings are listed under this line, e.g.:

Second Printing July 1979
Third Printing October 1980

"However, when the text is revised, the words Second Edition are substituted for the original First Edition line."

1988 Statement: "The practice we follow with respect to designating first editions is as follows:

"The first printing of a book originated by Stemmer House is designated First Edition on the copyright page. If the book was originally published by a foreign publisher, our own book bears the words First American Edition.

"When we go back to press for a new printing, unrevised, we delete the words First Edition and substitute First Printing with the date of this printing, and add Second Printing, along with the year of this printing. Subsequent printings are listed under this line, e.g.:

Second Printing 1979
Third Printing 1980

"When the text is revised, the words Second Edition are substituted for the original First Edition line."

STEMMER HOUSE PUBLISHERS INC
1988 Statement: *See* 1988 Statement of Stemmer House

STEPHEN-PAUL PUBLISHERS
1947 Statement: "In all our publications, first printings or editions are designated as such. Subsequent printings read—'second (or third) printing.' In the case of two of our publications this year, which slipped by without the designation 'First Edition,' second printings will be designated."

PATRICK STEPHENS LIMITED PUBLISHERS (ENGLAND)
1976 Statement: "We merely put on the verso of the title page of a new book, 'First published in (date).' This follows the usual copyright notice. If there is a second edition, we add the words 'Second edition (date).' "
1988 Statement: *See* 1988 Statement of Thorsons Publishing Group Ltd. (England)

STERLING PUBLISHING COMPANY, INC.
1976 Statement: "We merely put the copyright date in without any reference that it is a first edition. Should we print again without revisions,

we add 'Second Printing' etc. We have always used this particular wording. If revisions are made, we obtain a new copyright, and add this © date."

1981 Statement: *See* 1976 Statement

1988 Statement: "We merely put the copyright date in without any reference that it is a first edition. However, we insert a numerical impression series, normally 1 through 10, above the copyright notice at the time of first publication. The presence of '1' indicates the first impression. At the second run, the '1' is opaqued, and so on. If revisions are made and are sufficient to do so, we obtain a new copyright, add this © date, and a new numerical sequence of impressions begins."

GEORGE W. STEWART, PUBLISHER, INC.

1947 Statement: "With few accidental exceptions our second and subsequent printings and editions are so marked on the copyright pages. All others are first editions."

ELLIOT STOCK (ENGLAND)

1928 Statement: "The first editions of our publications are marked with the date thereof upon the title page. All later editions carry the record, *i.e.*, the date of the first edition, and of the subsequent editions or reprints as the case may be."

1937 Statement: *See* 1928 Statement

FREDERICK A. STOKES CO.

(Sometime between 1937 and 1949, Stokes publications were acquired by Lippincott, which publishes Stokes juveniles under the Stokes imprint.)

1928 Statement: "To date we have omitted putting any special mark or distinction upon first printings of any of our books, but in general these can very readily be distinguished from succeeding printings by the fact that on the Copyright Page (reverse of Title) no printing notice appears. After first printings we generally put the date of publication and the words 'Second Printing' and date of such printing."

1937 Statement: *See* 1928 Statement

STONE WALL PRESS, INC.

1988 Statement: "This is more or less what we do:
   Copyright [date] by Stone Wall Press, Inc.
   First Printing, November [date]
   Second Printing, January [date]"

STOREY COMMUNICATIONS, INC.

1988 Statement: "We publish how-to books on a variety of topics; not the type of books that will have value to collectors in later years. It is not generally our policy to designate first editions unless it is a big and important book in which case the copyright page would list both First Edition and the month and year of the first printing.

"The copyright page will list the number of the printing, and the month and year, regardless of what printing it is.

"When a title has 25 percent (or more) of new material, it then becomes a revised edition. Such will be printed on the cover and title page and the book will be issued a new ISBN number and will no doubt be reintroduced to the trade as a revised edition.

"Storey Communications, Inc., has two imprints: Garden Way Publishing and Storey Publishing."

STOREY PUBLISHING
1988 Statement: *See* 1988 Statement of Storey Communications, Inc.

STORM PUBLISHERS
1947 Statement: "Our printings are to be identified on the copyright page. Notes to that effect appear there irregularly in the case of first printings and systematically in the case of later printings. Storm books are hence *princeps* editions when they are identified as such and when they are not identified at all. We do not expect ever to deviate from this procedure."

STORMLINE PRESS INC.
1988 Statement: "We do not designate 1st printings of any editions. We do specify 2nd printing, 3rd printing, etc."

STRAWBERRY HILL PRESS
1981 Statement: "The only manner in which we *normally* indicate a first edition (first printing) is by stating on the copyright page the first printing information (for example: First Printing, June, 1981).

"The only time we have deviated from that was with a book entitled *The Closet*. With *The Closet*, we issued a small first printing of 1,000 copies which are designated 'Debut Edition' on both the front cover and the title page; the first commercial printing of the book (5,000 copies) does not show that 'Debut Edition,' nor is there any reference to the printing information on the copyright page.

"In the last few months only, we have changed our policy completely: we do not show first printing notices at all—rather, when a book is reprinted, the new printing information only is noted (for example: Second Printing, 1981)."

1988 Statement: "We do not show first printing notices at all—rather, when a book is *reprinted*, the new printing information only is noted on the copyright page (e.g.: Second Printing, February, 1988). When we issue a new edition of a book, as opposed to simply another printing, that is stated on the front cover and title page of the book, as: New Edition, Revised and Expanded.

"This policy applies to our imprints and subsidiaries (we do have both)."

STREET & MASSEY, LTD. (ENGLAND)
(Out of business prior to 1949.)
1937 Statement: "It is our rule to place on the title page of each book the year in which the book is last printed. On the back of the title page we clearly state:

First published in January, 1936
"This indicates the initial printing. After this:

Second Impression March, 1936
Third Impression June, 1936
Second Edition (Revision) January, 1937
Fifth Impression June, 1937

"We have adopted the use of the word revision in brackets after every new edition. Collectors are quite aware that a new edition is (or should be) a revision, but the general public is not so sure and we prefer to emphasise the fact."

STRETHER AND SWANN, PUBLISHERS

1976 Statement: "Our first editions are designated as such by the words First Edition on the copyright page. Subsequent printings are designated by number."

1981 Statement: *See* 1976 Statement

PAUL A. STRUCK, INC.

1947 Statement. "Our First Editions are just marked as such."

LYLE STUART, INC.

1976 Statement: "We have no policy about first editions. Sometimes we so identify them and at other times the only way that someone would know that a book is not a first edition is to find first printing and second printing dates and quantities on the copyright page."

1981 Statement: *See* 1976 Statement

1988 Statement: "We continue to follow the practice indicated in our 1976 statement. Frequently we use 2 through 10 numbers on a first printing and then drop a number in subsequent editions."

THE STUDIO LIMITED (ENGLAND)

1947 Statement: " 'Studio books always have the first year of publication printed on the back of their title pages, and subsequent reprints are noted thereunder with their respective year of publication. If, however, a book is re-set or revised, with new material added, it is our custom to list it as a 'new and revised edition,' but the notation to this effect still appears on the back of the title page under the previous listings of first publication and reprintings."

STUDIO PUBLICATIONS, INC.

1947 Statement: "We do not state Edition in first edition. Subsequent editions carry notation '2d. Edition,' etc.".

STUDIO VISTA (ENGLAND)

1988 Statement: *See* 1988 Statement of Cassell PLC (England)

SUFFOLK RECORDS SOCIETY (ENGLAND)

1988 Statement: *See* 1988 Statement of Boydell & Brewer, Ltd. (England)

GEORGE SULLY AND CO.
(Out of business prior to 1937.)

1928 Statement: "We do not mark the first editions of our books in any particular manner."

SUMMIT BOOKS

1981 Statement: "The first printing of a Summit book is identified on the copyright page, either by the words 'First Edition' or by the number '1' on the printing number line. This has been our practice since Summit Books began publishing in 1977."

1988 Statement: *See* 1981 Statement

SUMMIT BOOKS (AUSTRALIA)

1976, 1981 Statements: *See* 1976, 1981 Statements of Lansdowne Press (Australia)

1988 Statement: *See* 1988 Statement of Kevin Weldon and Associates Pty Ltd (Australia)

SUN & MOON CLASSICS

1988 Statement: *See* 1988 Statement of Sun & Moon Press

SUN & MOON PRESS

1988 Statement: "Sun & Moon Press designates both first editions and first printings. First editions are designated by the words FIRST EDITION on the copyright page. Second and further editions are designated in the same way, by the words SECOND EDITION and so on.

"Printings are designated by the line of numbers, from 10 to 1, running across the lower part of the copyright page. A first printing is designated by a complete series, from 10 to 1; each subsequent printing drops a number, e.g. a second printing bears the numbers 10-2, having dropped the '1.'

"Sun & Moon Press has used this method since 1980. Our imprints all use the same method."

SUN PUBLISHING COMPANY

1976 Statement: "We do not have any particular method of identifying first editions."

All printings of a first edition are indicated.

1981 Statement: "First printings say: 'First Sun Books Printing: (Date).' "

1988 Statement: "All printings of a first edition are indicated."

SUN RIVER PRESS

1976 Statement: "Sun River Press does not identify first editions—we do not identify first printing either."

The state of a book is never indicated.

1981 Statement: Sun River Press is no longer active.

SUNBURST BOOKS

1988 Statement: *See* 1988 Statement of Farrar, Straus & Giroux, Inc.

SUNDIAL (ENGLAND)

1989 Statement: *See* 1989 Statement of The Octopus Publishing Group PLC (England)

SUNDIAL BOOKS

1976, 1981, 1988 Statements: *See* 1976, 1981, 1988 Statements of The Sunstone Press

SUNNYSIDE

1981 Statement: *See* 1981 Statement of Sleepy Hollow Press

SUNSET BOOKS

1981, 1988 Statements: *See* 1981, 1988 Statements of Lane Publishing Co.

THE SUNSTONE PRESS

1976 Statement: "The Sunstone Press uses no distinguishing marks or symbols to identify first editions. As a general rule no edition statement is used at all for first editions. (Alas, there are one or two exceptions when 'First Edition' has been printed on the verso of the title page). Second editions carry the publishing history of the book on the verso of the title page as follows:

First Edition 1974
Second Edition 1976

"Being a small regional press we do not frequently produce more than one edition of a work. A second or third printing is so indicated on the verso of the title page. When reprinting an older title from another publisher we so indicate. If the printing has added material, illustrations, etc., we designate it a new edition and print the publishing history as above."

1981 Statement: "Yes, our methods have changed since we were last contacted by you. We now do state that a book is a first edition on the copyright page. The words First Edition appear in caps. At the bottom of the same page it will also state that the book is either a Sunstone Press title or a new imprint of ours, Sundial Books. Sundial Books are ones that we produce and distribute, but they are often published by other companies and individuals.

"In addition to the above, we also print a limited edition of each of our trade first edition books. In the back of these, usually on the last page in the book, there appears a colophon, which I am enclosing so you can see how we do it. For example:

RURAL ARCHITECTURE OF
NORTHERN NEW MEXICO
AND SOUTHERN COLORADO
Five hundred copies in
a limited edition
signed by the author
of which this is
number...

"And finally, our practice of stating second, third or fourth printings follows the same pattern described above in my first paragraph."

1988 Statement: "All books have edition statements. Most books are indicated as

First Edition

"For subsequent editions or reprintings, the printing history is given, i.e.,

First Edition, 1985
Second Edition, 1987

or

First Edition, 1985
Reprinted, 1987

"We no longer print limited editions of our trade books. If a limited edition of a title is printed, it is so noted."

SUPERIOR PUBLISHING COMPANY
(Seattle, Washington)

1947 Statement: "First printings of our books so far have had no identifying mark. On subsequent printings we include the words 'Second Printing,' 'Third Printing,' etc., as the case may be, directly under the copyright notice on the back of the title page."

1976 Statement: "We usually label our first editions on page 4 of our books and this would be our first printing also, on future printings the First Edition is taken off."

1981 Statement: *See* 1976 Statement

SUSQUEHANNA UNIVERSITY PRESS

1988 Statement: *See* 1988 Statement of Associated University Presses

SUSSEX UNIVERSITY PRESS (ENGLAND)

1976 Statement: "Readers may assume that all our books are first editions unless we specify on the copyright page that the book has been reprinted or is published in a new edition. The date after the copyright sign normally indicates when the book was first published."

ALAN SUTTON PUBLISHING LIMITED (ENGLAND)

1988 Statement: "The first edition would have the words 'First published 198-.' Subsequent editions would have the words 'Second edition 198-' and so on. If the text of a book has been revised, the word 'revised' is also inserted."

SUTTONHOUSE LTD.

1937 Statement: "Please note that all first printings of SUTTONHOUSE LTD., in the past have been identified by the appearance of the same date on both the title and the copyright page, unless 'second printing' appeared on the copyright page.

"In the future, however, 'first edition' will appear on the copyright page, so that there will be no confusion whatsoever. This means that all books published after May 1, 1936, will carry this marking. The second printings will have no such marking."

SWALLOW PRESS

1947 Statement: "First printings of our books carry only the copyright notice, except in a few instances the line
'FIRST PRINTING (month—year)'
below the copyright notice.

"All subsequent printings are marked 'Second Printing, Third Printing, Fourth Printing' as the case may be, and new editions of the book are clearly marked. A distinction should be made between an edition and a printing, edition having some material change in the text or format of the publication."

THE SWALLOW PRESS, INC.

1976 Statement: Both editions and printings are so indicated.
1981 Statement: *See* 1976 Statement
1982 Statement: "The Swallow Press, Inc., is now an imprint of Ohio University Press. The title pages will read either The Swallow Press or
The Swallow Press
Ohio University Press
Athens, Chicago, London
"The copyright page carries the Statement that 'Swallow Press/Sage books are published by Ohio University Press.'

"I believe that when the Press began in 1946 the name was Alan Swallow. The name may have changed to The Swallow Press, Inc., in 1966 or 1967, after the death of Alan Swallow.

"Ohio University Press took on the Swallow Press as an imprint in 1979.
"We mark the edition on subsequent printings on the copyright page."
1988 Statement: *See* 1988 Statement of Ohio University Press

SWEDENBORG FOUNDATION, INC.

1976 Statement: "Since our concern is exclusively with Swedenborgian theology and we have a copy of *A Bibliography of the Works of Emanuel Swedenborg* (743 pages) by the Rev. James Hyde, published in 1906 and contain-

ing a complete list and description of all these works in the original Latin and translations published prior to that date, we can easily identify any of these. We occasionally mention the date of original Latin publication, and the ordinal number of the particular reprint of ours, on the respective title page, but not always. Many of these works and extracts are also published by the Swedenborg Society, Ltd., London, which follows a similar practice."
1981, 1988 Statements: *See* 1976 Statement

SYDNEY UNIVERSITY PRESS (AUSTRALIA)

1976 Statement: "We have no particular method of identifying first edition printings, other than the stated year in which the book is first published and the copyright notice and date on the verso of the title page."
1981 Statement: *See* 1976 Statement
1988 Statement: Sydney University Press was inactive after 31 March 1988.

SYLVAN PRESS, INC.

1947 Statement: "First Editions of all of our books are (1) limited, (2) numbered by hand."

SYLVAN PRESS, LIMITED (ENGLAND)

1947 Statement: "We fall in line with the majority of established English publishers by printing the month and year of first publication on the back of the title page.

"The same imprint is used on reprints, retaining the date of the first edition and printing the date of reprint underneath.

"In the last twelve to fifteen months we have been obliged to abandon temporarily the insertion of the month in our imprint, production and binding delays being so acute; also, from the commercial standpoint, should a book be first published say in November, bearing the imprint of the previous April or May, this is liable to influence sales adversely.
"We are only too anxious to revert to the practice of including the month of publication as soon as production difficulties are more under control and timing can be fairly assessed."

SYRACUSE UNIVERSITY PRESS

1976 Statement: "The Syracuse University Press places the following information on the copyright page of the first edition:
Copyright notice
All rights reserved
First edition
"On subsequent editions, we add the new copyright date and indicate the number of the edition (second edition, etc.).
"The later printings give the number of the printing. i.e.:
1st
First Edition
2nd
First Edition
Second printing, 1976
3rd
First Edition
Third printing, 1977
etc."
1981 Statement: *See* 1976 Statement

1988 Statement: "In 1987 we did begin to use a new format to designate our first editions. However, in a few cases when we are relatively certain that a book will not require a second edition, we do still use the previous format.

"The Syracuse University Press places the following information on the copyright page of the first edition:

Copyright notice
First published 1987
All Rights Reserved
First Edition
97 96 95 94 93 92 91 90 89 88 87 6 5 4 3 2 1

"The above line of numbers refers to the year and the number of a particular reprint.

"If the book is the first edition of the paperback (that is, the book was initially published in cloth only), then it is designated as follows:

Copyright notice
First published 1986
All Rights Reserved
First paperback edition 1988
97 96 95 94 93 92 91 90 89 88 87 6 5 4 3 2 1

"On subsequent editions, we add the new copyright date and indicate the number of the edition (and other information as necessary), please see the following example:

Copyright notice
All Rights Reserved
First Edition 1984
Revised, Second Edition 1987
97 96 95 94 93 92 91 90 89 88 87 6 5 4 3 2 1

"We do not have any subsidiaries [or] imprints."

T

TABB HOUSE (ENGLAND)

1988 Statement: "Our policy is to print the year of a book's first edition at the top of the copyrights page, followed in chronological order by the years of further reprints or new editions."

TALBOT PRESS LIMITED (REPUBLIC OF IRELAND)

1976 Statement: "In the case of Talbot Press books the incidence of first edition is usually recognized by the year appearing at the foot of the title page following the imprint. Also on the verso of the title page you will invariably find reference to 'First published....' "

1981 Statement: *See* 1976 Statement

TRUMEN TALLEY BOOKS

1988 Statement: *See* 1988 Statement of E. P. Dutton & Co., Inc.

TALON BOOKS LTD. (CANADA)

1976 Statement: "We're primarily a literary publisher and we publish poetry, plays, fiction and short stories. For most books of poetry, they only have one printing, which sometime is dated by the month that the book was printing, but, more recently, only by the copyright date. Second printings usually are noted with an updated copyright page, on which it says, 'Second printing,' then the date. Our plays often go into numerous printings and these are noted on the copyright page, but only as the latest printing, i.e., the printing history is not given, although the original copyright date remains the same. Ditto for the fiction. If we do a second edition or a revised first edition, this too is noted, but as a continuum, i.e., 'Second printing (revised),' then the date. The third printing of a revised edition is noted only as 'Third printing,' however, the revision having earlier taken place."

1981 Statement: *See* 1976 Statement

TAMARACK PRESS

1981 Statement: A first printing is designated by the statement "First printing (year)" on the page bearing the copyright.

1988 Statement: "Tamarack Press is no longer involved in book publishing."

TANDEM PRESS, INC.

1976 Statement: "We identify our first editions by merely printing our Library of Congress and our ISBN numbers. Any edition following the first edition is then named as: Second edition and the date; third edition, date and so forth. This has been our policy and no other method was previously used."

1981, 1989 Statements: *See* 1976 Statement

THE TANTIVY PRESS (ENGLAND)

1947 Statement: "We send herewith a marked catalogue which may help, as our practice has varied greatly in the dating of our books, as a result of war-time difficulties.* At the outset it was often necessary to have the same book set up several times by different printers, in order to get paper. We were feeling our way and experimented with different methods of marking editions and impressions. We seem to have stabilized at the moment, however, in the method of indicating an edition or impression by a datemark in Roman characters within a bibliographical note at the foot of the verso of the title page.

"Often our first editions have several different kinds of binding, owing to the shortage of cloth, but there are so many variations here that to detail same would require a day's work and, frankly, we cannot afford that. We leave it to the eventual scholar with his university grant! And it will be an interesting job."

*According to the catalogue all first editions of books published by this Press carry the bibliographical details on the verso of the title page or of the bastard, except the following five titles, which carry the date on the title page: *The Pioneers, Satirical Verses, Representative Lyrics, Indiscretions of an Infant, Tubers and Taradiddle.*

1988 Statement: *See* 1947 Statement, but note that the company no longer publishes original works of a literary nature.

TAPLINGER PUBLISHING CO., INC.

1976 Statement: "Our current and continuing practice for designating all first printings of our original titles is to cite FIRST EDITION on the copyright page. Subsequent printings are so stated, as 'Second Printing,' 'Third Printing,' and so on.

"We also import a number of foreign titles (usually from England or Australia). These normally constitute a first American Edition although our copyright page rarely says so. These titles can usually be distinguished from our own original titles from the notice 'First published in the United States in... by Taplinger Publishing Company.' We often do subsequent printings of these books here in the United States, but not always; however, when we do, the copyright page will note the particular printing.

"I am sorry that I cannot verify if this has been standard policy or whether it does differ from previous methods in the company's early days. But of course we do indicate revised editions, printings with corrections and so forth."

1981, 1988 Statements: *See* 1976 Statement

J. P. TARCHER, INC.

1976 Statement: "To answer your question as to how we identify first editions: We identify it by the absence of any designation such as 'first edition.' In subsequent editions we designate it by 'revised edition' or '(title) No. 3' (or whatever edition).

"As for printings in each edition, we list the numbers 1 2 3 4 5 6 7 8 9 0 on the copyright page of our books and delete the number corresponding to the printing each time we reprint."

1981 Statement: "We have indeed changed the method of identifying first editions and printings:

"As of May 1979, J. P. Tarcher, Inc. identifies first editions by placing the designation 'First Edition' on the copyright page. In subsequent editions we do not indicate the edition on the copyright page but may place 'Revised edition' on the cover or jacket.

"We indicate the printings of an edition by listing '10 9 8 7 6 5 4 3 2 1' on the copyright page and deleting numbers so that the lowest number showing is the number of the printing.

"We also place a letter code before the printing numbers to help us quickly identify the manufacturer.

"These procedures apply to all our imprints."

1988 Statement: *See* 1988 Statement of Jeremy P. Tarcher, Inc.

JEREMY P. TARCHER, INC.

1988 Statement: As of 1985, Jeremy P. Tarcher, Inc. ceased placing a *letter* code before the printing number.

"Additionally, since *around* 1983 (nobody here is exactly sure of the date) the company name became Jeremy P. Tarcher as opposed to J. P. Tarcher. Certainly all books from 1984 on have that name on the title page."

TATSCH ASSOCIATES

1976 Statement: "We leave first editions unmarked, on the assumption that if no edition number is specified the reader will know that it is the first. Likewise, for the first printing of the first edition.

"These methods of identification do not differ from any previously used."

1981, 1988 Statements: *See* 1976 Statement

THE TAUNTON PRESS

1988 Statement: "We indicate a first printing with the words 'first printing, month, date' on the copyright page. Subsequent printings would be listed underneath that in the same manner. This has been our practice since 1978 when we first began publishing books. We have only one imprint, but if we ever create others or subsequent ones, they would follow the same practice."

TELEGRAPH PRESS

1947 Statement: "The Telegraph Press has adhered to no strict policy in the past, though usually its first printings have been marked 'First Edition'; but hereafter it will follow the same method as that used by Stackpole Sons, and its first printings will be identified by the lack of notice of subsequent reprintings."

C. & J. TEMPLE, LTD. (ENGLAND)

1947 Statement: "We usually give the required information on the reverse of the title page, together with the colophon of the printer.

"In the case of a first edition of a new book we print: 'First published by C. J. Temple, Ltd., etc. 1947.' In the case of subsequent reprints we add the words 'reprinted in 1948.'

"When we publish a new edition of a classic, or a new edition of a novel published by some other firm or firms in the past, we print: 'This edition was first published by etc., 194—.' "

TEMPLE HOUSE BOOKS (ENGLAND)

1988 Statement: *See* 1988 Statement of The Book Guild Limited (England)

TEMPLE UNIVERSITY PRESS

1988 Statement: "If we are publishing a book for the first time, the following information is inserted on the copyright page:

Temple University Press, Philadelphia 19122
Copyright (year) by Temple University. All rights reserved
Published (year)
Printed in the United States of America
(Any necessary acknowledgements)
(Library of Congress Cataloging in Publication Data box)

"If our book does *not* say 'Revised Edition,' 'Second Edition,' 'Third Edition,' etc., it is the first edition.

"We do not indicate second, third, etc. printings."

TEMPLEGATE PUBLISHERS

1988 Statement: "We adopt the same method to identify the first printings of our books as that employed by other leading publishers. The first edition would have the words 'First published 198-' and subsequent editions would have the words 'Second edition 198-' and so on. If the text of a book has been revised the word 'revised' is also inserted."

TEN SPEED PRESS

1976 Statement: "We have no special designation for first editions. We do sometimes indicate 'Tenth Printing' but not always, so that you cannot assume the lack of such identification means a first edition."

1981 Statement: *See* 1976 Statement

1988 Statement: "We now indicate the first printing with a number code from '1' and a year code, so the entry would come out

88 89 90 91 9 8 7 6 5 4 3 2 1

to indicate a first printing in 1988."

TEXAS A&M UNIVERSITY PRESS

1976 Statement: "We identify first editions by the statement 'First edition' on the copyright page. Subsequent printings are likewise identified: 'Second printing,' 'Third printing' and so on. This does not differ from any previous practice here."

1981 Statement: *See* 1976 Statement

1988 Statement: "Concerning first editions our press still follows the practice outlined in our last statement. The only difference involves second and following printings; we now add the year following the printing notice, as 'Second printing 1988.' "

TEXAS CHRISTIAN UNIVERSITY PRESS

1988 Statement: "We do not designate first printings as such, but simply put the copyright date on the copyright page. On subsequent printings that page also indicates second or third or whatever printing. This is not a policy adopted at any point in time by the press but a practice that has been followed over the years.

"We have no imprints other than our own and no subsidiaries."

TEXAS MONTHLY PRESS

1981 Statement: "The way we indicate the edition of a particular title is on the copyright page. [The phrase 'First Edition, (month) (year)' would be printed on the copyright page.] This has always been our practice. Also, we do not have any imprints.

"Starting [in the fall of 1980], we started indicating editions by setting on the copyright page, 'A B C D E F G H' When a book goes back for a second printing, we ask the printer to scratch out the 'A' Therefore, a 'B' indicates a second printing, a 'C' indicates a third printing, etc."

TEXAS TECH UNIVERSITY PRESS

1988 Statement: "We do not explicitly designate first editions or first printings. Second and subsequent editions are designated by 'Second edition; first edition 1972.' This represents no change in our practice since 1971, and it holds for all imprints under our control."

TEXAS WESTERN PRESS

1988 Statement: "Texas Western Press does not print the phrase 'first edition' in its books but does, on the verso of the title page, in the space which includes copyright data, indicate if a printing is anything but a first. We use the phrase 'second printing,' followed by the year, for a new printing of a book that is unaltered from the first, and 'second edition' for any book that is changed—added to, updated, etc.—in any significant way.

"This has not, however, been a consistent rule over the 35-year history of this press. The late J. Carl Hertzog, an eminent typographer and book designer, who was founder of this press, occasionally did print 'First Edition' in some of his elegant limited edition books and monographs.

"I would say the present practice has been consistently followed since about 1980."

THAMES AND HUDSON INC.

1981 Statement: First printings are indicated on the copyright page by the copyright date and the words "First published in (year corresponding to copyright year)."

"Subsequent printings are indicated by numbers at the bottom of the copyright page (e.g. 3 4 5 6 7 8 9 0).

"But—looking over a number of our books, there are exceptions and inconsistencies."

1988 Statement: "We do not make any special identification of first editions. On the other hand, we do indicate any edition which is a reprint. The result is that any of our books which do not have a reprint line can be taken to be first editions."

THAMES AND HUDSON LTD. (ENGLAND)

1976 Statement: "We do not make any special identification of first editions. On the other hand, we do indicate any edition which is a reprint. The result is that any of our books which do not have a reprint line can be taken to be first editions."

1981, 1988 Statements: *See* 1976 Statement

THEATRE ARTS BOOKS

1947 Statement: "Over the years Theatre Arts has published various volumes as they came up, and no consistent device was used to indicate first editions. Usually, however, the absence of any information in regard to the edition or the printing meant that the volume was a first edition."

1976 Statement: "Theatre Arts Books does not designate first editions. We do designate subsequent printings, so one can assume a book not so designated to be a first edition."

1981 Statement: *See* 1976 Statement

1988 Statement: "Theatre Arts Books, now an imprint of Routledge, does not identify first editions."

THE THEOSOPHICAL PUBLISHING HOUSE

1976 Statement: "We designate our first editions with a statement on the copyright page similar to the one below.

" 'First Quest Book edition 1975 published by the Theosophical Publishing House, Wheaton, Illinois, a department of The Theosophical Society in America.' "

1981 Statement: *See* 1976 Statement

1988 Statement: "The edition statement you list from 1976 is now obsolete. As of 1980 we started to develop a new format which currently encompasses two different types of Quest Books. For a title that has not been published before and thus is originated from Quest, our statement reads: 'A Quest Original. First Edition 19__.' If the book is a reprint, previously published by another publisher, then our statement will read: 'First Quest Edition 19__.' "

THISTLEDOWN PRESS LTD. (CANADA)

1989 Statement: "Most of our titles are published in a first edition only, and many are not reprinted. We are therefore not in the habit of indicating first editions in any way. We do, however, indicate second and subsequent printings and we also indicate if the book is a second edition. One can assume, then, that if there is no edition statement that the book in hand is a first printing of a first edition. This has been our practice throughout Thistledown's history.

"Thistledown Press is an independently owned company without subsidiaries or other imprints."

CHARLES C. THOMAS, PUBLISHER

1988 Statement: "We list on the Copyright Page each new edition but not reprintings."

S. EVELYN THOMAS (ENGLAND)

1947 Statement: "The first editions of my books are either not marked at all with the edition reference or they are marked 'First Edition.' All editions after the first have the edition number shown thereon."

THORNDIKE PRESS

1981 Statement: "We do not designate a 1st edition in any way, except that 2nd printings (and so on) will say, sometimes, '2nd Printing.' "
1988 Statement: "Thorndike Press no longer does 1st editions of any kind. We are exclusively a large print *reprint* house, and purchase those rights from other publishers."

THORSONS (ENGLAND)

1988 Statement: *See* 1988 Statement of Thorsons Publishing Group Ltd. (England)

THORSONS PUBLISHERS LIMITED (ENGLAND)

1981 Statement: "The administration of Turnstone is now run by Thorsons.

"The statement which appeared in [1976] for Turnstone Press still holds good although we differ slightly as you will see when comparing the final sentence.

"I have, therefore, set below the complete statement ready for publication.

"Our policy is to put 'First published 1981' as an indication for first editions of a book which we originate. 'First published in the United Kingdom 1981' would identify the first edition of a book which originated in America or elsewhere. 'This Edition first published 1981' would identify a title which has already appeared in another edition. Subsequent editions which have undergone updating, revision and resetting would appear as 'This Edition, completely revised and reset, 1981' and subsequent printings would appear as 'Fifth Impression 1981.' "
1988 Statement: *See* 1988 Statement of Thorsons Publishing Group Ltd. (England)

THORSONS PUBLISHING GROUP LTD. (ENGLAND)

1988 Statement: "Thorsons Publishing Group comprises the following imprints:

> THORSONS
> GRAPEVINE
> AQUARIAN PRESS
> CRUCIBLE BOOKS
> PATRICK STEPHENS LTD (PSL)
> EQUATION

All these imprints adopt the following rules:

" 'First published 1988' indicates a first edition of a book which we have originated.

" 'First published in the United Kingdom 1988' will identify the first edition of a book which was originated in America or other English language markets.

264

" 'This edition first published 1988' indicates a title which has already appeared in another edition; e.g. a trade paperback edition of a title first published in hardback.

" 'This edition completely revised and reset 1988' indicates a subsequent edition which has been completely updated, revised and reset.

"We now use the rub-off method to indicate the reprint history of a book."

THREE CONTINENTS PRESS, INC.

1976 Statement: "In all our publications to date, we state very clearly at the top of our copyright page, 'First Edition' and we expect to continue to do so in future books.

"A second printing of the 1st ed. will read: First Edition, 2nd printing (or 3rd or 4th etc. as appropriate).

"For us, a 2nd ed. signifies a basic change (one or more pgs. from the original 1st ed.) & 2nd printings of a second edition would be—2nd Ed-2nd printing."

1981 Statement: "As far as our statement is concerned, it still stands as is, with our imprints also."

1989 Statement: *See* 1981 Statement

THUNDER'S MOUTH PRESS

1988 Statement: "Subsequent to a first edition, the later editions of a book are so designated on the copyright page by its ordinal number and date (e.g. 'Seventh Printing April 1988'). This has been our policy since we began publishing in fall of 1981.

"We have no imprints or subsidiaries."

THURMAN PUBLISHING LTD (ENGLAND)

1989 Statement: *See* 1989 Statement of Price/Stern/Sloan Publishers, Inc.

TICKNOR & FIELDS

1988 Statement: "We use reverse numbers: e.g., '10 9 8 7 6 5 4 3 2 1' designates a first edition. For the second the '1' would be omitted, and so on. If we use up all 10, we start over using '20' through '11.'

"This is what our parent, Houghton Mifflin, does."

TIDEWATER PUBLISHERS

1976, 1981, 1988 Statements: *See* 1976, 1981, 1988 Statements of Cornell Maritime Press, Inc.

TIME-LIFE BOOKS INC.

1981 Statement: "Before I explain how we designate first printings of first editions, a brief history is in order. "Time-Life Books started as a division of Time Inc. 21 years ago. From the very beginning we have published books primarily in series. To date, we have published 28 series with a total of 620 titles. And now to the particulars about the manner in which we designate first printings of first editions.

"With the first series, LIFE WORLD LIBRARY, which started in September 1960 we designated first printings by a small hourglass symbol [**x**] published on the last page of the book. Second printings of the same title carried two hourglasses; third printings, three hourglasses, etc. This hourglass designation was used for all series through 1975. The book series that carried this hourglass design during that time were:

LIFE WORLD LIBRARY	1960
LIFE NATURE LIBRARY	1961

TIME READING PROGRAM	1962
LIFE HISTORY OF THE U.S.	1963
LIFE SCIENCE LIBRARY	1963
GREAT AGES OF MAN	1965
TIME-LIFE LIBRARY OF ART	1966
TIME-LIFE LIBRARY OF AMERICA	1967
FOODS OF THE WORLD	1968
THIS FABULOUS CENTURY	1969
LIFE LIBRARY OF PHOTOGRAPHY	1970
T-L ENCYCLOPEDIA OF GARDENING	1971
THE AMERICAN WILDERNESS	1972
THE EMERGENCE OF MAN	1972
THE ART OF SEWING	1973
THE OLD WEST	1973
WORLD'S WILD PLACES	1973
HUMAN BEHAVIOR	1974
TIME-LIFE LIBRARY OF BOATING	1975

"Starting in 1976 Time-Life Books no longer used the hourglass designation and in its place designated the particular printings of all books (even those that originally carried an hourglass and subsequently had additional printings starting in 1976) on the copyright page. The Time-Life book series that carry this latest designation since 1976 are:

THE GREAT CITIES	1976
HOME REPAIR AND IMPROVEMENT	1976
WORLD WAR II	1976
THE ENCYCLOPEDIA OF GARDENING	1978
THE SEAFARERS	1978
THE GOOD COOK	1979
CLASSICS OF THE OLD WEST	1980
THE EPIC OF FLIGHT	1980
LIBRARY OF HEALTH	1981

"Over our 21 year history, Time-Life Books has also published 84 single titles. The hourglass design was also used on these books through 1975 and the first printing designated on the copyright page was employed starting in 1976."

1988 Statement: *See* 1981 Statement. Note, though, that the following titles should be added to the post-1976 publication list:

COLLECTOR'S LIBRARY	
OF THE CIVIL WAR	1982
PLANET EARTH	1982
THE CIVIL WAR	1983
GREAT MEALS IN MINUTES	1983
THE KODAK LIBRARY	
OF CREATIVE PHOTOGRAPHY	1983
THE ENCHANTED WORLD	1983
YOUR HOME	1985
LIBRARY OF NATIONS	1985
UNDERSTANDING COMPUTERS	1985
HEALTHY HOME COOKING	1986
SUCCESSFUL PARENTING	1986
FITNESS, HEALTH & NUTRITION	1987
FIX IT YOURSELF	1987

TIME FRAME	 1987
MYSTERIES OF THE UNKNOWN	 1987
TIME-LIFE GARDENING GUIDE	 1988
VOYAGE THROUGH	
THE UNIVERSE (forthcoming)	 1988

"On both series and single titles from Time-Life Books, the printing number is always designated on the copyright page, and for printings other than the first, the date of the latest revision is shown."

TIMES BOOKS

1976, 1981 Statements: *See* 1976, 1981 Statements of Quadrangle / The New York Times Book Co., Inc.

1988 Statement: "Our method of identifying editions is as follows:

"The first edition/first printing is marked 'First Edition.' Subsequent printings are marked 2, 3, etc.

"A second edition will usually be identified as 'revised edition' and will have a printing identification, as with first editions."

TONGG PUBLISHING CO.

1947 Statement: "No special marks. Other than first editions carry indications of later printing."

THE TOUCHSTONE PRESS

1976 Statement: "Touchstone does not have a special way of identifying first editions . . . . We do identify different printings with the simple statement 'second printing' etc."

1981 Statement: *See* 1976 Statement

TRAIL'S END PUBLISHING CO.

1947 Statement: "*All* my books have the edition, year, etc., plainly printed on the copyright page. Second, third, etc., are likewise imprinted."

TRANSACTION BOOKS

1976 Statement: "Since we demarcate second and third editions, and second and third printings on the title page, the simplest way of identifying an original edition is that it will simply have the year of publication and the conventional Library of Congress markings."

1981 Statement: "The only revision I would make to [the 1976 Statement] is to note that the demarcation between editions now lists ISBN numbers.

"Since we demarcate second and third editions, and second and third printings on the title page, the simplest way of identifying an original edition is that it will have the year of publication, the ISBN listings, and the conventional Library of Congress markings."

1989 Statement: *See* 1981 Statement

TRANSATLANTIC ARTS, INC.

1947 Statement: "We identify first printings of our titles by the words:

First American Edition, 1900

"We identify second (and subsequent) printings of the same work by repeating the first line above and adding, beneath it:

Second Printing, 1900

"If a subsequent second or other printing is revised, instead of the immediate phrase reprintings, we note, beneath the last line of data:

Second American Revised Edition, 1900

"All the preceding apply to imported imprint editions that are not subject to copyright. On domestically produced titles, we follow the same plan but add the word 'Copyright' preceding the year for the first editions and revised editions. On every edition, we include all editions and all printings."
1982 Statement: *See* 1947 Statement

TRANSWORLD PUBLISHERS (AUSTRALIA) PTY LIMITED
(AUSTRALIA)
1988 Statement: "[This is] a copy of our standard imprint information which states the year in which the title is first published, subsequent reprints and new editions:
First published in Australasia in 19xx by
Doubleday, a division of Transworld Publishers (Aust.) Pty Ltd
15-23 Helles Avenue, Moorebank NSW 2170."

TRAVELLER'S PRESS (ENGLAND)
1989 Statement: *See* 1989 Statement of The Octopus Publishing Group PLC (England)

TREACLE PRESS
1988 Statement: *See* 1988 Statement of McPherson & Company

TREASURE PRESS (ENGLAND)
1989 Statement: *See* 1989 Statement of The Octopus Publishing Group PLC (England)

TREND HOUSE
1976 Statement: "First edition does not have any distinguishing features except that the single copyright line is an indication that it is a first edition. Later we use 'second printing' if no substantial editing or recopyright it in the event there is significant editing."
1981 Statement: *See* 1976 Statement

TRIAD EDITIONS
1947 Statement: *See* 1947 Statement of Falmouth Publishing House, Inc.

TRIGON PRESS (ENGLAND)
1988 Statement: "All title pages say 'first published in ...(year).' If [there are] 2nd or subsequent editions, then
'1st published ...[date]
2nd edition published ...[date]
3rd edition published ...'
etc."

TROUBADOR PRESS, INC.
1976 Statement: "We have had various methods for identifying first editions of our publications. 1) On most of our hard cover books we use the phrase 'first edition' on the © page. 2) On some of our paperback books we use the code '1 2 3 4 5 6 7 8 9 0,' erasing from the plate the last digit remaining on the left at each reprint. 3) Only when it seemed important, we've printed the edition number on reprints; esp. *The Fat Cat Coloring and Limerick Book* in which we printed 'Fourteenth printing' when that occasion arose. Another method of identifying editions of our books is the change of copy on the ad page (last page) in most of our books. This changes almost every reprinting, but there is no indication of sequence other than

noting the increased prices (i.e. you never know, necessarily, from the ad page which edition came before the other)."

1981 Statement: *See* 1976 Statement

1989 Statement: *See* 1989 Statement of Price/Stern/Sloan Publishers, Inc.

TUFTS UNIVERSITY

1988 Statement: *See* 1988 Statement of University Press of New England

TUNDRA BOOKS OF MONTREAL (CANADA)

1976 Statement: "We designate the edition only after the first. The only time we show it as a first is when it is a limited numbered edition. If there is only one entry—ex. © 1975, William Kurelek, it can be assumed it is the first edition."

1981, 1988 Statements: *See* 1976 Statement

TUNDRA BOOKS OF NORTHERN NEW YORK

1976 Statement: "We don't have a special way of designating first editions, except where we say 'This first edition is limited to — copies.' But since we always indicate in *later* editions the dates of previous editions, where there is no such listing, it can be assumed that the edition is the first."

1981 Statement: *See* 1976 Statement

1988 Statement: "We don't have a special way of designating first editions, except where we say 'This first edition is limited to — copies.' But since we always indicate in *later* editions the date of the first edition, where there is no such listing, it can be assumed that the edition is the first."

TUPPER AND LOVE, INC.

1947 Statement: "We do not make any difference between first and subsequent printings of our books. If there are changes in the manuscript, we show first or subsequent editions—but not printings of the same editions."

TURNER COMPANY

1937 Statement: "We purchased the assets of the Southwest Press in 1935 and continue to publish all titles formerly published by that concern.

"Since 1935 we use the following plan to differentiate first from subsequent printings of our books: On all editions except the first we run a line on the copyright page stating the number of printing, second printing, third printing, etc., as the case may be."

1947 Statement: *See* 1937 Statement

TURNSTONE PRESS LIMITED (ENGLAND)

1976 Statement: "Our policy is to put 'First published 1976' as an indication for first editions of a book which we originate. 'First published in Great Britain 1976' would identify the first edition of a book which originated in America or elsewhere. 'This edition first published 1976' would identify a title which had already appeared in another edition. Subsequent editions or printings in addition to the foregoing have 'Revised edition 1976' '5th printing 1976.' "

1981 Statement: *See* 1981 Statement of Thorsons Publishers Limited (England)

1988 Statement: *See* 1988 Statement of Thorsons Publishing Group Ltd. (England)

TUROE PRESS

1981 Statement: *See* 1981 Statement of Arlen House: The Women's Press (Republic of Ireland)

CHARLES E. TUTTLE CO., INC.

1976 Statement: "We normally indicate on the reverse of the title page for any book we publish, that this is the first printing. If we do not make this particular statement on a new printing, we do say 'second printing.'

"In other words, I think you can assume that anything we publish is a first edition, if it actually says so, or if there is no indication on the back that it is a second, third, fourth, etc. printing."

1981, 1988 Statements: *See* 1976 Statement

TWAYNE PUBLISHERS, INC.

1976 Statement: "Twayne has never designated a 'first edition'. Where a title does have a revised or second edition ('revised' indicates changes of 10% or less; 'second' indicates changes of more than 10% and usually nearly complete rewriting) the new editions are marked 'Revised Edition' on half-title and title pages; a new copyright covering the new material is entered; and a preface indicates the nature of changes.

"As for 'printings' it was only in 1976 that Twayne introduced the line *'First Printing'* on the copyright page; this line is deleted on subsequent printings. Otherwise, to identify a first printing of a first edition of a Twayne book is almost a book-by-book task that is complicated by the fact that until 1974, the common practice was to print twice as many copies as were first bound (e.g., print 2000, bind 1000), so there are variant bindings. Now we bind all copies."

TWENTIETH CENTURY FUND

1947 Statement: "We don't mark our first printings in any special way. The first printing is usually indicated as follows, on the copyright page:

Copyright 1939 by the Twentieth Century Fund

"Subsequent printings bear the following legends on the copyright page:

First published April 1942
Reprinted April 1942
Third printing April 1942
Fourth printing June, 1942, etc."

TYCOOLY PUBLISHING (ENGLAND)

1988 Statement: *See* 1988 Statement of Cassell PLC (England)

U

UNDERWOOD-MILLER

1988 Statement: "All Underwood-Miller and Brandywyne Books editions, since 1976, are noted FIRST EDITION, or FIRST HARDCOVER EDITION if the book is a reprint with only a previous paperback incarnation, or FIRST DELUXE EDITION if it is a special, limited signed edition of a title which has appeared elsewhere. Later printings are noted by 'Second' or 'Third' Printing, or nothing at all listed on the copyright page."

FREDERICK UNGAR BOOKS

1988 Statement: "The identifications for first editions or first printings in our books are the usual copyright line giving the year of publication plus the year of the printing at the top of the copyright page. We never use the words 'first edition' or 'first printing.' We do add 'second printing,' 'third printing,' and so on, whenever such printings are done.

"When a book is revised, enlarged, or substantially changed, we will include on the title page and/or the copyright page, either 'second edition,' 'enlarged edition,' etc., plus the year of this edition at the top of the copyright page. If these editions are reprinted, we also add 'second printing,' 'third printing,' etc.

"We have some reprints on our list. In such books the copyright information is different, depending on whether the book was in the public domain. These reprints or republications are, of course, not first editions, though they may have a new copyright line if we have added an introduction.

"[We] started printing the year at the top of the copyright page on 1 January 1986."

FREDERICK UNGAR PUBLISHING CO.

1947 Statement: "Our method of identifying the various printings of our books is to add the words 'Second Printing' or 'Third Printing' etc. on the copyright page.

"Revisions are indicated on the title page by 'Revised Edition' or a similar wording."

Statement for 1960: *See* 1982 Statement

1976 Statement: *See* 1982 Statement

1982 Statement: "The only identification for first editions or first printings in our books is the usual copyright line giving the year of publication. We never use the words 'first edition' or 'first printing.' We do add 'second printing,' 'third printing' and so on, whenever such printings are done.

"When a book is revised, enlarged, or substantially changed, we will include on the title page and/or the copyright page, either 'second edition,' 'enlarged edition,' etc. If these editions are reprinted, we also add second printing, 'third printing,' etc.

"We have some reprints on our list. In such books the copyright information is different, depending on whether the book was in the public domain. These reprints or republications are, of course, not first editions, though they may have a new copyright line if we have added an introduction."

1988 Statement: *See* 1988 Statement of Frederick Ungar Books

UNICORN PRESS (ENGLAND)

(Incorporating John Heritage, Publisher. Taken over by Richards Press, Ltd.)

1937 Statement: "It is our practice to put the date of publication of any book on the verso of the title-page. If the book is reprinted, the date of the reprint appears on the verso of the title-page under the original insertion. It should read so:

First printed February 1935

"In the case of a reprint, as above, but with the following appended:

Reprinted May 1935"

UNICORN PRESS, INC.

1976 Statement: "The editions (e.g., signed, numbered, cloth, etc.) of our hand-printed books are described on the colophon pages of each book, ac-

companied often by the names of the persons who typeset, printed, bound them. For our larger books, which are usually machine-printed but hand-bound, the info. you are interested in is on the © page."
1981, 1988 Statements: *See* 1976 Statement

UNITED NATIONS
1976 Statement: "All United Nations publications carry sales number iden-tification on both the back of the title page and in the tag line at the bot-tom of either the last page of text or the back cover. In the event of reprint of a publication, a statement to this effect is also indicated on the tag line."
1981, 1988 Statements: *See* 1976 Statement

UNITY PRESS
1976 Statement: "We have no special designation for indicating first edi-tions. Subsequent printings would not be so indicated. Should there be a revised edition of a work, it would be so indicated on the copyright page."
1981 Statement: "All 'First Editions' now carry the nomenclature on the copyright page. Subsequent editions are indicated by the lowest number appearing in a series located on the same page under the nomenclature 'Printed in the United States.' This practice was begun a couple of years ago."

UNIVERSE BOOKS
1976 Statement: "First printing contains no identification. Subsequent printings and editions are always stated."
1981 Statement: "In 1980 we changed our procedure. We now print the following type of line on the copyright page: 80 81 82 83 84 / 10 9 8 7 6 5 4 3 2 1. In reprints we drop the year (if necessary) and the number of the previous printing(s). Thus, a reprint of a 1980 book might contain the al-tered line: 81 82 83 84 / 10 9 8 7 6 5 4 3 2. A new book published in 1981 would contain the figures: 81 82 83 84 85 / 10 etc."
1988 Statement: *See* 1981 Statement

UNIVERSITY BOOKS, INC.
1976 Statement: "We show no designation for a first edition, but addition-al printings are identified."
1981, 1988 Statements: *See* 1976 Statement

THE UNIVERSITY OF ALABAMA PRESS
1988 Statement: "The Press does not use any special designation to iden-tify first editions. First editions and first printings can be assumed unless the copyright page carries a notice that the book is either a second or sub-sequent printing, or a second or subsequent edition.
"This method of designation does not differ from any previously used."

UNIVERSITY OF ALASKA PRESS
1988 Statement: "We have various way of designating first printings, edi-tions and reprints. On an unrevised reprint of another publisher's material we print 'Reprinted by the University of Alaska Press date' on the title page. On an original printing of our material we state 'First printing' on the back of the title page under the copyright date or year printed. For a second printing, we would so state 'Second Printing date.' In some cases [we] will do the first book printing of revised material and will note this on the back of title page as 'Revised Edition, Originally Published As: date.' For other

revised editions, we would state on the back of title page, 'Revised Edition, date,' etc."

UNIVERSITY OF ARIZONA PRESS

1976 Statement: "At our Press, a book which carries only the copyright date as *the* date information on the back of the title page is a first printing. All subsequent printings will carry an additional line showing the year of the printing (as well as the copyright date itself, of course)."

1981 Statement: *See* 1976 Statement

1988 Statement: "At the University of Arizona Press, a first edition carries the copyright date only. Subsequent editions carry an additional line giving the year and number of the printing.

"The policy applies equally to our imprints."

THE UNIVERSITY OF ARKANSAS PRESS

1988 Statement: "Until 1986 our first editions were distinguished only by the lack of any notation as to printing, which was added for subsequent printings. We now indicate the first printing of a first edition by serial notation, e.g.

92 91 90 89 88 5 4 3 2 1

dropping the single and double digits from the right as additional printings occur and years pass."

UNIVERSITY OF BRITISH COLUMBIA PRESS (CANADA)

1976 Statement: "In those titles which we have reprinted, we indicate the dates of the reprints on the copyright page."

1981 Statement: *See* 1976 Statement

1988 Statement: "Readers may assume that all our books are first editions unless we specify on the copyright page (page iv) that the book has been reprinted or is published in a new edition. The copyright line starts with the c in a circle symbol and is followed by 'The University of British Columbia Press' and the year of publication. Information about a reprint is put on a separate line below the original copyright year line, and consists of the word 'Reprinted' and the year in which the reprint was done.

"UBC Press adopted this method of designation when it was established in 1970. We have no subsidiaries."

UNIVERSITY OF CALGARY PRESS (CANADA)

1988 Statement: "The University of Calgary Press does not identify first printings in any particular way. Second or subsequent printings and/or revised editions are indicated on the copyright page. The UCP has followed this procedure since it was established in 1982."

THE UNIVERSITY OF CALIFORNIA PRESS

1937 Statement: "The few books that have gone into a second edition have had printed on the verso of the title page 'Second Edition' or 'Third Edition.' Such a notice will be printed on all editions after the first."

1947 Statement: "All new printings and revised editions are identified on the verso of the title page by a notice such as 'Second Edition,' 'Revised Edition,' or 'Third Printing.' A careful distinction is made between printings and editions."

1976 Statement: "We do not use any sort of identifying statement to designate first editions of our books. We print only a copyright date.

"We do print a line to indicate such things as second, third, revised, paperback, etc. editions, although the wording may vary according to particular circumstances.

"In the past, we did add a new printing line every time a book was reprinted ('Second printing, 1968' or 'Fourth printing, 1972'), but as that practice has been largely discontinued the absence of such a line no longer assures a first edition."

1981 Statement: "The numbers 1 to 9 are now included in the copyright statement to indicate the printing of the book. The lowest number appearing indicates the printing of the book".

1988 Statement: "Our process for identifying printings and editions remains the same as in our 1976 and 1981 statements."

UNIVERSITY OF CENTRAL FLORIDA
(Orlando)

1981, 1988 Statements: *See* 1981, 1988 Statements of University Presses of Florida

THE UNIVERSITY OF CHICAGO PRESS

1928, 1937 Statements: *See* 1947 Statement

1947 Statement: "You will notice that the publication date, and record of each new impression and new edition, is entered on the copyright page. Unless notice happens to be made in an occasional new preface, no other record is made in the book. This method has been used for at least thirty-one years."

Statement for 1960: *See* 1982 Statement

1976 Statement: "We have traditionally identified second and subsequent printings of a book, as well as second or later editions, on the verso of the title page. So if no such indication appears there, the reader can assume that the book is the first printing of the first edition.

"Currently, for some books, especially titles we expect to reprint frequently, we use a double sequence of numbers, the last of which indicates the year and number of the impression. That is, for the first impression of a book published in 1976 the sequence is as follows:

80 79 78 77 76   9 8 7 6 5 4 3 2 1

Then as new printings are ordered, numbers are removed from the plate or negative."

1982 Statement: "We have traditionally identified second and subsequent printings, as well as second or later editions, on the copyright page. If no such identification appears there, the reader can assume that the book is the first printing of the first edition.

"In recent years we have been indicating the year and number of the impression by means of a double sequence of numerals on the copyright page. These are easily altered to show subsequent impressions. The first impression of an edition published, for example, in 1980 would carry the following line:

87 86 85 84 83 82 81 80   54321

"For a second impression in 1982, the line would be altered to read as follows:

87 86 85 84 83 82   5432

"Second or later editions are identified as such on the copyright page and carry a new set of impression numbers."

1988 Statement: "The Press's practice for indicating edition and impression number remains as it last appeared in your publication."

UNIVERSITY OF CONNECTICUT
1988 Statement: *See* 1988 Statement of University Press of New England

UNIVERSITY OF DELAWARE PRESS
1976, 1981, 1988 Statements: *See* 1976, 1981, 1988 Statements of Associated University Presses, Inc.

UNIVERSITY OF FLORIDA
(Gainesville)
1976, 1981, 1988 Statements: *See* 1976, 1981, 1988 Statements of University Presses of Florida

THE UNIVERSITY OF GEORGIA PRESS
1976 Statement: "We do not use any specific identification; however, on later editions we designate them as second edition, third edition, and so on.

"Later printings are designated: Second Printing, 1976; Third Printing, 1980, etc.

"If there has been a revision of the book, the designation will be: second edition, 1976, etc."

1981 Statement: *See* 1976 Statement

1988 Statement: "In 1984 we changed our method designating editions and now uniformly use a line of numbers with years and editions for all new books. We block out numbers as required on subsequent editions.

"For our books published before 1984, we follow our older method of designation."

THE UNIVERSITY OF HAWAII PRESS
1988 Statement: "The University of Hawaii Press uses a numerical system to designate first and subsequent printings. For example:

First printing in 1988:	92 91 90 89 88	1 2 3 4 5
Second printing in 1990:	92 91 90	2 3 4 5
Third printing in 1991:	92 91	3 4 5

"We began this system in 1988. The information appears on the copyright page."

THE UNIVERSITY OF ILLINOIS PRESS
1976 Statement: "In general, books from this Press which do not indicate otherwise are first editions. Succeeding printings, impressions, revised editions, etc., are so indicated, either on the title page (occasionally) or on the back of the title page along with the copyright notice. There undoubtedly have been some lapses, but this has been the policy since 1950. For titles published during the years 1918-50, the earliest publication date is almost certain to indicate the first and only printing or impression in that year."

1981 Statement: *See* 1976 Statement

1988 Statement: "Since 1981 we have also included a printing code on the copyright page, which indicates which printing of *our* edition is the current one. This code will change with each reprinting, of course, and is relevant only for *our* edition (i.e. the *first* edition may have been published by another press—information that will also be clearly indicated on the copyright page, however)."

UNIVERSITY OF IOWA PRESS

1976 Statement: "Our press has no unusual method of identifying first editions of the works it publishes. Second printings and second editions are identified as such."

1981 Statement: *See* 1976 Statement

1988 Statement: "Since 1985 on our copyright page for first editions, we have stated, e.g. 'First edition, 1985.'

"Our imprints and subsidiaries follow our practices."

THE UNIVERSITY OF MASSACHUSETTS PRESS

1976 Statement: "We do not provide a specific statement to the effect that the volumes we publish are first editions.

"Printings are not identified. We identify only revised editions."

1981, 1988 Statements: *See* 1976 Statement

THE UNIVERSITY OF MICHIGAN PRESS

1988 Statement: "The first edition is not so stated. The copyright statement and the printing number and year indicate the printing history.

"Subsequent editions are designated in a statement preceding the copyright notice. The statement contains the edition and year, and the year is added to the copyright statement when necessary. The statement might be worded in the following ways:

> Revised Edition
> Second Edition
> New Edition
> First Paperback Edition
> First Edition as a Paperback."

UNIVERSITY OF MINNESOTA PRESS

1937 Statement: "University Press books, as you know, are usually published in small editions and, with no exception that I can think of, the *absence* of the words 'Second Edition' is enough identification for a first edition of our books. We do, however, make a distinction between a second edition and a second printing of the first edition, and almost invariably add the line 'Second Printing,' 'Third Printing' etc., under the copyright notice."

1947 Statement: *See* 1937 Statement

Statement for 1960: "Our 1976 statement on the identification of first editions applies to books published by this Press for the years between 1949 and 1976. The same statement also holds for the identification of impressions."

1976 Statement: "First editions of books published by this Press are not identified as such in the books themselves and may be distinguished from subsequent editions by the fact that the latter are identified as such. The same holds true for impressions."

1981 Statement: *See* 1976 Statement

1988 Statement: "The practice previously outlined (in 1976) for identifying editions and impressions stands without change. We have no other imprints or subsidiaries."

UNIVERSITY OF MISSOURI PRESS

1976 Statement: "We rarely do second or third editions of books (that is, with significant changes or revisions from the first). We do, however, reprint books as we run out of stock.

"The best way to determine the printing or edition of one of our books is to look at the copyright page. If there is no indication to the contrary, you probably have a book from the first printing. The appropriate information should be supplied in any other case."

1981, 1988 Statements: *See* 1976 Statement

UNIVERSITY OF NEBRASKA PRESS

1976 Statement: "The University of Nebraska Press does not identify the first printing of a work as a first edition. However, subsequent printings are identified as such on the copyright page. Thus, the absence of an edition statement indicates a first edition."

1981, 1988 Statements: *See* 1976 Statement

UNIVERSITY OF NEW HAMPSHIRE

1988 Statement: *See* 1988 Statement of University Press of New England

THE UNIVERSITY OF NEW MEXICO PRESS

1976 Statement: "It is presently our practice to use the words FIRST EDITION on the copyright page of each book. This is the verso of the title page, of course.

"Subsequent printings of the first edition usually carry the word *reprinted* and a date. A revised or enlarged edition has the words that so state. We do not use any alphabetical or numerical symbols such as A B C D, etc., or 1 2 3 4, etc.

"This press has been in existence since 1930 under a succession of directors, designers, and production managers. Regrettably, the words FIRST EDITION were not always used on earlier books. Seldom was a book reprinted within the same year, so the date of copyright would therefore indicate a first edition if there was no mention of a reprint with a later date.

"Our staff realizes that while the term 'edition' refers to an edition whose text remains unchanged, and may go through several printings, the average reader usually thinks of 'first edition, first impression, first issue, first state' as all the same thing. So we now state 'First edition' and add 'reprinted 1976' even if it remains unchanged, or if changed from cloth to paperback we will state this as well."

1981 Statement: "We identify a first edition by using the words *first edition* on the copyright page of each new book we publish. This practice seems to have been standard procedure since sometime in the late 1950s. Since we have generally indicated subsequent printings or editions on the copyright page (though not always by one particular method), any University of New Mexico Press book carrying only a copyright date can be identified reliably as first edition."

1988 Statement: *See* 1981 Statement

THE UNIVERSITY OF NORTH CAROLINA PRESS

1937 Statement: "We do not have any general rule by which a first edition of one of our books may be distinguished from a later edition.

"We sometimes reprint from type within a few weeks after the first printing, without distinguishing in any way the second from the first printing. We may indicate on the back of the title page, after the first printing, the dates of various subsequent printings, but we do not always do this.

"Whenever we publish a new edition of a work, we usually secure a copyright to cover the new matter. Both the new and the old dates will appear on the back of the title page."

1947 Statement: "We do not have any general rule by which a first edition of one of our books may be distinguished from a later edition.

"When we reprint without revising, we usually indicate on the copyright page, after the first printing, the dates of various subsequent printings. Whenever we publish a revised edition of a work, we secure a copyright to cover the new matter. Both the new and the old dates will appear on the copyright page."

Statement for 1960: "The UNC Press does not have any method of identifying first editions. Unless one of our books is clearly designated as either a second edition or a revised edition, the reader and bibliographer may assume that they are dealing with a first edition.

"This statement applies before and after 1976."

1976 Statement: "The Press does not have any method of identifying first editions. Unless one of our books is clearly designated as either a second edition or a revised edition, the reader and bibliographer may assume that they are dealing with a first edition."

1981, 1988 Statements: *See* 1976 Statement

UNIVERSITY OF NORTH FLORIDA
(Jacksonville)

1976, 1981, 1988 Statements: *See* 1976, 1981, 1988 Statements of University Presses of Florida

UNIVERSITY OF NOTRE DAME PRESS

1976 Statement: "We have no method of designating a first edition."

1981, 1988 Statements: *See* 1976 Statement

UNIVERSITY OF OKLAHOMA PRESS

1937 Statement: "All of our books contain on the copyright page a statement of the day, month, and year of first publication. This usually takes the following form: 'Set up and printed at Norman, Oklahoma, by the University of Oklahoma Press, Publishing Division of the University. First edition May 18, 1936.' If a second printing is issued, this information is always added to the material on the copyright page, though the day of second printing is usually not given. Notice of second printing is almost uniformly carried on our jackets as well. We have employed this method of differentiating first from subsequent printings since the founding of the Press in 1928."

1947 Statement: "The copyright pages on our books now customarily carry information arranged according to the following form: 'Copyright 1947 by the University of Oklahoma Press, Publishing Division of the University. All rights reserved. Set up and printed at Norman, Oklahoma, U.S.A., by the University of Oklahoma Press. First edition.' If a second printing is issued, we further particularize the information about the first edition and add the date for the second printing as follows: 'First edition, August, 1947. Second printing, October, 1947.' We frequently carry information about printings beyond the first on our jackets. This general method of differentiating first from subsequent printings as here described has been in use by the Press since its founding nearly twenty years ago. It is of particular importance that our colophon page, which always appears at the end of volume, be read in connection with the copyright page, especially for any notation of limited edition."

Statement for 1960: "The wording used to designate first printings in 1960 is as follows:

278

Copyright 1960 by the University of Oklahoma Press,
Publishing Division of the University. Composed and
printed at Norman, Oklahoma, U.S.A., by the University
of Oklahoma Press. First edition."
1976 Statement: "From the year, 1976, on, the form shown in new books
will be:
Copyright 19— by the University of Oklahoma Press,
Publishing Division of the University. Manufactured in
the U.S.A. First edition."
"At the time of the Press's founding, the form used was the following:
Copyright 1932 by the University of Oklahoma Press
All rights reserved
Manufactured in the United States of America. Set up
and printed by the University of Oklahoma Press at
Norman. First printed January, 1932
"The form used from the early 1940's until 1976 was the following:
Copyright 1975 by the University of Oklahoma Press,
Publishing Division of the University. Composed and
printed at Norman, Oklahoma, U.S.A., by the University
of Oklahoma Press. First edition."
1981 Statement: *See* 1976 Statement
1988 Statement: "As of January 1, 1988, the University of Oklahoma Press
copyright statement for the first printing of a new title reads as follows:
Copyright © 1988 by the University of Oklahoma Press,
Norman, Publishing Division of the University. All rights
reserved. Manufactured in the U.S.A. First edition.
"The changes in this statement were made in the interval between 1981
(the date of your last statement) and the present: the addition of ©, the addition of 'Norman' after the name of the Press, the addition of 'All rights
reserved,' and the change from 'Composed and printed at Norman, Oklahoma, U.S.A., by the University of Oklahoma Press' to 'Manufactured in
the U.S.A.'
"We have no subsidiaries; our imprints (titles in series) carry the same
copyright statement."

UNIVERSITY OF PENNSYLVANIA PRESS
1937 Statement: "All titles published by us are first printings unless otherwise noted on the copyright page. In the case of second and subsequent
printings, we give the date of publication and the dates of further printings."
1947 Statement: *See* 1937 Statement
1976 Statement: "If our book does not say 'Revised Edition,' 'Second Edition,' 'Third Edition,' etc., it is the first edition."
1981, 1988 Statements: *See* 1976 Statement

UNIVERSITY OF PITTSBURGH PRESS
1947 Statement: "We indicate second and third printings of our books as
follows:
Copyright 1937
University of Pittsburgh Press
Published 1937
Second Printing 1940
Third Printing 1947"

1976 Statement: "If we are publishing a book for the first time, the following information is inserted on the copyright page:
'Copyright © (date), University of Pittsburgh Press
(or author)
All rights reserved
Feffer & Simons, Inc., London
Manufactured in the United States of America
(Library of Congress Cataloging in Publication Data box)
(Any necessary acknowledgements)'
We do not indicate that it is the first edition or first printing.
"If we reprint the first edition, we add: 'Second printing (date)', 'Second printing (date) / Third printing (date),' etc.
"If we reprint a cloth book in paper, we add: 'First printing, (date) / Paperback reissue, (date)'.
"If we have bought the American rights of a British book, the usual wording is: 'First published in Great Britain (date) by (publishers) / Published in the U.S.A. (date) by the University of Pittsburgh Press.'
"I do not believe we have ever published a second edition.
"I do not believe the procedures are different from earlier ones, although minor aspects such as punctuation may vary."
1981, 1988 Statements: *See* 1976 Statement

UNIVERSITY OF QUEENSLAND PRESS (AUSTRALIA)
1981 Statement: "We don't actually designate that our books are the first printing of the first edition in any way. But their lack of identification marks them as such. All subsequent reprints or later editions are indicated as such, for example 'Second reprint of third edition'.
"Our imprints are not always the same. Our usual style is for the copyright line to read: Copyright University of Queensland Press. This is because our contracts assign the rights to us. However, there has grown up a loose tradition with creative writers that they always have copyright in their name, which legally speaking is incorrect."
1988 Statement: "All University of Queensland Press titles should carry both the year of first publication as well as the year any particular edition has been printed. If only one date is mentioned on the copyright page, and this is the date of first publication, then that clearly identifies the book as a first printing of a first edition. Should a reprint be issued in the same year, then the word 'reprinted' will also appear on the copyright page."

UNIVERSITY OF RHODE ISLAND
1988 Statement: *See* 1988 Statement of University Press of New England

UNIVERSITY OF SOUTH CAROLINA PRESS
1976 Statement: "Our first editions are identified on the copyright page with 'First Edition' and the date. All subsequent printings or revised editions are also identified on the copyright page. In short, we normally give all publishing information, including joint publishers abroad, if any."
1981 Statement: *See* 1976 Statement
1988 Statement: "Since about 1985, we have done an increasing number of simultaneous hard and paperback printings that do not indicate the first edition since this procedure is tantamount to two first editions. We do, however, indicate 'First Edition' in books initially published in hardback only.

"In all cases we do indicate the previous publishing history including copyrights, original publisher if other than the University of South Carolina Press, printing history, joint publishers, if any, and where published."

THE UNIVERSITY OF SOUTH DAKOTA PRESS

1988 Statement: "We never explicitly note the appearance of a first edition. Some books are printed in editions signed and numbered by the author, but these are infrequent. This information is carried on the copyright page."

(The Dakota Press at the University of South Dakota was renamed The University of South Dakota Press.)

UNIVERSITY OF SOUTH FLORIDA
(Tampa)

1976, 1981, 1988 Statements: *See* 1976, 1981, 1988 Statements of University Presses of Florida

THE UNIVERSITY OF TENNESSEE PRESS

1976 Statement: "On the copyright page of most of our books we carry the words 'First Edition' in addition to the customary copyright information. As a general rule we do not add 'First Edition' to the information given in scientific or technical studies; however, if the copyright page does not indicate that the volume is a 'Second' or 'Third Printing,' etc., bibliographers and book collectors can be assured that the volume is a first edition. If a title is a 'Second' or 'Third Edition' (a revision) that information is also noted on the copyright page."

1981, 1988 Statements: *See* 1976 Statement

UNIVERSITY OF TEXAS PRESS

1976 Statement: "We do not state that a book is a first edition. The date in the copyright notice indicates the year of first publication. Subsequent printings are marked 'Second Printing, date,' 'Third Printing, date,' etc. on the copyright page. A revised edition would be so identified on the title page. Paperback editions not published at the same time as the clothbound editions are identified as 'First Paperback Printing, date,' 'Second Paperback Printing, date' etc. on the copyright page."

1981 Statement: "Our new policy, effective 1/1/81, is to put 'First Edition' and the year on the copyright page. Subsequent printings and revised editions will be indicated as before."

1988 Statement: *See* 1981 Statement

UNIVERSITY OF TORONTO PRESS (CANADA)

1976 Statement: "We don't normally indicate that books are first editions. The date of publication is shown in the copyright notice, and if there are further printings or further editions the dates are listed on the copyright page. So that, as you suggest, when no designation is made, it may be assumed that it is a first printing and edition."

1981 Statement: *See* 1976 Statement

1988 Statement: "We do not designate first editions. Subsequent editions or printings are so indicated. It may be safely assumed that any book bearing the University of Toronto Press imprint is a first edition, unless otherwise indicated.

"This has always been the case.

"We have no subsidiary imprints."

UNIVERSITY OF UTAH PRESS

1976 Statement: "The University of Utah Press does not have a specific statement for identifying first editions. We do, however, identify a printing as a 2d, 3rd, etc., or as a 2d, 3rd, etc., edition. This information appears on the copyright page, usually beneath the copyright and rights statements, simply as: Second printing, 1976, or Second edition. Of course, subsequent editions beyond the first would have applicable copyright dates."

1981, 1988 Statements: *See* 1976 Statement

UNIVERSITY OF VERMONT

1988 Statement: *See* 1988 Statement of University Press of New England

UNIVERSITY OF WALES PRESS (WALES)

1988 Statement: "Where only one date of publication appears on the title page and/or the copyright page, it can be taken that the book is a first edition. Details of any subsequent editions or impressions are carried on the copyright page. (The Press was founded in 1922, and we cannot give an absolute guarantee that this was the invariable practice in the earlier years.)

"This information applies to all our imprints (University of Wales Press; Gwasg Prifysgol Cymru; GPC Books)."

UNIVERSITY OF WASHINGTON PRESS

1976 Statement: "This Press does not identify first editions as such. We do list reprintings and revised editions on the copyright page, so that the complete printing history of the book is given there."

1981, 1988 Statements: *See* 1976 Statement

UNIVERSITY OF WEST FLORIDA
(Pensacola)

1976, 1981, 1988 Statements: *See* 1976, 1981, 1988 Statements of University Presses of Florida

THE UNIVERSITY OF WESTERN AUSTRALIA PRESS (AUSTRALIA)

1988 Statement: "Our customary method is to indicate on the verso of the title page, in addition to the standard copyright notice and National Library of Australia Cataloguing-in-publication data (C.I.P.), that the book was 'First published in (year).' Reprints are noted thereunder as 'Reprinted (year),' or 'Reprinted with revisions/amendments (year).' A completely revised edition is treated as a new book with new ISBN number and C.I.P. data.

"Where a book is co-published we state 'First published in Australia (year).'

"This method has been unchanged (apart from the fairly recent innovation of the C.I.P. data) since the first book to be published under the imprint in 1954. Our trade title imprint 'Cygnet Books' adopts the same method."

THE UNIVERSITY OF WISCONSIN PRESS

1976 Statement: "The copyright page of each new title contains the year of publication and the words 'first printing.' Previous to 1970, the year of publication appeared on the title page. The copyright page of each reprint contains the year of first publication and the years of the subsequent printings."

1981 Statement: *See* 1976 Statement

1988 Statement: "With our Fall 1988 list the University of Wisconsin Press has instituted the practice of designating printings by a series of numbers in descending order from left to right:

5 4 3 2 1

"The number at the right represents the number of the printing.
"First editions are not labeled as such. Later editions are identified."

THE UNIVERSITY PRESS OF HAWAII

1976 Statement: "Editions and printings after the first are so indicated."
1981 Statement: *See* 1976 Statement
1988 Statement: See 1988 Statement of The University of Hawaii Press

UNIVERSITY PRESS OF KANSAS

1988 Statement: The Regents Press of Kansas changed its name to University Press of Kansas in June of 1982.

"The first printing does not say 'First printing.' The later printings are so labeled on © page.

"We label a second printing as 'Second printing (date).' It is not considered a new edition, even if a few corrections have been made."

THE UNIVERSITY PRESS OF KENTUCKY

1976 Statement: "Since the vast majority of our books appear in only one edition, we have had no occasion to develop a statement identifying first editions. Often when a book is reprinted we correct errors discovered too late in the first printing. But we have never to my knowledge identified such a reprint as a new edition, although I suppose that technically it is that."

The individual printings of a first edition are not identified.
1981 Statement: "Normally a book appears in only one edition, one printing; we do not identify it as a first edition, nor are the individual printings usually identified, although in one instance a corrected reprinting was so marked on the copyright page. Revised editions are identified as such."
1988 Statement: *See* 1981 Statement

UNIVERSITY PRESS OF MISSISSIPPI

1976 Statement: "First editions contain our normal copyright and imprint while later editions carry special notices such as 'second printing: (date).' "
1981 Statement: *See* 1976 Statement
1988 Statement: "[The] 1976 statement regarding first editions is still correct. In addition, we often use the five number/five date method—all five numbers and years indicate first printing; lowest remaining number and year indicates successive printing dates. (This method was begun in 1986; we do not use it for every book.)

"Imprints and subsidiaries follow this practice."

UNIVERSITY PRESS OF NEW ENGLAND

1976 Statement: "Our identification of a first edition is in our copyright notice. The first edition contains only the copyright year. Subsequent editions are identified by the added notice: 'Second edition, copyright—. Third edition, copyright—.' "
1981 Statement: *See* 1976 Statement
1988 Statement: "Our 1981 Statement . . . is correct. However, during 1987 we began to phase in a new method of identifying printings on new books as well as most backlist titles that happened to reprint during this period.

Under the new system, we place a series of numbers (5 4 3 2 1) toward the bottom of the copyright page. The printing is indicated by the lowest number in the string. Thus '5 4 3 2 1' is the first printing in an edition, '5 4 3' would be a third printing, and so on. We will be using this system on all our imprints."

THE UNIVERSITY PRESS OF VIRGINIA

1976 Statement: "Our first editions, first printings carry: *First published 19—* on the copyright page.

"A second printing would add: *Second printing 19—* to the above notice, or, in some cases, merely *Reprinted 19—*.

"A second edition would add: *Second edition 19—* to the above notice, and carry *Second edition* or some other qualifying statement on the title page."

1981, 1988 Statements: *See* 1976 Statement

UNIVERSITY PRESS OF WASHINGTON, D.C.

1988 Statement: *See* 1988 Statement of Larlin Corporation

UNIVERSITY PRESSES OF FLORIDA

Florida A&M University (Tallahassee), Florida Atlantic University (Boca Raton), Florida International University (Miami), Florida State University (Tallahassee), University of Central Florida (Orlando), University of Florida (Gainesville), University of North Florida (Jacksonville), University of South Florida (Tampa), University of West Florida (Pensacola)

To determine which of the following statements applies to the above universities, please refer to the individual entries for each of the universities.

1976 Statement: "*Printings.* There is no designation as such in a first printing. Subsequently we carry on the copyright page 'Second Impression,' 'Third Impression,' etc. Quantities and dates are not indicated.

"*Editions.* First editions have no special identity. If a work is revised it is designated 'Revised Edition' on the title page and on the copyright page. A *second* revision is called 'Third Edition.'

"The foregoing has been our practice for at least ten years."

1981 Statement: *See* 1988 Statement. The 1981 Statement previously provided was erroneous.

1988 Statement: The 1981 Statement was erroneous. The corrected statement reads as follows:

"*Printings.* There is no designation of a first or subsequent printing.

"*Editions.* First editions have no special identity. If a work is revised it is designated 'Revised Edition' on the title page and on the copyright page. A *second* revision is called 'Third Edition.'

"The foregoing has been our practice for at least ten years."

UNIVERSITY SOCIETY, INC.

1976 Statement: "The copyright date has always been the key to identifying first editions (our Company was founded in 1896). Our older anthologies generally indicated subsequent editions with new copyright dates, plus a note referring to earlier editions from which material was taken. There was no clear-cut method of identification, however.

"Today we use code numbers for each printing of a particular multi-volume anthology. For example, 'Pub. No. 1001' on the copyright page means that the volume in question is a first edition, '1002' a second printing, etc. The reason we do this is because in a 17 volume anthology, for example, the individual volumes are reprinted on a stagger system to accommodate our bindery. It would not do to have a set of books with one volume labeled 'third printing' and another volume labeled 'fourth printing;' yet sets with volumes from various printings do appear. The code is to prevent our customers from becoming alarmed at any apparent discrepancy.

"In the case of single volumes, we merely indicate 'First Edition' or 'Second Edition' on the copyright page."

UNWIN HYMAN, INC.

1988 Statement: "We do not identify first printings as such but identify all subsequent printings: 'Second printing, 1988,' and so on. This has been standard procedure for as long as I am aware. I believe that our imprints and subsidiaries follow this same practice, though to be honest, I cannot guarantee it.

"Please note that we have changed our name to: Unwin Hyman, Inc. We are the wholly owned subsidiary of Unwin Hyman Ltd of Great Britain, which now publishes titles under the former imprints of George Allen & Unwin, Allen & Unwin, Bell & Hyman, and Hutchinson."

UNWIN HYMAN LIMITED (ENGLAND)

1988 Statement: "1. First editions are designated by the line 'First published in Great Britain by ...' followed by the date, then the copyright line. Second and subsequent printings or editions contain an additional line so stating.

"2. This method has been in use for a number of years.

"3. Imprints and subsidiaries should follow the same practice."

URBAN & SCHWARZENBERG, INC.

1988 Statement: "First Printing is indicated by © date on the © page. This method was adopted in 1866. It does not differ from methods previously used. Subsidiary companies follow this practice."

URBAN INSTITUTE PRESS

1976 Statement: "The Urban Institute uses a code on the copyright page which shows the printing, year of printing, and the quantity printed. Thus, 'A/76/1M' would translate 'First printing, 1976, 1000 copies,' and 'B/78/1M' would translate as 'Second Printing, 1978, 1000 copies.' In that case, the date of the original printing is verified by the copyright notice."

1981 Statement: *See* 1976 Statement

1989 Statement: "The Urban Institute no longer has any special designation for a first printing."

URIZEN BOOKS, INC.

1981 Statement: "First printing on our first editions means first edition, further printings are indicated and it is also indicated whether revisions have been made by saying Revised New Edition on the title page. In the event we enter the reprint market we will write the book's past history on the copyright page."

U. S. NAVAL INSTITUTE

1976, 1981, 1988 Statements: *See* 1976, 1981, 1988 Statements of Naval Institute Press

V

VAGROM CHAP BOOKS

1976 Statement: "Our first editions have all been, so far, 'only' editions. We would only designate those editions after the first with proper numbering and information, to distinguish from first 'only' editions. All our issues may be taken as first editions."
1988 Statement: *See* 1976 Statement

VAN CORTLANDT MANOR

1981 Statement: *See* 1981 Statement of Sleepy Hollow Press

VAN NOSTRAND REINHOLD COMPANY

1976 Statement: "Since 1970, a numerical sequence, usually 16 through 1, has been used to indicate printings of a first edition. If the number 1 is present, the book in question is the first printing of a first edition. The words 'first edition' are not used.

"Second editions are noted and the sequence is started over again as well.

"The same practice is followed for the Professional and Reference books published by VNR."
1981, 1988 Statements: *See* 1976 Statement

VANCOUVER COMMUNITY PRESS (CANADA)

See 1988 Statement of New Star Books (Canada)

VANDERBILT UNIVERSITY PRESS

1976 Statement: Editions and printings are indicated only after the first.
1981, 1988 Statements: *See* 1976 Statement

THE VANGUARD PRESS

1937 Statement: "The Vanguard Press uses no special mark or wording to indicate its first editions, but states on the copyright page when a book is in any but the first printing."
1947 Statement: *See* 1937 Statement
1976 Statement: "Actually, there is no way to determine whether our books of the past were first editions or not. Some, not all, had second edition notices in them. However, if there was a rush to publication for a second edition or later this was often omitted. Thus, one could not tell the difference between the first edition and later printings. Presently, we do differentiate by numbering the edition on the copyright page with the numerals: 1 2 3 4 5 6 7 8 9 0. As each new edition is printed, the preceding number is deleted. Thus a second edition would bear the number 2, a third 3, etc."
1981 Statement: *See* 1976 Statement
1988 Statement: *See* 1937 Statement

VEDANTA PRESS

1976 Statement: "Our early titles simply had the copyright date for the first edition. Later editions would be so marked, i.e., '2nd printing, 1976.'

"Lately, we have been marking our books to designate the first edition, i.e., 'First Edition, 1976.' "
1981, 1988 Statements: *See* 1976 Statement

VENTURE PRESS

(See Simon and Schuster, Inc., who in 1945 added this as an imprint for work by beginning authors, as well as for first work in a new form by established authors.)

VERITAS PRESS

(Bought by Julian Messner in 1945.)

THE VESTAL PRESS LTD

1988 Statement: "We do not provide a statement in a first edition but we do identify subsequent editions and subsequent printings."

VIKING

1988 Statement: *See* 1988 Statement of Penguin Publishing Co Ltd. (England)

VIKING (ENGLAND)

1988 Statement: *See* 1988 Statement of Penguin Publishing Co Ltd. (England)

VIKING KESTREL

1988 Statement: *See* 1988 Statement of Penguin Publishing Co Ltd. (England)

VIKING KESTREL (ENGLAND)

1988 Statement: *See* 1988 Statement of Penguin Publishing Co Ltd. (England)

VIKING PENGUIN INC.

1989 Statement: "Our 1982 Statement is still accurate. We use a line of figures and strike out one of them with each new printing. Our subsidiaries (Viking Studio Books) follow this practice."
See also 1988 Statement of Penguin Publishing Co Ltd (England)

THE VIKING PRESS INC.

1928 Statement: *See* 1937 Statement
1937 Statement: "Our first editions can be distinguished by the fact that there is no indication to the contrary on the copyright page. That is, we indicate the date and number of each reprinting.

"This has always been our method and we shall continue it until further notice.

"The Viking Press and B. W. Huebsch, Inc., merged in August, 1925, to be known as The Viking Press Inc.

"The policy of B. W. Huebsch, regarding first editions, was the same as the present policy of The Viking Press."
1947 Statement: *See* 1937 Statement
1976 Statement: The usual practice is to have no printing line in the first printing of a book, and to add "second printing," etc., on reprints.
1981 Statement: *See* 1976 Statement
1982 Statement: "Our system of printing lines remains pretty much the same, but sometimes we add a line of figures (5 4 3 2 1, e.g.) and strike out one of them with each new printing."
1989 Statement: *See* 1989 Statement of Viking Penguin Inc.

VIKING STUDIO BOOKS

1989 Statement: *See* 1989 Statement of Viking Penguin Inc.

VILLAGE GREEN PRESS

1947 Statement: *See* M. Barrows and Company, Inc.

VILLAGE PRESS

1947 Statement: *See* 1947 Statement of The Press of James A. Decker

VILLARD BOOKS

1988 Statement: *See* 1988 Statement of Random House, Inc.

VINTAGE BOOKS

1988 Statement: *See* 1988 Statement of Random House, Inc.

VINYL SHOWER

1988 Statement: *See* 1988 Statement of Steam Press

VIRAGO PRESS LIMITED (ENGLAND)

1988 Statement: "We currently put, and have always put, on the title verso 'Published by Virago Press Limited 19—,' giving the date of first publication by ourselves.

"Should the book be reprinted, we keep the above line, but insert a further one saying 'Reprinted 19—' together with the word Twice or Three Times if necessary! So any book without an indication of a reprint is thus a first edition.

"We have no imprints or subsidiaries of a very separate nature, just different series within our whole list, and this practice is used on all the books we published and always has been."

VIRGINIA CENTER FOR THE CREATIVE ARTS

1988 Statement: *See* 1988 Statement of Associated University Presses

VISA BOOKS (AUSTRALIA)

1981 Statement: *See* 1981 Statement of Widescope International Publishers Pty. Ltd. (Australia)

W

WADSWORTH PUBLISHING COMPANY, INC.

1976 Statement: "EDITIONS
First Editions. Usually no designation is given in the title. Only designate editions after the first.
Subsequent *editions*. Ordinarily designated in the title as Second Edition, Third Edition, etc. Sometimes designated as Revised Edition, College Edition, etc.
 PRINTINGS
The particular printing of any edition of any book is currently designated by a printing line on the copyright page. The line looks like this:
1 2 3 4 5 6 7 8 9 10—80 79 78 77 76
The first number on the left indicates the printing (first printing in this case) and the last two digits on the right indicate the year the printing was made (1976 in this example). We did use a different method of indicating printings a number of years ago. We wrote it out (First printing: 1976)."
1981 Statement: "EDITIONS

First Editions. Usually no designation is given in the title. Only designate editions after the first.

Subsequent editions. Ordinarily designated in the title as Second Edition, Third Edition, etc. Sometimes designated as Revised Edition, International-al Edition, College Edition, etc.

PRINTINGS

The particular printing of any edition of any book is currently designated by a printing line on the copyright page. The line may look like this:

1 2 3 4 5 6 7 8 9 10—80 79 78 77 76

The first number on the left indicates the printing (first printing in this case) and the last two digits on the right indicate the year the printing was made (1976 in this example). Or the line may look like this:

10 9 8 7 6 5 4 3 2 1

The last digit on the right indicates the printing (first printing in this case). The year the printing was made is not indicated at all. We did use a different method of indicating printings a number of years ago. We wrote it out (First printing: 1976)."

WAKE FOREST UNIVERSITY PRESS

1989 Statement: "When we first publish a title, we indicate the publication date with the other copyright information. If the book will appear in England or Ireland before our edition is available, that publication date is usually mentioned as well. When a book is reprinted, the original date is included in the copyright information."

WAKE-BROOK HOUSE

1976 Statement: "Our first editions always state that they are first editions on the verso of the title page. Reprints are identified as such. We have not changed our practice in this since our founding in 1946."

1981, 1988 Statements: *See* 1976 Statement

WALNUT HILL BOOKS

1988 Statement: *See* 1988 Statement of Strawberry Hill Press

EDMUND WARD (ENGLAND)

1947 Statement: "As a general rule, first editions of our books can be iden-tified by the fact that no date or 'history' is shown on the title-page, verso of the titles, or opposite the title. Should a second edition or reprint be published then a 'history' such as:

First Edition October, 1947
Reprinted November, 1947

will be included on the verso of the title-page. It follows, therefore, that if no 'history' appears, then the book is a first edition."

WARD, LOCK & CO. LIMITED (ENGLAND)

1928 Statement: "We have no fixed method of designating our first edi-tions."

1935 Statement: "Generally speaking, at the present time we are placing on the back of the title page:

First published in.........."

1947 Statement: *See* 1935 Statement

1988 Statement: *See* 1988 Statement of Ward Lock Limited (England)

WARD LOCK LIMITED (ENGLAND)

1988 Statement: "Generally speaking, at the present time we are placing on the back of the title page:

First published in ...."

FREDERICK WARNE (ENGLAND)

1988 Statement: *See* 1988 Statement of Penguin Publishing Co Ltd. (England)

FREDERICK WARNE & CO., INC.

Statement for 1960: "In answer to your question, in the year 1960, we were not printing any information in our book to actually denote first printing so that, in other words, a book that did not state what the printing number was would actually be a first printing. If the book went into any subsequent printings then the legend 'First printing 1960' [was] followed by the legends 'Second printing 1962,' 'Third printing 1965,' etc. This would show which printing that particular volume came from."

1976 Statement: "We identify the first edition of our books by the following symbolic system on the copyright page.

1 2 3 4 5 6 7 8 9 10

"Each time we reprint, we eliminate the appropriate number—i.e. for the second edition, the symbol looks as follows:

2 3 4 5 6 7 8 9 10."

1981 Statement: "About our method of designating the first printing of a first edition: we have changed our method (this was done in the fall of 1978) and the entry should read as follows:

"We identify the first edition of our books by the following symbolic system on the copyright page:

1 2 3 4 5 85 84 83 82 81

"Each time we reprint we eliminate the appropriate numbers—i.e. for the second printing the symbols might be:

2 3 4 5 85 84 83

"The first digit represents that this is a second printing and the last digits represent the year of that second printing."

FREDERICK WARNE & CO., LTD. (ENGLAND)

1928 Statement: "We did at one time mark first editions of our publications with a private mark, but we are afraid the habit has been discontinued over a number of years now, and we have even lost trace of the private marks."

1937, 1947 Statements: *See* 1928 Statement

WARNER BOOKS, INC.

1981 Statement: "Warner First Editions are easily distinguished; they carry a line on the copyright page: first printing with date. Underneath that is a set of numbers from 10 down to one; the last number on the right is the number of the printing in your hand. This is the method we use for our mass market books, our trade paper backs and our hardcover publications. The hardcover edition is usually the first publication in any form in this country. Paperbacks are reprints unless they are marked as originals.

"We've been using this system for quite some time, but I couldn't tell you exactly when this first began."

1988 Statement: *See* 1981 Statement

THE WARTBURG PRESS

1947 Statement: "The policy which we are now following for identification of printings of our books·is to enter the number of the printing on the copyright page, thus, 'Second Printing,' 'Third Printing,' etc.

"This plan is not operative until the second printing—the original edition carries only the copyright notice, giving the year of the edition.

"With many of our older books, say those of five or more years ago, no identification of printings is possible. It would be difficult or even impossible to identify the original edition."

IVES WASHBURN INC.

1928 Statement: *See* 1937 Statement

1937 Statement: "We print the date of publication on the title page and on the reverse run a copyright date line but do not print 'first edition' or 'first printing' beneath it. When we make a second printing, we change the date on the title page, provided it is done in a subsequent year; otherwise, it remains the same.

"In making a second printing, whether new material is added to the book or not, we always print beneath the copyright date line on the reverse of the title page in italics the words 'first printing' followed by the month and year, and below 'second printing' with month and year, and so on for subsequent printings. In other words, unless we give this information on the reverse of the title page the buyer may know that he has bought the first editions of our books.

"We have used this method since 1927."

1947 Statement: "Our policy has changed somewhat. We print the year of publication on the copyright page but do not print 'first edition' or 'first printing' beneath it. When we make a subsequent printing we add the number, the month, and the year to the copyright page."

WATER ROW PRESS

1988 Statement: "First printings are identified with 'First Edition.' [This method was] adopted [in] 1981."

WATSON-GUPTILL PUBLICATIONS

1976 Statement: "Please note that we identify the first publication following the copyright. We follow this practice whether first published by ourselves or by someone else prior to our publication.

"Subsequent printings are identified at the bottom of the front matter by 1st printing, 1972, second printing, 1972, third printing, 1974, etc."

1981 Statement: *See* 1976 Statement

G. HOWARD WATT

(Out of business prior to 1949.)

1937 Statement: "On second printings we always mention the fact that it is the second edition. That is our only distinguishing mark."

FRANKLIN WATTS, INC.

1947 Statement: "We now have no distinguishing mark for first editions. When we publish books where there may be first edition interest we shall mark them 'first edition.'"

1981 Statement: "On the copyright page the numbers 5 4 3 2 1 are printed. The 1 indicates that it is only the first printing. This has always been our method for the various imprints we have used. Obviously, as each new printing run is done, we drop the number of the printing that has gone before it."

1988 Statement: *See* 1981 Statement

WAVERLY HOUSE

1947 Statement: "We have no special method for identification of first printings."

WAYNE STATE UNIVERSITY PRESS

1976 Statement: The first edition is not designated. The first printing of a first edition is not designated. All editions and printings after the first are indicated on the copyright page. These methods are not new.

1981 Statement: "The first edition is not designated as such. The title page carries the year of publication, indicating that the book is a first edition. All editions and printings after the first are indicated as such on the copyright page."

1988 Statement: *See* 1981 Statement

WAYNEBOOKS

1988 Statement: *See* 1988 Statement of Wayne State University Press

THE WEBB PUBLISHING COMPANY
(Including Itasca Press and Midland House.)

1947 Statement: "In the case of fiction and general nonfiction, our practice is to indicate first printings by the statement 'First Edition' in a small italic on the copyright page. In the case of text books and technical books this is not always done, although in most cases the month of publication is indicated on the copyright page and subsequent printings are listed in the editions as issued.

"The Midland House imprint appears only in those titles which we took over from the Midland House of Iowa City. Although we are privileged to use this imprint we do not contemplate doing so at the present time. We use, instead, The Itasca Press imprint."

GEORGE WEIDENFELD & NICOLSON LIMITED (ENGLAND)

1976 Statement: "We do not have any particular way of identifying first editions, except by the date and no mention of any edition. Subsequent editions state that they are reprints, second editions, or whatever."

1981, 1989 Statements: *See* 1976 Statement

SAMUEL WEISER, INC.

1988 Statement: "First editions carry the notice: 'First published in 1988 (or whatever year) by Samuel Weiser, Inc.' Subsequent printings carry a printing history such as 'third printing, 1988' or whatever the accurate printing history is for the title. The information about 2nd or more printings is listed under our address."

ROBERT WELCH PUBLISHING CO.

1948 Statement: "We differentiate between first printings and subsequent printings by stating on the copyright page of the subsequent printings the particular number that printing may be, such as, 'Second Printing' or 'Third Printing,' etc. In the case of First Printings the copyright page is left blank as to this information."

KEVIN WELDON AND ASSOCIATES PTY LTD (AUSTRALIA)

1988 Statement: "From September 1988 we will use the following imprint format for all new books.

A Kevin Weldon Production
Published by Kevin Weldon & Associates Pty Limited
372 Eastern Valley Way, Willoughby, NSW 2068, Australia
First published 1988
© Author

"For reprints and subsequent editions of books published by Weldon Publishing we would use the format as above with the addition of:

First published 1988
Reprinted 1989

"If a reprint has been first published by Ure Smith, Lansdowne Press or Rigby Publishers, we will keep the name and change the details on the imprint page as follows:

A Kevin Weldon Production
Published by Ure Smith
Lansdowne Press   use name appropriate to reprint
Rigby Publishers
a division of Kevin Weldon & Associates Pty Limited
372 Eastern Valley Way, Willoughby, NSW 2068, Australia
© Author
First published 1974
Reprinted 1975 (twice), 1976, 1988

"We will still continue to print some of our new titles under the Lansdowne Press and Rigby imprints.

"Limited editions are published under the imprint Lansdowne Editions. The print run and the number of the book are printed on a verso page in the preliminary pages."

WESLEYAN UNIVERSITY PRESS

1981 Statement: "As a rule, a 'printing' and an 'edition' are one and the same in Wesleyan books, and the fact that one is a first edition is so indicated on the copyright page."

1988 Statement: "While there has been some inconsistency in the past, 'printing' and 'edition' do not mean the same thing. 'Edition' is usually 'First Edition,' which is first printing. Later printings usually omit this and add: First printing, 19__; third printing, 19__. All of our poetry is published originally simultaneously in cloth and paper; usually (collected works often excepted) reprintings are in paper. Most of our nonfiction books, after 1982, have been published in cloth first, paperback later and these latter are designated, 'Wesleyan Paperback, first printing, 19__.' Most (but not all) reprintings of these titles are in paper only.

"Since 1984 we have been publishing a number of reissues of books out of print at their original publishers, usually in paper only (but in 1987 and 1988 in cloth also). In our *Books in Print* these are designated with original date bracketed. Copyright pages list the original publisher and also: 'Wesleyan Paperback, first printing, 19__.'

"We have no *imprints* as such, but several *series*, all with the Wesleyan name, such as Wesleyan Poetry, Wesleyan Paperback, Wesleyan Edition of the Works of Henry Fielding (co-published with Clarendon Press, Oxford), of which only the novels are in both cloth and paper."

WEST COAST POETRY REVIEW PRESS
1976 Statement: "We only designate edition and printings after the first—'First Printing, May, 1975/Second Printing, July, 1976' etc."
1981, 1989 Statements: *See* 1976 Statement

WESTERN PRODUCER PRAIRIE BOOKS (CANADA)
1989 Statement: "Regarding your inquiry about how our company designates the first printing of a first edition, up until now it has been indicated simply by giving the date of publication on the copyright page. Subsequent printings have been indicated by stripping in a new line: e.g. Second printing 1987. The original date of publication remains on the top line: e.g. Copyright © 1986 by Cora Taylor.

"Beginning with our spring 1989 books, however, we are starting a new system. A first printing will be indicated thusly: 10 9 8 7 6 5 4 3 2 1. The second printing will have the 1 deleted, the third, the 2 etc. The original date of publication will remain on the top line of the copyright page.

"Subsequent editions, as opposed to printings, are indicated by an edition statement plus year on the copyright page.

"We do not have any subsidiaries but in the case of co-publications, each publisher generally supplies its own copyright page and the style and form of these do not necessarily follow our practices."

WESTERN PUBLISHING COMPANY, INC.
1976 Statement: "First editions at Golden Press, which publishes children's books, cookbooks, craft books and science guides are never designated as first editions. Our printing code is shown on the last page or inside back cover of each book. First printings (first editions) bear the code ABCDE etc. Second prints then eliminate the letter A and so on."
1981 Statement: "The Western Publishing entry is basically correct, with a few minor changes:

"First editions at Golden Books, which publishes children's books, cookbooks, craft books and science guides are never designated as first editions. Our printing code is shown on the copyright page, the last page, or inside back cover of each book. First printings (first editions) bear the code ABCDE etc. Second printings then eliminate the letter A and so on."
1988 Statement: "First editions at Golden Books, which publishes children's books, cookbooks, craft books, and science guides, are never designated as first editions. Our printing code is shown on the copyright page, the last page, or inside back cover of each book. First printings (first editions) bear the code

ABCDEFGHIJKLMN
"Second printings then eliminate the letter A and so on.
"Our imprints and subsidiaries follow the same practice."

WESTERNLORE BOOKS
1976 Statement: "Westernlore first editions are undesignated as such. Unless subsequent editions are typographically so noted it is a first edition."

WESTERNLORE PRESS
1988 Statement: First editions are not designated.

JOHN WESTHOUSE (PUBLISHERS) LIMITED (ENGLAND)
1947 Statement: "We generally use the phrase—'First published in....' in the preliminary pages of our first editions."

THE WESTMINSTER PRESS

1947 Statement: "We do not attempt to identify first printings of all of our books. However, those which have a distinctly scholarly use and which are possibly changed from edition to edition or printing to printing are identified on the copyright page by 'First Printing,' 'Second Printing,' etc."

Statement for 1960: *See* 1976 Statement

1976 Statement: "Prior to 1974 there was no way to distinguish one printing from another on most Westminster Press publications. "Starting in 1974 all but the first printings are identified on the copyright page with the printing and the year of the printing, i.e., Second Printing, 1974."

1981 Statement: "To the information you have, please add that starting in 1977 Westminster Press first printings are identified with a line of figures 9 through 1.

"The lowest figure is deleted on all future printings so that the printing may be identified by the lowest number showing. The date of the printing is not shown."

1988 Statement: *See* 1988 Statement of Westminster / John Knox Press

WESTMINSTER / JOHN KNOX PRESS

1988 Statement: "Starting January 1, 1989, titles from The Westminster Press and from the John Knox Press will bear the same imprint: Westminster / John Knox Press, and the city will be Louisville, Kentucky. *See* the 1981 Statement of The Westminster Press."

WESTVIEW PRESS, INC.

1976 Statement: "We in no way designate a first edition or a first printing of a first edition. Only if it *isn't* a first edition do we say anything at all."

1981 Statement: *See* 1976 Statement

1988 Statement: "Westview Press does not label its first editions as such; however, the reader is notified of a second (or any subsequent) edition on both the copyright page and the title page. As to printings of a given edition, the copyright page carries a series of numbers descending from 10 to 1 or from 6 to 1. A second printing lacks the number '1' in that sequence, a third printing lacks numbers '2' and '1,' and so on."

WESTWATER PRESS

1988 Statement: *See* 1988 Statement of Howe Brothers

WHEATON (ENGLAND)

1981 Statement: *See* 1981 Statement of Pergamon Press Ltd. (England)

WHEATSHEAF BOOKS LIMITED (ENGLAND)

1988 Statement: *See* 1988 Statement of The Harvester Press Ltd. (England)

J. WHITAKER & SONS, LTD. (ENGLAND)

1988 Statement: "We do not identify first editions. We do identify second and subsequent editions, reprints and so forth, by a statement on the history page (verso of title page)."

WHITCOMB AND BARROWS

(Early name [1904-?] of M. Barrows and Company, Inc.)

WHITE PINE PRESS

1988 Statement: "We use no special designation for first editions but mark subsequent printings as such."

WHITMAN

1988 Statement: *See* 1988 Statement of Western Publishing Company, Inc.

ALBERT WHITMAN & CO.

1947 Statement: "The only way that our books are marked is the printing date on the title page and the copyright date on the reverse side, which must agree in order for the book to be the first edition. All extra printings are marked underneath the copyright. Any book that carries the second printing with the year of date would not be the first edition. Where this does not appear the book would be the first edition if printed by us."

Statement for 1960: "Our first edition has no special marking but subsequent printings are indicated by a note (e.g., Second Printing 1960) above or below the copyright notice. Revised editions are identified as such when they occur."

1976 Statement: "Our first edition has no special marking but subsequent printings are indicated by a note (e.g., Second Printing 1976) above or below the copyright notice. Revised editions are identified as such when they occur."

1981 Statement: *See* 1976 Statement

1988 Statement: *See* 1988 Statement of Albert Whitman & Company

ALBERT WHITMAN & COMPANY

1988 Statement: "For each first edition, a row of numbers is printed beneath the copyright notice in descending order from 10 through 1. With each reprinting, the number of the previous printing is deleted from the row. The number of the printing will be the lowest number in the row.

"We began using the method of designation in 1984.

"We do not have other imprints or subsidiaries."

WHITMAN GOLDEN LTD. (CANADA)

1988 Statement: *See* 1988 Statement of Western Publishing Company, Inc.

THE WHITNEY LIBRARY OF DESIGN

1976 Statement: "I'm afraid we have no special way of designating a first edition. The copyright page simply says 'Copyright (©) 1976 by Watson-Guptill Publications,' or whoever the copyright holder may be. This is then followed by a line that says: 'first published in the United States 1974 by Watson-Guptill Publications' or 'by the Whitney Library of Design.' "

1981 Statement: *See* 1976 Statement

WHITSON PUBLISHING COMPANY

1989 Statement: "1st Printing—copyright date.

"Second printings have new date added to the page, i.e.:
Second printing 1989."

WHITTLESEY HOUSE

1937 Statement: "The first printing of the first edition of Whittlesey House books has the words 'first edition' under the statement of copyright, which, of course, includes the year of publication. Subsequent printings have 'second printing,' 'third printing,' etc. Considerably revised editions are designated 'second edition,' 'third edition,' etc. This statement is run on the verso of the title page of all Whittlesey House books."

1947 Statement: "The first printing of the first edition of Whittlesey House books has no indication of edition or printing anywhere in the book. The first edition may be identified only in a negative manner. Subsequent printings have 'second printing,' and subsequent editions 'second edition,' etc., on the verso of the title page under the copyright statement."

WIDESCOPE INTERNATIONAL PUBLISHERS PTY., LTD. (AUSTRALIA)

1981 Statement: "Our imprint details always commence with the notation 'First published 19....' with the dates of reprints or other subsequent editions shown in chronological order.

" 'First published' means the first Australian edition. We rarely republish in Australia books first published abroad although, when we do, we do not indicate the book's foreign publishing record.

"We have not changed our method of designation except by adding the Cataloguing in Publication data supplied by the National Library of Australia.

"This information applies to the following four imprints: Commemorative Editions, Visa Books, Cavalier Press and Widescope Publishers."

WILD & WOOLLEY PTY. LIMITED (AUSTRALIA)

1981 Statement: "Most of our books—we've published 45 so far—have had only one edition. Those that have had additional printings are: *WRAPPINGS* by Vicki Viidikas. 1 was cloth, 2nd paperback. *Cobb Book* by Ron Cobb 6th or 7th printing, I'm not sure. 1st printing had a poor reproduction of the back cover cartoon, which we corrected in the 2nd printing when we located the original.

Cobb Again by Ron Cobb. Uses form 5 4 3 2 1 to denote printing.

"That's about all I can tell you. I've tried to standardise with the 5 4 3 2 1 style, but it seems silly when you know there'll only be the one printing."

1988 Statement: *See* 1981 Statement

W. A. WILDE COMPANY

1947 Statement: "We do not have any specific method of identifying our first printing of a book but refer you to a sample copyright page for the method employed in additional printings:

Copyright 1945

W. A. WILDE COMPANY

All rights reserved

Sixth Edition

Fourth Printing

MADE IN THE UNITED STATES OF AMERICA"

WILDERNESS PRESS

1976 Statement: "A first edition of ours is indicated by the fact that it does not say 'Xth revised edition' or 'Xth revised printing' or 'Xth printing.' When it is a revised edition, a revised printing or a subsequent printing, the copyright page says so."

1981, 1988 Statements: *See* 1976 Statement

JOHN WILEY & SONS, INC.

1976 Statement: "There is no designation of our first edition titles. Only subsequent editions carry a designation. To my knowledge, this has always been our practice.

"As for the printing, since 1969 we have placed the numbers from 10 through 1 on the bottom line of the copyright page. If all of these numbers appear it is the initial printing; if the 1 has been deleted, it is the first print-

ing; the 2, the second printing, etc. Prior to 1969 the system called for specifically spelling out the printing. The absence of a printing designation should indicate that it is the first printing. How diligent we have been in following this routine over the years, I can't be certain. For the past fifteen years, I know for certain that we have emphasized the need to follow this system and I *suspect* such has been the case all along."
1981 Statement: *See* 1976 Statement

WILLETT, CLARK & COLBY
(Became Willett, Clark & Company on Oct. 22, 1930.)
See Willett, Clark & Company

WILLETT, CLARK & COMPANY
1937 Statement: "Any book published by Willett, Clark & Company that goes into a second edition has the designation 'second edition' under the copyright notice or at least on that page. The first edition is never given any distinctive marking of any kind, therefore, any book not designated as second, third, or fourth edition is a first edition."
1947 Statement: *See* 1937 Statement

WILLIAMS & NORGATE LTD. (ENGLAND)
1937 Statement: "Our usual practice, adopted a good many years ago, is to put the date of original publication and particulars of any reprint on the back of the title page. Thus:
First printed in Great Britain in 1934
Second impression (or) Reprinted
Third (revised) edition, 1935
"Very occasionally the date appears on the title page itself."
1947 Statement: *See* 1937 Statement

WILLING PUBLISHING CO.
1947 Statement: "Printings are listed on copyright page."

WINCHESTER PRESS
1976 Statement: "It is not the practice of Winchester Press to differentiate between or among first and subsequent editions. If there is no indication on the title page, the work is a first printing, however; other printings are identified by number."
1981 Statement: "We have changed our methods and the [1976] statement is no longer accurate. The new practice was begun in Jan. 1980.
"Winchester Press does indicate Revised Edition on the copyright page of any such book. A printing history line also runs on the copyright page and is revised with each reprint. This line will indicate a first printing."
1988 Statement: *See* 1981 Statement

WINDSWEPT PRESS
1988 Statement: *See* 1988 Statement of Heart of the Lakes Publishing

WINDWARD HOUSE
(Out of business prior to 1949.)
1937 Statement: "All books published under this imprint are trade editions. Unless they are new editions of Derrydale Press books, they are first editions of the text, though this is not stated in the book. In the case of a second edition this is so stated on the back of the title page."
See also The Derrydale Press, Inc.

ALLAN WINGATE (PUBLISHERS), LIMITED (ENGLAND)

1947 Statement: "With reference to your letter, I can supply you with the following information. When any of our titles is first published, it is printed on the imprint page in the following manner—

'First Published in MCMXLVII
by Allan Wingate, Publishers, Ltd.,
64 Great Cumberland Place,
London, W.1'

and when the title is reprinted, the second impression is mentioned in this manner—

'First Published in MCMXLVII,
second impression February MCMXLVIII
by Allan Wingate, Publishers, Ltd.,
64 Great Cumberland Place, London, W.1' "

WINGBOW PRESS

1976 Statement: "Any second printing or second edition is always clearly marked."

1981 Statement: "A first edition is noted by either 'First edition,' or 'First printing,' followed by the date."

1988 Statement: *See* 1981 Statement. "Wingbow Press publishes only under its own imprint and has no subsidiaries."

JOHN C. WINSTON CO.

1928 Statement: "We publish books in a number of different classes and have private marks on some of our editions, notably on our text-books, which give us the date of each edition for our own information.

"We have not, however, made a practice of marking the first editions of our trade publications and should we decide to do so we will probably adopt a symbol which would not mean anything to the public, as I can think of at least one good reason why it might not be desirable to have first editions indicated.

"I must confess that this is undesirable from a book collector's standpoint but other considerations unfortunately outweigh this to such an extent that we are not as yet prepared to establish a permanent system of marking our first editions."

1937 Statement: *See* 1928 Statement

1948 Statement: "We have realized now for some time the importance of distinguishing first editions of trade books, and are endeavoring to include the notification on the copyright page of every new book we publish. If it does not appear in all publications issued from 1948 on, it is an oversight, and not a change in policy."

WINSTON-DEREK PUBLISHERS, INC.

1988 Statement: "We do not use any specific identification; however, on later editions we designate them as second edition, third edition, and so on.

Second Printing, 1989;
Third Printing, 1990, etc."

WISCONSIN HOUSE, LTD.

1976 Statement: "At present, Wisconsin House merely indicates a First Edition with the statement 'First Edition' on the copyright page. Subsequent editions carry the number of each printing."

WM. H. WISE & CO., INC.

1976 Statement: "We do not especially designate first editions."

1981 Statement: *See* 1976 Statement

WISHART AND CO., LTD. (ENGLAND)

1928 Statement: "The title page carries the date of the edition. On the back of the title page there are the words 'First published in....' The date of the second and subsequent editions and impressions is printed below this. First editions are therefore not specifically marked as such."

1935 Statement: "We do not print any bibliographical information on the back of the title page, unless the book goes into a second impression, in which case we give details as to date. The absence of such information implies therefore that the copy is a first edition."

1948 Statement: "Wishart Books Ltd. (formerly Wishart and Co., Ltd.), although technically still in existence has not actually carried on any publishing business for the last eight or nine years, and no titles have been published. Any information given you in 1939 would hold good since there have been no further publications after that date."

H. F. & G. WITHERBY, LTD. (ENGLAND)

1937 Statement: "Our usual practice is always to give a full biblio on the reverse of the title page. In certain cases the date appears in the title page, but more usually the date of publication appears on the biblio."

1947 Statement: *See* 1937 Statement

WITTENBORN ART BOOKS, INC.

1981 Statement: "No method is used. Only the reprint/reissue date is noted."

1988 Statement: "[We] have no special mark for 1st edition. [We] do note later printings."

WIZARDS BOOKSHELF

1988 Statement: "We specialize in 19th century scholarly reprints, but have done a number of first editions. In most we state in the introductory note to the book that it is the first edition, or the first translation. There is no immediate obvious way to determine it is a first edition, and we have never thought this an important point, since our runs are 2,000 copies, and we don't have enormous turnover as popular novels might.

"We have a few heavily annotated reprints such as the *Zohar*, which has undergone extensive revisions to the notes, in which case we put '2nd edition,' or '3rd edition' on the title page.

"We have no subsidiaries."

ALAN WOFSY FINE ARTS

1988 Statement: "There will usually be an indication on the copyright page for printings or editions after the first."

WOLFHOUND PRESS (REPUBLIC OF IRELAND)

1981 Statement: "Wolfhound Press has only one imprint to date, Wolfhound Press. First editions from Wolfhound Press can be identified by reference to the verso of the title page. The copyright date given will be the date of the first edition unless a statement to the contrary is contained on that page. Reprints in the same year as the first edition have not to date been separately identified but reprints in the year after that of the first edition carry that information on the title verso page. First Wolfhound editions of previously published works include the relevant bibliographical information."

1988 Statement: *See* 1981 Statement. Wolfhound Press now has two imprints: Wolfhound Press and Monarch Line.

THE WOMAN'S PRESS

1947 Statement: "When we have a revised edition of a book, we state the number of the edition and the year, for example, 'First Edition, 1945,' 'Second Edition, 1947.'

"The first printing of a book is not specifically designated, although the copyright is stated. Usually our second printing is marked 'Second Printing.' In other words, first printings of any of our books are not so designated, but subsequent printings are designated from the first printings."

WONDER / TREASURE BOOKS

1989 Statement: *See* 1989 Statement of Price/Stern/Sloan Publishers, Inc.

WOOD LAKE BOOKS INC. (CANADA)

1988 Statement: "We tend to publish in very small quantities, since our market is a) religious, and b) entirely Canadian. Therefore we rarely expect to go into second or subsequent printings.

"When we do have a second printing, we identify it on the credits page (verso of title page) with the notation, Second Printing 1989. Or Third, etc.

"We don't have any plans for changing the system."

WOODBRIDGE PRESS PUBLISHING COMPANY

1976 Statement: "First Edition if no indication otherwise.

"Subsequent editions and/or printings identified by No."

1981 Statement: *See* 1976 Statement

1988 Statement: "First Edition if no indication otherwise.

"Subsequent editions and/or printings identified by number and/or date."

WORLDWIDE LIBRARY (CANADA)

1989 Statement: "First printings of Worldwide Library books are designated:

A Worldwide Library Book / (month and year of publication)
"Worldwide Library also holds a number of imprints, including Worldwide Mysteries, Worldwide Science Fiction and Gold Eagle Books. First printings of Worldwide Mysteries are designated:

A Worldwide Mystery / (month and year of publication)
"Worldwide Science Fiction is designated in the same manner as the general Worldwide Library publications.

"Books in the Gold Eagle imprint, which are all paperback originals, are designated:

First edition (month and year of publication)."

WORLDWIDE MYSTERIES (CANADA)

1989 Statement: *See* 1989 Statement of Worldwide Library (Canada)

WORLDWIDE SCIENCE FICTION (CANADA)

1989 Statement: *See* 1989 Statement of Worldwide Library (Canada)

WRIGHT (ENGLAND)

1988 Statement: *See* 1988 Statement of Butterworth Scientific, Ltd. (England)

JOHN WRIGHT OF BRISTOL (ENGLAND)
See 1988 Statement of Wright (England)

THE WRITER, INC.
1981, 1988 Statements: *See* 1981, 1988 Statements of Plays, Inc., Publishers

A. A. WYN, INC.
1947 Statement: "First printings of our books may be identified by the fact that the copyright page carries no reference to the printing. Subsequent printings are identified by the number, as 'Second Printing,' 'Third Printing,' etc.

"A. A. Wyn, Inc. is distributor for books published under the imprints of Current Books, Inc., A. A. Wyn, Inc. and The L. B. Fischer Publishing Corporation. Since the L. B. Fischer Corporation was purchased by A. A. Wyn, the imprint will not be used on any further printings of Fischer books."

X

XANADU PUBLICATIONS LIMITED (ENGLAND)
1988 Statement: "We do not designate editions. At this point most of our reprints are indistinguishable from our first editions, due to the cost of making that alteration. However, we hope to indicate new editions and reprints for book clubs and the like by changing the date. For the foreseeable future we will not be attempting anything more sophisticated."

Y

YACHTING
1947 Statement: "Yachting Publishing Company has only three active titles at present. They are: *The Gaff Rigged Yachtsman* by Darrell McClure; *Gadgets and Gilhickies* by Ham deFontaine; *Ocean Racing* by Alfred F. Loomis.

"Second and third printings of the above, if any, are so noted.

"Books published by Kennedy Brothers, later Yachting Publishing Corporation, are now published by Dodd, Mead and Company."

YALE UNIVERSITY PRESS
1928 Statement: "We do not print the words 'First Edition' in any of our books, but on the reverse of the title-page, under the copyright notice, we indicate the subsequent printings as follows:

First Published, 1915.
Second Printing, 1916.
Third Printing, 1919.
Second and Enlarged Edition, 1922.
Third Edition with Many New Chapters, 1924.

"It is therefore safe to assume that any of our publications which have no designation below the copyright notice are first editions."
1936 Statement: "The statement of method as used by us is correct as far as it goes. In the case of some of our earlier books, we ran a line under the

302

copyright line reading, 'First published January 1921.' In most cases, and on all books which we are now publishing, the first edition simply carries the copyright line, but some first editions carry a second line as indicated above."

1947 Statement: *See* 1936 Statement

1976 Statement: "We do not identify first editions as such, but any edition except the first has that fact displayed on the title page or the copyright page or both. Second and subsequent printings of a first edition contain a line stating which printing it is on the copyright page. This method of identification has not changed over the years."

1981, 1988 Statements: *See* 1976 Statement

YANKEE, INC.

1976 Statement: "Usually we simply include the words FIRST EDITION on the title or colophon page."

Printings of a first edition may not be distinguished.

1981 Statement: "Now that our books have gone into a number of printings and continue to do so, we have changed our policy as follows:

"For the first printing of the first edition of any book, usually we simply include the words FIRST EDITION on the title or colophon page. Successive printings of a first edition are distinguished by the number of the printing underneath the words 'First Edition,' i.e.:

FIRST EDITION
2nd Printing

"I would say roughly that this practice has been our habit for the past three years."

YE GALLEON PRESS

1988 Statement: "This is a small book deal working in the university-college-public library market. Most of my list is reprint material, mildly scarce to excessively rare, going down in some cases to one known original copy.

"We rarely reprint hard case books. When we do it is usually in a different format and different typesetting. This is especially the case with limited, numbered editions. We have not had a special policy of identification of first and second editions, but we could watch this and put in a printed explanation. We have sometimes printed a facsimile edition and then later reset the title and printed in a different format.

"However, we do reprint booklets where there is continued demand. Sometimes we have reset the booklet and sometimes not. Some of the booklets are backlist and have been printed several times but it is rare to reprint hard cased material.

"We could easily have a policy of designating second or third printings on the reverse of the title page with an explanation of reset type or other changes but have not had such a policy as hard case material has rarely been reprinted."

BRIGHAM YOUNG UNIVERSITY PRESS

1976 Statement: A line similar to the following appears on the copyright page:

76 2M 12735

On initial printings, the last two digits of the copyright date agree with the number at the left.

1981 Statement: A line similar to the following appears on the copyright page:

8/76   12735
(month/year)   (job number)

On initial printings, the last two digits of the copyright date agree with the second number at the left (following the slash).

YOUNG SCOTT BOOKS

1937, 1947 Statements: *See* 1937, 1947 Statements of William R. Scott, Inc.

Z

Z PRESS

1988 Statement: "Z Press does not identify a first edition as such. On the colophon page, the date of printing and the size of the edition, as well as the number of signed copies (usually twenty-six, A to Z) are specified. The year of each printing appears on the title page, and is changed in case of subsequent printings. In one case (*3 Plays*, by John Ashbery), in the second printing, the colophon page was dropped, and the information regarding first and second printing appeared on the copyright page. But this is an exception. The tradition of the colophon page continues, and began with *Miltie is a Hackie* by Edwin Denby, the first Z Press book, in 1973."

ZEPHYRUS PRESS, INC.

1981 Statement: "On the copyright page we specify that it is the first edition and the first printing. Reprintings are labeled as such, e.g, second printing. New editions are labeled as such and have a second copyright date."

ZIFF DAVIS, LIMITED (ENGLAND)

1947 Statement: "Our bibliographical notices follow the usual English practice, namely:—
"First printing will be identified:—
    First published..........
"Subsequent printings will be identified with the different number of impressions as follows:—
    First published..........
    New impression........"

ZIFF-DAVIS PUBLISHING COMPANY

1947 Statement: "Our first printings and first editions have no marks to distinguish them as such. Second and subsequent printings are referred to on the copyright page as SECOND PRINTING, THIRD PRINTING, etc. Second or revised editions are mentioned as such on either the title page or the copyright page.
"The above applies to both ZIFF-DAVIS and ALLIANCE books."

ZONDERVAN PUBLISHING HOUSE

1947 Statement: "We have no particular method of differentiating between various printings and editions of our publications. We indicate the edition on the title page whenever an edition is printed."
1976 Statement: "As new editions are printed (or new printings are scheduled) we indicate the number of the printing on the copyright page.

"This does not differ markedly from our previous practice. On certain books, where the printing history is rather overwhelming (such as *Halley's Bible Handbook*), we do indicate a complete printing history on a separate page."

1981, 1988 Statements: *See* 1976 Statement

IDENTIFYING BOOK CLUB EDITIONS

We have included this brief summary of book club edition identification practices in response to readers' queries regarding techniques for differentiating a book club edition from the trade edition. Generally, book club editions do not attract the interest of collectors; neither are they usually the true first edition, though there are exceptions.

A book club edition is a book issued by a book club to its members. The book club edition may or may not be part of a special edition. Because some book club editions are taken from the first printing of the trade edition, it is not uncommon for a book club edition to be mistaken for a first printing of the trade edition. For example, a book club edition may be marked as a first edition or first printing. In other cases, it may seem to be such by the absence of any identifying marks to the contrary. The collector, then, needs to ensure that the book at hand is indeed a first printing from the trade edition, and not a first printing issued as a book club edition.

IDENTIFYING BOOK-OF-THE-MONTH CLUB® EDITIONS

Probably the most well-known of the major book clubs in the United States, the Book-of-the-Month Club offers to its members several books each month. Among these offerings, books by a number of collected modern authors inevitably appear. All of the following points relate to the identification of Book-of-the-Month Club editions, though some of the points relate also to the identification of editions issued by other book clubs.

- Look at the lower right-hand corner of the back cover board of the book. Book-of-the-Month Club editions can usually be identified by a small circle, square, or other geometric form on the lower right-hand corner of the back cover board. In past years, this mark was printed on the cover cloth. More recently, however, the mark has been indented, or debossed.
- Check the dust jacket for reference to a book club. A book club edition is sometimes identified as such at the top and/or the bottom of the front or back jacket flap. For example, a Book-of-the-Month Club edition may be identified as "A Selection of the Book-of-the-Month Club."
- Does the dust jacket carry a price? Book club editions sometimes carry no price on the dust jacket.
- Does the book have headbands? These are the small decorative bands, usually of cloth, fastened inside the top and sometimes also the bottom of the back, or spine, of a book. Generally, Book-of-the-Month Club editions lack headbands.
- Are the top edges of the pages stained, or colored? On Book-of-the-Month Club editions, the top page edges usually are not stained.

Book club editions also often feel lighter. Because of the use of paper stocks and cover stocks that are different from those used for the trade edition, book club editions may weigh less.

There are, of course, exceptions to all of the above general guidelines.

IDENTIFYING LITERARY GUILD EDITIONS

Literary Guild editions state "Literary Guild" on the title page and spine.

IDENTIFYING EDITIONS OF OTHER BOOK CLUBS
IN THE UNITED STATES

Many book clubs, especially the smaller book clubs, buy their books from the publisher's general run. On receiving the books, they sell them directly to their members, making no changes whatsoever to the books or their jackets. These books are indistinguishable from the publisher's books sold, say, through a retail trade outlet such as a general bookstore. In gathering information on the identification of book club editions, we queried all of the book clubs in the United States, Canada, and England. The following book clubs in the United States responded, in 1988, that the titles issued by them were bought from the publisher's general run and not marked as a book club edition in any way: Aviators Guild, Books of Light, The Computer Book Club, Computer Professionals Book Society, Dance Book Club, Electronics Book Club, Electronics Engineers and Designers Book Club, Evangelical Book Club, How-To Book Club, Intercultural Book Club, Interior Design Book Club, The Jewish Book Club, Mechanical Engineers' Book Club, Thomas More Book Club, Music Book Society, Mystic Arts Book Society, Performing Arts Book Club, Prevention Book Club, Publisher's Choice Book Club, Semontodontics, Inc., The Troll Book Club, Writer's Digest Book Club.

The following book clubs in the United States responded with more specific information.

EPISCOPAL BOOK CLUB

1988 Statement: In the years 1980 to 1984, books from the trade edition served as club editions, with the publisher's price on them. The book usually carried a club emblem and corporate name inside the dust jacket. This also sometimes appeared on the front cover, along with the words "Selection of the Episcopal Book Club."

FRAGGLE ROCK BOOK CLUB

1988 Statement: "As you can see, we:
-identify Weekly Reader Books on the back cover, the spine and copyright page
-do not have an ISBN
-do not have a retail price
-are a different size
-use different paper and cover stock

"This same method holds true for all of our book clubs and in some we even print Weekly Reader Books on the end pages. As far as I know, we have been doing this type of identification as long as we have had book clubs and book club editions (about 35 years)."

GUIDEPOSTS

1988 Statement: "On most of our Book Club and Book Service selections we use a cross enclosed in a circle on the spine of the book itself, as well as on the dust jacket. And the Guideposts registered name along with the words 'Carmel, New York 10512,' are often printed on the back of the dust jacket.

"As far as I've been able to determine, we've been using the Guideposts cross inside a circle at least since 1953. I can not say what methods were used to designate our Book Club and Book Service selections prior to that year, however."

MUPPET BABIES BOOK CLUB
1988 Statement: *See* 1988 Statement of Fraggle Rock Book Club

WEEKLY READER CHILDREN'S BOOK CLUB
1988 Statement: *See* 1988 Statement of Fraggle Rock Book Club

IDENTIFYING EDITIONS OF BOOK CLUBS
IN THE UNITED KINGDOM
Among queried book clubs in the United Kingdom, the following offered helpful statements:

THE ARTISTS BOOK CLUB LTD. (ENGLAND)
1988 Statement: "The Artists' Book Club is a small specialist Club and as such, rarely buys 'own editions' from its suppliers, but rather smaller quantities which are either extra to the originating publisher's print-run, if the book is a new title, or from publisher's stock for a backlist item. In these cases, nothing distinguishes the Club editions from the trade one.

"In the case where the quantity ordered (currently 1500 copies in the UK, though renegotiations of the Book Club Regulations will put the maximum for an exclusive Book Club Edition up to 3500) is sufficient to warrant the extra cost, the two editions are distinguished in that
  a) the Book Club colophon appears on the jacket spine and possibly on the spine of the binding;
  b) the Book Club name appears on the title page in the position usually occupied by the Publisher's name;
  c) the Book Club is sometimes mentioned in the verso of the title page with a separate ISBN number.
"This has been a practice used widely in the UK from at least the late '60s onwards."

BOOKMARX CLUB (ENGLAND)
1988 Statement: "We almost always use the regular trade edition. Stickers were applied to some early titles, with Bookmarx Club on them. Nowadays we don't usually bother."

THE POETRY BOOK SOCIETY (ENGLAND)
1988 Statement: "We do not have special book club editions. Books are not distinguished from trade editions."